CONSCIOUSNESS:
Brain,
States of Awareness,
and Mysticism

CONSCIOUSNESS:
Brain,
States of Awareness,
and Mysticism

DANIEL GOLEMAN
Psychology Today Magazine

RICHARD J. DAVIDSON
State University of New York,
College at Purchase

EDITORS

HARPER & ROW, PUBLISHERS
New York   Hagerstown   Philadelphia   San Francisco   London

Please refer to page v for acknowledgments and credits.

Sponsoring Editor: Bhagan Narine
Project Editor: Julie Segedy
Production Manager: Marian Hartsough
Cover and Interior Designer: Karen Emerson
Illustrator: Karen Emerson
Compositor: Nancy Cranwell
Printer and Binder: Malloy Lithographing

**CONSCIOUSNESS: Brain, States of
Awareness, and Mysticism**

Library of Congress Cataloging in Publication Data
Main entry under title:

Consciousness: brain, states of awareness, and mysticism

Includes bibliographical references.
1. Consciousness—Addresses, essays, lectures.
2. Brain—Addresses, essays, lectures. I. Goleman,
Daniel. II. Davidson, Richard J. [DNLM: 1. Consciousness—Collected works. BF311 P974]
BF311.C65   153   78-12678
ISBN   0-06-383045-0

Cover Photo: George Roos
"Le chef d'oeuvre ou les mystères de l'horizon," Rene Magritte,
  © A.D.A.G.P., Paris 1978.
From the collection of L. Arnold Weissberger, New York.

Acknowledgments

Part I photograph, © David Powers 1978/Jeroboam, Inc.
Part II photograph, by Nacio Jan Brown/BBM.
Part III photograph, by Hide Shibata.
Part IV photograph, © Suzanne Arms 1978/Jeroboam, Inc.

I THE BRAIN & CONSCIOUSNESS

1 The Human Brain, Steven Rose
From *The Conscious Brain*, by Steven Rose. Copyright©
1973 by Steven Rose. Reprinted by permission of Alfred
A. Knopf, Inc.

2 The Brain's Three Principal Functional Units, A. R. Luria
Excerpted from *The Working Brain: An Introduction to
Neuropsychology*, by A. R. Luria, translated by Basil
Haigh, pp. 43, 45-47, 67-74, 78-84, 99-101,© Penguin
Books Ltd. 1973, translation © Penguin Books Ltd.
1973, Basic Books, Inc., Publishers, New York.

3 How the Brain Works—A New Theory, E. Roy John
Reprinted from *Psychology Today Magazine.* "How the
Brain Works" by E. Roy John, Copyright © 1976
Ziff-Davis Publishing Company.

**4 The Two Modes of Consciousness and
the Two Halves of the Brain,** David Galin
From *Symposium on Consciousness*, copyright © 1976
by Philip Lee, Robert E. Ornstein, Charles Tart, Arthur
Deikman and David Galin. Reprinted by permission of
The Viking Press.

5 The Paranoid Streak in Man, Paul MacLean
Reprinted with permission of Macmillan Publishing Co.,
Inc. From *Beyond Reductionism* by Arthur Koestler and
J. R. Smythies (eds.). Copyright © 1969 by The
Hutchingson Publishing Group Ltd.

6 The Mind-Brain Question, Wilder Penfield
From: "Relationship of Mind to Brain—A Case Exam-
ple," in *The Mystery of the Mind: A Critical Study of
the Consciousness and the Human Brain* by Wilder
Penfield. With discussions by William Feindel, Charles
Hendel, and Charles Symonds (Copyright © 1975 by
Princeton University Press): pp. 67-71. Reprinted by
permission of Princeton University Press.

II ORDINARY STATES OF CONSCIOUSNESS

7 What Is Perception? S. H. Bartley
From pp. 17-22, 216-218, 235-237, 275-281 in *Perception in Everyday Life* by S. Howard Bartley. Copyright©
1972 by S. Howard Bartley. By permission of Harper &
Row, Publishers, Inc.

8 On the Sources of Pleasure, Jerome Kagan
From "On the need for relativism" by Jerome Kagan in
American Psychologist (22), © 1967 by American
Psychological Association. Reprinted by permission.

9 The Varieties of Attention, William James
From *The Principles of Psychology* by William James.
Copyright©1950 by Dover Publications, Inc.

10 Good-Me, Bad-Me, Not-Me, Harry Stack Sullivan
Reprinted from *The Interpersonal Theory of Psychiatry*
by Harry Stack Sullivan, M.D. By permission of W. W.
Norton & Company, Inc. Copyright © 1953 by The
William Alanson White Psychiatric Foundation.

11 Anomalies of Attention, Graham Reed
From *The Psychology of Anomalous Experience: A
Cognitive Approach* by Graham Reed. Copyright 1972
by Graham Reed. Boston: Houghton-Mifflin Co.

12 The Importance of Daydreaming, Jerome L. Singer
Reprinted from *Psychology Today Magazine.* "Fantasy:
The Foundation of Serenity" by Jerome Singer. Copy-
right©1976, Ziff-Davis Publishing Company.

13 The Conditions of Creativity, Jerome Bruner
Reprinted by permission of the author and publishers
from *On Knowing: Essays for the Left Hand* by Jerome
S. Bruner, Cambridge, Mass.: The Belknap Press of
Harvard University Press, Copyright©1962 by President
and Fellows of Harvard College.

14 The Flow Experience, Mihaly Csikszentmihalyi
From "Play and Intrinsic Rewards" by Mihaly Csikszent-
mihalyi. Copyright © 1975, *Journal of Humanistic
Psychology*, Vol. 15, #3.

15 The Psychology of Tiredness, E. L. Hartmann
From *The Functions of Sleep*, © 1973 Yale University
Press.

16 Two Kinds of Sleep, William Dement
From *Some Must Watch While Some Must Sleep* by William C. Dement (New York: Norton, 1978)

17 The Nature of Dreams, Wilse B. Webb
From Wilse B. Webb, *Sleep: The Gentle Tyrant* ©1975, pp. 137-143. Reprinted by permission of Prentice-Hall, Inc., Englewood Cliffs, New Jersey.

18 The Meaning of Dreams, Calvin S. Hall
Reprinted by permission of the author.

III ALTERED STATES OF CONSCIOUSNESS

19 The Systems Approach to States of Consciousness,
Charles T. Tart
From *States of Consciousness* by Charles T. Tart. Copyright © 1975 by Charles T. Tart. Reprinted by permission of the publishers, E. P. Dutton.

20 Altered States of Awareness, Ernest R. Hilgard
From Ernest R. Hilgard, "Altered States of Awareness," *Journal of Nervous & Mental Disease,* Vol. 149. Copyright ©1969, The Williams & Wilkins Co. Reproduced by permission.

21 State-Bound Knowledge, Roland Fischer
Reprinted from *Psychology Today Magazine.* "I Can't Remember What I Said Last Night. . .But It Must Have Been Good" by Roland Fischer, Copyright © 1976, Ziff-Davis Publishing Company.

22 The Psychopharmacological Revolution, Murray E. Jarvik
Reprinted from *Psychology Today Magazine.* "The Psychopharmacological Revolution" by Murray E. Jarvik, Copyright © 1976, Ziff-Davis Publishing Company.

23 The Doors of Perception, Aldous Huxley
From pp. 14-26 in *The Doors of Perception* by Aldous Huxley. Copyright © 1954 by Aldous Huxley. By permission of Harper & Row, Publishers, Inc.

24 The True Speed Trip: Schizophrenia, Solomon Snyder
Reprinted from *Psychology Today Magazine.* "The True Speed Trip" by Solomon Snyder, Copyright © 1971, Ziff-Davis Publishing Company.

25 Living with Schizophrenia, Norma MacDonald
From *Canadian Medical Association Journal, 82,* 1960.

26 The Shattered Language of Schizophrenia, Brendan A. Maher
Reprinted from *Psychology Today Magazine.* "The Shattered Language of Schizophrenia" by Brendan A. Maher, Copyright © 1968, Ziff-Davis Publishing Company.

27 Shamans and Acute Schizophrenia, Julian Silverman
Reproduced by permission of the American Anthropological Association, from *American Anthropologist,* 69:1 (21-31), 1967.

28 The Relaxation Response,
Herbert Benson, et. al.
From "Historical and Clinical Considerations of the Relaxation Response," *American Scientist* 65, July 1977.

29 A Map of Inner Space, Daniel Goleman
From *The Varieties of the Meditative Experience* by Daniel Goleman. Copyright © 1977 by Daniel Goleman. Reprinted by permission of the publishers, E. P. Dutton.

30 Biofeedback, Gerald Jonas
From *Visceral Learning* by Gerald Jonas. Copyright © 1972, 1973 by Gerald Jonas. Reprinted by permission of The Viking Press.

31 Tuning in on the Twilight Zone, Thomas Budzynski
Reprinted from *Psychology Today Magazine.* "Tuning in on the Twilight Zone" by Thomas Budzynski, Copyright ©1977, Ziff-Davis Publishing Company.

32 The Hypnotic State, Ernest R. Hilgard
From *Divided Consciousness* by Ernest R. Hilgard, Copyright © 1977 by Ernest Hilgard. Reprinted by permission of John Wiley & Sons, Inc.

33 Hypnosis and Dissociation, Kenneth Bowers
From *Hypnosis for the Seriously Curious* by K. S. Bowers. Copyright © 1976 by Wadsworth Publishing Company, Inc. Reprinted by permission of the publisher, Brooks/Cole Publishing Company, Monterey, California.

34 Self-Exploration in the Hypnotic State, Milton H. Erickson
Abridged from the January 1955 *Journal of Clinical and Experimental Hypnosis.* Copyrighted by The Society for Clinical and Experimental Hypnosis, January 1955.

35 Social Isolation: A Case for Interdisciplinary Research, Peter Suedfeld
From *Canadian Psychologist,* January 1974, pp. 1-2, 4-15.

36 The Painful Ecstasy of Healing, Richard Katz
Reprinted from *Psychology Today Magazine.* "The Painful Ecstasy of Healing" by Richard Katz, Copyright ©1976, Ziff-Davis Publishing Company.

37 The High Dream, Charles Tart
From *Altered States of Consciousness* by Charles T. Tart, Copyright ©1969 by Charles T. Tart. Reprinted by permission of John Wiley & Sons, Inc.

38 The Experience of Dying, Raymond Moody, Jr.
From *Life After Life* by Raymond Moody, Jr. Copyright © 1976. By permission of Bantam/Mockingbird Books, New York.

IV   THE POLITICS OF CONSCIOUSNESS

39 Are We a Nation of Mystics?
Andrew Greeley and William McCready
©1975 by The New York Times Company. Reprinted by permission.

40 Transcendental Experience, R. D. Laing
From *The Politics of Experience* by R. D. Laing, pp. 131-134, 137-145 (U.S. ed.). Copyright©1967 by R. D. Laing. Reprinted by permission of Penguin Books, Ltd.

41 What Mysticism Is, Group for the Advancement of Psychiatry
From *Mysticism: Spiritual Quest or Psychic Disorder,* by the Group for the Advancement of Psychiatry, Copyright©1976.

42 Comments on the GAP Report on Mysticism, Arthur J. Deikman
From Arthur Deikman, "Comments on the GAP Report on Mysticism," *Journal of Nervous and Mental Disease,* Vol. 165, No. 3. Copyright © 1977, The Williams & Wilkins Co. Reproduced by permission of the publisher and author.

43 Schizophrenia—The Inward Journey, Joseph Campbell
From *Myths to Live By* by Joseph Campbell. Copyright ©1972 by Joseph Campbell. Reprinted by permission of The Viking Press.

44 The Six Realms of Existence, Chögyam Trungpa
Reprinted by special arrangement with Shambhala Publications, Inc., 1123 Spruce St., Boulder, Colorado 80302. From *The Myth of Freedom,* by Chögyam Trungpa. Copyright©1976 by Chögyam Trungpa.

45 Psychiatry and the Sacred, Jacob Needleman
From *On the Way to Self-Knowledge* by Jacob Needleman, Professor of Philosophy, San Francisco State University.

46 Eastern and Western Models of Man, Ram Dass
From the *Journal of Transpersonal Psychology,* Vol. 2, No. 2, 1970 and Vol. 3, No. 1, 1971. Reprinted with permission.

47 The Way Things Are, Huston Smith
From pp. 1-11, 14-18 in *Forgotten Truth: The Primordial Tradition* by Huston Smith. Copyright ©1976 by Huston Smith. By permission of Harper & Row, Publishers, Inc.

Contents

v   Acknowledgments
xvii   Preface

| PART I | 1 | **THE BRAIN AND CONSCIOUSNESS** |

Section 1   2   **How the Brain Works**

Steven Rose   3   **The Human Brain**   From *The Conscious Brain* by Steven Rose, Knopf, 1973.
The brain is the biological basis of consciousness. Biochemist Steven Rose outlines how the brain is put together, from neurons—the brain's cells—to the large brain areas that regulate mental life.

A. R. Luria   10   **The Brain's Three Principal Functional Units**   From *The Working Brain* by A. R. Luria, Basic Books, 1973.
Different areas of the brain work together so that we can perceive, think, and act. The eminent Russian neuropsychologist, A. R. Luria, maps the zones of the brain responsible for each major mental function.

E. Roy John   14   **How the Brain Works—A New Theory**   From *Psychology Today,* May 1976.
The view that a single part of the brain controls a single mental function is outdated. A noted neuropsychologist shows that the brain works in a coordinated orchestration of all its parts together, and that the frequency at which brain cells fire can be more important than where they are located.

Section 2   18   **Brain and Mind**

David Galin   19   **The Two Modes of Consciousness and the Two Halves of the Brain**   From *Symposium on Consciousness* by Philip Lee, Robert E. Ornstein, Charles Tart, Arthur Deikman, David Galin, Viking Press, 1976.
Each half of the human brain duplicates most functions of the other half, and each hemisphere has some special abilities. In most people, for example, the left hemisphere specializes in verbal skills and logical analysis, while the right half excels at spatial and holistic tasks.

Paul MacLean   24   **The Paranoid Streak in Man**   From *Beyond Reductionism,* Arthur Koestler and J. R. Smythies, Eds., 1969.
Human history is marred by the "paranoid streak" that leads people to view others with hatred and suspicion. Paul MacLean, the neurologist who first identified the limbic system as the brain's emotional center, links it to the "paranoid streak."

Wilder Penfield   27   **The Mind-Brain Question**   From *The Mystery of the Mind* by Wilder Penfield, Princeton University Press, 1975.
The exact relationship of brain to mind is a mystery. An eminent neurosurgeon describes a man's recovery from coma to full awareness, and poses the question: Where does consciousness begin?

PART II	**33**	**ORDINARY STATES OF CONSCIOUSNESS**

Section 1   **34**   **The Mechanics of Experience**

S. H. Bartley   **35**   **What Is Perception?**   From *Perception in Everyday Life* by S. Howard Bartley, Harper & Row, 1972.
Our five modes of perception differ from what are commonly thought of as "the five senses." Together they construct the world "out there," but that world exists for us only as our senses portray it.

Jerome Kagan   **40**   **On the Sources of Pleasure**   From *"On the need for relativism"* by Jerome Kagan, American Psychologist, 1967
One person's pleasure is another person's boredom. To understand why, we need to consider how we find meaning in the world through inner mental models called "schema."

William James   **43**   **The Varieties of Attention**   From *The Principles of Psychology* by William James, Dover Publications, 1950.
The founding father of American psychology refelcts on the vagaries of attention, the searchlight of consciousness.

Harry Stack Sullivan   **46**   **Good-Me, Bad-Me, Not-Me**   From *The Interpersonal Theory of Psychiatry,* by Harry Stack Sullivan, M.D., Norton, 1953.
A major theorist in psychiatric thought describes the splits within us in the way we experience reality, and how they defend us against anxiety.

Section 2   **48**   **Ordinary Waking States**

Graham Reed   **49**   **Anomalies of Attention**   From *The Psychology of Anomalous Experience* by Graham Reed, Houghton Mifflin, 1974.
Attention determines what we notice, but we rarely notice attention itself. Lapses in attention cause a variety of strange moments, and explain what makes professors "absent-minded," time evaporate, and impending threats disappear.

Jerome L. Singer   **53**   **The Importance of Daydreaming**   From *Psychology Today,* 1976.
Daydreams intrude into everyone's waking thoughts from time to time, especially in "off" moments when we are quiet and alone. There are many kinds of daydreams, a noted expert tells us, and all of them serve a useful psychological purpose.

Jerome Bruner   **58**   **The Conditions of Creativity**   From *On Knowing: Essays for the Left Hand* by Jerome Bruner, Belknap Press, 1962.
The creative act can occur in anything we do, whether it be business, painting, or expressions of affection. Creativity grows out of placing the familiar in new perspectives. Cognitive psychologist Jerome Bruner spells out the conditions of the creative state.

Mihaly Csikszentmihalyi   **63**   **The Flow Experience**   From the *Journal of Humanistic Psychology,* 1975.
We experience flow whenever we engage in what we do with total attention and involvement. When we flow we're at our best, performing at our peak, and enjoying what we do. Flow is a "natural high."

Section 3 | **68** | **Sleep and Dreams**

E. L. Hartmann | **69** | **The Psychology of Tiredness** From *The Functions of Sleep* by E. L. Hartmann, Yale University Press, 1973.
There are two kinds of tiredness, one purely from physical exertion, the other from emotional stress. Psychiatrist Ernest Hartmann tells us why physical tiredness can be pleasant, but the mental kind can make us irritable and childish. It takes different stages of sleep to restore us from each.

William Dement | **72** | **Two Kinds of Sleep** From *Some Must Watch While Some Must Sleep* by William C. Dement, Norton, 1978
As we sleep, we go through a cycle of stages that vary in depth and in brain function. William Dement, a pioneer in sleep research, describes the stages, how they are measured, and what each is like.

Wilse B. Webb | **76** | **The Nature of Dreams** From *Sleep: The Gentle Tyrant* by Wilse B. Webb, Prentice-Hall, 1975.
The dreams we remember are more interesting on the whole than most of our other dreams. While sleep researchers have learned much about the standard dream by waking volunteers as they finished dreaming, the outstanding feature of most dreams is their commonplaceness.

Calvin Hall | **79** | **The Meaning of Dreams**
Our dreams reveal much of our psychological underlife, especially basic concepts and conflicts we rarely admit to waking awareness. Psychologist Calvin Hall makes a plea that we take our dreams more seriously, and use their wisdom to solve problems in living.

PART III | **85** | **ALTERED STATES OF CONSCIOUSNESS**

Section 1 | **86** | **The Nature of Altered States**

Charles T. Tart | **87** | **The Systems Approach to States of Consciousness** From *States of Consciousness* by Charles T. Tart, Dutton, 1975.
Out ordinary state of consciousness is a complex structure built from an interplay of psychological processes. As any of these processes change, our state of consciousness shifts. Ordinary states are constantly shifting; a major change puts us into a dramatically altered state.

Ernest R. Hilgard | **89** | **Altered States of Awareness** From the *Journal of Nervous and Mental Disease,* 1969
Although we all know from experience that our consciousness can undergo extreme alterations, when it comes to the hard criteria of science, the borderlines of altered states are hard to define. A pioneer in hypnosis research proposes that the hypnotic trance is as altered a state as dreaming, but we do not as yet know how to measure the physiological changes it brings.

Roland Fischer | **92** | **State-Bound Knowledge** From *Psychology Today,* August 1976.
As the brain changes, so does consciousness. Each unique level of change seems to have its distinctive state, with its own skills, perceptions, and memories.

Section 2   94   **Drug-Induced Altered States**

Murray E. Jarvik   95   **The Psychopharmacological Revolution**   From *Psychology Today,* May 1967.
The most immediate and striking altered states come about when drugs change the chemistry of the brain. A noted psychopharmacologist sketches the range of brain-changing drugs, from alcohol to LSD to the chlorpromazines, the anti-psychotic chemicals that revolutionized psychiatry.

Aldous Huxley   102   **The Doors of Perception**   From *The Doors of Perception* by Aldous Huxley, Harper & Row, 1954.
Aldous Huxley recalls how mescaline admitted him to experience "Mind at Large," muting for a time the reducing effects of the brain and expanding his universe of perception.

Solomon H. Snyder   105   **The True Speed Trip: Schizophrenia**   From *Psychology Today,* January 1971.
The nightmare world of schizophrenia seems most certainly the product of aberrant brain chemistry. Drug researcher Solomon Snyder traces the evidence that a natural analog of amphetamine—popularly known as "speed"—is the chemical key to schizophrenia.

Section 3   110   **Psychotic States**

Norma MacDonald   111   **Living with Schizophrenia**   From the *Canadian Medical Association Journal,* 1960.
A young nurse describes her plunge into the hellish world of schizophrenia, and her re-entry into a sometimes precarious normality.

Brendan A. Maher   115   **The Shattered Language of Schizophrenia**   From *Psychology Today,* November 1968.
Clinicians agree widely when it comes to recognizing the word salad of schizophrenics as a hallmark of the condition. Brendan Maher, a researcher on psychopathology, finds that the unique flavor of schizophrenic language comes from a combination of spastic attention and free association gone wild.

Julian Silverman   120   **Shamans and Acute Schizophrenia**   From the *American Anthropologist,* 1967.
How a given altered state is valued can differ greatly from culture to culture. A psychiatrist culls the anthropological literature and finds that a psychotic episode is a prerequisite of training to become a shaman.

Section 4   126   **The Self-regulation of Consciousness**

Herbert Benson   127   **The Relaxation Response**   From the *American Scientist,* July 1977.
Jamie B. Kotch
Karen D. Crassweller   The pressures of industrialized society needlessly trigger the "fight-or-flight"
Martha M. Greenwood   response, where the body mobilizes to defend itself. Spiritual traditions have long used meditation to evoke the "relaxation response," where the body and mind can restore themselves.

Daniel Goleman   132 **A Map of Inner Space**   From *Varieties of the Meditative Experience* by Daniel Goleman, E. P. Dutton, 1977.
Although most casual meditators never experience them, there are dramatic altered states one can enter through meditation. An ancient Buddhist manual spells out the nature of altered states in meditation and what one must do to enter them.

Gerald Jonas   137 **Biofeedback**   From *Visceral Learning* by Gerald Jonas, Viking, 1973.
By feeding a person information on the subtle bioelectric currents that pulse through the body, biofeedback allows us to extend our control of bodily functions usually beyond sensing or changing.

Thomas Budzynski   141 **Biofeedback and the Twilight States of Consciousness**   From *Psychology Today,* 1977.
When we apply biofeedback to our brain wave patterns, we can learn to maintain ourselves in a state of consciousness at the borderline between wakefulness and sleep. A pioneer in biofeedback research tells us that in this twilight zone we have easier access to our creative processes, and possibly to the unconscious itself.

Section 5   146 **Hypnosis, Dissociation, and Trance**

Ernest R. Hilgard   147 **The Hypnotic State**   From *Divided Consciousness* by Ernest R. Hilgard, Wiley, 1977.
The nature of the hypnotic state varies with the hypnotist's instructions. Yet during deep self-hypnosis, the sharp break with waking awareness seen in meditation is also at the core of the hypnotic trance.

Kenneth Bowers   151 **Hypnosis and Dissociation**   From *Hypnosis for the Seriously Curious* by K. S. Bowers, Brooks/Cole, 1976.
People who are easily hypnotized are better able to register and respond to information they receive out of their awareness. This ability to passively attend may be a key to the mystery of the hypnotic trance.

Milton H. Erickson   155 **Self-Exploration in the Hypnotic State**   From *The Journal of Clinical and Experimental Hypnosis,* January, 1955.
Under hypnosis a person can sometimes recall and recover from a psychologically crippling trauma from the past. Psychiatrist Milton Erickson, the dean of clinical hypnosis, recounts a dramatic self-cure by a medical student in hypnotic trance.

Section 6   160 **Isolation, Healing, Dreaming, and Dying**

Peter Suedfeld   161 **Social Isolation: A Case for Interdisciplinary Research**   From *The Canadian Psychologist,* January, 1974.
Humans seem to have a primal fear of isolation, and accounts by stranded sailors and explorers reaffirm our fear that complete isolation can drive one mad. Yet when people are prepared for isolation, as with religious hermits or Indian vision quests, it can yield a rich inner reward.

Richard Katz 165 **The Painful Ecstacy of Healing**   From *Psychology Today,* December 1976.
Among the !Kung Bushmen of Africa's Kalahari Desert, healing of all sorts takes place during an all-night marathon dance and chant. The best healers enter an altered state where healing energy surges through them; by dawn the dance restores the whole community to a sense of closeness.

Charles T. Tart 169 **The High Dream**   From *Altered States of Consciousness* by Charles T. Tart, Wiley, 1969.
Altered states of consciousness do not occur only during waking awareness; any state can be the baseline for a shift in awareness. Psychologist Charles Tart recalls his experience of an altered state during dreaming.

Raymond Moody, Jr. 171 **The Experience of Dying**   From *Life After Life* by Raymond Moody, Jr., Mockingbird Books, 1976.
As a person dies, a progression of changes in consciousness unfolds. Psychiatrist Raymond Moody, Jr. has collected accounts by people who were clinically dead and then resuscitated. Their testimony reveals that for many, dying can be an uplifting, rather than frightening, event.

PART IV 175 **THE POLITICS OF CONSCIOUSNESS**

Section 1 176 **Mysticism and Madness**

Andrew Greeley 178 **Are We a Nation of Mystics?**   From the *New York Times Magazine,* January 16, 1975.
William McCready A national poll reveals that two out of five Americans have had a mystical experience, but almost all who did were afraid to tell anyone what had happened to them.

R. D. Laing 184 **Transcendental Experience**   From *The Politics of Experience* by R. D. Laing, Ballantine, 1967.
A controversial psychiatrist draws a parallel between the psychotic and the mystic states, and suggests that both may be valid responses to modern man's predicament.

Group for the Advancement 187 **What Mysticism Is**   From *Mysticism: Spiritual Quest or Psychic Disorder?* 1976.
of Psychiatry A committee of psychiatrists investigates the nature of the mystical experience, and concludes that it is difficult to draw the line between mysticism and psychosis. Their training in psychiatry, however, does not seem to be suitable for a full understanding of mysticism.

Arthur J. Deikman | 191 | **Comments on the GAP Report on Mysticism** From the *Journal of Nervous and Mental Disease,* 1977.
The GAP report contends psychologist Arthur Deikman, reveals more about the limits of the psychiatric profession than the mystical experience, reducing it to ''comfortable'' terms.

Joseph Campbell | 195 | **Schizophrenia—The Inward Journey** From *Myths to Live By* by Joseph Campbell, Viking Press, 1972.
A noted expert on myths finds that the schizophrenic, the LSD tripper, the shaman, and the mystic all follow the same basic route through the uncertain terrain of altered states.

Section 2   204   Other Visions, Other Realities

Chögyam Trungpa | 205 | **The Six Realms of Existence** From *The Myth of Freedom* by Chögyam Trungpa, Shambhala Press, 1975.
There are many states of consciousness that people experience in an ordinary day, each with its unique reality. A Tibetan Buddhist teacher describes six such realms of experience, suggesting that each of them offers a distorted view of reality.

Jacob Needleman | 209 | **Psychiatry and the Sacred** From *On the Way to Self-Knowledge* by Jacob Needleman, Knopf, 1976.
The once-hopeful promise that psychotherapy could transform people has been dimmed, observes philosopher Jacob Needleman, and many, including therapists themselves, are turning to ancient spiritual traditions. Therapy differs in a fundamental way from these sacred traditions: therapy concentrates on the contents of consciousness, and spiritual techniques seek to transform consciousness itself.

Ram Dass | 213 | **Eastern and Western Models of Man** From the *Journal of Transpersonal Psychology,* 1971.
A psychologist turned yogi details the rigors of meditation and the spiritual route to liberation. Eastern systems of thought are less judgmental than our own; from their vantage point rational waking awareness is but one—and by no means the best—of innumerable states of consciousness from which truth can be perceived.

Huston Smith | 217 | **The Way Things Are** From *The Forgotten Truth* by Huston Smith, Harper & Row, 1976.
The scientific method is powerful, but it is a tool that loses sights of its own limits. The more significant human issues—values, purpose, and the meaning of life—cannot be settled by science, but may require a voyage through consciousness.

Preface

During the formative years of psychology in America, William James proposed as the discipline's prime goal the study of states of consciousness. But the then-primitive grasp of brain function and the ascendency of more fruitful avenues of research and theory combined to make the study of consciousness beyond psychology's pale. Now, almost three-quarters of a century later, methods and technologies have arrived that make it possible for psychologists to take up James' challenge.

Even so, in the sociology of professions it is a natural law that those in established branches tend to look askance at innovative fields, either with benign disinterest or outright hostility. So it is that the study of consciousness as yet has no sure perch anywhere in psychology. Rather, it is emerging as a field of study because of the ardent interest of people scattered throughout the many arms of psychology and well beyond to other disciplines. This multidisciplinary spread is inevitable, too, because of the nature of the subject itself: consciousness is too vast a phenomenon to become the sole property of any single field of study.

For this reason we have tapped numerous areas in psychology and other disciplines in assembling this book of readings. Within psychology, among the areas we have drawn from are neuropsychology, perception, cognition, psychodynamics, human development, and psychophysiology. Outside psychology we have tapped disciplines ranging from psychopharmacology and psychiatry to anthropology, philosophy, and mythology. A subject like consciousness is so vast that it touches on virtually every human science; to do it justice, then, requires a convergence of views from a wide variety of methods and through many theoretical lenses.

Although introductory psychology may be helpful in understanding this book, we have chosen and edited the selections so that readers with little or no psychology background will understand them with ease. The scope of these readings is intentionally wide, going well beyond the bounds of psychology *per se,* as the topic of consciousness demands. We assume that most readers will be unfamiliar with at least some of the disciplines from which selections have come, so the book is actually an introduction to the many facets of consciousness.

Our first look at consciousness is from the viewpoint of the brain, its key organ. While we are learning at an ever-increasing rate about how the workings of the brain connect to consciousness, we have yet to understand fully the link between the brain and the mind. Our next perspective on consciousness is in terms of the major psychological processes that combine to shape it: perception, cognition, attention, and the like. We also survey states of consciousness that are experiences common to us all. This gives us a background for understanding the radical shifts in consciousness surveyed in the third section. When the usual ebb and flow of our brain and mind are significantly transformed—whether by drugs, mental illness, meditation, hypnosis, or some other means—we experience an altered state of consciousness; the third part of the book surveys the major altered states. Whether or not a given state of consciousness is valued depends to a large extent on personal and cultural tastes. The final section deals with the politics of consciousness—the judgments we place on altered states.

Each part represents a different focus for the study of consciousness. To facilitate comprehension of these foci, we have added introductions to each of the part and section openings, that discuss the background and scope of the topics, and suggest guidelines for the actual reading of the text. This format should be helpful to the reader with a limited background in psychology and, for classroom use, allows flexible adaptation in order to make an optimal fit with the particular emphasis of any given psychology course. Thus the first part, on brain function, could be easily incorporated into a course emphasizing psychobiology; the second part, on the psychological processes that shape awareness, would fit with a focus on cognition and perception; the third part, on altered states, could stand by itself as a comprehensive unit in a course on that topic; and the final part, on the politics of consciousness, can be used as source material for a course oriented around issues in psychology. And besides its intended use as a sourcebook on the psychology of consciousness, any or all of these readings could supplement a course on introductory psychology.

Daniel Goleman
Richard J. Davidson

CONSCIOUSNESS:
Brain,
States of Awareness,
and Mysticism

THE BRAIN AND CONSCIOUSNESS

Our states of consciousness are an intricate tapestry woven from the workings of the brain. William James, a founding father of American psychology, saw that the brain was the organ of behavior and experience, and theorized that for every mental change there was a corresponding change in the brain. This early focus faded from psychology, however, for knowledge of the brain was then sparse and primitive. During most of its history psychology has been a human science without an organ. The workings of the brain have been an elusive mystery, with a vast gap between the states we observe and what we know of their underlying brain activity. Only very recently have advances in technology allowed researchers to begin to bridge the brain-behavior gap. Working both with humans and animals, researchers the world over are piecing together a tapestry of findings that connect what happens in the brain with what we think and do.

HOW THE BRAIN WORKS

To understand how the brain works we must first see the role of the parts of the brain in consciousness. In this section, biochemist Steven Rose gives a detailed anatomy of the brain, an organ that very much resembles a huge, greyish, three-pound walnut. To the anatomist, it breaks down into large regions that control different aspects of consciousness, such as movement and sensing. These anatomical areas are themselves built from an astronomical number of neurons, the cells that compose and tie together the various regions of the brain. Although we can identify the parts of the brain, we still don't understand exactly how they work together to create consciousness. The mass of possible interactions among the brain's cells and zones is so complex, says Rose, it "beggars both description and mathematicization."

The eminent Russian neuropsychologist A. R. Luria shows how scattered zones of the brain work together as functional units to perform a specific job. These functional zones are mainly in the cortex, the brain's topmost layer. Below the cortex, in the lower brain, is the reticular formation, a series of interconnected structures surging up in a nerve network to virtually every zone of the upper brain. This nerve net is like a brain rheostat; it controls the level of activity throughout the brain over the whole range of consciousness, from the frenetic activity of alert excitement to the somnolent stillness of quiet sleep. At the back of the cortex the third unit reacts to this information by planning and making the body act on these plans. All three functional units act together to orchestrate the complexities of human consciousness.

While the brain's various zones are conveniently talked of as being the source for a specific mental function, this is an oversimplification of how the brain actually works. A more accurate view, according to brain researcher E. Roy John, is that vast regions of the brain take part in every mental act, although some parts are more involved than others. Clinicians have long known of cases where patients suffered the loss of a part of their brains, but did not lose the ability which that brain area was thought to control. Even so, the prevailing view of how the brain works has been a strict "localization" theory, that each brain area does a specific mental job. John proposes that this localization model is only partly true: certain zones of the brain have many more cells concentrated there that are active in a particular task, but many cells scattered throughout the brain also join in that task. Thus the visual cortex has the highest concentration of brain cells active in seeing, but other parts of the brain also have such cells. It is more important that cells fire at a rate in harmony with all the other cells active in the same mental task than where any of the cells are located. The rhythms of cell activity count for more than their location. No brain region makes an all-or-nothing contribution to a given mental job; rather, some regions are more involved on the average than are others. Every mental activity, including consciousness itself, is due to cells at work throughout the brain.

The Human Brain

Steven Rose

THE FORM OF THE BRAIN

The brain is a machine for communicating, receiving information, storing it, issuing instructions based on it. The most elaborate and elegant theoretical descriptions of the way the machine works must in due course come to terms with the real brain rather than model ones. . . . We describe the brain, what it looks like to the naked eye and to the microscope, what its components are. . . .

We begin with a visual inspection of the brain, of what can be seen by the naked eye or be separated by scissors and scalpel and forceps. Having toured the brain on this macro-scale we then return to the start once more and look at it again, this time with the additional tools of the light microscope, the electron microscope and some of the formidable machinery of contemporary biochemistry. Only then is it possible to consider how the whole apparatus is wired up. But note that throughout . . . we are considering the brain as an object, a static, dead thing to be cut up and observed, analysed by whatever appear to be the most relevant tools. In this analysis there is no room for questioning of *process,* for a consideration of the brain as even a working machine still less the seat of thought, emotion or consciousness. But to understand the brain at work and in operation it must first be seen as a static, three-dimensional fixed and stained object. Only then will it be clear what are the operating units which must be assembled in order to make a working brain.

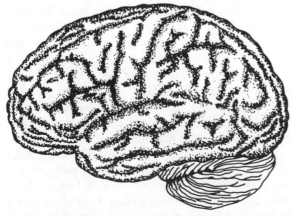

A drawing of the surface of the human brain. The cortex is greatly infolded with more than half of the surface hidden from view.

THE CEREBRUM

Removed from its skull and weighed, a human brain tops the scale at some three pounds, heavier than most organs in the body. Its appearance, dominated by the massive cerebrum, is roughly walnut like; its colour is pinkish grey on the outside, yellowish white within. Even the crudest inspection reveals that the cerebrum is like a walnut in another way than just its wrinkles: it divides neatly in half down its mid-line. To visual inspection (and to microscopic inspection as well) each half is very nearly the mirror image of the other. . . . In addition, it soon became clear to early anatomists, from the ease with which the mass of tissues could be divided, that the brain was composed of a number of readily separable parts, mini-organs so to say. . . .

First there is the division between 'grey' and 'white' matter. . . . The grey matter lies largely on the surface of the brain, the white below, in the interior. This surface is known as the cortex. Three to four millimetres thick, it wraps, wrinkled and fissured, around the entire external surface of the most prominent feature of the human brain, the two massive infolded *cerebral hemispheres.*

The curves and wrinkles, folds and grooves of the cortex are characteristic. The same wrinkles appear almost in the same place in any human brain examined. They represent a series of landmarks whereby particular cortical regions can be demarcated, enabling the cerebrum to be divided into a number of major separate regions or lobes: that at the rear is the occipital lobe; at the side, above the ear when the brain is in its skull, is the temporal lobe; at the front behind the forehead is the frontal lobe; the region running over the top under the hair is the parietal lobe. The anatomical divisions also correspond approximately to a set of regions with particular functions in the control of bodily activity and in the processing of sensory information. . . .

In general terms the parietal cortex contains those areas which are responsible for the coordination and control of sensory input and motor output, while the frontal and temporal lobes have much more diffuse and less understood functions relating to speech, learning, memory, intelligence and performance, and other, even more hard to define—but nonetheless real—human attributes. Around the primary areas concerned with the direct processing of sensory information or the organization of motor output are diffuse zones which . . . are concerned with more sophisticated treatment and analysis of sensory input or motor output. These are the so-called association areas of the cortex. . . . Stimulation of particular cortical regions evokes appropriate responses: stimulation of the motor area produces movement, of the visual area the sensation of light, the auditory area of sound, and so on. Yet despite these effects, large areas of cortex can be removed without apparent deficit in performance in experimental animals. In humans, some areas are occasionally destroyed by disease, and large regions of some of the lobes can be removed in operations without easy-to-see dificits in performance. In particular, the role of the association areas is not revealed by studying the consequences of such removals. On the other hand, animals whose primary visual cortex region has been removed behave as if they are virtually blind; they cannot analyse shapes or patterns, although some relearning is possible.

The cerebrum . . . is a bilaterally symmetrical structure. That is, it consists of two halves, each the mirror image of the other. The input from half of the body, and output to it, goes to and comes from one half of the cerebrum. However, rather surprisingly, the left half of the brain is concerned with the right half of the body, and the right half of the brain with the left half of the body. Sensory input, too, in general goes to the opposite side of the brain from that of the body from which it came (in the visual system it is the information from the left and right

halves of the visual field which cross, however.) Thus stimulation of the left motor cortex results in movement of the right side of the body. . . . However, there are exceptions to the statement that every function in one half of the cerebrum is mirrored in the other. For a number of brain functions it does seem as if there is only one cortical site of control. This is particularly true for speech. The speech centres of the brain . . . are, in adults, confined to one hemisphere, the so-called dominant hemisphere, while the equivalent regions in the other hemisphere, which are anatomically identical so far as can be observed, are functionally silent. In humans, it is generally the left hemisphere, which is connected to the right side of the body, which contains the speech centre and is said to be dominant. It is possible that this dominance has something to do with handedness as well. In left-handed people the dominant hemisphere, containing the speech centre, is often, though not always, found to be the right one.

Both the symmetry and asymmetry are important. How does information present in one cerebral hemisphere become transferred to the other—that is, how does the right-hand side of the body know what the left-hand side is doing? There is one major connection between left and right hemispheres . . . the corpus callosum. To split the brain down the middle . . . it is necessary to cut the callosum, and such cuts, when they occur in the living organism, produce a split brain, a brain which is double, in which the left-hand side does not know what the right-hand side is doing. Both halves of the body and brain then operate with a fair degree of autonomy. This autonomy is not obvious under normal circumstances, partly because a lot of bodily activities are controlled, as we shall see, from lower in the brain than the cerebral hemispheres, and partly because under normal circumstances a split-brain individual can, for instance, see what both halves of his body are doing, and so compensate for the lack of transfer of information in his brain. . . .

In adults, if particular brain regions are destroyed, unlike the situation with say, skin or liver, they will not regrow. The function of the region is permanently lost. This is an example of . . . the specificity of the brain. Nonetheless, as time goes by, it is often found that an individual who has been damaged can regain some of his lost capacities, and relearn lost skills. This is not because new brain tissue has regrown to replace the old, but because other parts of the brain have taken over the functions lost with the destroyed tissue. . . . It is as if the result of damage to one part is to make other parts of the brain system work overtime. The fact of the redundancy of function in the brain, so that at a pinch many different regions can fulfill a particular task, is another important unifying principle. . . .

This redundancy, while important in the adult, is even more important in the young child. Even in the young child if damage or loss of brain tissue occurs the brain region cannot regrow, but often, provided the lesion is not

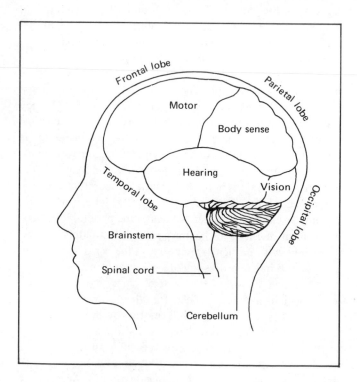

The four lobes of the right hemisphere of the cortex. The left hemisphere is similarly divided into four lobes.

too severe, and only occurs in one half of the brain, considerable recovery of function is possible. Other bits of the brain—perhaps the equivalent region to the destroyed one, but in the opposite hemisphere—are called into play to fulfill the function of the destroyed area. This is notably the case with damage which affects the speech areas, where if the left hemisphere has been dominant and is damaged, then almost complete takeover of the function can be made by the equivalent region in the right hemisphere. Thus plasticity of function, achieved by virtue of the tremendous redundancy of structure in the brain, can triumph over specificity of pathways.

THE CEREBELLUM

Behind the cerebral hemispheres, and practically covered by them above, lies a smaller, fist-sized structure which is even more convoluted than the cerebrum, the cerebellum. A third of the cerebral surface is exposed to the outside of the brain, but only one sixth of the cerebellar surface is. The rest lies buried deep in the convoluted folds. Like the cerebrum, the cerebellum is covered with its own cortex and is bilaterally symmetrical. . . . The cerebellum is one of the few brain regions which can be ascribed a precise and specific function and whose structure can in a sense be related to that function. If the cerebellum is removed, or the nerve tracts linking it to the rest of the brain are severed, then there is a loss of control of fine movement,

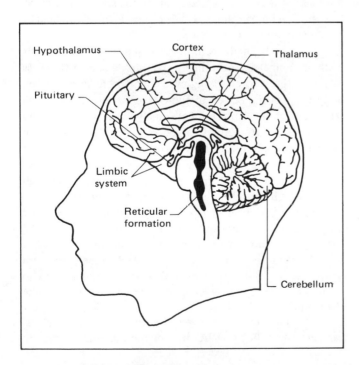

A cross section of the human brain.

that degree of muscular coordination which makes it possible, for example, to reach out and pick up a distant object accurately, not to overshoot it or for the hand to shake so violently as to upset it. The cerebellum appears to monitor all of those tiny muscular movements that are made in purposeful action and to ensure that they are adapted to the intention; that they are not too wild, too gentle, too far or too near for the purpose. It is disorders of this function of fine control of muscular coordination (in the cerebellum or a connected region, the basal ganglia) that occur particularly in elderly people and lead to characteristic shaking and hand tremors.

THE BRAIN STEM

Cerebrum and cerebellum can be plucked off the rest of the brain like apples, large and small. And indeed when they are plucked like apples they leave a stalk behind them, a thick white tube which runs up the centre of the brain and from which the other structures branch. This tube or brain stem, largely white matter, is in fact the continuation of the spinal cord which runs from the brain right through the spine to its end at an animal's tail or the residual human equivalent. In humans, the cord is . . . in cross-section the shape of a butterfly. The butterfly's body is made of grey matter, its wings of white. The white carries the nerve fibres running to and from the brain, while along the cord at varying points branch the nerves which run to the periphery of the body, bringing every distant point in communication with the cord and, through the cord, the brain. It is the spinal cord and the brain which together constitute the central nervous system of the human, and of all other vertebrates. Indeed it is from the cord that the other structures so much more prominent in the human brain originally evolved.

The brain stem itself begins to thicken as it emerges from the spine into the skull cavity which contains the brain. It broadens out, first into a region which in section is rather like a slice of cake, the medulla, and then beyond the medulla into an arched region a little like a humpbacked bridge—at least so must have thought the old anatomist who called it the pons, which is Latin for bridge. Beyond this bridge it is difficult to trace the brain stem easily because it merges into a number of structures which are attached to it by subsidiary stems: little spheres or spheroids. . . . One, above the pons, is the pineal gland which is where Descartes located the seat of the soul. A second, the pituitary, hangs down like a plum below the brain stem, and is known to be the organ which produces a large number of different hormones controlling a wide range of body activities, including growth and sexual development.

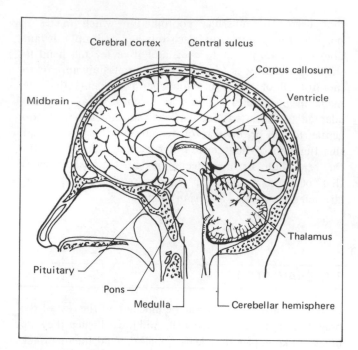

Cerebral cortex Central sulcus
Corpus callosum
Midbrain
Ventricle
Pituitary
Pons
Medulla
Thalamus
Cerebellar hemisphere

The human brain in section

CEREBROSPINAL FLUID AND BLOOD

The second important feature is revealed by considering what separates the various structures of the brain—the corpus callosum, the cerebrum and so on. Each is distinct, joined only in defined places by stems or stalks. The spaces between these structures are themselves a set of inter-communicating cavities, like a chain of caves. They form a continuation of the central canal which runs right through the spinal cord. These spaces are known as ventricles and, in the living brain, are filled with a particular liquid, the cerebrospinal fluid, whose composition is not dissimilar to that of blood from which red and white blood cells have been filtered off. It is this cerebrospinal fluid which the early theorists of brain action considered as the reservoir of the vital spirits of the nerves. In fact it is an internal circulatory system for the brain, helping bring nutrients to regions distant from a blood supply and in turn washing out waste products.

Not that the brain is without a blood supply of course. Over its surface and within its interior runs an arterial system which carries a large portion of the total blood supply of the body. The brain is indeed urgently dependent upon two of the vital substances carried within the blood—oxygen and glucose. Although the adult brain makes up only 2 percent of the body weight, its oxygen consumption is 20 percent of the total—and as much as 50 percent in the young infant. Twenty percent of the body's glucose consumption occurs in the brain. Fully one fifth of the blood pumped by the heart passes through the brain—eight hundred millilitres a minute. If the brain is deprived of its oxygen or glucose for more than a few seconds, fainting results. If the period is more prolonged the results can be disastrous. Unlike the liver or muscle tissue, for example, the brain maintains almost no reservoirs of stored glucose on which it can draw; it is absolutely dependent on that supplied by the circulating blood supply. In the absence of glucose or of oxygen, fainting, followed by coma and death, occur. Fainting in itself could be regarded as a righting mechanism by the body. By lowering the head it helps ensure that blood can arrive at the brain without being pumped up-hill. The sequence of fainting, coma and death will also follow an overdose of insulin (the hormone missing in diabetics), for it causes a rapid uptake of glucose from the circulating blood into liver and muscle, to the detriment of the brain.

THE NEURON

... If one just takes a microscope and looks at the surface, cut or natural, of the brain, one can see very little. It is necessary to bathe the surface in a dye which is selectively taken up by some parts of the brain and not others, or to cut and prepare thin sections and stain them. Then the cellular structure of the brain is revealed. The difference between grey and white matter becomes obvious. The grey regions are seen to be packed with cells, the *nerve cells* (known as neurons); the white regions are bundles of nerve fibres, nerve tracts running from one part of the brain to another. The most obvious cells to be seen in the grey matter are frequently quite large—from ten to one hundred microns* in diameter—which is big by the standard of many cells in the human body. The red blood cell, for instance, has a diameter of only seven microns.

The body of the neuron often appears to take quite a distinct geometric form, like a pyramid, a star, a rhombus or a pear, but more striking even than the form of the cell body (the central region of the cell, containing, as we shall see, most of its 'conventional' biochemical apparatus) are the numerous projections, or processes like fingers, which can be seen running off from the cell in all directions. ... It is estimated that there are some ten thousand million (10^{10}) such neurons in the human cerebral cortex (though figures which put the numbers at up to a hundred times higher have also been quoted). The neurons pack together in layers in the cortex of the cerebrum and of the cerebellum, and in clusters, each containing perhaps 10^7-10^8 cells, in the mini-organs attached to the brain stem below the cerebral hemispheres. Diffuse sets of neurons also occur in some regions which are largely white matter, like the medulla.

... The cell body is seen to contain a large nucleus, carrying the cellular DNA, the genetic material ultimately

*A micron is one ten-thousandth (10^{-4}) cm.

responsible for directing the synthesis of the protein on which the day-to-day running of the cellular economy depends. Packed into the cytoplasm which surrounds the nucleus are numerous ovalshaped structures: the mitochondria, which are responsible for providing the bulk of the cell's energy requirements by oxidizing substances derived from glucose to carbon dioxide and water, and the granular ribosomes, containing the ribonucleic acid (RNA) on which the cell proteins are continuously fabricated. The cell is surrounded by a membrane, which under the electron microscope, has a characteristic sandwich-like appearance, of two parallel dark lines with a lighter space between them. It is across this membrane that much of the cell's business with the outside world is conducted. Except in the large size of its nucleus and the very large number of ribosomes, indicating an active protein-synthesizing capacity, a typical neuron under the electron microscope does not differ too much from any other cell of the body. Even its characteristic shape is harder to see in the vanishingly thin section it is necessary to cut in order to observe it with the electron microscope.

CELL PROCESSES

What of the cell processes? Even within the brain they may be many millimetres long. Those running along the spinal cord or from the cord outwards into the periphery of the body, forming the nerve fibres, may be many centimetres long, though only a few microns in diameter. As a percentage of the total cell volume, the processes may indeed contribute the majority. In one type of neuron in the cerebellum, for instance, the volume of the cell processes is up to 95 percent, the cell bodies only 5 percent, of the total.

One of the great debates among neuroanatomists at the end of the nineteenth century related to these processes, or dendrites as they are called (i.e. 'little fingers'). One school of thought . . . maintained that they were continuous within the brain, so that every neuron was connected by dendrites to all others to form a complete tissue web. . . . A second school maintained that each cell and its processes were separate. At points the processes touched, but there was not continuity of tissue. One cell stopped, with its border close to that of the next cell. These border points, or junctions, were called synapses by Charles Sherrington in 1897 (from the Greek word meaning 'to clasp'). . . .

Each neuron is composed of a cell body, branching processes, or dendrites, and one generally longer process which can branch in its turn called an axon. It is down this axon that . . . the nerve impulses are propagated. Higher power magnification of the dendrites shows that many of them branch into innumerable little twiglets, known as dendritic spines. The axon branches at its ends to

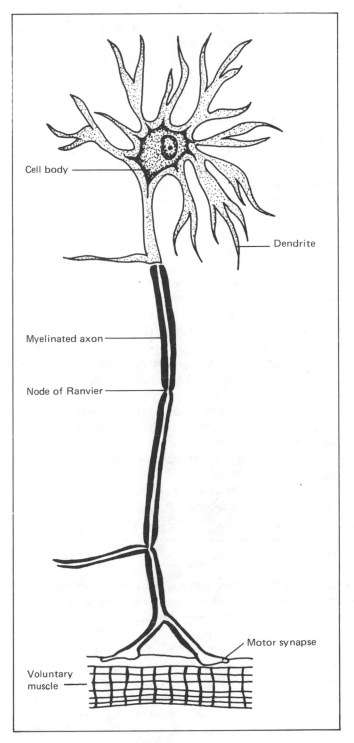

Schematic drawing of a single motor neuron, showing its functional components: cell body, axon, dendrites, and synapses onto the muscle.

make synaptic contacts with the dendritic spines or cell bodies of other neurons, and it is across these synapses that one neuron signals to another. The message travels in turn down the dendrites and through the cell body to the second neuron, resulting, under the appropriate circumstances, in an impulse travelling down the axon of the second neuron. The synapses between the cells can be seen under high-power magnification as swellings at the end of the axonal branches. The synapses are the points at which signals pass between cells, providing the brain with the possibility of coding, classifying and operating upon information arriving at it from the outside world. Most theories of brain action . . . depend upon the idea of the operation of these synapses as devices for processing information. If the number of nerve cells within the brain is large, the number of synapses is astronomical. In some brain regions in the monkey each neuron may make upwards of ten thousand synaptic connections with its neighbours. With 10^{10} neurons, this would be equivalent to a total of 10^{14} synaptic contacts in a single human cortex, or thirty thousand times as many synapses as there are people in the world.

It requires the electron microscope though, to show the reality . . . of synaptic junctions between cells. . . . The axon swells at its terminal into a capsule-like shape. The capsule contains mitochondria, the cellular energy providers, and a mass of small almost circular objects known as synaptic vesicles, which are believed to be related to the process of transmission between cells across the synaptic junction.

Away on the other side of the synapse, the post-synaptic side, the membrane of the dendrite of the second cell can be seen lying alongside the membrane of the synapse itself. The gap between them, the synaptic cleft, only two millionths of a centimetre across, is that which the message, running down the axon of the first cell, must jump to arrive at the second cell. . . .

AXONS

Each nerve cell then consists of four major parts, the dendrites on which other cells synapse, the cell body, the axon down which the messages accumulated at the cell-body pass, and the synapses at which the cell communicates with others. We need to say a little more about the axon and its relationship to those structures that have so far been referred to rather loosely as 'nerves' running up through the spinal cord, from cord to periphery and from region to region of the brain in the white matter. These too are axons, but outside the grey regions of the brain each axon is surrounded by a sheath which provides a thick outer tube around it, like the plastic or rubber insulation of an electric cable. These sheaths are composed of a fatty material known as myelin and are much thicker than the axon itself. One of the functions of these sheaths is precisely that suggested by the comparison with the rubber tube, to insulate each axon from its neighbours, thus preventing confusing the message passing down each. It is the great mass of myelin surrounding the axons running between the

brain regions which gives the white matter of the brain its characteristic appearance, by contrast with the grey, and also helps account for the large amount of fatty substances like cholesterol which are found as so striking a feature of any chemical analysis of the brain.

Outside the grey region of the brain axons travel together in organized bundles, or nerve tracts, connecting a group of neurons in one region with those in another. Nerves running into the brain, like the optic nerves, or to and from the spinal cord, are bundles of such myelin-sheathed axons, each connected to individual cells. A single bundle, such as the optic nerve, passing from the eye to the brain, may contain as many as 10^6 such individual axons.

THE STRUCTURE OF THE CORTEX: GLIA

The neurons, however, are not the only cells present in the cortex. In fact, in large regions it is difficult to see neurons at all. Although some entire layers are almost filled with cell bodies and others with their twising dendritic and axonal processes, embedded within them or closely adjacent to the neurons themselves lie quite different cells, smaller than the neuron, either unbranched or surrounded with an aura of short stubby processes like a sea urchin.

These cells are known as glia (from the Latin for 'glue') for they appear to stick and seal up all the available space in the cortex, outnumbering the neurons by about ten to one. Their real function in the brain system is far from clear. It has been proposed that, curling around the neuron and its processes as they do, they provide it with essential nutrients which it cannot synthesize itself, or that they serve to regulate the immediate micro-environment of the neuron, mopping up unwanted substances and keeping it cushioned and insulated from the outside world. . . . One of the few functions that can with certainty be ascribed to them is that of fabricating the myelin sheaths in which the long-distance axons are wrapped. . . .

With neurons and their processes, glia and blood capillaries, the brain's grey matter is a fairly crowded place. More crowded with cells indeed than any other tissue in the body. Take a typical tissue, like the liver, say, and from electron microscopic and biochemical studies it would seem that some 20 percent or more of the total volume of the tissue is outside the cells; an extracellular space which surrounds individual cells with a bathing fluid which resembles filtered blood or cerebrospinal fluid in composition. It is through this extracellular space that nutrients diffuse to the cell from the circulating blood, and waste products or chemicals synthesized for export, hormones for instance, leave the cell and enter the circulation.

By contrast, the brain's extracellular space is very small. Estimates vary, but a consensus would put it at around 7 to 12 percent of the total volume (about the theoretical minimum possible for the packing together of more or less spherical objects). This means that the processes, cell bodies and synapses are extremely close-packed and intertwined, leaving almost no room for material to enter or leave the tissue by way of the extracellular space. This presents the brain a considerable problem in obtaining nutrients or removing waste matter. It is almost as if a barrier existed between brain and blood (some workers have indeed referred to a blood-brain barrier). One effect of this barrier is to make the brain more resistant than it might otherwise be to assault by toxic or unpleasant substances in the circulating bloodstream, which find it harder to enter the brain than, say, the liver. The close-packing has even led some to propose, improbably in my view, that for any substance to enter a neuron from the blood it must pass into the glial cells, and then out again. I think otherwise: there is space enough between the cells—but only just. Be that dispute as it may, the close-packing of the brain contributes to its almost frightening complexity when looked at under the electron microscope.... The mass of processes, structures and interactions possible within this web beggars both description and mathematicization. The fascination is almost akin to terror, of such complexity, multiplied so many times, within every individual human's head.

The Brain's Three Principal Functional Units

A. R. Luria

I have said that human mental processes are complex functional systems and that they are not 'localized' in narrow, circumscribed areas of the brain, but take place through the participation of groups of concertedly working brain structures, each of which makes its own particular contribution to the organization of this functional system. Accordingly, the first essential must be to discover the basic functional units from which the human brain is composed, and the role played by each of them in complex forms of mental activity.

There are solid grounds for distinguishing *three principal functional units of the brain* whose participation is necessary for any type of mental activity. With some approximation to the truth they can be described as a unit for *regulating tone or waking,* a unit for *obtaining, processing and storing information* arriving from the outside world and a unit for *programming, regulating and verifying mental activity.* Man's mental processes in general, and his conscious activity in particular, always take place with the participation of all three units, each of which has its role to play in mental processes and makes its contribution to their performance.

Another important feature is that each of these basic units itself is *hierarchical in structure* and consists of at least three cortical zones built one above the other: the *primary* (projection) area which receives impulses from or sends impulses to the periphery, the *secondary* (projection-association), where incoming information is processed or programmes are prepared, and finally, the *tertiary* (zones of overlapping), the latest systems of the cerebral hemispheres to develop and responsible in man for the most complex forms of mental activity requiring the concerted participation of many cortical areas. Let us examine the structure and functional properties of each unit separately. . . .

For human mental processes to follow their correct course, the waking state is essential. It is only under optimal waking conditions that man can receive and analyse information, that the necessary selective systems of connections can be called to mind, his activity programmed, and the course of his mental processes checked, his mistakes corrected, and his activity kept to the proper course.

It is well known that such precise regulation of mental processes is impossible during sleep; the course of reminiscences and associations which spring up is dis-organized in character, and properly directed mental activity is impossible.

'Organized, goal-directed activity requires maintenance of an *optimal level of cortical tone,'* Pavlov stated many years ago, asserting hypothetically that if it were possible to see the system of excitation spreading over the cortex of a waking animal (or man), we would observe a moving, concentrated 'spot of light,' moving over the cortex with the change from one activity to another, and reflecting a point of optimal excitation, without which normal activity is impossible.

The credit not only for indicating the need for such an optimal state of the cortex for any form of organized activity to take place, but also for establishing the fundamental neurodynamic laws characterizing such an optimal state of the cortex, is due to Pavlov. As many of his observations showed, processes of excitation taking place in the waking cortex obey a *law of strength,* according to which every strong (or biologically significant) stimulus evokes a strong response, while every weak stimulus evokes a weak response. It is characterized by a certain degree of *concentration* of nervous processes and a certain balance in the relationships between excitation and inhibition and, finally, by high *mobility* of the nervous processes, so that it is easy to change from one activity to another.

It is these fundamental features of optimal neurodynamics which disappear in sleep or in the state preceding it, when cortical tone diminishes. In these states of inhibition or, as Pavlov calls them, these 'phasic' states the law of strength is broken, and weak stimuli may either evoke equally strong responses as strong stimuli (the 'equalizing phase'), or may evoke stronger responses than strong stimuli (the 'paradoxical phase'), or they may even continue to evoke a response whereas strong stimuli altogether cease to do so (the 'ultraparadoxical phase'). It is also known that in a state of lowered cortical tone the normal relationship between excitation and inhibition is disturbed, and the mobility of the nervous system, so necessary for mental activity to pursue its normal course, is lost. These observations show that maintenance of the *optimal level of cortical tone is essential for the organized course of mental activity.* This raises the question of which brain structures are responsible for maintaining the optimal level of cortical tone we have just mentioned. What parts of the brain regulate and modify cortical tone, maintain it at the proper time and raise it should it become necessary to do so.

A most important discovery, made only thirty years ago, was that the *structures maintaining and regulating cortical tone do not lie in the cortex itself, but below it, in the subcortex and brain stem;* it was also discovered that these structures have a *double relationship with the cortex, both influencing its tone and themselves experiencing its regulatory influence.*

The year 1949 initiated a new period in our knowledge of the functional organization of the brain. In that year two outstanding investigators, Magoun and Moruzzi, showed that there is a special nervous formation in the brain stem which is specially adapted, both by its morphological structure and by its functional properties, to play the role of a mechanism regulating the *state of the cerebral cortex,* changing its tone and maintaining its waking state. Unlike the cortex, this formation does not consist of isolated neurons, capable of sending single impulses along their long processes (axons) and, operating according to an 'all or nothing' law, generating discharges and leading to the innervation of muscles. This formation has the structure of a *nerve net,* among which are scattered the bodies of nerve cells connected with each other by short processes. Excitation spreads over the net of this nervous structure, known as the *reticular formation,* not as single, isolated impulses and not in accordance with the 'all or nothing' law, but *gradually,* changing its level little by little and thus modulating the whole state of the nervous system.

Some of the fibres of this reticular formation run upwards to terminate in higher nervous structures such as the thalmus, caudate body, archicortex and, finally, the structures of the neocortex. These structures were called the *ascending reticular system.* As subsequent observations showed, it plays a decisive role in *activating the cortex and regulating the state of its activity.* Other fibres of the reticular formation run in the opposite direction: they begin in higher nervous structures of the neocortex and archicortex, caudate body, and thalamic nuclei and run to lower structures in the mesencephalon, hypothalamus and brain stem. These structures were called the *descending reticular system* and, as subsequent observations showed, they subordinate these lower structures to the control of programmes arising in the cortex and requiring modification and modulation of the state of waking for their performance.

These two sections of the reticular formation thus constitute a single vertically arranged functional system, a single self-regulating apparatus built on the 'reflex ring' principle, capable of changing the tone of the cortex, but itself also under cortical influence, being regulated and modified by changes taking place in the cortex and adapting itself readily to the environmental conditions and in the course of activity.

With the discovery of the reticular formation, a new principle was thus introduced: the *vertical organization of all structures of the brain.* This put an end to that long period during which the attention of scientists attempting to discover the nervous mechanisms of mental processes was concentrated entirely on the cortex, the work of whose systems was deemed to be independent of the lower or deeper structures. With the description of the reticular formation, the *first functional unit of the brain* was discovered—an apparatus maintaining cortical tone and the waking state and regulating these states in accordance with the actual demands confronting the organism.

The unit for receiving, analysing and storing information

We have discussed the systems of the first functional unit of the brain which plays a role in the regulation of the state of cortical activity and the level of alertness. As we have seen, this unit has the structure of a 'non-specific' nerve net, which performs its function of modifying the state of brain activity gradually, step by step, without having any direct relationship either to the reception and processing of external information or to the formation of complex goal-directed intentions, plans and programmes of behaviour.

In all these considerations the first functional unit of the brain, located mainly in the brain stem, the diencephalon, and the medial regions of the cortex, differs essentially from the system of the *sound functional unit of the brain,* whose primary function is the *reception, analysis and storage of information.*

This unit is located in the lateral regions of the neocortex *on the convex surface of the hemispheres,* of which it occupies the *posterior regions,* including the *visual (occipital), auditory (temporal)* and *general sensory (parietal)* regions.

In its histological structure it consists, not of a continuous nerve net, but of *isolated neurons,* which lie in the parts of the cortex already described and which, unlike the systems of the first unit, do not work in accordance with the principle of gradual changes, but obey the 'all or nothing' rule, by receiving discrete impulses and relaying them to other groups of neurons.

In their functional properties, the systems of this unit are adapted to the reception of stimuli travelling to the brain the peripheral receptors, to their analysis into a very large number of very small component elements, and to their combination into the required dynamic functional structures (or in other words, their synthesis into whole functional systems).

Finally, it is clear from what has been said above that this functional unit of the brain consists of parts possessing *high modal specificity,* i.e. that its component parts are adapted to the reception of visual, auditory, vestibular or general sensory information. The systems of this unit also incorporate the central systems of gustatory and olfactory reception, although in man they are so overshadowed by the central representation of the higher exteroceptive systems, receiving stimuli from objects at a distance, that they occupy a predominantly minor place in the cortex. . . .

The primary zones of the individual cortical regions composing this unit also contain cells of a multimodal character, which respond to several types of stimuli, as well as cells which do not respond to any modally-specific type of stimuli, and which evidently retain the properties of non-specific maintenance of tone; however, these cells form only a very small proportion of the total neuronal composition of the primary cortical areas (according to some figures, not more than 4 percent of the total number of cells present). . . .

The principal modally-specific zones of the second brain system . . . are thus built in accordance with a single *principle of hierarchical organization* . . . which applies equally to all these zones, each of which must be regarded as the *central, cortical apparatus of a modally-specific analyser.* . . .

All the zones described above are in fact adapted so as to serve as an *apparatus for the reception, analysis and* (as we shall see) *the storage of information arriving from the outside world* or, in other words, *the cerebral mechanisms of modally-specific forms of gnostic processes.*

As we have discussed, human gnostic activity never takes place with respect to one single isolated modality (vision, hearing, touch); the perception—and still more, the representation—of any object is a *complex* procedure, the result of polymodal activity, originally expanded in character, later concentrated and condensed. Naturally, therefore, it must rely on the combined working of a complete system of cortical zones.

It is the *tertiary* zones of this second brain system or, as they are generally called, the *zones of overlapping* of the cortical ends of the various analysers, which are responsible for enabling groups of several analysers to work concertedly. These zones lie on the boundary between the occipital, temporal, and post-central cortex; the greater part of them is formed by the inferior parietal region which, in man, has developed to a considerable size, occupying just about one-quarter of the total mass of the system we are describing. It can therefore be considered that the tertiary zones or, as Flechsig described them, the 'posterior associative centre,' are *specifically human structures.* . . . The principal role of these zones is connected with the *spatial organization* of discrete impulses of excitation entering the various regions and with the conversion of *successive stimuli into simultaneously processed groups.* . . .

This work of the tertiary zones of the posterior cortical regions is thus essential, not only for the successful integration of information reaching man through his visual system, but also for the *transition from direct, visually represented syntheses to the level of symbolic processes*—or operations with word meanings, with complex grammatical

and logical structures, with systems of numbers and abstract relationships. It is because of this that the *tertiary zones of the posterior cortical region play an essential role in the conversion of concrete perception into abstract thinking,* which always proceeds in the form of *internal* schemes, and for the *memorizing of organized experience* or, in other words, not only for the reception and coding of information, but also for its storage.

We have therefore every reason for regarding the whole of this functional system of the brain as a system for the reception, coding and storage of information. . . .

Conversely, in the *adult* person, with his fully formed higher psychological functions, the *higher cortical zones have assumed the dominant role.* Even when he perceives the world around him, the adult person organizes (codes) his impressions into logical systems, fits them into certain schemes; *the highest, tertiary zones of the cortex thus begin to control the work of the secondary zones* which are subordinated to them, and if the secondary zones are affected by a pathological lesion, the tertiary zones have a compensatory influence on their work. This relationship between the principal, hierarchically organized cortical zones in the adult led Vygotsky to the conclusion that in the late stage of ontogeny the main line of their interaction runs 'from above downward,' and that the work of the adult human cerebral cortex reveals not so much the dependence of the higher zones on the lower as the opposite—dependence of the lower (modally specific) zones on the higher.

This suggests that the *hierarchical principle of the working of individual zones of the second brain unit* is the first fundamental law which provides a clue to its functional organization. . . .

The unit for programming, regulation and verification of activity

The reception, coding, and storage of information constitute only one aspect of human cognitive processes. Another of its aspects is the organization of conscious activity. This task is linked with the third of the fundamental functional systems of the brain, responsible for programming, regulation and verification.

Man not only reacts passively to incoming information, but creates *intentions,* forms *plans* and *programmes* of his actions, inspects their performance, and *regulates* his behaviour so that it conforms to these plans and programmes; finally, he *verifies* his conscious activity, comparing the effects of his actions with the original intentions and correcting any mistakes he has made.

All these processes of conscious activity require quite different brain systems from those which we have already described. Whereas even in simple reflex tasks there are both afferent and effector sides as well as a feedback system, acting as a controlling servo-mechanism, special neuronal structures of this type are even more essential to the work of the brain when regulating complex conscious activity. These tasks are met by the structures of the third brain unit, whose functions we have just described.

The structures of the third functional unit, the system for programming, regulation and verification, are located in the *anterior regions* of the hemispheres. . . .

The most important part of this third functional unit of the brain is the *frontal lobes* or, to be more precise, the *prefrontal divisions of the brain* which, because they do not contain pyramidal cells, are sometimes known as the *granular frontal cortex.* It is these portions of the brain, belonging to the tertiary zones of the cortex, which play a decisive role in the formation of intentions and programmes, and in the regulation and verification of the most complex forms of human behaviour. . . .

Interaction between the three principal functional units of the brain

We have examined modern ideas regarding the three principal functional units of the brain and have tried to show the role of each of them in the organization of complex mental activity. We must now consider a fact which is essential to the understanding of the work of all the functional units of the brain we have examined.

It would be a mistake to imagine that each of these units can carry out a certain form of activity completely independently—for example, that the second functional unit is entirely responsible for the function of perception and thought, while the third is responsible for the function of movement and for the construction of action.

It will be clear from what has been said already regarding the *systemic structure of complex psychological processes* that this is not so. Each form of conscious activity is always a *complex functional system* and takes place through the *combined working of all three brain units,* each of which makes its own contribution. The well established facts of modern psychology provide a solid basis for this view.

Many years have passed since psychologists regarded mental functions as isolated *faculties,* each of which could be localized in a certain part of the brain. However, the time has also passed when it was thought that mental processes could be represented by models of a *reflex arc,* the first part of which was purely afferent in character and performed the function of sensation and perception, while

the second, effector part, was entirely concerned with movement and action.

Modern view regarding the structure of mental processes are completely different in character and are based more on the model of a *reflex ring* or *self-regulating system,* each component of which embodies both afferent and effector elements, so that on the whole, *mental activity assumes a complex and active character.*

As an example let us examine the structure, first, of perception and, second, of movement or action. We shall do so only at the most general level. . . .

It would be a mistake to imagine that sensation and perception are purely passive processes. Sensation has shown to include motor components, and in modern psychology sensation and, more especially, perception are regarded as active processes incorporating both afferent and efferent components. . . . Adequate proof that sensation is complex and active in character is given by the fact that even in animals it incorporates a process of selection of biologically significant features, while in man it also includes the active coding influence of speech. . . .

The active character of the processes in the perception of complex objects is more obvious still. It is well known that perception of objects not only is polyreceptor in character and dependent on the combined working of a group of analysers, but also that it always incorporates active motor components. The vital role of eye movements in visual perception was described originally by Sechenov (1874-8), but it is only recently that psychophysiological investigations have shown that the stationary eye is virtually incapable of the stable perception of complex objects and that such perception is always based on the use of active, searching movements of the eyes, picking out the essential clues, . . . and that these movements only gradually become contracted in character in the course of development. . . .

These facts clearly show that *perception takes place through the combined action of all three functional units of the brain;* the first provides the necessary cortical tone, the second carries out the analysis and synthesis of incoming information, and the third provides for the necessary controlled searching movements which give perceptual activity its active character. . . .

It is clear that *all three principal functional brain units work concertedly,* and that it is only by studying their interactions, when each unit makes its own specific contribution, that an insight can be obtained into the nature of the cerebral mechanisms of mental activity.

How the Brain Works – A New Theory

E. Roy John

Most modern theories of brain function relate specific physical and mental activities to certain places in the brain. In this view, we need particular parts of our brain to perform specific functions—our visual system to see, our motor system to move, and so on. I think this view is only partly right. My research leads me to believe that vast regions of the brain are involved in every thought process, although some parts are more involved than others.

By basing the treatment of brain disorders on the theory of highly specialized brain areas, we may be cheating ourselves of the most effective therapies. If my view is correct, people who lose some of their mental capacities because of brain damage can recover much more fully than we give them credit for or encourage them to try.

The old theories that brain functions are localized assume that when we learn something, such as how to play the piano, new connections are made between nerve cells in different parts of the brain. Our memory that a certain note on the page means we should strike a black key in the middle of the keyboard, such theories hold, lies in these connections. Remembering the correct note means that the connected cells have been reactivated.

These views of learning and memory persist despite telling evidence to the contrary. The strongest contradiction is the failure of generations of physiological psychologists to find undeniable evidence for these supposed connections. Some researchers have erased memory by cutting parts of animals' brains. But a careful look at these experiments usually shows that the brain damage caused less specific deficits—changes in motivation, attention, or sensory sensitivity—and not the loss of a specific memory.

Also, a great deal of research has shown that when brain damage that would normally cause a loss of certain capacities is inflicted in stages, there is little or no loss. For example, if both sides of the visual system of a rat's brain are destroyed in the same operation, the rat loses the ability to recognize visual patterns. But if the second side is destroyed two weeks after the first, the rat can still recognize patterns. Apparently, during the two-week interval, the rat learns to use other parts of the brain for recognition; the localization theory provides no explanation for this whatever. Nor can it explain why people with severe brain damage sometimes recover lost functions completely. Since destroyed brain cells and nerve tissue do not regenerate, such recovery should be impossible. Yet the medical literature is sprinkled with many such cases.

Stroke Victims. For a long time, others have questioned these localization theories. Perhaps the best known skeptic was the American psychologist Karl Lashley. In the early 1930s he proposed that many different regions of the brain carry out the same function. Lashley's arguments have been dismissed or ignored and the one-region one-function idea has prevailed. Perhaps the strongest arguments in favor have come from the work of modern neurophysiologists, who identified cells in the visual system that reacted with precision to specific sights, and cells in the motor system that seemed to control particular muscles. Localization also seems the best explanation for stroke victims or others with brain damage who permanently lose the functions associated with the damaged parts of their brains.

My own experiments over the last 25 years have led me to propose a theory which reconciles these seemingly contradictory outlooks. This statistical configuration theory proposes that many brain functions are distributed throughout most brain regions, but that some regions contribute more than others to any given function. For example, the motor system has the biggest role in movement and the visual system in seeing, but many other parts of the brain play a role in these functions.

The earliest electrophysiological indications that memories do not consist of new connections between cells came when Keith Killam and I implanted 34 electrodes in different parts of the brain of a cat. These electrodes let us see the electrical rhythms recorded from many parts of the brain as the cat watched a light that flashed repeatedly. Some of the regions showed electrical waves the same frequency as the flashing light. We called these waves "labeled rhythms." These labeled rhythms were the response of the cat's brain to the flashing light; the other regions showed only random activity.

When the cat first saw the flashing light, labeled rhythms showed up in only a few parts of the brain, mainly in areas included in the classical anatomical sketch of the visual system. But as the cat learned to associate the lights with the need to jump a hurdle to avoid shock, the lights took on new meaning. The labeled rhythms spread to other parts of the brain. When the cat was merely registering that a light was flashing, only the visual system was involved. When the light acquired a specific meaning for the cat, the rest of the brain got into the act.

We Were Seeing Memory. Once the labeled rhythms spread to other parts of the brain, the cat's brain would sometimes emit them when the light was off. Quite often, between trials, when the cat was expecting the lights to flash, the labeled rhythms showed up in abundance. Sometimes the cat accompanied these bursts of labeled rhythms with hurdle jumps, as though rehearsing for the next flashing light.

We next trained our cats to do two different things, depending on the pattern of flashing lights. If the lights flashed at the rate of one flash per second, the cat would press a lever to get milk; if the flashes were five per second, the cat would jump a hurdle to avoid shock. If the cat got confused, and performed a hurdle jump in response to the first flash rhythm, the cat's brain showed the labeled pattern for the second flash rhythm. If it mistakenly performed a lever press in response to the second flash rhythm, the one-per-second brain response showed up. We were seeing memory, and it was spread throughout the brain.

We wanted to sort out the brain rhythms of memory that came from inside the brain from those caused by the brain's responses to what it was sensing from outside, through its visual system. Frank Bartlett and I set out to see if the waves in a given region were due to internal or external causes. This new approach depended on a computerized measure, the average evoked potential (EP). The EP calculates the average electrical response pattern from a brain region. This response pattern occurs within a few hundred milliseconds after a sensory stimulus, such as a light flash. The computer shows the detailed pattern of the brain's response to incoming information.

Predicting Mistakes. When we used the EP, we again found that as the cats learned specific responses to the flashing lights, new regions of the brain became involved. Each stimulus caused electrical activity in the brain, which the computer depicted as a specifically shaped wave. Daniel Ruchkin and Paul Easton devised computer programs that could recognize the wave shape associated with each stimulus. These programs allowed us to predict what the cat would do in response to a particular light pattern. We could know beforehand that the cat was going to make a mistake, and what mistake it would be.

These same waveshape-recognition programs allowed us to separate internal and external influences. We could tell which part of the waveshape came from the brain's receiving a sensory message, and which from memory. Using these programs, Bartlett and I recorded waveshapes from many different brain regions in hundreds of cats, separating the internal and external portions. We found a

lawful relationship between the senses and memory in each region: the more a brain region senses an event, the more it remembers it.

We also found that brain regions do not make an all-or-nothing contribution to mental operations. Each brain region makes an average contribution to practically every operation, but these contributions are graded, each region more involved on the average in some operations than in others.

To see just how involved in a given function each region was, we devised a tiny movable microelectrode that could record a single cell's activity for a period, then move on down through the brain to do the same for a different cell. In this way we mapped cell activity throughout the brain while a cat performed the same hurdle-jump or lever-press tasks described earlier. Every cell we looked at responded in unpredictable ways to a new stimulus, in more predictable ways to a familiar stimulus, and in different ways to different stimuli. Each cell also showed much random activity. Further, well-separated cells in distant parts of the brain sometimes responded to the same stimulus with identical firing rhythms. In many cases, the firing pattern reflected what the cat would later do, and not the stimulus we were giving it.

The Statistical Brain. If, as most theories assume, cells form connections during learning, they should reliably react to the learned stimulus and not to another. If remembering consists of the activation of a specific group of cells, the activity of a cell in the group should be predictable, or at least fall into some recognizable pattern. Certainly, according to most theories, cells should not activate randomly. But I found the firing of any single cell is random and variable. Remembering requires the average pattern of a great many cells, not the dependable activation of any one cell. Such averages even predict future behavior.

David Kleinman and I used those results to test my idea about the statistical functioning of the brain. After identifying the pattern for a specific stimulus, we used an electrical replica of the pattern to stimulate cells where the electrodes were implanted. Again, the cat was taught to make two different responses to two patterns of flashing lights. When the cat's brain was stimulated directly in the pattern typical of its response to one pattern of flashing lights, the cat performed the appropriate response, even though the light itself had not flashed.

Once we knew that we could make the cat perform as though it were experiencing a familiar event when it was not, we tried a conflict study. We showed the cat the first pattern of light while stimulating its brain in the cell-firing rhythm characteristic of the second light pattern. As we increased the strength of the direct brain stimulation, the internal signals overpowered the external flash and the cat behaved as though it were seeing the internally signaled light.

We were able to make a cat react even when we split the internal signal, sending part of the pattern to some sections of the brain, and the rest to the others. The cat's response was appropriate to the total pattern of stimulation. Apparently, the brain put the split signals together, combining different timing patterns from different parts of the brain into an integrated whole.

Noise in the Brain.   It is not the location of cells that matters, but rather the rhythm at which they fire. Any given cell is important insofar as it contributes to the average behavior of a large group of cells spread throughout the brain. Cells combine to perform mental functions by a statistical process, and the rhythm of their average firing pattern controls the function. The pattern of all cells involved causes us to see, move a finger, or remember our first bicycle ride.

Each brain region has a characteristic signal-to-noise ratio for a particular operation. "Noise" refers to random cell firing, and "signal" to cell firing in rhythm with other cells performing the same operation. The more signal and the less noise, the greater the contribution of a given region of cells to a specific function. The regions conventionally thought to control a given function are actually those with the most signal and least noise for that function. Almost every other region of the brain is involved in the same function, but with comparatively more noise and less signal. For example, when we see something, the visual system has the most cells firing at a specific rhythm and the least firing at random. But the motor system also has many cells firing at the same rhythm, although relatively more fire at random.

One implication of this is that no one function can be attributed to activity in any specific cell or group of cells. Every mental operation, including consciousness itself, is due to activity throughout the brain. The experiments that showed visual cells reacting to a particular stimulus and not to others told only part of the story. They may have been the cells with the highest signal-to-noise ratio for that function, but there were innumerable other cells throughout the brain firing in synchrony with them.

When we learn something, small groups of cells do not form new connections. Rather, cells in many parts of the brain learn a new rhythm of firing corresponding to the learning. The memory of what is learned is not to be found in any specific brain region, but rather in its unique cell-firing rhythm. As the brain works, it is not just the connections between its parts that matter. The brain's rhythms count for as much or more than the way it is put together.

BRAIN AND MIND

The perennial puzzle in the study of consciousness is the relationship of the brain to the mind. The puzzle is complicated by the fact that different parts of the brain contribute to different qualities of consciousness. Neurologist David Galin describes the ways in which we have two brains, each half excelling in certain abilities in which the other is not as skilled. In most of us, the right half of the brain, which controls the left half of the body, sees things more as a whole; the left half, which controls the right half of the body, analyzes things into their parts. Thus the right half of the brain is better at jobs like recognizing faces, while the left half excels in rational, logical tasks such as mathematics and writing. Each mode of handling information complements the other; the left hemisphere rationally analyzes a problem, the right intuits the pattern that can solve it. The differences in functions between the hemispheres are not all-or-none; in actuality the dominance of one or the other in any given mental task is only relative. This means that many cells in the nondominant hemisphere are also active in a task where the other hemisphere dominates. As we will see, no mental function is due to cell activity isolated in only one part of the brain, but involves cells throughout many disparate brain zones.

A more sinister aspect of brain function is what neurologist Paul MacLean calls the "paranoid streak"—our proneness to outbursts of rage and selfish violence. While normal people enter this state from time to time, this psychological attitude of mistrust and hostility characterizes the paranoid psychotic. The key to localizing the part of the brain most to blame for this state is in the emotional tone of paranoia, free-floating fear. The part of the brain that triggers such feelings is the limbic system, which MacLean himself was among the first to study. The limbic system, which man shares with all other mammals and reptiles, is a series of structures that rise up from the brain's base toward the cortex at the top. As the source of all strong emotions like fear, anger, and lust, the limbic system is by no means the center for only sinister feelings; it is also the brain's source of feelings of pleasure, sexual desire, and satiation.

We know that what happens in the brain is essential for consciousness, but we are mystified when it comes to specifying exactly what aspect of brain function makes us conscious. Neurologist Wilder Penfield recounts the case of a Russian Nobel Prize-winning physicist who was pulled from the brink of death back to full awareness. As he recovered, the physicist regained the use of more and more of his damaged brain. At what point, Penfield asks, did he become fully "conscious?" Which brain centers, if any, are essential to human consciousness? What exactly is the connection between brain and mind? Penfield offers no easy answers, for at the moment there are none. Another Nobel Prizewinner, biochemist Paul Weiss, considered the same problem, and concluded that all we can say of the brain-mind relation is that consciousness does not reduce simply to the sum of brain cell activity. Here, as with all living organisms, the maxim applies: the whole is more than the sum of its parts.

The Two Modes of Consciousness and the Two Halves of the Brain

David Galin

HEMISPHERIC SPECIALIZATION

It has been known for one hundred years that in typical right handers the left hemisphere is specialized for spoken language and its derivatives, reading and writing. A large injury to the left hemisphere will usually destroy these behaviors. An injury to the right hemisphere does not usually interfere with speech, and for a long time the right hemisphere was considered to be just a rather stupid spare for the left. The specialization of the right hemisphere has only recently been widely recognized; it is very good at dealing with novel complex spatial and musical patterns. A person with a large right-hemisphere injury might have trouble copying a geometric figure, or matching a design with wooden blocks, or recognizing faces (even his own), or recognizing melodies. These tasks all require that you keep in mind an *over-all pattern of relations,* not just the separate parts.

It is important to emphasize that what most characterizes the hemispheres is not that they are specialized to work with different types of material (the left with words and the right with spatial forms); rather, each hemisphere is specialized for a different cognitive style; the left for an analytic, logical mode for which words are an excellent tool, and the right for a holistic, Gestalt mode, which happens to be particularly suitable for spatial relations.

THE TWO COGNITIVE MODES CHARACTERIZED

We have called the style of the left hemisphere "analytical;" i.e., it is adept at taking things apart, and dealing with the separated parts one at a time. In this mode, therefore, boundaries are very important, because boundaries are what define a part.

Words serve to establish boundaries. When we name an object (or a person) we separate it from its context, and label it in accord with some of its attributes, of necessity neglecting other attributes. For example, if I say "give me the hammer," I have focused attention on the functional aspects of the tool (hammer, rather than the pliers) and not on its size, color, ownership, sentimental or cash value, etc. In this sense labeling is a way of excluding aspects or relations which are not wanted. This is why people often resent being "labeled;" the label of necessity excludes some aspect, and they do not want any aspect of themselves to be denied. This is exemplified currently in the feminists' concern over labels pertaining to gender.

Sequence or temporal ordering is also very important in the analytic mode. In verbal analysis, for example, word sequence is critical to meaning in sentences (compare "John loves Mary" versus "Mary loves John"). Injuries to the left hemisphere interfere with the perception of temporal sequences. Patients with such injuries may not be able to tell which of two lights flashed first, or if they flashed at the same time. We have speculated that this specialization for temporal ordering in simple perceptual and motor performance may be related to a focus on time in more complex behavior. For example, this mode might emphasize concern with outcome and sequences of actions, focusing on the future, or the past, rather than focusing on processes and the present (what Gestalt therapists call "staying in the now").

The verbal-analytic style is extremely efficient for dealing with the object world. Our modern technology, standard of living, and scientific achievements depend heavily on highly developed linear, analytic methods. Communication of some concepts is very difficult without verbal propositions; for example, "Democracy requires informed participation." On the other hand, some concepts are not handled well with words. Consider what most people do when asked to define a spiral staircase: they begin to say a few words haltingly, and then make a twirling gesture with an upraised finger. For most people this complex concept is better handled with this visual-kinesthetic representation than with a verbal representation. (One of our associates whose earlier training was in nuclear physics answered with the sine and cosine equations for a helix, without moving his hands, but this is not a common response.) This sort of nonverbal representation seems to be more characteristic of right-hemisphere thinking.

We have called the special style of the right hemisphere "holistic." It is particularly good at grasping patterns of relations. This mode seems to integrate many inputs simultaneously, rather than operating on them one at a time, sequentially, like the analytic mode. This is important for the many situations in which the essential meaning is given by the overall pattern of relations between the elements not by the elements themselves. A simple example of this is a stew; its nature depends on the mutual interactions of its parts. A piece of meat, a potato, a carrot, an onion, a clove of garlic, cooked and served separately in sequence would not be stew; they must simultaneously act on each other.

The holistic mode of information processing is very good for bridging gaps; we can perceive a pattern even when some of the pieces are missing. In contrast, a logical, sequential mode cannot skip over gaps. Since we are usually trying to operate in this world with incomplete information, we very badly need to have a capacity to perceive general patterns and jump across gaps in present knowledge.

HEMISPHERIC DISCONNECTION SYNDROME— "THE SPLIT BRAIN"

The two hemispheres have been surgically separated for the treatment of certain rare cases of epilepsy. It has been found that after all the connecting nerve-fiber bundles have been cut, each hemisphere is independently conscious and can carry out the complex cognitive processes of the type for which it is specialized. In short, there appear to be two separate, conscious minds in one head. Sperry has summarized the hemisphere disconnection syndrome as follows:

The most remarkable effect of sectioning the cerebral commissures continues to be the apparent lack of change with respect to ordinary behavior. [The patients] ... exhibit no gross alterations of personality, intellect or overt behavior two years after operation. Individual mannerisms, conversation and bearing, temperament, strength, vigor and coordination are all largely intact and seem much as before surgery. Despite this outward appearance of general normality in ordinary behavior ... specific tests indicate functional disengagement of the right and left hemispheres with respect to nearly all cognitive and other psychic activities. Learning and memory are found to proceed quite independently in each separated hemisphere. Each hemisphere seems to have its own conscious sphere for sensation, perception, ideation, and other mental activities and the whole inner realm of gnostic experience of the one is cut off from the corresponding experiences of the other hemisphere—with only a few exceptions. . . .

To understand the method of testing and interviewing each half of the brain separately, two points of functional anatomy must be kept in mind. The first is that since language functions (speech, writing) are mediated predominantly by the left hemisphere in most people, the disconnected right hemisphere cannot express itself verbally. The second point is that the neural pathways carrying information from one side of the body and one-half of the visual field cross over and connect only with the opposite side of the brain. This means that sensations in the righ hand and images in the right visual space will be projected almost entirely to the *left* hemisphere. Similarly, the major motor output is crossed, and the left hemisphere controls mainly the movements of the right hand. Therefore, patients with the two hemispheres disconnected can describe or answer

questions about objects placed in their right hands, or pictures flashed to the right visual fields with a tachistoscope, but can give no correct verbal response when the information is presented to the left hand or the left visual field (they will, in fact, often confabulate). However, the mute right hemisphere can indicate its experience with the left hand, for example, by selecting the proper object from an array.

The human brain, from the top, is something like a walnut, wrinkly and divided down the middle into two distinct halves by a deep fissure. At the bottom of the fissure, the two halves are connected by a great bridge of nerve fibers called the Corpus Callosum. From a side view the brain is more like a mushroom, with the hemispheres forming the cap, and the lower parts of the brain forming a stem which connects below with the spinal cord. The Corpus Callosum contains 200,000,000 nerve fibers, more than the combined total of all the sensory fibers entering the cerebrum and all the descending fibers controlling movement. From its relative size, it would appear to be a very important part of the brain. Nevertheless, when this connecting bridge was surgically cut, the patients seemed quite ordinary unless tested in the very special ways described above.

The dissociation between the experiences of the two disconnected hemispheres is sometimes very dramatic. Dr. Roger Sperry and his colleagues at the California Institute of Technology have photographed illustrative incidents.

One film study shows a female patient being tested with a tachistoscope as described above. In the series of neutral geometrical figures being presented at random to the right and left fields, a nude pin-up was included and flashed to the right (nonverbal) hemisphere. The patient blushes and giggles. Sperry asks "What did you see?" She answers "Nothing, just a flash of light," and giggles again, covering her mouth with her hand. "Why are you laughing then?" asks Sperry, and she laughs again and says, "Oh, Dr. Sperry, you have some machine." The episode is very suggestive; if one did not know her neurosurgical history one might see this as a clear example of perceptual defense and think that she was "repressing" the perception of the disturbing sexual material—even her final response (a socially acceptable non sequitur) was convincing.

In another film a different patient is performing a block-design task; he is trying to match a colored geometric design with a set of painted blocks. The film shows the left hand (right hemisphere) quickly carrying out the task. Then the experimenter disarranges the blocks and the right hand (left hemisphere) is given the task; slowly and with great apparent indecision it arranges the pieces. In trying to match a corner of the design the right hand corrects one of the blocks, and then shifts it again, apparently not realizing it was correct; the viewer sees the left hand dart out, grab the block to restore it to the correct position—and then the arm of the experimenter reaches over and pulls the intruding left hand off camera.

HOW DO THE TWO HEMISPHERES GET ALONG UNDER NORMAL CIRCUMSTANCES?

Two facts have been presented: the cerebral hemispheres are specialized for different kinds of thinking, and when they are surgically disconnected, each one is capable of being independently conscious. When these two facts are considered together they lead to a number of important questions. In the normal person with intact connections between the hemispheres, are these systems smoothly integrated? Can these two half-brains to some extent sustain separate parallel consciousnesses as they do when the connecting fibers are surgically severed? Or do they alternate in control, taking turns in directing behavior? If they can operate independently, there are possibilities for both cooperation and for conflict. Bogen has pointed out some of the implications of these two facts, summarizing the main propositions very elegantly and with proper historical perspective, under the title of "Neowiganism." The essentials of this theory and its implications were first developed by A. L. Wigan in a book called *The Duality of the Mind* published in 1844. Wigan was first led to his theory by the postmortem observation of a man whom he had known well before the man's death from unrelated causes. At autopsy one cerebral hemisphere was found to be totally absent. Wigan was not only astounded by this finding, but had the wits to see its meaning: only one hemisphere is required to have a mind or to be a person. Therefore Wigan concluded: if only one cerebrum is required to have a mind, possession of two hemispheres (the normal state) makes possible or perhaps even inevitable the possession of two minds; and however synchronous these two minds may be most of the time, there must inevitably be some occasion when they are discrepant. This provides the anatomical-physiologic basis for that division of self, that internal struggle which is characteristic of so much of mankind's ill health and unhappiness. This magnificent speculation was accorded very little notice at the time . . . . What Wigan did not know [was that] . . . whereas the two hemispheres of a cat or monkey may sustain two duplicate minds, the lateralization typical of man requires that the two minds must *necessarily* be discrepant. "Neowiganism" means that . . . each of us is possessed of two minds which differ in content, possibly even goals, but most certainly in respect to mode of organization. The evolutionary advantage of having two different minds is obvious; possession of two independent problem solving organs increases mightily the likelihood of a creative solution to a novel problem. At the same time there is an enormous increase in the likelihood of internal conflict. And so we have man, the most innovative of species and at the same time the most at odds with himself.

LEFT AND RIGHT MODES: COMPLEMENTARY OR IN CONFLICT

The analytic and holistic modes are complementary; each provides a dimension which the other lacks. Artists, scientists, mathematicians, writing about their own creativity, all report that their work is based on a smooth integration of both modes. If we want to cultivate creativity it appears that we must first develop each mode, both the rational-analytic and the intuitive-holistic; second, we must develop the ability to inhibit either one when it is inappropriate to the task at hand; and finally we must be able to operate in both modes in a complementary fashion.

However, the two modes may also be in conflict; there seems to be some mutual antagonism between the analytic and the holistic. For example, the tendency of the left hemisphere to note details in a form suitable for expression in words seems to interfere with the perception of the over-all pattern. This mutual interference has been suggested as the reason why our brains evolved with these two systems segregated into separate hemispheres.

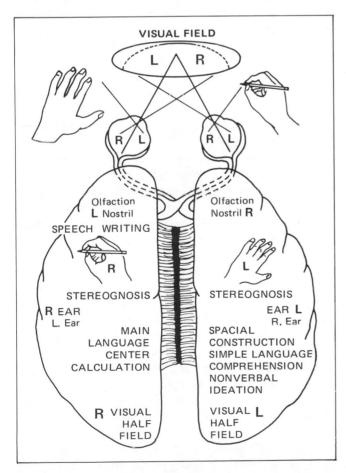

VISUAL FIELD

Schema showing the way in which the left and right visual fields are projected onto the right and left visual cortices, respectively. The schema also shows other sensory inputs from right limbs to the left hemisphere and that from left limbs to the right hemisphere.

Use of the inappropriate mode for a task may account for some common problems. My difficulties with dancing may be related to my excessive reliance on analytic sequential processes; instead of allowing a smooth synthesis of the separate parts, I have not been able to progress past counting "one . . . two . . . THREE . . . , one . . . two . . . THREE." Similarly, an excessive or inappropriate use of the holistic mode could interfere with learning to read, or with carrying out sequential arithmetic calculations such as are required in balancing a checkbook.

The specialization of the hemispheres and their potential for independent functioning may play some role in psychiatric conflict as well. Freud had reluctantly abandoned the attempt to relate the functioning of the parts of the mental apparatus to specific anatomical locations because the neurology of his time was insufficient. It may be useful to reconsider these questions now.

There is a compelling formal similarity between some dissociations seen in the split-brain patients (such as the pin-up sequence described above) and the phenomena of repression. According to Freud's early "topographical" model of the mind, repressed mental contents functioned in a separate realm which was inaccessible to conscious recall or verbal interrogation. This realm of the unconscious had its own rules, and developed its own goals. It could affect the viscera, and could insinuate itself into the stream of ongoing consciously directed behavior. Certain aspects of right-hemisphere functioning are similar to "primary process," the form of thought which Freud originally assigned to the unconscious realm: both depend mainly on non-verbal image representations, with nonsyllogistic logic, and are more concerned with multiple simultaneous interactions than with temporal sequencing.

When the two hemispheres are surgically disconnected the mental process of each one is inaccessible to deliberate conscious retrieval from the point of view of the other. However, the operation does not affect them as symmetrically with respect to overt behavior. Sperry and his collaborators have found that "in general, the postoperative behavior [of the patients] has been dominated by the major [left] hemisphere . . ." except in tasks for which the right hemisphere is particularly specialized. In these respects there seems to be a parallel between the functioning of the isolated right hemisphere and mental processes which are repressed, unconscious, and unable directly to control behavior.

These similarities suggest the hypothesis that in normal, intact people mental events in the right hemisphere can become disconnected functionally from the left hemisphere (by inhibition of neuronal transmission across the Corpus Callosum) and can continue a life of their own. This hypothesis offers a neurophysiological mechanism for at least some instances of repression, and an anatomical locus for the unconscious mental contents.

HOW INTEGRATED ARE THE TWO HEMISPHERES UNDER NORMAL CONDITIONS?

We do not know the usual relation between the two hemispheres in normal adults, but we can speculate on several possible arrangements. One possibility is that they operate in alternation, i.e., taking turns, depending on situational demands. When one hemisphere is "on" it may inhibit the other. A variant of this relationship might be that the dominating hemisphere makes use of one or more of the subsystems of the other hemisphere (e.g., memory), inhibiting the rest (e.g., planning, motivation). The inhibition thus may be only partial, suppressing enough of the subordinate hemisphere so as to render it incapable of sustaining its own plan of action. Our EEG studies of normal people are consistent with this view: when subjects performed verbal tasks (left hemisphere) we observed an increase in alpha waves (an idling rhythm) over the right hemisphere; when they performed spatial tasks (right hemisphere) the idling rhythm shifted to the left hemisphere. Another variant is the one hypothesized above in relation to "repression;" one hemisphere dominates overt behavior, but can only disconnect rather than totally inhibit (disrupt) the other hemisphere, which remains independently conscious. The fourth possible condition, in which the two hemispheres are fully active and integrated with each other, is the condition which Bogen associates with creativity. Unfortunately this does not seem to occur very often. In fact, he suggests that one of the reasons that the commissurotomy patients appear so normal to casual observation is because the activities of daily life do not demand much creativity.

If the usual condition is either alternation between the two modes, or parallel but independent consciousnesses with one of them dominating overt behavior, what factors determine which hemisphere will be "on"? Which will gain control of the shared functions and dominate overt behavior? There are two factors suggested by experiments with split-brain monkeys and humans. One could be called "resolution by speed;" the hemisphere which solves the problem first gets to the output channel first. This seems the most likely explanation for the observations in the human patients that "when a hemisphere is intrinsically better equipped to handle some task, it is also easier for that hemisphere to dominate the motor pathways."

For example, Sperry and his collaborators have found that the right hemisphere dominates behavior in a facial recognition task. Recognition of faces requires a perception of the Gestalt, and is relatively resistant to analytical verbal description.

A second factor determining which hemisphere gets control could be called "resolution by motivation;" the one who cares more about the outcome pre-empts the output.

This was demonstrated by Michael Gazzaniga in a series of ingenious experiments with split-brain monkeys. He taught each hemisphere (separately) the opposite solutions to a discrimination task, and then tested them at the same time in conflict. He found that he could change which hemisphere dominated behavior by changing the amount of reward that each hemisphere got for a correct answer. Gazzaniga concluded, "Cerebral dominance in monkeys is quite flexible and subject to the effects of reinforcement. . . . The hemisphere which is most successful in earning reinforcement comes to dominate." This may apply to intact humans as well. As the left hemisphere develops its language capability in the second and third year of life it gains a great advantage over the right hemisphere in manipulating its environment and securing reinforcements. It seems likely to me that this is the basis for the left hemisphere's suzerainty in overt behavior in situations of conflict with the right hemisphere.

CONDITIONS FAVORING THE DEVELOPMENT OF SEPARATE STREAMS OF CONSCIOUSNESS

There are several ways in which the two hemispheres of an ordinary person could begin to function as if they had been surgically disconnected and decrease their exchange of information.

The first way is by active inhibition of information transfer because of conflict. Imagine the effect on a child when his mother presents one message verbally but quite another with her facial expression and body language; "I am doing it because I love you, dear," say the words, but "I hate you and will destroy you," says the face. Each hemisphere is exposed to the same sensory input, but because of their relative specializations, they each emphasize only one of the messages. The left will attend to the verbal cues because it cannot extract information from the facial Gestalt efficiently; the right will attend to the nonverbal cues because it cannot easily understand the words. In effect, a different input has been delivered to each hemisphere, just as in the laboratory experiments in which a tachistoscope is used to present different pictures to the left and right visual fields. I offer the following conjecture: in this situation the two hemispheres might decide on opposite courses of action; the left to approach, and the right to flee. Because of the high stakes involved each hemisphere might be able to maintain its consciousness and resist the inhibitory influence of the other

side. The left hemisphere seems to win control of the output channels most of the time, but if the left is not able to "turn off" the right completely it may settle for disconnecting the transfer of the conflicting information from the other side. The connections between hemispheres are relatively weak compared to the connections within hemispheres, and it seems likely that each hemisphere treats the weak contralateral input in the same way in which people in general treat the odd discrepant observation which does not fit with the mass of their beliefs; first they ignore it, and then, if it is insistent, they actively avoid it.

The mental process in the right hemisphere, cut off in this way from the left-hemisphere consciousness which is directing overt behavior, may nevertheless continue a life of its own. The memory of the situation, the emotional concomitants, and the frustrated plan of action all may persist, affecting subsequent perception and forming the basis for expectations and evaluations of future input.

DICHOTOMANIA

The notion that there is a relation between the duality of the human brain and other dualities in human nature has been taken up by people in many different fields besides neuropsychology: for example, in education, sociology, the creative arts, philosophy. Like many productive ideas, this one is sometimes applied overenthusiastically. The specialization of the two halves of the brain is being offered as the mechanism underlying everybody's favorite pair of polar opposites: scientist-artist, obsessive-hysteric, rational-mystical, conscious-unconscious, masculine-feminine. Marcel Kinsbourne has labeled this phenomenon in its excesses "dichotomania."

The problem is a new version of "naive localizationism," which grew up with the phrenologists of the eighteenth century. The phrenologists made an important contribution to neuropsychology in advancing the idea that the different parts of the brain were not functionally identical. This idea was expanded, however, into the thesis that if certain capacities were more developed in an individual the corresponding part of the brain would be larger, and this would be detectable in a corresponding bump on the skull. They produced detailed maps, localizing complex psychological qualities to minute areas of the scalp. We can avoid slipping into a neophrenology by keeping in mind that we are talking about styles of information processing, not specific contents.

The Paranoid Streak in Man

Paul MacLean

In the denouement of his book *The Ghost in the Machine* (1967) Koestler refers repeatedly to the inherent "paranoid streak" in man. He concludes that "the damages wrought by individual violence for selfish motives are insignificant compared to the holocausts resulting from self-transcending devotion to collectively shared belief-systems." "We have seen," he says, "that the cause underlying these pathological manifestations is the split between reason and belief—or more generally, insufficient coordination between the emotive and discriminative faculties of the mind." "I believe that if we fail to find . . . (the) cure, the old paranoid streak in man, combined with his new powers of destruction, must sooner or later lead to genosuicide." "Before the thermonuclear bomb, man had to live with the idea of his death as an individual; from now onward, mankind has to live with the idea of its death as a species" (Koestler, 1967).

If, as Koestler claims, the "paranoid streak" is so indelibly a part of man's nature that it now threatens his very existence, it deserves to be singled out for special consideration. As pinpointing the site of a disorder in a mechanism is the first step in fixing it, I wish to search for the neural substrate of the "paranoid streak" in man. For conducting this search, we must first describe the demon and how he disguises himself. Then we shall try to track him down in the evolution of the mammalian brain in the hope that this will lead us to the part of the cerebrum in which he may be lurking. But we should be forewarned that there is little hope that we shall lay our hands on him. With his reputation as one of the most elusive demons of all time, let us be satisfied if we can only find his hideaway.

That paranoid reactions show up so regularly in the psychoses from generation to generation supports Koestler's contention that the "paranoid streak" is inherent in the nature of man. The adjectival form of the word as it is now used usually refers to a mental condition characterized by false beliefs which predispose to delusions of persecution or grandeur.

The Emotive Element. How does the emotive element, as Koestler correctly assumes, enter into the system of false beliefs? The answer requires a brief analysis of what is meant by emotion.

We commonly speak of the subjective and expressive aspects of emotion. As the subjective aspect is purely private it needs to be distinguished by some such word as "affect." Only we as individuals can experience affects. The public communication of affects requires expression through some form of verbal or other behavior. The expression of affect is appropriately denoted by Descartes' word "emotion."

In considering the "paranoid streak" it is important to make the distinction that it refers to a subjective state rather than to a form of behavior.

Affects differ from other forms of psychic information in so far as they are subjectively recognized as being either agreeable or disagreeable. There are no neutral affects, because emotionally speaking, it is impossible to feel unemotionally.

The traditionally regarded "emotions" such as love, anger, etc., are included among the general affects. I call them general because they are feelings that may pertain to situations, individuals, or groups. All the general affects may be considered in the light of self-preservation or the preservation of the species (MacLean, 1961).

If we exclude verbal behavior, we can identify in animals and man six types of behavior that are inferred to be guided by the general affects (MacLean, 1966b). These six behaviors are recognized as searching, aggressive, protective, dejected, gratulant, and caressive. Verbally, they may be respectively characterized by such words as desire, anger, fear, sorrow, joy, and affection. Symbolic language makes it possible to identify many variations of these affects, but in working with animals inferences about emotional states must be largely based on the six mentioned types of behaviour.

The emotive element in the "paranoid streak" answers the description of a general affect. Essentially, it amounts to an unpleasant feeling of fear attached to something that cannot be clearly identified. The feeling has the capacity to persist or recur long after the inciting circumstance and may apply to a situation or thing, an individual or group of individuals. It has survival value because it puts the organism on guard against the unexpected—hence, the words apprehension and suspicion often used in describing the paranoid state. A few examples will illustrate how inadequate information received by way of one of the sensory systems may arouse fear and suspicion, and how suspicion may often be quickly allayed by comparison with information from one or two other sensory systems. The horse which has a keen olfactory sense, but relatively poor vision, is uncommonly fearful of ill-defined objects. One might say it is particularly "paranoid" about paper bags! The sight of one, as riders well know, will often cause a horse to shy or come to a sudden halt. If, however, it can be coaxed to approach and smell the bag, its fear and suspicion seem suddenly to melt away, and it will proceed as though nothing had happened. Information from its most trusted sense reveals the object to be lifeless and harmless.

Man, on the contrary, relies largely on vision to relieve his uncertainty about the nature of things. Poorly visualized objects are under suspicion until he can bring them clearly into focus. But perhaps his greatest suspicions are aroused by things he cannot see at all. Consequently darkness has always held its particular terrors for him. Unexplained muted house sounds at night become amplified in the mind into the footsteps of a burglar. The faint smell of smoke explodes into a blaze of fire. Man's inherent fear of the dark is brought into clear relief under pathological conditions. Patients suffering from high fever or toxic poisoning not uncommonly become delirious with the approach of darkness. I remember a man with lead poisoning who became so terrified at the onset of darkness that he leapt from his bed, ran headlong down the hospital corridor, and was apprehended only in time to save him from jumping from a balcony.

Some individuals become hypochondriacal in a somewhat similar manner. Unable to visualize the source of a recurring internal ache or pain, they are led, according to their social background, to suspect all manner of deleterious processes. The more primitive the individual the more primitive may be his explanation. I recall a young man of primitive background who had a belly ache and came to the hospital complaining of fighting cats and dogs in his stomach. While I was examining him and listening to his heart with a stethoscope, he asked me, "Can you hear them?" Given the seed of suspicion, the human mind is capable of developing any kind of paranoid hybrid.

There is yet another form of the unseen that besets man and distinguishes him from all other animals. This is the poorly outlined and uncertain picture of future events which he is forever striving to see. When nature gave him the prefrontal neocortex for anticipation and connected it with his visual cortical areas, she failed to provide a radar antenna and viewing screen. Consequently, all his probings into the future must be done with obscured, remembered images of the past combined with his picture of the present. As the future is always generating more "futures" *ad infinitum* it is apparent why its uncertainties are responsible for most of man's chronic forms of suspicion.

The emphasis given to the capacity of vision both to arouse and allay suspicion should not imply an insignificant role of the other senses in this respect. There are, for example, situations where one can clearly see what is taking place, but where hearing only in part, or not at all, what is happening or being said results in uncertainty and suspicion. For such reasons deaf people are especially prone to develop paranoid tendencies. Receiving a chance smile or look from someone in a group conversation, they may gain the impression that they are being talked about. In the paranoid psychoses auditory illusions and hallucinations are more frequent than those in the visual sphere. I recently saw an epileptic patient with schizophrenic symptoms who claimed to hear clicking sounds and imagined that people were snapping pictures of her.

Stripped to nakedness, the paranoid demon steps forth from the foregoing analysis as *a general affect characterized as an unpleasant feeling of fear attached to something that cannot be clearly identified.* Seen in this pristine state, he is hardly an impressive figure. The thing, obviously, that gives him mystique is his capacity to assume as many disguises as there are individuals. He could thus be compared to a plot that lends itself to as many stories as there are potential authors.

Evolutionary considerations.   With this brief description and characterization of our protagonist we are now in a position to look for signs of him in the evolution of the mammalian brain. Our starting point is 200 million years ago in the age of reptiles when animals which never learned to talk, began to work their way into the brain of man (MacLean, 1964). Perhaps the most revealing thing about the study of man's brain is that he has inherited the structure and organization of three basic cerebral types which for purposes of discussion I label reptilian, old mammalian, and new mammalian (MacLean, 1962, 1964, 1966b, 1967). Despite their great differences in structure and chemistry all three must interconnect and function together. Man's brain of oldest heritage is basically reptilian. It forms the matrix of the brain stem and comprises much of the reticular system, midbrain and basal ganglia.

But in contrast to mammals there is only an incipient cortex. The evolving old mammalian brain is distinctive because of the marked expansion and differentiation of a primitive cortex which, as will be explained, is synonymous with the limbic cortex. Finally, there appears late in evolution a more highly differentiated form of cortex called neocortex, which is the hallmark of the brains of higher mammals and which culminates in man to become the brain of reading, writing and arithmetic.

In the popular language of today, the reptilian and the old and new mammalian brains might be regarded as biological computers, each with its own subjective, gnostic, time-measuring, memory, motor and other functions (Mac-Lean, 1966b). On the basis of behavioural observations of ethologists, it may be inferred that the reptilian brain programmes stereotyped behaviours according to instructions based on ancestral learning and ancestral memories. In other words, it seems to play a primary role in instinctually determined functions such as establishing territory, finding shelter, hunting, homing, mating, breeding, imprinting, forming social hierarchies, selecting leaders and the like. In the experimental situation the presentation of a dummy or a fragment of a dummy may release the sequential acting out of an instinctual form of behaviour. Indeed, a mere phantom is sometimes sufficient to trigger the entire copulatory act.

The reptilian brain seems to be a slave to precedent. If, for example, having found a safe way home, it is thereafter inclined to follow that route even though it means going around Robin Hood's barn. It would be satisfying to know to what extent the reptilian counterpart of man's brain determines his obeisance to precedent in ceremonial rituals, legal actions, political persuasions, and religious conviction. Obeisance to precedent is the first step to obsessive compulsive behaviour, and this is well illustrated by the turtle's always returning to the same place year after year to lay its egg. The reptilian brain appears to have inadequate machinery for learning to cope with new situations.

The evolutionary development in lower mammals of a respectable cortex might be regarded as Nature's attempt to provide the reptilian brain with a "thinking cap" and emancipate it from inappropriate stereotypes of behaviour. In all mammals most of the primitive cortex is found in a large convolution which Broca called the limbic lobe because it surrounds the brain stem (Broca, 1878). From the standpoint of behavioural implications it is significant that this lobe is found as a common denominator in the brains of all mammals.

The functions of this brain play an important role in emotional, viscero-somatic, and endocrine functions (Mac-Lean, 1949, 1958). In 1952 I suggested the term "limbic system" as a designation for the limbic cortex and brain stem structures with which it has primary connections (MacLean, 1952). Broca's simple descriptive term "limbic" has the advantage, as he stated, that it implies no theory as regards function. It should be emphasized that the limbic cortex has similar features in all mammals and is structurally primitive compared with the neocortex. From this it can be inferred that it continues to function at an animalistic level in man as in animals. Also in marked contrast to the neocortex, it has strong connections with the hypothalamus which plays a basic role in integrating emotional expression and viscero-somatic behaviour.

Functions of the limbic system. Case histories of psychomotor epilepsy provide crucial evidence that the limbic cortex is implicated in the generation of affective states.

Irritative lesions in or near the limbic cortex of the lower part of the ring give rise to epileptic discharges accompanied by basic and general affects that under ordinary conditions are important for survival. The basic affects include feelings of hunger, thirst, nausea, suffocation, choking, retching, cold, warmth, and the need to defecate or urinate. Among the general affects are feelings of terror, fear, foreboding, familiarity, strangeness, unreality, wanting to be alone, sadness, and feelings of a paranoid nature. The automatisms that follow these aural affects often seem to be an acting out of the subjective state: for example, eating, drinking, vomiting, urinating, running and screaming as if afraid.

As already noted, paranoid feelings may occur in conjunction with the initial discharge of psychomotor epilepsy. I once treated a young man, for example, who at the beginning of his seizure had a feeling of fear that someone was standing behind him. If he turned to see who it was, the feeling of fear became intensified. During inter-seizure periods some patients are tormented by persistent paranoid feelings. One such patient was continually obsessed by the feeling that God was punishing her for over-eating. While she was expressing such thoughts, the basal electroencephalogram showed random spiking at the site of the electrode just underneath the temporal lobe. I referred earlier to the patient with epilepsy and schizophrenic manifestations who claimed to hear clicking sounds and imagined that people were taking pictures of her.

Final comments. In considering the genesis of paranoid feelings under normal and psychotic conditions let us begin with an illustration of the experience of a young man returning from Europe on the SS United States. One

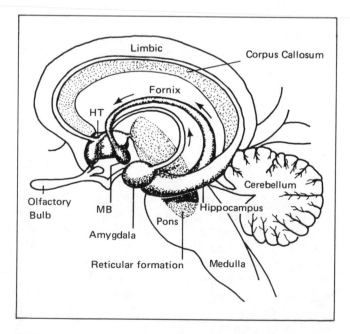

Representation of the limbic system, upper brain stem, and cerebellum.

morning when the ship was off the Newfoundland Banks he walked out on deck and had a vivid feeling that it had been snowing. Presumably the appearance of sky and the temperature and the moisture of the air affecting his skin and respiratory passages added up to this snowy feeling. In communicating the nature of this feeling to his fellow passengers he found that they readily agreed with him. A short time later a news bulletin reported that it had been snowing in Newfoundland.

But let it be supposed that the young man had experienced and communicated similar feelings while cruising in the subtropical waters of the Caribbean. And suppose further, that the feeling persists. Would he not perhaps become suspicious of fellow passengers who failed to agree with his inappropriate feeling or challenged his sanity? We may imagine that the schizophrenic patient with his persistent delusional symptoms finds himself in a comparable situation. Affective feelings provide the connecting bridge between our internal and external worlds and perhaps more than any form of psychic information assure us of the reality of ourselves and the environment around us: hence the statement that "a crazy man would be crazy not to believe in the reality of his crazy feelings" (MacLean, 1958). Beset by a chronic fearful feeling, the psychotic individual utilizes his preserved intellectual faculties to "explain away" his feelings. He may conclude that his fellow workers despise him and wish him to lose his job because they somehow learned that he had been involved in an unnatural sexual act. Less commonly in paranoid psychoses, there are chronic feelings of elation and delusions of grandeur which require some divine explanation.

The neurological condition that appears to distinguish the persisting affect of the epileptic from that of the schizophrenic is the presence in the former of a demonstrable irritative focus. What it is that accounts for the neural reverberation in the case of schizophrenia is entirely a matter of speculation. When a nagging, unpleasant feeling affects an entire social group, it may be concluded that it arises from something in the environment. Here the question of sanity does not arise because the group shares a feeling, which unlike that of the psychotic individual, lends itself to a collective belief-system.

What are some of the conditions that generate persisting unpleasant feelings among a society? Today, illustrations abound on every side. Perhaps the most generally prevailing disturbing factor is the pressure arising from over-population. Evidence is accumulating with respect to several animal species that aggressiveness increases with increasing density of population. It is often stated that man is uncommonly aggressive, and he is compared unfavourably with lower primates because of this and his propensity to kill. But the peaceful coexistence of groups of sub-human primates in the wild is possibly attributable to an abundance of living space and food; under conditions of captivity, crowding has been observed to result in violent and deathly struggle. Among animals, however, it is usually not death from combat that reduces population density to tolerable levels. Rather, nature appears to have ruled that aggression should take its toll indirectly through wasting diseases and loss of fertility. Surpassing other animals in intelligence and inventiveness, man has found an additional solution. The use of weapons, he discovered, works more quickly and just as effectively. The price of this discovery has been an enhancement of his natural paranoid tendencies, because since the slaying of Able he has had to live with the realization that his fellow man holds over him the power of life or death.

REFERENCES

BROCA, P. (1878) Anatomie comparée des circonvolutions cérébrales. Le grande lobe limbique et la scissure limbique dans la série des mamiféres. *Rev. Anthrop., I:* pp. 385-498.

JACKSON, J. HUGHLINGS and COLMAN, W. S. (1989) Case of epilepsy with tasting movements and "dreamy state"–Very small patch of softening in the left uncinate gyrus. *Brain, 21:* pp. 580-590.

KOESTLER, A. (1967) *The Ghost in the Machine.* Hutchinson and Co., London, and Macmillan, New York.

KRAFFT-EBING, R. (1904) *Test-book of Insanity.* Trans by C. G. Chaddock, F. A. Davis Co., Philadelphia.

MACLEAN, P. D. (1949) Psychosomatic disease and the "visceral brain" Recent development bearing on the Papez theory of emotion. *Psychosom. Med., II:* pp. 338-353

—— (1952) Some psychiatric implications of physiological studies on frontotemporal portion of limbic system (visceral brain). *Electroenceph. Clin. Neurophysiol., 4:* pp. 407-418.

—— (1954) The limbic system and its hippocampal formation. Studies in animals and their possible application to man. *J. Neurosurg., II:* pp. 29-44.

—— (1958) Contrasting functions of limbic and neocortical systems of the brain and their relevance to psychophysiological aspects of medicine. *Amer. J. Med., 25:* pp. 611-626.

—— (1961) Psychomatics. In Field J. (ed.) *Handbook of Physiology, Neurophysiology III.* American Physiol. Soc., Washington D.C., pp. 1723-1744.

—— (1962) New findings relevant to the evolution of psychosexual functions of the brain. *J. Nerv. Ment. Dis., 135:* pp. 289-301.

—— (1964) Man and his animal brains. *Mod. Med., 32:* pp. 95-106.

—— (1966a) The limbic and visual cortex in phylogeny: Further insights from anatomic and microelectrode studies. R. Hassler and H. Stephan (eds.) in: *Evolution of the Forebrain.* Georg Thieme, Stuttgart. pp. 443-453.

—— (1966b) Brain and vision in the evolution of emotional and sexual behavior. *Thomas William Salmon Lectures,* New York Academy of Medicine.

—— (1967) The brain in relation to empathy and medical education. *J. Nerv. Ment. Dis., 144:* pp. 374-382.

MALAMUD, N. (1966) The epileptogenic focus in temporal lobe epilepsy from a pathological standpoint. *Arch. Neurol., 14:* pp. 190-195.

MEYER, A. (1928) The evolution of the dementia praecox concept. *Res. Publ. Ass. nerv. ment. Dis., 5:* pp. 3-15.

PAPEZ, J. (1937) A proposed mechanism of emotion. *Arch Neurol. Psychiat. (Chicago), 38:* pp. 725-743.

PENFIELD, W. and JASPER, H. (1954) *Epilepsy and the Functional Anatomy of the Human Brain.* Little, Brown and Co., Boston.

REEVES, A. G., SUDAKOV, K. and MACLEAN, P. D. (1968) Exploratory unit analysis of exteroceptive inputs to the insular cortex in awake, sitting, squirrel monkeys. *Fed. Proc., 27:* pp. 388.

WIENER, N. (1948) *Cybernetics, or Control and Communication in the Animal and the Machine.* Wily New York.

The Mind-Brain Question

Wilder Penfield

Consciousness can be present whenever the highest brain-mechanism is normally active, even though adjacent parts of the brain are inactivated by some abnormal influence. A patient, whom I was called upon to see in Moscow under dramatic circumstances in 1962, illustrated the fact that conscious understanding may be present when motor control has been lost completely, or almost completely, and when the brain is not capable of making a permanent record of the stream of consciousness.

The patient was the brilliant physicist, Lev Landau. Only intensive nursing had kept him alive during six weeks of complete unconsciousness following a head injury in an automobile crash. On my first examination of the patient, I agreed that he was completely unconscious. I then recommended a minor diagnostic operation (ventriculography). His limbs were paralyzed; his eyes were open but apparently unseeing. Next morning, when I entered his room to examine him again, I was accompanied by his wife. She preceded me and, sitting down at the bedside, she talked to him, telling him that I had suggested to the Soviet surgeons that he should have a brain operation. As I stood silent, watching over her head, I became aware of a startling change in the patient. He lay unmoving still, as on the previous night. But his eyes, which had been deviated from each other then were focused now in a normal manner. He seemed to be looking at her. He appeared to hear, and see, and to understand speech! How could this be? She came to the end of her explanation and was silent. His eyes then moved upward to focus quite normally on me. I moved my head from side to side. The eyes followed me. No doubt about it! Then they swung apart again and he appeared, as he had the night before, to be unconscious.

It was clear that the man had returned to consciousness. He had been able to hear, see, understand speech, but not to speak. He could not move, except to focus and turn his eyes briefly. Perhaps I should explain that he and his wife had been separated for a time. It was our talk of possible operation that had led to her being summoned to Moscow and to the hospital. She was seeing him that morning for the first time since the accident.

It was thrilling to realize what had happened. He had been roused by her presence and probably understood her message. Evidently the hemispheres above the higher brain-stem, with their speech and visual and auditory mechanisms, had not been injured. The to-and-fro exchange between brain-stem and cortex was free, but when he sent neuronal messages out to the peripheral motor nuclei in the lower brain-stem and spinal cord, none could pass the block at the level of the hemorrhage in the midbrain. None, that is, except those to the eye movement center, which is highest of all the peripheral centers for motor control. If he was conscious, he must have sent down many other messages that would normally have flashed outward to the muscles. His wife was an appealingly handsome women. His mind may well have sent a message intended to cause his hand to take hers. But his lay motionless.

However that may be, I went back to the other doctors and we decided that no operation was necessary. I had seen the first sure sign of recovery. He was transferred at once from the outlying hospital, in which he had been nursed so magnificently, to the Moscow Neurosurgical Institute, where he would have the great advantage of supervision by Professor B. G. Egorov. Physiotherapy was begun at once, and I learned later that there was slow but continuous and progressive recovery from that day onward.

For the first six weeks after the accident, Landau's fellow physicists, most of them his disciples, had joined the nurses and doctors in their gallant effort to keep the patient breathing and capable of recovery if that should prove possible. This man, who had already been awarded the Lenin Prize for his contributions to physics, was given the Nobel Prize during his convalescence. He and his wife were happy together and she was with him on the special occasion of his acceptance of the award.

I saw him nine months later, on my return from a visit to the university hospitals of China. He had been transferred to a convalescent hospital. The neurologist, Professor Propper Graschenkov, took me, in company with Landau's collaborator, the brilliant Professor Lifshitz, who had shared the Lenin Prize with his master, to visit him. I quote now from my journal note, made a few days later: "Landau was sitting up in bed in a fresh white shirt looking at me anxiously. He was a handsome person with a fine head. He had an air of understanding. He was stubborn in his confusion and I could appreciate why, several months earlier, he had been depressed and had even asked Lifshitz to bring him poison." Laudau spoke excellent English and did so eagerly. "When I asked him if he had received the Lenin Prize, he said 'yes,' but he could not tell me when. When I asked him if someone had shared it with him he looked around and, finding Lifshitz standing with the others, smiled and pointed to him—'I think he and I shared it.' " The relationship of the two men was somewhat like that of David and Jonathan. "Lifshitz feels he has lost his closest friend and his leader."

The final diagnosis was as follows: A head injury that resulted in a small hemorrhage in the conducting tracts (white matter) of the higher brain-stem. During the six weeks following his accident, the hemorrhage had gradually absorbed through the brain's own circulation. Eventually, neuronal communcation had been restored through the nerve fibers of the brain-stem. There remained only a difficulty in recalling the recent past. His confusion was due to that.

It is, of course, only a matter of conjecture exactly when consciousness did return. Before he could show that he was conscious, it was necessary for him to regain control of some portion of his motor system. Evidently, control of the movement of his eyes returned before anything else. During our first interview, while Mrs. Landau was explaining the situation to him, and when he looked at me so searchingly, I concluded that the whole explanation continued to be clear in his mind. He was remembering what she had said at the beginning as well as what she was saying at the close of her explanation. For that, the mind does not need the brain's mechanism of experiential recall. It needs only the mechanism of the stream of consciousness, which was normally active.

When I saw him at the second interview nine months later he did not remember me or anything that had happened to himself for some months after his transfer to the Moscow Neurosurgical Institute. The scanning and recall of past experience can only be carried out by the mechanism in which at least one hippocampus of one temporal lobe must play an essential role. And that mechanism can carry out this recall only for periods in which it had been normal and, thus, able to form its own clues to the stream of consciousness, its duplicate "keys-of-access."

I learned still later that Landau did continue to improve in the year that followed, and was able to tutor his son in preparing for his university entrance examinations. Great recognition came to this man whose mathematical genius had been likened to that of Einstein. His countrymen rejoiced at his recovery but the "depression" returned to him. Perhaps he realized that his brain could no longer serve him as it had.

I have described this case in some detail because it, like many others, demonstrates how it is that when consciousness is present, the highest brain-mechanism is used to activate and employ other brain-mechanisms that are capable of normal function. Beyond that, it bears out our conclusion that the mind can hold the data that have come to it during this focusing of attention and while the mechanism of the stream of consciousness is moving forward. But the mind, by itself, cannot recall past experience unless the brain's special mechanism of scanning and recall is functioning normally. In such a case as this, in which damage brings to the brain a small area of paralyzing interference, one's knowledge of how brain mechanisms coordinate and integrate is put to the test. More than that, such accidental experiments point the way toward clearer understanding of how the business of the brain is transacted. Human physiology can only wait for guidance from such accidental experiments.

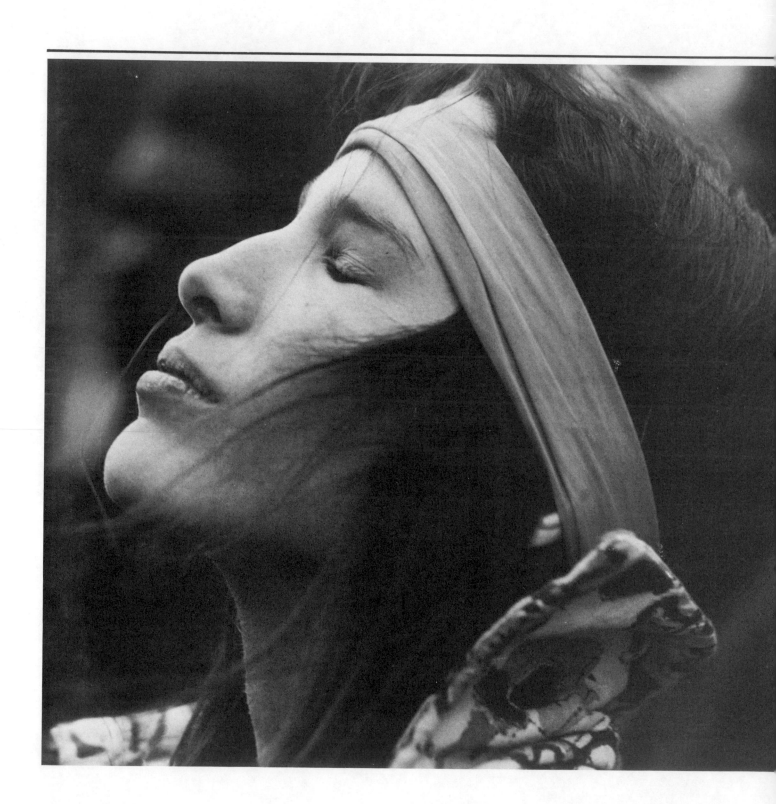

ORDINARY STATES OF CONSCIOUSNESS

Our normal states of consciousness are the product of a complex interplay of psychological processes. We usually are unaware of these processes themselves, since they are embedded in our awareness as background. Just as when we watch a movie we rarely, if ever, trouble to notice the screen or the beam of light that carries the image to it, so in life do we rarely notice our senses, our thinking, or the way we attend. What we *do* notice are the *contents* of these processes—*what* we sense, think, and notice—instead of the processes themselves. In this section we will review some of the basic psychological processes that work together to form a state of consciousness, and survey some notable, though ordinary, states of consciousness.

THE MECHANICS OF EXPERIENCE

To speak of "the five senses" is technically incorrect, perceptual psychologist S. H. Bartley informs us. More accurately we ought to speak of five "basic perceptual systems." These five modes of perceiving do not correspond to what is popularly meant by the five senses, but instead group together two of them—taste and smell—in a single savory system, and add another, the "basic orienting system"—our sense of balance. When we perceive something, all the senses come into play, although for example, we are rarely aware that we "see" with more than our eyes alone. Other senses such as posture and balance mingle with what we see to round out our perception. What's more, the world is not as we perceive it to be; our senses solidify a universe that physics tells us is fluid and at base a mass of insubstantial wavelengths. The human-scale sensory world is, however, a conceit essential to our survival; even though its dimensions do not correspond with the objective universe, it gives us the information we need to make our way through it.

The perceiver is active, constructing his perception from the vast array of available possibilities. From the myriad random messages our senses send to the brain, our cognitive processes sort and select to find meaningful patterns. A "schema" is such a mental program for selecting useful information and acting on it. Developmental psychologist Jerome Kagan shows how schema can be an essential source of pleasure, and how changes in children's schema as they grow up influence what they think is funny at different ages. A full understanding of states like pleasure, cautions Kagan, must take into account elements in the mechanics of experience such as schema.

The key element that shapes our awareness is attention; where and how we direct our attention defines our world of reality at each moment. Many of the changes in consciousness—both minor and major—that we undergo are the result of attentional shifts. William James, the founding father of American psychology, enumerates the varieties of attention with which we are all familiar: focused activity, passive wandering, and the distractedness that comes when we are facing a task we want to avoid. James placed a high value on the ability to concentrate, placing it at the very root of will and character. Nevertheless, he despaired of giving practical instructions for improving this capacity.

We experience ourselves very differently depending on the state of mind we are in. This shifting sense of self psychiatrist Harry Stack Sullivan calls a "personification." There are three such kinds of "me," each tied to a certain quality of experience. The "me" that is rewarded and receives tender love and kindness is the "good-me." The experience of feeling anxious and unworthy of love is the "bad-me." Moments of practically obliterating sudden anxiety or terror create the "not-me"—a feeling of being so filled with dread that one psychologically disconnects the experience itself from one's being. The original source of these personifications is in the infant's relation to his mother, but these ways of organizing experience last throughout a lifetime. Because it is much more pleasant to feel the "good-me" than either of the other two sorts of experience, a psychological mechanism called the "self-system" evolves employing a range of defensive maneuvers—particularly attentional distortions—to minimize threatening facts, and so to keep anxiety at a minimum. The self-system mobilizes a variety of mental tricks to avoid anxiety, and in so doing keeps a person from squarely facing normal waking reality.

What Is Perception?

S. H. Bartley

It has been long taken for granted that there are five senses. Now we know that there are more than twice that many. However... they may be grouped into at least five major functional clusters called perceptual systems. Hence, it is not that we have just five senses, but five modes of perceiving.... They are as follows:

The Basic Orienting System. The vestibular mechanism in the inner ear reacts to forces of acceleration which indicate the direction of gravity and also the forces involved when one moves in diverse directions and various rates. This includes information about the beginnings and endings of body movements. The gravitational input to the vestibular mechanism is accompanied by haptic inputs from touch and kinesthesis (muscle, tendon, and joint information). The basic orienting system participates with the four other perceptual systems since it is a ground or frame of reference for them.

The Haptic System. This system utilizes the receptors in the skin and in the muscles and joints of touching and handling things. Thus, it is the prime system dealing with mechanical contact and its consequences such as the appreciation of temperature and of injurious forces via pain. Haptic inputs (stimuli) specify an astonishing variety of facts about the environment and the perceiver himself. Much of this information is not fully appreciated because vision usually receives the most attention in descriptions of sensation and perception.

The Savor (Taste-Smell) System. This is the perceptual system whereby the individual detects, discriminates, and appreciates materials that reach the interior of the nose and mouth. In general, the receptors in the nose, when stimulated, provide experiences we call smells, odors, or fragrances. Likewise, putting something into the mouth results in what we call taste. There is such an intimate functional connection between what affects smell and taste receptors that it is logical to speak of them together as being components of a *savor* system. In addition to these two sets of receptors, the system also contains the receptors for touch, temperature, and pain that line the nasal and oral cavities. Certain foods taste very different depending upon whether the nose is clamped so as to exclude the volatile component of the food from entering the nostrils. It is also known that cold whipped potatoes taste different from warm or hot ones. The mechanical features of food (hardness, softness, lumpiness, etc.) also affect its taste. The savor system is both a defensive and appreciative system, as will be seen later when we give examples....

The Auditory System. This system deals with minute vibrations reaching the ear. Vibratory events are propagated over long distances; hence, auditory perception deals with events apart from the body. It identifies the nature and direction of acoustic sources. Since organisms themselves can act as acoustic sources, the vibrations manufactured can be used for communication by means of the distinct patterns that are produced. Communication is more than a transmission of literal effects; it is an exchange of symbolic effects. Hence, hearing and language go hand in hand....

The Visual System. So much is made out of vision that the viewer hardly realizes all that is involved. This mechanism combines with all others in registering environmental conditions and events. The available information gained by vision is enormous....

Muscle Systems in Perception

...Muscle systems function in connection with the receptors and by their states provide a form of information as to body position, and tensional states. Muscle movement is of two sorts, *exploratory* (thus, informational) and *performatory.*

One may speak of *systems* in ways other than those used in classifying perceptual systems. Muscles are involved in the organized activity that can be given system labels. For example, there is the *postural system* whereby the organism relates itself to the acting mechanical forces, primarily those of gravity. There is the *orienting-exploratory system*—which moves the head, mouth, eyes, hands for gaining information about the mechanical and other features of the surroundings. Another system is the *locomotor system,* by which approach, avoidance, and transportation in general are accomplished. The *appetitive system* involves give-and-take between the organism and the environment such as eating, breathing, eliminating, and sexual interaction. The *expressive system* produces gestures, facial expressions and vocalization, as well as other movements which manifest personalistic attitudes and emotion. And, lastly, there is the *language* or *semantic system* which signals by movements of all sorts.

In all of these systems, it is evident that not separate mechanisms but, instead, separate kinds of activity are being manifested; some of it *perfunctory,* some *exploratory.*

Sensation and Perception

... Starting with Aristotle more than two thousand years ago, it has been thought that there are five classes of sensations: seeing, hearing, tasting, smelling, and touching. Along with the mediating body mechanisms, these were called senses or sense modalities. Continued use of the analytic method applied skillfully and persistently, with the help of instruments, had disclosed ten sense mechanisms. Some workers call the results ten senses. Additional classes of receptors (sensitive tissue) have even been discovered but for some reason they have not yet led to an expansion in the number of senses definitely labelled and described.

All this time, despite the discovery of additional sense mechanisms, the idea of five senses has persisted among nontechnical people, which seems strange, indeed. Within the last four or five years a resolution of this apparent contradiction has been achieved. Gibson (1966) has made it clear that whereas there may be ten or more senses as judged by specific classes of body mechanisms, there still are probably only five *perceptual* systems. This involves a new distinction between perception and sensation.

Whereas sensation is defined in relation to sensory mechanisms, perception is regarded in terms of the tasks imposed upon the organism by the nature of the environment ("the nature of Nature").

Each of the perceptual systems is composed of the cooperative action of several sense mechanisms and extracts information from the environment. . . .

WHAT DO WE SEE WITH?

... When you look about you, you use your eyes, and it is easy to suppose that seeing is nothing but the consequences of the reception of patterns of photic radiation ("light") on your retinas. Seeing is the combined result of using ears and body muscles and even the skin as well as the eyes. Such statements are often made, and it may be that many people accept them as fact, but it is a great deal more convincing and satisfying to have at least some of this participation spelled out.

First of all, it is to be expected that if one were totally paralyzed from birth, seeing would be something

PERCEPTION, SENSATION, AND ENVIRONMENTAL STIMULI

Perceptual System	Senses	Stimuli
Basic Orienting System	vestibular	forces of gravity and acceleration
	visual	
	kinesthetic	mechanical contacts with supports
Haptic System	tactual kinesthetic	feedback from: passive and active mechanical
	deep pressure	contact and mechanical
	pain	manipulation of objects,
	thermal	including people
Savor System	smell	gases
	taste	liquids, foods
	tactual	—
	thermal	—
	pain	—
Auditory System	auditory	vibrations in air and in cranial bone
Visual System	sight	photic radiation ("light") (plus other senses)

very different from what it is in normal individuals. Whereas we can often tell the difference between smooth and rough surfaces just by looking at them, we would not have been able to tell if we had not used both the visual and tactual (haptic) mechanisms together to begin with. Whereas we can often tell by sight the difference between what is soft and what is hard, we could not have done so had we not had tactual experiences. These and other properties that are essentially and primarily mediated by sense mechanisms other than vision become fully visual as a result of several sense modalities being used together.

There is still another way in which vision is contributed to or made possible and that is by the way things look as various tensions are applied to skeletal muscles. The prime involvement of skeletal muscles is in maintaining static posture, or in changes in the kinesthetic feedback to the central nervous system as body movements are made. These tensions are the result of static or changing patterns of skeletal muscle activity that position you with relation to the earth and the gravitational field. Two things are involved, namely, patterns of muscle tension and geometrical orientation to objects around you including the earth itself. These two factors are not independent of each other but are lawfully related. For example, if you bend over and look backward between your legs to the horizon, you are seeing the "world upside down," and are producing a particular pattern of tension in most if not all of your skeletal muscles. If the tensions were suddenly relieved, one would experience a different overall reality. The assurance that what you were looking at is upside down would lessen or cease.

Two novel sets of conditions can be brought about, wherein the muscle, tendon and joint (kinesthetic) contributions to the sensory input are radically changed. This one case is the artifical application of tension to a group of skeletal muscles, and the other is by the production of weightlessness. The latter set of conditions is very difficult to produce. It is reached by certain stunt conditions in aviation or in rocketry which carry man far enough from the earth and other planets to make their gravitational effects negligible.

[One] . . . observation that links space perception and muscle activity is to be found in golf stance. Individuals who change from handling clubs left-handed to right-handed note this especially. Obviously, as you view the fairway off your right shoulder, you are looking at it differently from when you view it off your left. The shift from the one stance to the other emphasizes the intimate relation between the feel of the one posture and the other. The one posture places the elements of the scene somewhat differently in front of you than the other. Proper driving of the ball involves making a connection between how the fairway looks and execution of the proper motions. It can as well be said that executing the proper motions depends on how the fairway looks. One of the most conspicuous features of it all is how you feel. Once you become a good golfer, it is possible that this self-consciousness disappears, but it is there to begin with.

Many other examples of muscle involvement in the act of looking and seeing may be found, all illustrating that we see with the whole body.

WHAT IS A STAIRCASE?

. . . In describing the difference between the blind and the sighted I have often used an example of what the two classes of persons can imagine. Of course, what they can imagine is derived from what they can directly experience in the first place. Imagination is thus an indicator of what their direct experiences (sensation and perception) are like.

Take the example of imagining a staircase. The sighted, of course, will imagine how it looks. When he does so, he can "see" the whole staircase instantaneously. He does not have to imagine it, part by part. This is because he was able to look at a staircase in the first place and see all of it at once.

The blind person can walk up and down a staircase, but he cannot see it. The sensory contact he has with the staircase is haptic (tactual and kinesthetic). To imagine it, he must go through some sort of a sequential remembrance of what his actual contacts with the staircase have been like. From the sensory standpoint, to the sighted, a staircase in mainly what he can see. In a secondary way, it is also what it is to him in climbing and descending it (something haptic). It could be that if the subject of stairs comes up in conversation, his impression of stairs is expressed in imagery of muscular exertion and shortness of breath. In this respect he would be much like a blind person who has the same exertional limitations.

In any case, a staircase is to a person what it is to him sensorially and perceptually.

Recently, in a penetrating conversation with a congenitally blind man, I brought up the question of how the blind can imagine a staircase. In what constituted a surprise remark, he said to me that a blind person might imagine what the stairs felt like if he laid down on them so that various parts of his body would touch different steps. Truly enough, he had given me an example in which the person was using the maximal possibility of experiencing a large part of the total staircase simultaneously. While the blind could do this, the more typical imagery would have to do with his usual experience, namely, climbing and descending the stairs.

The experience of lying on the staircase would, as the blind man said, give the person a feeling of the structure's tilt from the perpendicular. It would tell him its slope or "steepness," hence he would be exercising his basic orientation system.

The blind person could extend his tactual and haptic exploration of the staircase by manual exploration, going from one step to another and by sitting on successive steps, and so forth. But, here again, sequential rather than simultaneous and comprehensive experience is involved.

The typical sighted person at this point is likely to think that this exploration would provide for an overall image of the staircase, such as the visual image that he has, but this is not to be expected. . . .

Thus we can suppose that the imaginal life of the blind and the sighted are very different in this one essential feature—their sensory content. In the sighted, it covers a comprehensive portion of externality and in the blind it covers externality more nearly piecemeal.

The stairs or the maze are only what they can be experienced or imagined to be.

ILLUSIONS, PERCEPTUAL CONSTANCY, AND OBJECTIVITY

. . . We have been dealing with sensory processes and perception from the standpoint of the individual. There is still another pertinent and interesting problem—that of *veridicality,* which has to do with what is ordinarily called truth-telling. . . .

The present problem has to do with the concept of *illusion.* In vision there has long been a group of geometrical figures which have been known as illusions. Illusions also occur in other senses. So, to round out our examination of the senses and perception, we shall discuss the various ways sensory experience is related to the world outside of the individual. This is where the question of whether perceptions "tell the truth" comes in.

We live in a world of things (objects). Objects are what they are to us by reason of the way our sensory response mechanisms are affected by the energies the physicist and chemist describe. The ancients believed in a universe of entities with independent existence and that these entities were made known to us by a kind of ghostlike emanation that left us and sent to external objects and brought back to us information about them. This was called the *emanation theory.* Today, this sounds absurd. We believe we know better. Nevertheless, recently a man 'phoned me to find out why hunters perceive other hunters as deer. He seriously and with some self-satisfaction proposed a reason to see what I thought of it. It was nothing but the old emanation theory, in scarcely a new dress. . . .

Most people today still believe in the independent existence of objects, and that our senses make known these objects to us. For example, if we can't see color in the dark, the color is believed to still be there, but we just can't see it. The sophisticated view is not that at all, but that certain physical conditions may be independent of the perceiver and be existent when the individual is prevented from being affected by them, and thus does not perceive. In case of color, it is generally seen as a property of an object. The physical conditions that constitute the object may exist independently of the presence of a human observer. But, for the observer to see color, an additional "ingredient" or factor must exist, namely, photic radiation ("light") which reflects certain wavelengths more than others. So, the painting of a beautiful scene or the portrait of a friend exists only in the physical properties that make up the material of the canvas and paint. Color comes and goes as variably as the levels and wavelengths of illumination change.

What I have just said has been repeated countless times by a few people, but it doesn't seem real or understandable by most people.

Through the senses a physical world is made known to us, and it is a world describable in terms of what we see, hear, taste, smell, and touch. But this is a different description from what physicists and chemists give us. Physicists and chemists describe the world with man left out. And, when they do this, what is the description like? It is a world of energy manifestations having no trees, no cities, no people, no color, nor objects. It is a universe of "particles" or manifestations of energy. We have no reason

to reject this description. It is a universal one which the people in science and technology of all nations accept. It involves no language barrier, no political biases, no nationalism. Man as man (a sensing, experiencing creature) is left out. Though this description has been taught even in some high schools for over a half century, it is not a view that is consistently held by most people even today. The other views make one feel better. Most people cannot readily comprehend a universe that is *not* describable in the sensory (experiential) words they have at their command. They cannot stand to accept a world as empty as physicists and chemists describe it. In fact, chemists don't always avoid sensory description since they are constrained by some of the very conditions that apply to all humans. They describe the chemical elements as materials having the properties we sense, like color and solidity. But this is not the ultimate description to which I've just referred. The ultimate and basic description they use daily in their work is given in structural formulae of molecules, etc., and in terms of certain kinds of "reactions."

But what do we do when we come to the study of man? There are two or three major choices, at least hypothetically. One is the ancient choice of conceiving of man as being apart from Nature, and that to study him one does not resort to what we have learned about Nature to account for anything he does. The other is to consider him a part of Nature. This implies that the same general understandings that apply to all else in Nature are to be applied in the study of man.

Most people straddle the two alternatives and, among other things, provide themselves with an additional problem. This straddling view assumes that man's body can be studied as a part of Nature, but that man is something else than his body. So, we have what is called dualism—a mind-body dichotomy.

The emergence of things or objects is most clearly pictured in the way our visual system performs. For this, let's consider the following example. We look and see a dark gray surface. On it a lighter area emerges which may be seen as simply as a spot. In the present case, we see it as a small *disk,* an independent object. We see it as something that looks solid that we can touch and pick up. Before we attempt to do this, it looks hard and, of course, has edges which can be grasped or traced with one's fingers. When we reach to touch it, we find the edges missing, and we can't pick it up. Whatever it is, it is part of the surface on which it exists. Soon we find that it is only a spot of light which perchance has been focused on the gray surface. Thus, when the photic radiation ("light beam") is intercepted, the disk disappears. It can be made to appear and disappear as many times as we wish simply by intercepting the photic beam. Thus we see that what was a real object visually does not have all the properties that we were led to believe it had by looking at it. It is not something that has independent existence. The texture (if any) that we see by looking at it is simply something visual. So are its hardness and tangible edge.

Now what are we going to say or do? Since it failed to have all of the properties expected of it, many people would be satisfied simply to call it an illusion and forget it, looking elsewhere for *reality*. This is the very way the advanced student of perception doesn't act.

Let us look at the light spot again. In spite of the knowledge we have just obtained, it still looks like the little hard disk that could be picked up. What the sense of vision first supplied, it still supplies.

Since we could not gain tactual corroboration for what we saw, the spot is not quite the full-fledged object it would have been had we obtained it. But, whatever it is, it is only what our senses make out of it. Both the initial object properties given by vision and the negation of any kind of object properties by touch were the products of sensory mechanisms. We have nothing out side of what the senses provide to go on. While this case would be counted by some as an illusion, a "mistaken perception," it is an example of what happens every minute of an individual's waking life as he looks about. Visual perception is making something out of the data provided by photic radiation. When the radiation ceases as we turn off the "light," we see nothing. It eliminates visual existence. What we *see* is thus only what is provided by the photic form of stimulus energy.

What you experienced visually, you called an illusion because when you touched the spot, it did not have the solid properties that a tactual thing would have. But what if it had had them? You would not have questioned your visual perception. You would have "known" you were right.

Let us turn the matter around, and use as an illustration an experience of a touchable (tangible) object, a raised spot on a surface. It is in the dark. The photic radiation (stimulation) for vision is absent. So, since you don't see what you touched, you still wonder about it. You want to see it. You know that since you experience darkness, your eyes are not stimulated and you have learned not to expect to see under such conditions. Knowing this, you "turn on the light" and examine what you touched. But let's say the raised area is so slight that it can't be seen. It still has tactile existence, and since you can't move or separate it from the surface or because it doesn't have a sharp edge, it can't be called a thing with the same meaning as if it were independent from the surface. But, since language is loose, you call it a thing, not an illusion. Since you tactilely experience it, though don't see it, you excuse the visual failure by saying the bump is *too*

slight to see. This precludes its being an illusion for you. You have found a way to excuse vision for failing to give testimony.

However, if you were to use some sort of instrumentation (magnifying glass, for example) and couldn't visually perceive a raised place on the surface, you would conclude that you had experienced a tactual (haptic) illusion. However, with the excuse you originally used, you likely didn't feel the need of using a device to supplement naked vision. You just relied on touch.

These two cases show that you relied on visual perception and tactual perception in different ways. It is as if you were saying that touch is more real than vision.

Be this as it may, when touch or full haptic perception is all that one has to rely on when vision is precluded, one cannot fully determine the identity and apprehend the nature of something placed in the hand. One wants to see it so that he can obtain additional information. This is strange, for we have just said that touch is in some respects more real than vision. Here we are asking for a "less real" form of evidence to supplement this "more real" kind of evidence.

We could continue this procedure by examining the results obtained from employing the other forms of perception. Were we to do so, we would find that they are related to each other and participate in the daily moment-to-moment affairs of life in various ways, mostly supporting, but at times contradicting each other.

Illusions have been defined in textbooks as *mistaken perceptions*. This is an assertion that deserves a close look. Where was the mistake? On what basis can it be said that any mistake was made? We have pointed out the contradiction between the properties of a thing looked at and a thing touched. Even so, can we say that the visual experience was false? We have been taught in natural science not to expect something for nothing and not to expect nothing for something. Basically, we expect justifiable quantitative relations. By calling an experience an illusion and defining illusion as a mistake, we believe in a result without a cause.

The "mistake" must lie in the implied *use* one makes of the raw sensory data. The visual experience was real—as real as anything could be. So was the tactual one. If we look upon the perceptual end result as a bona fide result of the conditions producing it, we can say that when one is using visual perception, he is employing one set of conditions; when he is using touch, he is employing another set. If he respects the results each of these sets of conditions produces, he need not imply mistakes in the relations between cause and effect.

On the Sources of Pleasure

Jerome Kagan

The joint ideas that man is a pleasure seeker and that one can designate specific forms of stimulation as sources of pleasure are central postulates in every man's theory of behavior. Yet we find confusion when we seek a definition of pleasure. The fact that man begins life with a small core set of capacities for experience that he wishes to repeat cannot be disputed. This is a pragmatic view of pleasure and we can add a dash of phenomenology to bolster the intuitive validity of this point of view. A sweet taste and a light touch in selected places are usually pleasant. Recently, we have added an important new source of pleasure. It is better to say we have rediscovered a source of pleasure, for Herbert Spencer was a nineteenth-century progenitor of the idea that *change in stimulation* is a source of pleasure for rats, cats, monkeys, or men. But, change is short-lived, quickly digested, and transformed to monotony. Popping up in front of an infant and saying peek-a-boo is pleasant for a 3-month-old infant for about 15 minutes, for a 10-month-old infant for 3 minutes, and for a 30-month-old child, a few seconds. This pleasant experience, like most events that elicit their repetition a few times before dying, is usually conceptualized as a change in stimulation. The source of the pleasure is sought in the environment. Why should change in external stimulation be pleasant? The understanding of pleasure and reinforcement in man is difficult enough without having to worry about infrahuman considerations. Let us restrict the argument to the human. The human is a cognitive creature who is attempting to put structure or create schema for incoming stimulation. A schema is a representation of an external pattern; much as an artist's illustration is a representation of an event. A schema for a visual pattern is a partial and somewhat distorted version of what the photograph would be. Consider the usefulness of the following hypothesis:

The creation of a schema for an event is one major source of pleasure. When one can predict an event perfectly, the schema is formed. As long as prediction is not perfect the schema is not yet formed. The peek-a-boo game works for 15 minutes with a 12-week-old for it takes him that long to be able to predict the event—the "peek-a-boo." Charlesworth (1965) has demonstrated the reinforcing value of "uncertainty" in an experiment in which the peek-a-boo face appeared either in the same locus every trial, alternated between two loci, or appeared randomly in one of two loci. The children persisted in searching for the face for a much longer time under the random condition than under the other two conditions. The random presentation was reinforcing for a longer period of time, not because it possessed a more optimum level of external stimulation than the other reinforcement schedules, but because it took longer for the child to create a schema for the random presentation and the process of creating a schema is a source of pleasure.

Consider another sign of pleasure beside persistence in issuing a particular response. Display of a smile or laugh is a good index of pleasure. Indeed, Tomkins' (1962) scheme for affect demands that pleasure be experienced if these responses appear. Consider two studies that bear on the relation between pleasure and the creation of schema. In our laboratory during the last 2 years, we have seen the same infants at 4, 8, and 13 months of age and have shown them a variety of visual patterns representative of human faces and human forms. In one episode, the 4-month-old infants are shown achromatic slides of a photograph of a regular male face, a schematic outline of a male face, and two disarranged, disordered faces. The frequency of occurrence of smiling to the photograph of the regular face is over *twice* the frequency observed to the regular schematic face—although looking time is identical—and over *four times* the frequency shown to the disordered faces. In another, more realistic episode, the 4-month-old infants see a regular, flesh-colored sculptured face in three dimensions and a distorted version of that face in which the eyes, nose, and mouth are rearranged. At 4 months of age the occurrence of smiling to the regular face is over three times the frequency displayed to the distorted version, but looking time is identical. There are two interpretations of this difference (Kagan, Henker, Hen-Tov, Levine, & Lewis, 1966). One explanation argues that the mother's face has become a secondary reward; the regular face stands for pleasure because it has been associated with care and affection from the mother. As a result, it elicits more smiles. An alternative interpretation is that the smile response has become conditioned to the human face via reciprocal contact between mother and infant. A third interpretation, not necessarily exclusive of these, is that the smile can be elicited when the infant matches stimulus to schema—when he has an "aha" reaction; when he makes a cognitive discovery. The 4-month-old infant is cognitively close to establishing a relatively firm schema of a human face. When a regular representation of a face is presented to him there is a short period during which the stimulus is assimilated to the schema and then after several seconds, a smile may occur. The smile is released following the perceptual recognition of the face, and reflects the assimilation of the stimulus to the infant's schema—a small, but significant act of creation. This hypothesis is supported by the fact that the typical latency between the onset of looking at the regular face (in the 4-month-old) and the onset of smiling is about 3 to 5 seconds. The smile usually does not occur immediately but only after the infant has studied the stimulus. If one sees this phenomenon live, it is difficult to avoid the conclusion that the smile is released following an act of perceptual recognition.

Additional data on these and other children at 8 months of age support this idea. At 8 months, frequency of smiling to both the regular and distorted faces is *reduced dramatically,* indicating that smiling does not covary with the reward value of the face. The face presumably has acquired more reward value by 8 months than it had at 4 months. However, the face is now a much firmer schema and recognition of it is immediate. There is no effortful act of recognition necessary for most infants. As a result, smiling is less likely to occur. Although smiling is much less frequent at 8 than 4 months to all faces, the frequency of smiling to the distorted face now *equals* the frequency displayed to the regular face. We interpret this to mean that the distorted face is sufficiently similar to the child's schema of a regular face that it can be recognized as such.

The pattern of occurrence of cardiac deceleration to the regular and distorted three-dimensional faces furnishes the strongest support for this argument. A cardiac deceleration of about 8 to 10 beats often accompanies attention to selected incoming visual stimuli in adults, school-age children, and infants. Moreover, the deceleration tends to be maximal when the stimuli are not overly familiar or completely novel, but are of intermediate familiarity. One hypothesis maintains that a large deceleration is most likely to occur when an act of perceptual recognition occurs, when the organism has a cognitive surprise. Let us assume that there is one trial for which this type of reaction occurs with maximal magnitude. If one examines the one stimulus presentation (out of a total of 16 trials) that produces the largest cardiac deceleration, a lawful change occurs between 4 and 8 months of age. At 4 months of age more of the infants showed their largest deceleration to the regular face (45% of the group: $n = 52$) than to the scrambled (34%), no eyes (11%), or blank faces (10%). At 8 months, the majority of the infants ($n = 52$) showed their largest deceleration to the scrambled face (50% to scrambled versus 21% to regular face). This difference is interpreted to mean that the scrambled face now assumes a similar position on the assimilation continuum that the regular face did 16 weeks earlier.

At 13 months of age these infants are shown six three-dimensional representations of a male human form and a free form matched for area, coloration, and texture with the human form. The stimuli include a faithful representation of a regular man, that same man with his head placed between his legs, the same man with all limbs and head collaged in an unusual and scrambled pattern, the man's body with a mule's head, and the mule's head on the man's body, the man's body with three identical heads, and a free form. The distribution of smiles to these stimuli is leptokurtic with over 70% of all the smiles occurring to the animal head on the human body and the three-headed man, forms that were moderate transformations of the regular man, and stimuli that required active assimilation. The free form and the scrambled man rarely elicited smiles from these infants. These stimuli are too difficult to assimilate to the schema of a human form possessed by a 13-month-old infant. It is interesting to note that the regular human form sometimes elicited the verbal response "daddy" or a hand waving from the child. These instrumental social reactions typically did not occur to the transformations. The occurrence of cardiac deceleration to these patterns agrees with this hypothesis. At 13 months of age, the man with his head between his legs, the man with the animal head, or the three-headed man, each elicited the largest cardiac decelerations more frequently than the regular man, the scrambled man, or the free form ($p < .05$) for each comparison. Thus, large cardiac decelerations and smiles were most likely to occur to stimuli that seemed to require tiny, quiet cognitive discoveries—miniaturized versions of Archimedes' "Eureka."

It appears that the act of matching stimulus to schema when the match is close but not yet perfect is a dynamic event. Stimuli that deviate a critical amount from the child's schema for a pattern are capable of eliciting an active process of recognition, and this process behaves as if it were a source of pleasure. Stimuli that are easily assimilable or too difficult to assimilate do not elicit these reactions.

A recent study by Edward Zigler[1] adds important support to the notion that the smile indicates the pleasure of an assimilation. Children in grades 2, 3, 4, and 5 looked at cartoons that required little or no reading. The children were asked to explain the cartoon while an observer coded the spontaneous occurrence of laughing and smiling while the children were studying the cartoons. It should come as no surprise that verbal comprehension of the cartoons

---

[1] Unpublished paper; personal communication.

increased in a linear fashion with age. But laughing and smiling increased through grade 4 and then declined markedly among the fifth-grade children. The fifth graders understood the cartoons too well. There was no gap between stimulus and schema and no smiling. Sixteen-week-old infants and 8-year-old children smile spontaneously at events that seem to have one thing in common—the event is a partial match to an existing schema and an active process of recognitory assimilation must occur.

The fact that a moderate amount of mismatch between event and schema is one source of pleasure demands the conclusion that it is not always possible to say that a specific event will always be a source of pleasure. The organism's state and structure must be in the equation. . . .

REFERENCES

CHARLESWORTH, W. R.   Persistence of orienting and attending behavior in young infants as a function of stimulus uncertainty. Paper read at Society for Research in Child Development, Minneapolis, March 1965.

KAGAN, J., HENKER, B. A., HEN-TOV, A., LEVINE, J., & LEWIS, M.   Infants' differential reactions to familiar and distorted faces. Child Development, 1966, 37, 519-532.

TOMKINS, S. S.   *Affect imagery consciousness. Vol. I The positive affects.* New York: Springer, 1962.

The Varieties of Attention

William James

The things to which we attend are said to *interest* us. Our interest in them is supposed to be the *cause* of our attending. What makes an object interesting we shall see presently; and later inquire in what sense interest may cause attention. Meanwhile attention may be divided into kinds in various ways. It is either to

1. Objects of sense (sensorial attention); or to
2. Ideal or represented objects (intellectual attention).

It is either

3. Immediate; or
4. Derived: immediate, when the topic or stimulus is interesting in itself, without relation to anything else; derived, when it owes its interest to association with some other immediately interesting thing. What I call derived attention has been named 'apperceptive' attention. Furthermore, attention may be either

5. Passive, reflex, non-voluntary, effortless; or
6. Active and voluntary.

Voluntary attention is always derived; we never make an *effort* to attend to an object except for the sake of some remote interest which the effort will serve. But both sensorial and intellectual attention may be either passive or voluntary.

In *passive immediate sensorial attention* the stimulus is a sense-impression, either very intense, voluminous, or sudden—in which case it makes no difference what its nature may be, whether sight, sound, smell, blow, or inner pain—or else it is an *instinctive* stimulus, a perception which, by reason of its nature rather than its mere force, appeals to some one of our normal congenital impulses and has a directly exciting quality.

Sensitiveness to immediately exciting sensorial stimuli characterizes the attention of childhood and youth. In mature age we have generally selected those stimuli which are connected with one or more so-called permanent interests, and our attention has grown irresponsive to the rest. But childhood is characterized by great active energy, and has few organized interests by which to meet new impressions and decide whether they are worthy of notice or not, and the consequence is that extreme mobility of the attention with which we are all familiar in children, and which makes their first lessons such rough affairs. Any strong sensation whatever produces accommodation of the organs which perceive it, and absolute oblivion, for the time being, of the task in hand. This reflex and passive character of the attention which, as a French writer says, makes the child seem to belong less to himself than to every object which happens to catch his notice, is the first thing which the teacher must overcome. It never is overcome in some people, whose work, to the end of life, gets done in the interstices of their mind-wandering.

The passive sensorial attention is *derived* when the impression, without being either strong or of an instinctively exciting nature, is connected by previous experience and education with things that are so. These things may be called the *motives* of the attention. The impression draws an interest from them, or perhaps it even fuses into a single complex object with them; the result is that it is brought into the focus of the mind. A faint tap *per se* is not an interesting sound; it may well escape being discriminated from the general rumor of the world. But when it is a signal, as that of a lover on the window-pane, it will hardly go unperceived.

Passive intellectual attention is immediate when we follow in thought a train of images exciting or interesting *per se;* derived, when the images are interesting only as means to a remote end, or merely because they are associated with something which makes them dear. Owing to the way in which immense numbers of real things become integrated into single objects of thought for us, there is no clear line to be drawn between immediate and derived attention of an intellectual sort. When absorbed in intellectual attention we may become so inattentive to outer things as to be 'absent-minded,' 'abstracted,' or *'distraits.'* All revery or concentrated meditation is apt to throw us into this state.

Archimedes, it is well known, was so absorbed in geometrical meditation that he was first aware of the storming of Syracuse by his own death-wound, and his exclamation on the entrance of the Roman soldiers was: *Noli turbare circulos meos!* In like manner Joseph Scaliger, the most learned of men, when a Protestant student in Paris, was so engrossed in the study of Homer that he became aware of the massacre of St. Bartholonew, and of his own escape, only on the day subsequent to the catastrophe. The philosopher

Carneades was habitually liable to fits of meditation so profound that, to prevent him sinking from inanition, his maid found it necessary to feed him like a child. And it is reported of Newton that, while engaged in his mathematical researches, he sometimes forgot to dine. Cardan, one of the most illustrious of philosophers and mathematicians, was once, upon a journey, so lost in thought that he forgot both his way and the object of his journey. To the questions of his driver whether he should proceed, he made no answer; and when he came to himself at nightfall, he was surprised to find the carriage at a standstill, and directly under a gallows. The mathematician Vieta was sometimes so buried in meditation that for hours he bore more resemblance to a dead person than to a living, and was then wholly unconscious of everything going on around him. On the day of his marriage the great Budaeus forgot everything in his philological speculations, and he was only awakened to the affairs of the external world by a tardy embassy from the marriage-party, who found him absorbed in the composition of his *Commentarii.*

The absorption may be so deep as not only to banish ordinary sensations, but even the severest pain. Pascal, Wesley, Robert Hall, are said to have had this capacity. Dr. Carpenter says of himself that

he has frequently begun a lecture whilst suffering neuralgic pain so severe as to make him apprehend that he would find it impossible to proceed; yet no sooner has he by a determined effort fairly launched himself into the stream of thought, than he has found himself continuously borne along without the least distraction, until the end has come, and the attention has been released; when the pain has recurred with a force that has overmastered all resistance, making him wonder how he could have ever ceased to feel it.

Dr. Carpenter speaks of launching himself by a determined *effort.* This effort characterizes what we called *active or voluntary attention.* It is a feeling which every one knows, but which most people would call quite indescribable. We get it in the sensorial sphere whenever we seek to catch an impression of extreme *faintness,* be it of sight, hearing, taste, smell, or touch; we get it whenever we seek to *discriminate* a sensation merged in a mass of others that are similar; we get it whenever we *resist the attractions* of more potent stimuli and keep our mind occupied with some object that is naturally unimpressive. We get it in the intellectual sphere under exactly similar conditions: as when we strive to sharpen and make distinct an idea which we but vaguely seem to have; or painfully discriminate a shade of meaning from its similars; or resolutely hold fast to a thought so discordant with our impulses that, if left unaided, it would quickly yield place to images of an exciting and impassioned kind. All forms of attentive effort would be exercised at once by one whom we might suppose at a dinner-party resolutely to listen to a neighbor giving him insipid and unwelcome advice in a low voice, whilst all around the guests were loudly laughing and talking about exciting and interesting things.

There is no such thing as voluntary attention sustained for more than a few seconds at a time. What is called sustained voluntary attention is a repetition of successive efforts which bring back the topic to the mind. The topic once brought back, if a congenial one, *develops;* and if its development is interesting it engages the attention passively for a time. Dr. Carpenter, a moment back, described the stream of thought, once entered, as 'bearing him along.' This passive interest may be short or long. As soon as it flags, the attention is diverted by some irrelevant thing, and then a voluntary effort may bring it back to the topic again; and so on, under favorable conditions, for hours together. During all this time, however, note that it is not an identical *object* in the psychological sense, but a succession of mutually related objects forming an identical *topic* only, upon which the attention is fixed. *No one can possibly attend continuously to an object that does not change.*

Now there are always some objects that for the time being *will not develop.* They simply *go out;* and to keep the mind upon anything related to them requires such incessantly reviewed effort that the most resolute Will ere long gives out and let its thoughts follow the more stimulating solicitations after it has withstood them for what length of time it can. There are topics known to every man from which he shies like a frightened horse, and which to get a glimpse of is to shun. Such are his ebbing assets to the spendthrift in full career. But why single out the spendthrift when to every man actuated by passion the thought of interests which negate the passion can hardly for more than a fleeting instant stay before the mind? It is like 'memento mori' in the heyday of the pride of life. Nature rises at such suggestions, and excludes them from the view:—How long, O healthy reader, can you now continue thinking of your tomb?—In milder instances the difficulty is as great, especially when the brain is fagged. One snatches at any and every passing pretext, no matter how trivial or external, to escape from the odiousness of the matter in hand. I know a person, for example, who will poke the fire, set chairs straight, pick dust-specks from the floor, arrange his table, snatch up the newspaper, take down any book which catches his eye, trim his nails, waste the morning *anyhow,* in short, and all without premeditation,—simply because the only thing he *ought* to attend to is the preparation of a noonday lesson in formal logic which he detests. Anything but *that!*

And now we can see why it is that what is called sustained attention is the easier, the richer in acquisitions and the fresher and more original the mind. In such minds, subjects bud and sprout and grow. At every moment, they please by a new consequence and rivet the attention afresh. But an intellect unfurnished with materials, stagnant, unoriginal, will hardly be likely to consider any subject long. A glance exhausts its possibilities of interest. Geniuses are commonly believed to excel other men in their power of sustained attention. In most of them, it is to be feared, the so-called 'power' is of the passive sort. Their ideas coruscate, every subject branches infinitely before their fertile minds, and so for hours they may be rapt. *But it is their genius making them attentive, not their attention making geniuses of them.* And, when we come down to the root of the matter, we see that they differ from ordinary men less in the character of their attention than in the nature of the objects upon which it is successively bestowed. In the genius, these form a concatenated series, suggesting each other mutually by some rational law. Therefore we call the attention 'sustained' and the topic of meditation for hours 'the same.' In the common man the series is for the most part incoherent, the objects have no rational bond, and we call the attention wandering and unfixed.

It is probable that genius tends actually to prevent a man from acquiring habits of voluntary attention, and that moderate intellectual endowments are the soil in which we may best expect, here as elsewhere, the virtues of the will, strictly so called, to thrive. But, whether the attention come by grace of genius or by dint of will, the longer one does attend to a topic the more mastery of it one has. And the faculty of voluntarily bringing back a wandering attention, over and over again, is the very root of judgment, character, and will. No one is *compos sui* if he have it not. An education which should improve this faculty would be *the* education *par excellence.* But it is easier to define this ideal than to give practical directions for bringing it about. The only general pedagogic maxim bearing on attention is that the more interest the child has in advance in the subject, the better he will attend. Induct him therefore in such a way as to knit each new thing on to some acquisition already there; and if possible awaken curiosity, so that the new thing shall seem to come as an answer, or part of an answer, to a question pre-existing in his mind.

Good-Me, Bad-Me, Not-Me

Harry Stack Sullivan

Three aspects of interpersonal cooperation are necessary for the infant's survival, and dictate learning. That is, these aspects of interpersonal cooperation require acculturation or socialization of the infant. Infants are customarily exposed to all of these before the era of infancy is finished. From experience of these three sorts—with rewards, with the anxiety gradient, and with practically obliterative sudden severe anxiety—there comes an initial personification of three phases of what presently will be *me,* that which is invariably connected with the sentience of *my body*—and you will remember that *my body* as an organization of experience has come to be distinguished from everything else by its self-sentient character. These beginning personifications of three different kinds, which have in common elements of the prehended body, are organized in about mid-infancy—I can't say exactly when. I have already spoken of the infant's very early double personification of the actual mothering one as the good mother and the bad mother. Now, at this time, the beginning personifications of *me* are *good-me, bad-me,* and *not-me.* So far as I can see, in practically every instance of being trained for life, in this or another culture, it is rather inevitable that there shall be this tripartite cleavage in personifications, which have as their central tie—the thing that binds them ultimately into one, that always keeps them in very close relation—their relatedness to the growing conception of "my body."

Good-me is the beginning personification which organizes experience in which satisfactions have been enhanced by rewarding increments of tenderness, which come to the infant because the mothering one is pleased with the way things are going; therefore, and to that extent, she is free, and moves toward expressing tender appreciation of the infant. Good-me, as it ultimately develops, is the ordinary topic of discussion about "I."

Bad-me, on the other hand, is the beginning personification which organizes experience in which increasing degrees of anxiety are associated with behavior involving the mothering one in its more-or-less clearly prehended interpersonal setting. That is to say, bad-me is based on this increasing gradient of anxiety and that, in turn, is dependent, at this stage of life, on the observation, if misinterpretation, of the infant's behavior by someone who can induce anxiety. The frequent coincidence of certain behavior on the part of the infant with increasing tenseness and increasingly evident forbidding on the part of the mother is the source of the type of experience which is organized as a rudimentary personification to which we may apply the term bad-me.

So far, the two personifications I have mentioned may sound like a sort of laboring of reality. However, these personifications are a part of the communicated thinking of the child, a year or so later, and therefore it is not an unwarranted use of inference to presume that they exist at this earlier stage. When we come to the third of these beginning personifications, *not-me,* we are in a different field—one which we know about only through certain very special circumstances. And these special circumstances are not outside the experience of any of us. The personification of not-me is most conspicuously encountered by most of us in an occasional dream while we are asleep; but it is very emphatically encountered by people who are having a severe schizophrenic episode, in aspects that are to them most spectacularly real. As a matter of fact, it is always manifest—not every minute, but every day, in every life—in certain peculiar absences of phenomena where there should be phenomena; and in a good many people—I know not what proportion—it is very striking in its indirect manifestations (dissociated behavior), in which people do and say things of which they do not and could not have knowledge, things which may be quite meaningful to other people but are unknown to them. The special circumstances which we encounter in grave mental disorders may be, so far as you know, outside your experience; but they were not once upon a time. It is from the evidence of these special circumstances—including both those encountered in everybody and those encountered in grave disturbances of personality, all of which we shall presently touch upon—that I choose to set up this third beginning personification which is tangled up with the growing acquaintance of "my body," the personification of *not-me.* This is a very gradually evolving personification of an always relatively primitive character—that is, organized in unusually simple signs in the parataxic mode of experience, and made up of poorly grasped aspects of living which will presently be regarded as 'dreadful,' and which still later will be differentiated into incidents which are attended by awe, horror, loathing, or dread.

This rudimentary personification of not-me evolves very gradually, since it comes from the experience of intense anxiety—a very poor method of education. Such a complex and relatively inefficient method of getting acquainted with reality would naturally lead to relatively slow evolution of an organization of experiences; furthermore, these experiences are largely truncated, so that what they are really about is not clearly known. Thus organizations of these experiences marked by uncanny emotion—which means experiences which, when observed, have led to intense forbidding gestures on the part of the mother, and induced intense anxiety in the infant—are not nearly as clear and useful guides to anything as the other two types of organizations have been. Because experiences marked by uncanny emotion, which are organized in the personification of not-me, cannot be clearly connected with cause and effect—cannot be dealt with in all the impressive ways by which we explain our referential processes later—they persist throughout life as relatively primitive, unelaborated, parataxic symbols. Now that does not mean that the not-me component in adults is infantile; but it does mean that the not-me component is, in all essential respects, practically beyond discussion in communicative terms. Not-me is part of the very 'private mode' of living. But, as I have said, it manifests itself at various times in the life of everyone after childhood—or of nearly everyone, I can't swear to the statistics—by the eruption of certain exceedingly unpleasant emotions in what are called nightmares.

These three rudimentary personifications of *me* are, I believe, just as distinct as the two personfications of the objectively same mother were earlier. But while the personifications of me are getting under way, there is some change going on with respect to the personification of mother. In the latter part of infancy, there is some evidence that the rudimentary personality, as it were, is already fusing the previously disparate personifications of the good and the bad mother; and within a year and a half after the end of infancy we find evidence of this duplex personification of the mothering one as the good mother and the bad mother clearly manifested only in relatively obscure mental processes, such as these dreamings while asleep. But, as I have suggested, when we come to consider the question of the peculiarly inefficient and inappropriate interpersonal relations which constitute problems of mental disorder, there again we discover that the trend in organizing experience which began with this duplex affair has not in any sense utterly disappeared.

THE DYNAMISM OF THE SELF-SYSTEM

From the essential desirability of being good-me, and from the increasing ability to be warned by slight increases of anxiety—that is, slight diminutions in euphoria—in situations involving the increasingly significant other person,

there comes into being the start of an exceedingly important, as it were, secondary dynamism, which is purely the product of interpersonal experience arising from anxiety encountered in the pursuit of the satisfaction of general and zonal needs. This secondary dynamism I call the *self-system*. As a dynamism it is secondary in that it does not have any particular zones of interaction, any particular physiological apparatus, behind it; but it literally uses all zones of interaction and all physiological apparatus which is integrative and meaningful from the interpersonal standpoint. And we ordinarily find its ramifications spreading throughout interpersonal relations in every area where there is any chance that anxiety may be encountered.

The essential desirability of being good-me is just another way of commenting on the essential undesirability of being anxious. Since the beginning personification of good-me is based on experience in which satisfactions are enhanced by tenderness, then naturally there is an essential desirability of living good-me. And since sensory and other abilities of the infant are well matured by now—perhaps even space perception, one of the slowest to come along, is a little in evidence—it is only natural that along with this essential desirability there goes increasing ability to be warned by slight forbidding—in other words, by slight anxiety. Both these situations, for the purpose now under discussion, are situations involving another person—the mothering one, or the congeries of mothering ones—and she is becoming increasingly significant because, as I have already said, the manifestation of tender cooperation by her is now complicated by her attempting to teach, to socialize the infant; and this makes the relationship more complex, so that it requires better, more effective differentiation by the infant of forbidding gestures, and so on. For all these reasons, there comes into being in late infancy an organization of experience which will ultimately be of nothing less than stupendous importance in personality, and which comes entirely from the interpersonal relations in which the infant is now involved—and these interpersonal relations have their motives (or their motors, to use a less troublesome word) in the infant's general and zonal needs for satisfaction. But out of the social responsibility of the mothering one, which gets involved in the satisfaction of the infant's needs, there comes the organization in the infant of what might be said to be a dynamism directed at how to live with this significant other person. The self-system thus is an organization of educative experience called into being by the necessity to avoid or to minimize incidents of anxiety.

ORDINARY WAKING STATES

Awareness is the most slippery of faculties. Slips and twists of attention play havoc with our awareness, even during our normal waking state. Psychologist Graham Reed shows how attentional shifts of different sorts cause anomalous moments of consciousness. When we concentrate intently on a mental problem, the result is the preoccupation of the absent-minded professor. While engaged in a routine task such as driving, we let our minds gather wool, then suddenly snap to attention only to find that we have lost minutes or even hours in reverie, with no memory at all of what happened in the meanwhile. Under extreme pressure we may selectively distort or even freeze our attention into a sort of tunnel vision that blocks out an impending threat.

A much more mundane evasion of the reality around us is the common daydream. Daydreams intrude into the waking state of almost everyone during a normal day, and surge into prominence in quiet moments when we are alone. The word "daydream" has negative connotations in our action-oriented culture, but, claims psychologist Jerome Singer, these moments of self-absorption can have both practical and psychological value. Although some daydreams can be neurotic and anxiety-filled, more often these bouts of fantasy are sources of pleasure and an opportunity to try out possible solutions to pressing problems.

Such moratoriums of active wakefulness may be part of the core of creativity. It is in such moments that we are open to inspiration for what cognitive psychologist Jerome Bruner calls "effective surprise," the placing of things in new perspectives in such a way that it takes the beholder beyond common ways of experiencing the world. The conditions in which creativity flourishes require a state of mind that Bruner loosely defines by its main features: a detachment from the obvious, conventional ways of construing the situation; a motivation to render a new order of things; passionate involvement with a respect for technique; and the openness to let the object being created take one over.

A state connected with such creative moments is "flow," the experience of being totally absorbed in an act that is pleasant in itself, and which one does well. We all fall into such moments from time to time, when things go just right, when we're "on," when we perform at our peak. A typical situation where flow occurs is during play and games, but the state is possible during any task we're prepared for. Psychologist Mihaly Csikszentmihaly has studied the elements of flow: a person's attention is centered in what he is doing, he loses his self-consciousness and forgets himself in the moment, his pleasure comes from the activity itself rather than some external reward, and the person's skills are sufficient for the demands of the moment. Flow is a "natural high" that flourishes in the domain of consciousness between boredom and anxiety.

Anomalies of Attention

Graham Reed

'Every one,' asserted William James, 'knows what attention is.' Perhaps they do; but, at least as far as psychologists are concerned, the trouble is that their knowings do not match. And dictionary definitions, such as: 'The act of applying one's mind, notice, consideration . . ' *(Pocket Oxford Dictionary)*, raise more questions than they answer. So we may profitably start by considering some of the varieties of attention and the ways in which the word is used.

Clearly, a distinction must be made between *passive* and *voluntary* attention. The first of these terms refers to situations where our attention is 'arrested' or 'captured,' despite ourselves. This passive attention is a function of the event or stimulus, and many studies have been made to determine the characteristics which make a stimulus attention-gaining. These include size, motion, colour, repetition, contrast and novelty, features which are deliberately employed by advertisers whose aim of course is to attract maximum attention.

Voluntary attention refers to situations where we deliberately focus upon some particular feature or train of events. This may be the most interesting among the whole array of those available for inspection. But it may be only one of many equally arresting items, or indeed something to which we pay attention *despite* the fact that it is dominated or masked by other features or events.

Let us look briefly at some of the ways in which the word 'attention' has been used, and some of the key concepts and terms employed in its study:

(1)   Perhaps the most commonly recognized type of attention in everyday life is that where we *concentrate,* with more or less success, upon some particular task. Thus we speak of concentrating upon a textbook, the presentation of an argument, driving a car in heavy traffic or swinging a golf club. Later, the anomalous experience of *absent-mindedness* as related to this type of attention will be considered. Ironically, absent-mindedness is generally taken to involve a lack of concentration, whereas in fact it describes the opposite.

Our level of concentration may be diminished when we are distracted from the task in hand by events irrelevant to the task or simply by our own thoughts or day-dreams as in 'wool-gathering.' This will affect our performance most seriously in unfamiliar tasks or those in which we are relatively unskilled. We may be able to perform habitual activities or ones in which we are highly skilled with minimal conscious attention. The *time-gap experience* will be discussed as an anomaly related to this question of level of skill.

(2)   In referring to 'voluntary attention' above it was noted that we can attend to one particular signal or sequence when there are many others equally or more interesting, all competing for our attention. Under the title of *selective attention* this phenomenon has excited the interest of experimental psychologists since the 1950s, after an interval of some forty years during which the whole area of attention had received relatively little examination.

(3)   A third usage of the word 'attention' is in relation to *arousal.* For instance, when we are frightened, delighted, amazed, curious or sexually aroused, our attention is heightened. We become acutely attentive if we are approached by a belligerent drunk or a provocative and attractive member of the opposite sex. Dependent upon our cultural background, we may exhibit similar attention changes when we are faced with a sonnet by Shakespeare, a Rembrandt etching or a wine bottle whose label lays claim to a particular vintage. Or an unexpected cheque, or a severed hand. . . . In such cases, arousal is associated with intensity of attention. We have mentioned the 'focussing' of attention; this implies differential distribution or *deployment* of attentional resources. Arousal involves the focussing of attention, but crucially it affects the *degree* of attention. Arousal theory states that the activation of the organism varies along a continuum from sleep to drowsiness through optimally effective functioning to diffuse over-excitation. Clearly this is an example of what we have referred to as 'passive' or 'primary' attention because it is involuntary and consequent upon the effects upon us of external events. We are aroused by the situation despite ourselves. Subsequently, of course, we may employ voluntary attention also.

With reference to this type of attention, responses to *stress* are discussed, but later on such experiences as 'possession,' which can also be considered from the attentional point of view, are covered.

(4)   The cat at the mouse-hole displays highly focused and intense attention. But she is not attending to

the mouse-hole as such. She is waiting for the appearance of the mouse itself. Similarly, the industrial meter-watcher must be highly attentive, not so much to the display currently before him, but in anticipation of occasional *changes* in the display. Study of the decrements in performance of radar operators during World War II initiated a mass of research into this sort of attention, which was termed *vigilance* by Mackworth (1950).

ABSENT-MINDEDNESS

The traditional picture of the 'absent-minded professor' (AMP) portrays an unkempt, white-haired figure shambling along the centre of King's Parade, Cambridge, blissfully unaware both of the traffic screaming to a halt around him and of the fact that he is carrying a vacuum cleaner instead of his brief-case.

This sort of behaviour is regarded by the observer as highly anomalous but it is not seen as pathological, despite the fact that it has much in common with lay presumptions about lunatics. Far from being associated with mental illness or intellectual impairment, it is usually cited (with elaborations) as evidence of the eccentricity associated with genius. This is particularly so when the individual behaves in this way so consistently as to suggest that it reflects a relatively stable personality variable rather than temporary abberation.

The true AMP himself is not aware that his behaviour is unusual. Indeed, were he aware, he could not be said to be absent-minded. For the whole point about absent-mindedness is that the individual is so preoccupied with his own thoughts that he closes out much of the external information which is currently available to him. He may engage in many habitual activities such as seizing his brief-case and setting off at the time he usually leaves to deliver his lecture. But he is not responsive to feed-back regarding changes in his routine. Thus, in the way that Henri Bergson asserted was the crux of humour, his actions are machine-like. If the vacuum cleaner happens to be standing where his brief-case usually is, then he seizes that on his way out. Furthermore, he may not regulate the details of his on-going habitual behaviour in accordance with environmental demands. If his goal is the college gates he may make directly for them, regardless of traffic conditions across his route. In short, the AMP's *level* of attentiveness is low for what are to him distracting stimuli. But it must be remembered that not only is he very attentive to his thinking, but he may also attend closely to any external activity related to that thinking. One variant of the AMP is the absent-minded scientist who is so involved in his experiment that he fails to notice that his beard is on fire. Thus, the *level* of his attention is associated with his *deployment* of attentiveness which will be considered in a later section. It may be presumed that absent-mindedness is

a threshold phenomenon. The AMP's diminished level and scope of attention to external events are directly but inversely related to the degree of his preoccupation with those events of concern to him. If the competing signals from the environment suddenly increase in intensity or significance it may be anticipated that his general attentiveness will increase to a more appropriate level. Indeed, although there are many stories of AMPs disappearing down uncovered manholes, there are no recorded instances of any who actually failed to skip out of the way at the last moment as the omnibuses bore down upon them. And it is difficult to believe that the classic AMP would remain quite so absent-minded were he to be confronted by an equally absent-minded lady professor sauntering down King's Parade in the nude.

THE 'TIME-GAP' EXPERIENCE

After a long drive the motorist will quite commonly report that at some point in the journey he 'woke up' to realize that he had no awareness of some preceding period of time. People often describe this, with some justification, as a 'gap in time,' 'a lost half-hour,' or 'a piece out of my life.' The strangeness of the experience springs partly from 'waking up' when one is already awake. But mainly it is due to the knowledge of a blank in one's temporal awareness. Doubtless the uneasiness associated with such a realization is largely culturally determined. For in our culture our everyday lives are sharply structured by time requirements. For most of us there are conventional times for commencing and finishing work, for taking breaks, for eating, sleeping and enjoying leisure pursuits. We talk about 'wasting time' as opposed to 'spending time profitably.' We are continually consulting our watches or turning on the radio to check our subjective estimates of the passage of time, and in many jobs 'clock-watching' has a very real significance. Only when we are on holiday can most of us indulge in the luxury of ceasing to bother about clock time. But furthermore, our consciousness of self is closely related to the sense of *continuity* in the passage of time. To miss a period of time can be very disturbing; it has been used as the theme of several stories and films, as in the alcoholic's 'lost week-end.'

A little reflection will suggest, however, that our experience of time and its passage is determined by *events*, either external or internal. What the time-gapper is reporting is not that a slice of time has vanished, but that he has failed to register a series of events which would normally have functioned as his time-markers. If he is questioned closely he will admit that his 'time-gap' experience did not involve his realization at, say, noon that he had somehow 'lost' half an hour. Rather, the experience consists of 'waking up' at, say, Florence and realizing that he remembers nothing since Bologna. It is now noon, whereas he left

Bologna at eleven-thirty. The time-gapper describes his experience in terms of *time,* whereas he could just as well describe it in terms of *distance.* To understand the experience, however, it is best considered in terms of the absence of *events.* If the time-gapper had taken that particular day off, and spent the morning sitting in his garden undisturbed, he might have remembered just as little of the half-hour in question. He might still describe it in terms of lost time, but he would not find the experience unusual or disturbing. For he would point out that he could not remember what took place between eleven-thirty and twelve simply because nothing of note occurred. Doubtless there were many events during that time—clouds moved across the sky, sparrows twittered, leaves fluttered across the lawn. But none of these represented any drastic change in the situation, and none had any alerting significance for our man. Why then is he puzzled about his failure to remember anything between Bologna and Florence? Simply because he knows very well that he has driven his car from one place to the other, which demands continual personal events in the form of on-going skilled activity, which naturally presents a continual shift of visual scene and which normally involves events related to other road-users. But the point is that the time-gap experienced when a portion of the journey lacks events of significance. There is little traffic, clear visibility, a good road surface, no warning signs and so on. In short, the demands of the task are relatively unchanging.

Now our performance of complex skills involves perfecting the basic elements, the integration of these into a new level of skill, then the further integration of several such levels and so on in a hierarchical progression of *schemata.* Our mastery of the overall skill is facilitated by the fact that, when we have perfected each component or level, its performance becomes 'automatic,' in the sense that we can withdraw active attention from that level of activity and concentrate on the next. We seldom 'attend' to our execution of habitual, life-long skills such as grasping, walking or talking. We become conscious of them only when our functioning is impaired by injury of ill-health. On the other hand, we do have to attend to the ways in which these basic skills must be organized in response to environmental demands, particularly when these are stressful or unfamiliar. We may walk for miles along a smooth track without noticing what we are doing. Matters become very different when the track surface deteriorates or the path winds along the edge of a cliff. In the performance of more formal activities, much depends upon the amount of change involved in the task. The skilled boxer cannot afford to relax his concentration because, however habitual the *elements* of his performance, his opponent is continually introducing changes which demand the reorganization of these elements. But when the task is relatively 'closed' and strategic reorganization unlikely, then the skilled person can perform it with a minimum of active attention. Thus

the experienced knitter can execute a complex activity whilst conversing or watching the television or listening for the baby. The pianist can play familiar music whilst discussing audience reactions with his colleagues and the carpenter can operate a lathe whilst instructing his apprentice.

The relevance of the above to the time-gap experience is obvious. The task of driving is itself highly skilled, but its component activities are over-learned and habitual to the experienced driver. Steering, changing gear, adjusting speed, giving signals and so on all become automatic acts which do not require his conscious attention. Their organization and integration at the tactical level also become habitual within a certain range of requirements. (Indeed, a major danger in motorway driving, where the road is straight, wide and well surfaced and where constant speeds over long distances are possible, is that drivers can afford to diminish their conscious attention to the point where the task becomes boring and they fall asleep.) However, traffic conditions usually demand continual reorganization of skilled responses at the strategic level and this requires constant alertness and conscious attention.

The key to the time-gap experience, then, is the level of organization or schematization required by the situation. But why is it that the driver realizes that he has been driving 'automatically?' Simply that the situation *does* change and events demanding his active attention do intrude. As he approaches Florence, he encounters more traffic, warning signs, traffic lights and so on. His on-going routine activity is now insufficient; the situation suddenly demands responses to new information and feed-back, in the form of continual strategic reorganization of his skills. He must, in fact, 'wake up,' relatively speaking. And, in waking up, his reactivated conscious attentiveness enables him to register among many other things that he is now in Florence. In one sense he is correct in describing what has happened as a 'gap.' But the gap is not in time, but in alertness or high conscious attention.

CHANGES IN ATTENTION AS RESPONSE TO STRESS

Absent-mindedness reflects the failure of signals from the environment to engage attention. What happens when signals are maximally attention-gaining? Let us take the example of a stressful situation, where signals have heightened impact because of their fear- or anxiety-provoking significance. Just as danger signals elicit bodily changes which are accompanied by changes in performance, so are our *cognitive* processes modified in characteristic ways.

For us all, our attention becomes heightened and relatively restricted. As our muscles gird themselves for maximal activity, so we tend to *focus* awareness in a way which must originally have had clear survival value. In physically dangerous situations the threatening features demand all our attention, and other matters are put to one side. Up to a point, this is most appropriate; we are harnessing all our resources in preparation for action. But there is for each of us a breaking point. Either our attention becomes so narrowed that we 'freeze' (physically and mentally) or our behaviour disintegrates and we panic. When a driver sees another car skidding towards him, he immediately experiences several cognitive changes. A moment before he may have been driving automatically, his mind far away. Suddenly, he is very conscious of himself, the controls, his speed, the road ahead. This necessarily involves the submergence of his previous train of thought as well as the normal balance of his physical control over his vehicle. He is now very conscious of his own position in space and time relative to the approaching car. Similarly, he acquires a sort of 'tunnel vision'—he perceives only the other vehicle and the area between. What was a global field is suddenly articulated. What was an interrelated overall pattern of road, sky, hedgerows, houses and hills breaks down. Just as his earlier stream of thought has been ousted, so the general visual scene is blurred into what the Gestalt psychologists described as 'ground' totally dominated by the relevant 'figure' of threat.

Now in civilized urban life we rarely meet actual physical danger. Stress is more usually related to social demands and intra-psychic conflict. In other words, we provide our own danger signals, which are usually the product of the ways in which we construe our own behaviour and the situations in which we find ourselves. And our construing is the product of our interpretations of and predictions about any given situation and our learned standards, aspirations, self-images and so on. But whether these signals are external and refer to actual danger or are internal and spring from our 'state of mind,' our cognitive responses tend to be the same.

Not only do we differ radically according to our individual kinds of learning and previous experiences, but we vary in our degrees of autonomic reactivity. Some autonomic nervous systems are more reactive than others; so some people's emergency response thresholds are lower than others and can be triggered off more easily. When such people are also liable to be over-sensitive in their construing of situations, they are continually vulnerable to anxiety and impaired performance. This leads to further tension and doubts, so that a vicious circle is set up. When the person no longer feels able to cope he may seek psychiatric help; he may well now be termed 'neurotic' and diagnosed as suffering from an 'anxiety state.'

The attentional changes noted as occurring in stressful situations are common to all of us, though in varying degrees. But each person probably has his individual attention pattern which is sufficiently consistent to allow it to be given the status of a personality characteristic.

The Importance of Daydreaming

Jerome L. Singer

George, I've asked you three times to empty the garbage and you haven't moved."

"Sorry, Darling, I guess I didn't hear you. I must have been daydreaming."

"But you were looking straight at me!" Mrs. Brown hears voices coming from five-year-old Timmy's bedroom. Momentarily startled, she soon realizes that Timmy merely is playing a game by himself, acting out the roles of the good guys and the bad guys.

The mother smiles proudly at Timmy's cleverness in shifting voices. Then she feels a pang of anxiety. Is something wrong with her son? Should he be talking to himself at his age? Isn't this a symptom of some emotional conflict?

These two cases illustrate a phenomenon most common to human experience. Daydreams intrude suddenly into the waking thoughts of almost everyone during a normal day and certainly surge into prominence in those quiet or solitary moments when we ride on trains, sit in waiting rooms, or prepare for bed.

The nocturnal dream, more vivid and dramatic, has been the focus of much attention in folklore, literature and science from the days of Joseph in Pharaoh's court to the recent flurry of neurophysiological experimentation on sleep. Its paler cousin, the fleeting fantasy or distracting image we call the daydream, has always been of interest to creative artists but has been virtually ignored by scientific researchers.

These two hypothetical but typical cases point up some of the unkowns about daydreaming. Is George's reverie simply an escape from the unpleasant reality of taking out the garbage? Is his failure to hear his wife the sign of worthwhile, creative thinking, or is it a psychological defense against the humdrum character of his life?

And what is the nature of the fantasy play activity in which young Timmy is indulging? Is he abnormal? Is his taking of several roles the creation in effect of a world around Timmy which is not really there; is it something that prepares him for skills in later life, or is it a passing characteristic of childhood. What kinds of cultural patterns foster such imaginative play or prevent its continuation?

Clearly, some systematic scientific understanding of the scope and function of daydreaming in children and in adults is called for. But how does one catch hold of so insubstantial a bit of fluff as a daydream for any kind of scientific study? Science usually requires objectivity, repeatability of the phenomenon, measurement and experimental control. How to squeeze a daydream into that mold has so baffled psychologists that very little formal research on daydreaming has been done.

Well before the turn of the century, Sir Francis Galton proposed to study the range of human imagery and William James called attention to the stream of thought as a significant human phenomenon. Psychoanalysts have of course made frequent use of their patients' daydreams in diagnosis and therapy. But behavioral scientists have devoted surprisingly little effort to examining daydreams or related types of self-generated internal stimulation experienced by the average person.

Indeed, in our action-oriented nation, the term "daydreaming" has assumed a negative connotation. But it does not seem likely that fantasizing is inherently pathological or even defensive. It seems more reasonable that daydreaming is a fundamental human characteristic, an autonomous ego function. Daydreaming is more than a readily available defense or escape; it is a valuable method we all use to explore a variety of perspectives.

My own interest in daydreaming evolved out of an earlier interest in the nature of imaginative behavior as shown clinically in such "projective techniques" as the Rorschach inkblots and the Thematic Apperception Test. Both of these techniques require a person to project his own feelings and ideas into an interpretation of ambiguous images—inkblots in the first case and nondescript drawings in the second. Presumably in doing so he reveals his general behavioral style and his dominant motivational pattern.

Especially interesting to me was Herman Rorschach's observation that people who look at inkblots and report seeing human beings in action—the so-called M determinant—are imaginative people, inclined to an original, rich inner life. The Rorschach M response has interesting implications for an understanding of imagination. Nevertheless, with the Rorschach data we still are dealing with an inferred measure of imagination based on reactions to inkblots—several steps removed from the underlying process which is of primary interest: the daydream itself.

Rather than attempting to explore daydreaming simply by making inferences from the Rorschach data, we decided to begin again and examine the phenomenon more directly. For some time now a program of research has been carried on under my direction at the City College of the City University of New York, with the close collaboration of various colleagues, in particular Professor John Antrobus.

My first step was to devise a questionnaire, based on what I could learn from clinical literature and from the experiences of friends, relatives and patients, as well as from my own introspections. This questionnaire consisted of a large number of actual daydreams; the person answered it by indicating how frequently he indulged in the various kinds of daydreams described. Over a period of time the questionnaire was improved and polished, and administered to almost 500 men and women, most of them college-educated. No data on persons of other socioeconomic levels are available at this time.

The questionnaire included such sample daydreams as these:

"I have my own yacht and plan a cruise of the Eastern seaboard."

"I suddenly find I can fly, to the amazement of passersby."

"I see myself in the arms of a warm and loving person who satisfies all my needs."

"I picture an atomic bombing of the town I live in."

"I see myself participating with wild abandon in a Roman orgy."

In analyzing the responses to the questionnaire, we saw at once that almost all adults engage in some form of daydreaming every day. Most of these daydreams take the form of fairly clear visual images. They occur chiefly during private moments, just before bedtime or during rides on buses or trains.

Most people report that they enjoy their daydreams. In content their fantasies stick fairly close to simple possibilities, although a very high proportion admit wildly improbable dreams such as inheriting a million dollars. A sizable minority report such fantasies as "being the Messiah," obtaining homosexual satisfactions, and murdering family members. Those individuals with a pronounced tendency to daydream seem to run the gamut of both realistic and bizarre fantasies. Apparently nothing human is alien to the imaginative realm of the accomplished daydreamer.

Men and women vary little in the frequency of their daydreams, but there is an understandable difference in the content of their fantasies. Women's daydreams clearly show their interest in fashions, while those of men display their enthusiasm for heroics and athletics. A recent independent study by Morton Wagman of the University of Illinois, using the same questionnaire, indicates that men report more explicitly sexual daydreams than women, while women have daydreams involving passivity, narcissism, affiliation (need for personal contact), and physical attractiveness.

Marriage precipitates no special pattern of daydreaming, but there are changes in the frequency of fantasy as people grow older. The peak of daydreaming seems to be in mid-adolescence, and then it falls off gradually, although fantasy persists well into old age. In later years daydreaming takes on a retrospective quality, for future possibilities are not only limited but rather frightening to the aged.

We compared the daydream responses of adults from several socio-cultural groups—people from Italian, Irish, Jewish, Negro, Anglo-Saxon, and German subcultures. All of them were well-educated, middle-class Americans born of at least the second generation, but with both parents from the same national-origin background.

The order of daydreaming frequency reported was, from high to low, Negro, Italian, Jewish, Irish, German and Anglo-Saxon. This order strikingly reflects the relative upward mobility, insecurity and even the pattern of immigration of the various groups to the United States. The latter three groups represent subcultures which have pretty well "made it," socially and economically, in America.

Interesting differences in the content of the fantasies also emerged. The Irish showed a tendency toward religious, extremely fantastic or heroic daydreams. The Negroes fantasized about sensual satisfactions, eating well, comfort, fine clothes and cars.

What other personality characteristics, we asked, might be associated with the tendency toward frequent daydreaming? Psychoanalytic theory suggested one hypothesis: that relative closeness to one's mother might lead to greater inhibition and fantasy.

In order to examine this theory and to evaluate relevant personality factors, we gave the subjects a series of additional tests. All subjects answered a questionnaire designed to explore their attitudes about self, mother, father and ideal self. They also filled out Cattell and Minnesota Multaphasic questionnaires which provided information on anxiety, repressive defenses and self-awareness. They kept logs of their night dreams for a month, a technique developed by Rosalea Schonbar of Columbia University. In addiiton they wrote Thematic Apperception Test stories or gave accounts of fantasies which were scored by judges for imaginativeness and creativity.

In general, findings with the questionnaire and with projective measures support psychoanalytic theory. Men and women who report closeness to or identification with their mothers, or a rejection of their fathers' values, tend to daydream more frequently. They also remember more of their night dreams. On the projective tests, such individuals rate as more creative storytellers, are generally more self-aware and anxiously sensitive, and are less inclined to employ defense mechanisms such as repression.

When we analyzed the results of some 40 personality tests taken by college freshmen and matched them with the subjects' daydreaming patterns, we discovered that there were seven categories of daydreaming.

General daydreaming reflected a predisposition to fantasy with great variety in content and often showed curiosity about other people rather than about the natural world.

Self-recriminating daydreaming was characterized by a high frequency of somewhat obsessional, verbally expressive but negatively-toned emotional reactions such as guilt and depression.

Objective, controlled, thoughtful daydream displayed a reflective, rather scientific and philosophically inclined content, and was associated with masculinity, emotional stability and curiosity about nature rather than about the human aspects of environment.

Poorly controlled, kaleidoscopic daydreaming reflected scattered thought and lack of systematic "story lines" in fantasy, as well as distractibility, boredom and self-abasement.

Autistic daydreaming represented the breakthrough into consciousness of material associated with nocturnal dreaming. It reflected the kind of dreamy, poorly controlled quality of inner experience often reported clinically by schizoid individuals.

Neurotic, self-conscious daydreaming revealed one of the clearest patterns—the one most closely associated with measures of neuroticism and emotional instability. It involved repetitive, egocentric and body-centered fantasies.

Enjoyment of daydreaming was characterized by a generally positive and healthy acceptance of daydreaming, an enjoyment of fantasy and the active use of it for both pleasure and problem solving.

People who scored high on introversion showed a strong inclination to respond to internally generated material. Their daydreams were either fantastic and fanciful or controlled, orderly and objective. This vividly calls to mind C.P. Snow's much discussed contrast of the literary-humanist scholar with the scientist-engineer. Both are given to inner activity, but they are very likely at opposite poles of the daydreaming dimension.

Daydreaming is not confined to adults; it also enters into the games of children. If we observe young children in a nursery or at a playground, those whose play is directly involved with physical reality can be separated from those who introduce make-believe characters, scenes or times into their play.

In one of our investigations, children between six and nine years of age were interviewed and observed in a series of situations. From their responses to questions about play habits, imaginary companions, and "pictures in your head," we classified them into high- and low-fantasy groups. We then told the children that we were looking for "astronauts of the future." We pointed out that astronauts have to sit quietly in a confined space for long periods of time and asked the children to remain seated in a simulated space capsule as long as possible.

The high-fantasy group were far better at sticking it out, presumably because they could create internal games to pass the time. These children also showed more creativity in storytelling and more achievement motivation. They were more likely to be firstborn or only children; they reported greater closeness to one parent, and they indicated that their parents played fantasy games with them and told them bedtime stories.

Clinically, the high-fantasy children were evaluated as more obsessional in character structure, with greater likelihood of Oedipal conflicts. The low-fantasy children more often were rated as hysterical personalities with pre-Oedipal conflicts—that is, problems with need satisfaction or aggression control, rather than problems relating specifically to parental figures.

Another study in this series, carried out by Bella Streiner and me, compared the dreams and fantasies of congenitally blind children with a matched group of sighted children. As could be anticipated, the variety and complexity of the dreams, daydreams and imaginative play of the blind children was greatly limited. Their dreams, cast of course in verbal and kinesthetic imagery, stayed close to their own immediate life stiuations. The sighted children were off on rocket ships of flying carpets, but for the blind children a trip to the supermarket became a source of adventure in fantasy.

The contrast emerged when two children, one blind and one sighted, imagined an airplane flight. The blind child spoke of the fact that the boy in his fantasy did not know what an airplane was but that he had a pleasant trip and enjoyed traveling with his mother. The sighted child told of the plane hitting an air-pocket, the pilot's unconsciousness, and the parents taking over controls of the ship.

Blind children, we discovered, were more likely to have imaginary companions, and to keep them to a later age than the sighted children. This is understandable when one remembers how dependent these children are on their parents or siblings for even simple maneuvers outside the home. Clearly, they develop make-believe companions, invariably sighted, as a comfort for the times when they are left alone.

Still another study, carried out under my direction by Sybil Gottlieb of the City University of New York, sought to determine whether children imitate adults in producing fantasy material. Several hundred children, who differed initially in fantasy predisposition, were divided into three groups. They were shown an experimental color movie involving a lot of activity by abstract figures. After they had seen the movie, an adult discussed the film with each group. One group was given a very *imaginative* interpretation of the film; the second group was provided with a *realistic* type of story, and the third was given merely a literal description of the "events" of the movie with a *neutral* content.

Then a second abstract film was shown and the children were instructed to write something about it. We were looking for answers to these questions: (1) In describing the second film, to what extent would the children imitate the adult interpretations of the first film? (2) What effect would their initial imaginative predisposition have on their response? and (3) Would the age level of the children make a significant difference?

Results were rather clearcut. The elementary-school-age children showed a strong imitative effect. Direct mimicry was rare, but the story content which emerged showed that the adults' versions of the first film had a decided impact on the way the children responded to the second. Their fantasy predisposition was less influential than the content of the adults' stories.

The older children were less influenced by the adult models. Rather, their imaginative predisposition was the deciding factor in how they described the second movie. Regardless of which adult version they had heard, those junior-high-school children who were rated high in fantasy showed far more imagination in their stories.

These and other experiments lead us to believe that fantasy play is indeed a kind of cognitive skill, a fundamental potentiality of all children. Normal development seems to require some aspects of imaginative play. The child combines novel associations with scraps of adult behavior and weaves them into his limited repertory of concepts. Fantasy play is one way in which a child carries out his explorations, not only through interaction with his environment but also through playful combinations and reexaminations of new ideas.

As a child develops a game such as "house" or "knights attacking a castle," he acquires mastery over the elements of the game and thinks of better ways to play it. Whether alone and talking to himself or with a companion, he gains verbal feedback from the game and he may develop a more differentiated vocabulary and a wider repertory of images.

As he grows older and the pressure increases for socializing his play, the child gradually "internalizes" his fantasy. When parents accept his imaginative play, or when the child is not shamed away from such activity, he may continue his fantasy play into late puberty, becoming quite skillful at this form of self-entertainment.

Predictably, children in the middle of large families are less inclined toward fantasy play. They are caught up in direct imitation of other children. It takes time and solitude to develop a rich imaginative life. Indeed, the indications that slum children show less complex fantasy play than other children may be attributed to the facts that their lives are spent in crowded conditions and that they lack consistent adult models for imaginative activity.

Freud theorized that fantasy processes grew out of early hallucinatory experiences of children during periods of drive arousal when gratification was delayed. The child gradually would experience the fantasy of gratification, partially reducing the drive and enabling him to "hold out" until sustenance arrived.

Seymour Feshback made some ingenious attempts to test Freud's theory that fantasy partially reduces an aroused aggressive drive. His subjects, having been angered by insults from the experimenters, showed less residual resentment after being given an opportunity to write aggressive Thematic Apperception Test stories or to view an aggressive prize-fight film.

Richard Rowe and I applied this approach specifically to daydreaming rather than to projective fantasy. In our study we aroused anxiety instead of aggression. Our subjects were students who had to take surprise midterm examinations. Immediately after their test papers were collected, some of the students were allowed to engage in daydreaming. Others were assigned a distracting task. Results suggested that daydreaming did not reduce anxiety. If anything, daydreaming increased anxiety because the subjects could not avoid thinking about the situation in fantasy form.

But in other situations, daydreaming can reduce anxiety. In another study, Rowe placed subjects in a medical laboratory, taped electrical wires to them, and told them they shortly would receive an electric shock. Those subjects who daydreamed to divert themselves showed a reduction of the aroused heart rate caused by the threat of shock. But subjects who had no chance to daydream continued to show an accelerated heart rate. The subjects who were strongly predisposed to daydreaming, as measured by the daydream questionnaire, showed significantly less arousal in response to the experimental situation than those with little inclination to fantasy.

An elaborate study by Ann Pytkowicz, Nathaniel Wagner and Irwin Sarason of the University of Washington used subjects rated high and low in daydreaming. They were subjected to insults, then given a chance to daydream or to tell Thematic Apperception Test stories. The experimenters found that both TAT fantasy and daydreaming worked equally well in reducing anger, but they worked best for those persons already inclined toward daydreaming. Contrary to a simple drive-reduction hypothesis, the investigators noted that the amount of aggression was not reduced. As the subjects engaged in fantasy activities, they shifted their aggression from the experimenter to themselves.

It may be that practiced daydreamers can engage in distracting imagery in the fantasy realm, or work out resolutions of their fear or anger. Thus, fantasy changes their mood, rather than reducing the amount of drive energy. Those not skilled in the use of fantasy, who are left to their own devices during a period of stress or while angered, actually may become more uncomfortable.

The issue of the functional role of daydreaming in relation to motivational or emotional processes is far from resolved. Moreover, the problem has broader implications, such as the effects of violence or sex in literature, art or movies. There is a general belief that sexual fantasy material is arousing and therefore ought to be limited to "mature audiences." But no restrictions are imposed on aggressive material presented to children. In effect, our folklore seems to argue that fantasy is drive-arousing in the sexual area, and drive-reducing in the area of aggression.

This latter notion has been seriously questioned by the work of several researchers. But it is still not known whether predispostion to fantasy might be a critical factor. Perhaps the daydreaming child is less likely to be aroused to direct action after witnessing violence in life or in a movie than the child who has little experience in fantasy play.

Another series of studies in this program dealt with daydreams in relation to information processing. Let us assume that daydreaming represents a special case of "noise" produced by the unceasing activities of our active brains. Ordinarily we are forced to ignore these "signals" in order to steer our way through our physical and social environments.

But when the flow of external information to be processed is markedly reduced, as when we prepare for sleep, there is a dramatic upsurge in awareness of one's interior monologues, self-generated imagery, or elaborate fantasy. Memories of the day's events flood into consciousness, touching off associations to earlier events or important unfinished business, leading to fantasies about what tomorrow will bring.

The results of a series of experiments, designed to examine fantasy processes, suggested distinct values in daydreaming and unearthed a wealth of materials about the process of fantasizing and free-association. In one experiment subjects seated in a small, dark, sensory-restriction chamber reported their thought content every 15 seconds. These signal detection and vigilance studies gave us a sample of thought that was independent of any stimulus and unrelated to any task. Reports were filled with fantasy like content, following the predictions of information theory. In another experiment, the electroencephalograph was used to record the eye-movement of subjects. Each person was left to think naturally, but whenever the polygraph showed periods of little or of considerable eye-movement, he was interrupted and asked to report his thought content. Tests were also made during periods of instructed fantasy, when the subject was asked to imagine that his deepest secret wish was coming true, and during conscious suppression, when he was asked to suppress his secret wish as if he wanted no one to read his mind. The Rapid-Eye-Movement studies made under the opposed conditions were compared. As a result of the study of these comparisons, we now can make a number of generalizations.

Daydreaming can keep us entertained or reasonably alert under dull, monotonous conditions, but at the cost of missing some of what is going on "outside." When extreme alertness is demanded in a complex environment, daydreaming is less useful and may even become dangerous. It is as if the individual makes rapid estimates of the degree to which he will have to pay attention to his environment, and than allows himself some appropriate margin of time or "channel space" to indulge in fantasies, interpretative glosses on the scenery or his situation, or some other form of self-stimulation.

The situation is analogous to that of a driver. On a road he knows well, with little traffic, he feels free to drift off into an extensive daydream. On an unfamiliar city street where external information is irregular and not readily anticipated, too much attention to his thought-stream could be fatal.

To engage in a daydream, a person must withdraw part of his attention from his environment. When he is awake and in a normal environment, he somehow must screen out the material surrounding him. Perhaps he does this by fixing his gaze steadily at a spot in front of him, so that the image fades. With less external material to process, he can deal more effectively with internal material. This may account for the blank stare which tells us that someone with whom we're conversing really isn't listening but is lost in thought.

One of the important conclusions drawn from our program of research is that the ephemeral fantasy need not be so elusive a phenomenon. The properties of man's inner experience can be systematically studied by formal methods as well as by clinical observation. While the scientist may never see the actual inner imagery any more than he can see an electron, it should be possible to employ certain physiological or reporting measures in a sufficiently systematic fashion to ensure that we are indeed zeroing in on private experience.

The early psychoanalytic view that daydreaming is compensatory, defensive or drive-reducing does not seem either general enough or precise enough to become the basis of a model. Today it seems more reasonable to regard daydreaming as a consequence of the on-going activity of the brain, and to apply models that relate to man's cognitive and affective environmental adaptation and his requirements for varied stimulation.

Very likely man's capacity to daydream is a fundamental characteristic of his constitution. Like other abilities—perceptual, motor or cognitive—it is there to be developed depending on circumstances.

The practiced daydreamer has learned the art of pacing so that he can shift rapidly between inner and other channels without bumping into too many obstacles. He has developed a resource that gives him some control over his future through elaborate planning, some ability to amuse himself during dull train-rides or routine work, and some sources of stimulation to change his mood through fanciful inner play.

This heightened self-awareness also may bring to consciousness many things that less internally sensitive persons can avoid: awareness of faults, failures or the omnipresent threat of global destruction. The daydreamer thus pays a price for his highly-developed inner capacity. But perhaps it is well worth it.

The Conditions of Creativity

Jerome Bruner

There is something antic about creating, although the enterprise be serious. And there is a matching antic spirit that goes with writing about it, for if ever there were a silent process it is the creative one. Antic and serious and silent. Yet there is good reason to inquire about creativity, a reason beyond practicality, for practicality is not a reason but a justification after the fact. The reason is the ancient search of the humanist for the excellence of man: the next creative act may bring man to a new dignity. . . .

The artist, the writer, and to a new degree the scientist . . . create or they seek to create, and this in itself endows the process with dignity. There is "creative" writing and "pure" science, each justifying the work of its producer in its own right. It is implied, I think, that the act of a man creating is the act of a whole man, that it is this rather than the product that makes it good and worthy. So whoever seeks to proclaim his wholeness turns to the new slogan. There is creative advertising, creative engineering, creative problem solving—all lively entries in the struggle for dignity in our time. We, as psychologists, are asked to explicate the process, to lay bare the essence of the creative. Make no mistake about it: it is not simply as technicians that we are being called, but as adjutants to the moralist. My antic sense rises in self-defense. My advice, in the midst of the seriousness, is to keep an eye out for the tinker shuffle, the flying of kites, and kindred sources of surprised amusement.

We had best begin with some minimum working definition that will permit us at least to look at the same set of things. An act that produces *effective surprise*—this I shall take as the hallmark of a creative enterprise. The content of the surprise can be as various as the enterprises in which men are engaged. It may express itself in one's dealing with children, in making love, in carrying on a business, in formulating physical theory, in painting a picture. I could not care less about the person's intention, whether or not he intended to create. The road to banality is paved with creative intentions. Surprise is not easily defined. It is the unexpected that strikes one with wonder or astonishment. What is curious about effective surprise is that it need not be rare or infrequent or bizarre and is often none of these things. Effective surprises, and we shall spell the matter out in a moment, seem rather to have the quality of obviousness about them when they occur,

producing a shock of recognition following which there is no longer astonishment. It is like this with great formulae, as in that for the conservation of energy or for the brilliant insight that makes chemistry possible, the conservation of mass. Weber's stunning insight into the nature of a just noticeable sensory difference is of this order, that before a difference will be noticed it must be a constant fraction of the sensory intensity presently being experienced: $\Delta I/I=K$.

I think it is possible to specify three kinds of effectiveness, three forms of self-evidence implicit in surprise of the kind we have been considering. The first is predictive effectiveness. It is the kind of surprise that yields high predictive value in its wake—as in the instance of the formula for falling bodies or in any good theoretical reformulation in science. You may well argue that predictive effectiveness does not always come through surprise, but through the slow accretion of knowledge and urge—like Newton with his *hypothesis non fingo*. I will reply by agreeing with you and specifying simply that whether it is the result of intuitive insight or of slow accretion, I will accept it within my definition. The surprise may only come when we look back and see whence we have come.

A second form of effectiveness is best called formal, and its most usual place is in mathematics and logic—possibly in music. One of the most beautiful descriptions of the phenomenon is to be found in G. H. Hardy's engaging *A Mathematician's Apology*. It consists of an ordering of elements in such a way that one sees relationships that were not evident before, groupings that were before not present, ways of putting things together not before within reach. Consistency or harmony or depth of relationship is the result. One of the most penetrating essays that has ever been written on the subject is, of course, Henri Poincare's in his *Science and Method*. He speaks of making combinations that "reveal to us unsuspected kinship between . . . facts, long known, but wrongly believed to be strangers to one another."

Of the final form of effectiveness in surprise it is more difficult to write. I shall call it metaphoric effectiveness. It, too, is effective by connecting domains of experience that were before apart, but with the form of connectedness that has the discipline of art.

It is effective surprise that produces what Melville celebrated as the shock of recognition. Jung speaks of art that can produce such metaphoric connectedness as "visionary" in contrast to the merely psychological. It is, for example, Thomas Mann's achievement in bringing into a single compass the experiences of sickness and beauty, sexuality and restraint in his *Death in Venice*. Or it is the achievement of the French playwright Jean Anouilh who in *Antigone* makes Creon not only a tyrant but a reasonable man. What we are observing is the connecting of diverse experiences by the mediation of symbol and metaphor and image. Experience in literal terms is a categorizing, a placing in a syntax of concepts. Metaphoric combination leaps beyond systematic placement, explores connections that before were unsuspected.

I would propose that all of the forms of effective surprise grow out of combinatorial activity—a placing of things in new perspectives. But it is somehow not simply a taking of known elements and running them together by algorithm into a welter of permutations. One could design a computer to do that, but it would be with some embarrassment, for this is stupid even for a computer, and an ingenious computer programmer can show us much more interesting computer models than that. "To create consists precisely in not making useless combinations and in making those which are useful and which are only a small minority. Invention is discernment, choice." If not a brute algorithm, then it must be a heuristic that guides one to fruitful combinations. What is the heuristic? Poincare goes on to urge that it is an emotional sensibility: "the feeling of mathematical beauty, of the harmony of numbers and forms, of geometric elegance." It is this that guides one in making combinations in mathematics. But it is surely not enough. One hears physicists speak of "physical intuition" as distinguishing the good theorist from the mere formalist, the mathematician. I suspect that in each empirical field there is developed in the creating scientist a kind of "intuitive familiarity," to use a term that L. J. Henderson was fond of, that gives him a sense of what combinations are likely to have predictive effectiveness and which are absurd. What precisely this kind of heuristic consists of is probably difficult to specify without reference to the nature of the field in question, which is not to say that the working models are utterly different in different areas of empirical endeavor, for there is obviously some generality, too.

It seems unlikely that the heuristic either of formal beauty or of intuitive familiarity could serve for the artist, the poet, and the playwright. What genius leads Faulkner to created and combine a Temple Drake and a Popeye in *Sanctuary?* How does Dostoevsky hit upon the particular combination of the Grand Inquisitor and the Christ figure in *The Brothers Karamazov?* What leads Picasso to include particular objects in a painting? Picasso says to Christian Zervos: "What a sad thing for a painter who loves blondes but denies himself the pleasure of putting them in his picture because they don't go well with the basket of fruit! What misery for a painter who detests apples to have to use

them all the time because the harmonize with the table-cloth! I put in my pictures everything I like. So much the worse for the things—they have to get along with one another."[1] However maddening such a remark may be coming from a painter, it does point up the essentially emotive nature of the painter's work and his criteria for judging the fitness of combination. So Yeats may write:

> God guard me from those thoughts men think
> In the mind alone;
> He that sings a lasting song
> Thinks in a marrow-bone.

But marrow-bones are not really enough for lasting songs. For if it is true, as Picasso and many before have said, that "a picture lives only through him who looks at it," then the artist must speak to the human condition of the beholder if there is to be effective surprise. I, for one, find myself compelled to believe that there are certain deep sharings of plight among human beings that make possible the communication of the artist to the beholder, and, while I object to the paraphernalia that Jung proposes when he speaks of the collective unconscious, I understand why he feels impelled to proffer the idea. The artist—whatever his medium—must be close enough to these conditions in himself so that they may guide his choice among combinations, provide him with the genuine and protect him from the paste.

The triumph of effective surprise is that it takes one beyond common ways of experiencing the world. Or perhaps this is simply a restatement of what we have been meaning by effective surprise. If it is merely that, let me add only that it is in this sense that life most deeply imitates art or that nature imitates science. Creative products have this power of reordering experience and thought in their images. In science, the reordering is much the same from one beholder of a formula to another. In art, the imitation is in part self-imitation. It is the case too that the effective surprise of the creative man provides a new instrument for manipulating the world—physically as with the creation of the wheel or symbolically as with the creatio of $e=mc^2$.

One final point about the combinatorial acts that produce effective surprise: they almost always succeed through the exercise of technique. Henry Moore, who is unusually articulate both as craftsman and artist, tells us that he was driven to the use of holes in his sculpture by the technical problem of giving a sense of three-dimensionality to solid forms—"the hole connects one side to the other, making it immediately more three-dimensional," a discovery made while fretting over the puzzle of how to avoid relief carving on brittle material like stone. Joseph Conrad and Ford Madox Ford sat before a scene trying to describe it to each other in the most economical terms

[1] "Conversation with Picasso," *Cahiers d'Art* (Paris), 1935. Translated by Brewster Ghiselin in *The Creative Process* (New York: Mentor Books, 1952), p. 56.

possible. Katherine Anne Porter sat on a camp stool before a landscape trying to jot down everything before her—and finally decided that she could not train her memory that way. Technique, then, and how shall we combine it eventually with the doctrine of inspiration?

As soon as one turns to a consideration of the conditions of creativity, one is immediately met by paradox and antimony. A "determinant" suggests itself, and in the next pulse its opposite is suggested. I shall honor these antinomies and what I have to say will, as a result, seem at times paradoxical.

Detachment and commitment.   A willingness to divorce one-self from the obvious is surely a prerequisite for the fresh combinatorial act that produces effective surprise. There must be as a necessary, if not a sufficient, condition a detachment from the forms as they exist. There are so many ways in which this expresses itself in creative activity that one can scarcely enumerate them. Wallace Stevens, among many, has written of the alienation of the poet from society and reality, and the spirit of this alienation is caught in his searching poem, "Notes Towards a Supreme Fiction." It is in part a condition for exploring one's own individu-ality, in part a means of examining the possibilities of human connection. The University as an institution, pro-tected within its walls, should and sometimes does provide a basis for detachment insofar as it recognizes the inviolate privacy of those who inhabit it. The preoccupation of the scholar, gating out all but what seems relevant to his theme—this too is a vehicle of detachment. The creative writer who takes his journey without maps or his voyage into the interior, whether in the subjective Africas of Graham Greene or Joseph Conrad or in the interior jungles of Henry James or Marcel Proust—again it is detachment.

But it is a detachment of commitment. For there is about it a caring, a deep need to understand something, to master a technique, to rerender a meaning. So while the poet, the mathematician, the scientist must each achieve detachment, they do it in the interest of commitment. And at one stroke they, the creative ones, are disengaged from that which exists conventionally and are engaged deeply in what they construct to replace it.

Passion and decorum.   By *passion* I understand a willingness and ability to let one's impulses express themselves in one's life through one's work. I use it in the sense, "he has a passion for painting," or "she has a passion for cooking." I do not wish to raise or explore the Bohemian dilemma—whether the condition for passion in work is its expression in other forms of life. I happen to believe that Freud's fixed quantity of libido (express it here and it must be withdrawn from there) is a kind of first-order nonsense. Passion, like discriminating taste, grows on its use. You more likely act yourself into feeling than feel yourself into action. In any case, it is true of the creative man that he is not indifferent

to what he does, that he is moved to it. For the artist, if not for the scientist, there is a tapping of sources of imagery and symbolism that would otherwise not be available—as expressed in the beautiful refrain line of Rimbaud's *Les Illuminations:* "J'ai seul la clef de cette parade sauvage." As for the scientist and the scholar, it is perhaps the eighteenth-century French philosopher, Helvetius, who, in his *Treatise on Man,* has put it best: "A man without *passions* is incapable of that degree of attention to which a superior judgment is annexed: a superiority that is perhaps less the effect of an extraordinary effort than an habitual attention."

But again a paradox: it is not all urgent vitality. There is a decorum in creative activity: a love of form, an etiquette toward the object of our efforts, a respect for materials. Rimbaud's wild beasts in the end are caged. For all that *Lord Jim* is a turbulent book, with the full range of human impulse, its raw power is contained by the decorum of the dispassionate gentlemanly narrator, Marlow. Herakles of the myth was not a hiary ape expressing his mastery indiscriminately: his shrewd trickery is the decorum. The wild flood of ideas that mathematicians like Hardy have described: eventually they are expressed in the courtesy of equations.

So both are necessary and there must surely be a subtle matter of timing involved—when the impulse, when the taming.

Freedom to be dominated by the object.   You begin to write a poem. Before long it, the poem, begins to develop metrical, stanzaic, symbolical requirements. You, as the writer of the poem, are serving it—it seems. Or you may be pursuing the task of building a formal model to represent the known properties of single nerve fibers and their synapses: soon the model takes over. Or we say of an experiment in midstream that *it* needs another control group really to clinch the effect. It is at this point that we get our creative second wind, at the point when the object takes over. I have asked about a dozen of my most creative and productive friends whether they knew what I meant as far as their own work was concerned. All of them replied with one or another form of sheepishness, most of them commenting that one usually did not talk about this kind of personal thing. "This is when you know you're in and—good or bad—the thing will compel you to finish it. In a long piece of work it can come and go several times." The one psychologist among my informants was reminded of the so-called Zeigarnik completion tendency, suggesting that when the watershed was reached the task then had a structure that began to require completeness.

There is something odd about the phenomenon. We externalize an object, a product of our thoughts, treat it as "out there." Freud remarked, commenting on projection, that human beings seem better able to deal with stimuli from the outside than from within. So it is with the externalizing of a creative work, permitting it to develop its own being, its own autonomy coming to serve *it*. It is as if *it* were easier to cope with there, as if this arrangement permitted the emergence of more unconscious impulse, more material not readily accessible.

There is still another possibility. Observing children in the process of learning mathematics, I have been struck repeatedly by the economical significance of a good mode of representing things to oneself. In group theory, for example, it is extraordinarily difficult to determine whether a set of transformations constitutes a closed group so that any combination of them can be expressed by a single one. The crutch provided by a matrix that gets all the combinations out of the head on to paper or the blackboard makes it possible to look at the group structure as a whole, to go beyond it to the task of seeing whether it has interesting properties and familiar isomorphs. Good representation, then, is a release from intellectual bondage.

I have used the expression "freedom to be dominated" by the object being created. It is a strange choice of words, and I should like to explain it. To be dominated by an object of one's own creation—perhaps its extreme is Pygmalion dominated by Galatea—is to be free of the defenses that keep us hidden from ourselves.

As the object takes over and demands to be completed "in its own terms," there is a new opportunity to express a style and an individuality. Likely as not, it is so partly because we are rid of the internal juggling of possibilities, because we have represented them "out there" where we can look at them, consider them. As one friend, a novelist and critic, put it, "If it doesn't take over and you are foolish enough to go on, what you end up with is contrived and alien."

Deferral and immediacy.   There is an immediacy to creating anything, a sense of direction, an objective, a general idea, a feeling. Yet the immediacy is anything but a quick orgasm of completion. Completion is deferred. Let me quote at some length from the conversation of Christian Zervos with Picasso:

With me a picture is a sum of destructions. I make a picture, and proceed to destroy it. But in the end nothing is lost; the red I have removed from one part shows up in another.

It would be very interesting to record photographically, not the stages of a painting, but its metamorphoses.[2] One would see perhaps by what course a mind finds its way towards the crystallization of its dream. But what is really very curious is to see that the picture does not change basically, that the initial vision remains almost intact in spite of appearance. I see often a light and a dark, when I have put them in my picture, I do everything I can to "break them up," in adding a color that creates a counter effect. I perceive, when this work is photographed, that what I have introduced to correct my first vision has disappeared, and that after all the photographic image corresponds to my first vision, before the occurrence of the transformations brought about by my will.[3]

This is not to say that there is not the occasional good luck, the piece that comes off lickety-split and finished, the theory hit upon at first fire. If ever Georges Simenon is acclaimed a great writer—and that he is more than simply competent is plain—then we will say he brings it off in a gush, in a quantum of pure energy and with such intensity, Carvel Collins tells us, that he has developed the custom of getting clearance from his doctor before he flings himself into a new novel.

Having read a good many journals and diaries by writers, I have come to the tentative conclusion that the principal guard against precocious completion, in writing at least, is boredom. I have little doubt that the same protection avails the scientist. It is the boredom of conflict, knowing deep down what one wishes to say and knowing that one has not said it. One acts on the impulse of boredom, to defer. Thus Virginia Woolf, trying to finish *Orlando* in February 1928: "Always, always, the last chapter slips out of my hands. One gets bored. One whips oneself up. I still hope for a fresh wind and don't very much bother, except that I miss the fun that was so tremendously lively all October, November, and December."[4]

The internal drama.   There is within each person his own cast of characters—an ascetic, and perhaps a glutton, a prig, a frightened child, a little man, even an onlooker, sometimes a Renaissance man. The great works of the theater are decompositions of such a cast, the rendering into external drama of the internal one, the conversion of the internal cast into dramatis personae. Freud, in his searching essay on "The Poet and the Daydream," is most discerning about this device of the playwright.[5] There have been times when writers have come too close to their own personal cast in constructing a play, and even so able a craftsman of the theater as Goethe stumbled in his *Torquato Tasso,* an embarrassingly transparent autobiographical piece about the conflict between Tasso the poet and Antonio the politician. It is, perhaps, Pirandello among modern playwrights who has most convincingly mastered the technique, although a younger Italian dramatist, Ugo Betti, showed promise of carrying it further before his premature death a few years ago. In his brilliant *The Queen and the Rebels,* Betti includes an unforgettable scene at the political frontier of a mythical fascist state, the frontier guards searching a bus party for the fleeing queen. As the scene progresses, it becomes patent that the queen is a spineless nonentity; it is the prostitute in the party who emerges as the queen.

As in the drama, so too a life can be described as a script, constantly rewritten, guiding the unfolding internal

---

[2]My colleague Professor George Miller is now engaged in doing just this.—J. S. B.

[3]*The Creative Process,* pp. 56-57.

[4]*A Writer's Diary* (New York: Harcourt, Brace, 1953), p. 121.

[5]For a discussion of Freud's use of the same device in the development of psychoanalysis, see the chapter on "Freud and the Image of Man."

drama. It surely does not do to limit the drama to the stiff characters of the Freudian morality play—the undaunted ego, the brutish id, the censorious and punitive superego. Is the internal cast a reflection of the identifications to which we have been committed? I do not think it is as simple as that. It is a way of grouping our internal demands and there are idealized models over and beyond those with whom we have special identification—figures in myth, in life, in the comics, in history, creations of fantasy.

There are some scripts that are more interesting than others. In some, there is a pre-empting protagonist in the center to the stage, constantly proclaiming, save for those moments when there are screamed intrusions from offstage, at which point the declaimer apologized by pointing out that the voices are not really in the play. In others there is a richness, an inevitability of relationship, a gripping and constant exchange—or perhaps one should call it "in-change." These are dramatic personalities, producers of surprise.

I would like to suggest that it is in the working out of conflict and coalition within the set of identities that compose the person that one finds the source of many of the richest and most surprising combinations. It is not merely the artist and the writer, but the inventor too who is the beneficiary.

The dilemma of abilities.   We have now looked at some of the paradoxical conditions that one might assume would affect the production of effective surprises—creativity. Nothing has been said about ability, or abilities. What shall we say of energy, of combinatorial zest, of intelligence, of alertness, of perseverance? I shall say nothing about them. They are obviously important but, from a deeper point of view, they are also trivial. For at any level of energy or intelligence there can be more or less of creating in our sense. Stupid people create for each other as well as benefiting from what comes from afar. So too do slothful and torpid people. I have been speaking of creativity, not of genius.

The chapter in Henry Adams' *Education,* "The Dynamo and the Virgin," is urbane, but beneath the urbanity there is a deep perplexity about what moves men, what moves history, what makes art. Adams spent the summer and fall of 1900 haunting the Great Exposition in Paris, particularly the hall of dynamos, until the dynamos "became a symbol of infinity . . . a moral force, much as the early Christians felt the Cross." During the same summer he made excursions to Notre Dame of Amiens and to Chartres, and it was then that he came to realize that the Virgin as symbol was also a source of energy: "All the steam in the world could not, like the Virgin, build Chartres." I end with the same perplexity in attempting to find some way of thinking reasonably about the creative process. At the outset I proposed that we define the creative act as effective surprise—the production of novelty. It is reasonable to suppose that we will someday devise a proper scientific theory capable of understanding and predicting such acts. Perhaps we will understand the energies that produce the creative act much as we have come to understand how the dynamo produces its energy. It may be, however, that there is another mode of approach to knowing how the process generates itself, and this will be the way in which we understand how symbols and ideas like the Virgin capture men's thoughts. Often it is the poet who grasps these matters most firmly and communicates them most concisely. Perhaps it is our conceit that there is only one way of understanding a phenomenon. I have argued that just as there is predictive effectiveness, so is there metaphoric effectiveness. For the while, at least, we can do worse than to live with a metaphoric understanding of creativity.

The Flow Experience

Mihaly Csikszentmihalyi

There is a common experiential state which is present in various forms of play, and also under certain conditions in other activities which are not normally thought of as play. For lack of a better term, I will refer to this experience as "flow." Flow denotes the wholistic sensation present when we act with total involvement. It is the kind of feeling after which one nostalgically says: "That was fun," or "That was enjoyable." It is the state in which action follows upon action according to an internal logic which seems to need no conscious intervention on our part. We experience it as a unified flowing from one moment to the next, in which we feel in control of our actions, and in which there is little distinction between self and environment: between stimulus and response; or between past, present, and future.

The most typical kind of flow experience is play, and games are the most common forms of play activity. Excellent descriptions of what we here call flow have been given by Murphy (1972) in his book on golf, Herrigel (1953) in regards to Zen archery, Abrahams (1960) on chess, and Unsworth (1969) on rock climbing.

But play is not synonymous with flow. Experiential states undistinguishable from those we have called "flow" and that are reported in play are also reported in a great variety of other contexts. What Maslow (1962, 1965, 1971) has called "peak experiences," and de Charms (1968) has called the "origin" state, share many distinctive features with the process of flow.

The working out of creative ideas also involves analogous experiences. In fact, almost any description of the creative experience (e.g., Dillon, 1972; Getzels & Csikszentmihalyi, 1974; Ghiselin, 1952; Montmasson, 1939) gives experiential accounts which are in important respects analogous with those obtained from people at play.

It is quite obvious that certain states of rapture which are usually labelled "religious" share the characteristics of flow with play and creativity. These include almost any account of collective ritual (e.g., Deren, 1953; Turner, 1969; Worsley, 1968); of the practice of Zen, Yoga, and other form of meditation (e.g., Eliade, 1969; Herrigel, 1953; Narango & Ornstein, 1971); or of practically any other form of religious experience (e.g., Laski, 1962; Moltman, 1972; Rahner, 1967).

While flow is often experienced in play, in creativity, or in religious ecstasy, it is not always present in these activities, nor is it limited to them. In fact, part of the problem with this phenomenon is that previously what here is called flow has been identified with the behavioral pattern within which it has been experienced. Thus flow has been described as play, as creativity, as religious ecstasy, etc., and its explanation has been sought in these activities which define different behavioral patterns. It is my task to analyze out the experience of flow as a conceptually *independent process* which might or might not underlie these activities.

ELEMENTS OF THE FLOW EXPERIENCE

Merging Action and Awareness

Perhaps the clearest sign of flow is the experience of merging action and awareness. A person in flow does not operate with a dualistic perspective: he is very aware of his actions, but not of the awareness itself. A tennis player pays undivided attention to the ball and the opponent, a chess master focuses on the strategy of the game, most states of religious ecstasy are reached by following complex ritual steps, yet for flow to be maintained, one cannot reflect on the act of awareness itself. The moment awareness is split so as to perceive the activity from "outside," the flow is interrupted.

Therefore, flow is difficult to maintain for any length of time without at least momentary interruptions. Typically, a person can maintain a merged awareness with his or her actions for only short periods interspersed with interludes (from the Latin *inter ludes,* "between plays") in which the flow is broken by the actor's adoption of an outside perspective.

These interruptions occur when questions flash through the actor's mind such as "am I doing well?" or "what am I doing here?" or "should I be doing this?" When one is in a flow episode these questions simply do not come to mind.

Steiner (1972) gives an excellent account of how it feels to get out of the state of flow in chess, and then back into it again:

The bright arcs of relation that weld the pieces into a phalanx, that make one's defense a poison-tipped porcupine shiver into vague filaments. The chords dissolve. The pawn in one's sweating hand withers to mere wood or plastic. A tunnel of inanity yawns, boring and bottomless. As from another world comes the appalling suggestion . . . that this is, after all, "only a game." If one entertains that annihilating proposition even for an instant, one is done for. (It seemed to flash across Boris Spassky's drawn features for a fraction of a second before the sixty-ninth move of the thirteenth game.) Normally, the opponent makes his move and in that murderous moment addiction comes again. New lines of force light up in the clearing haze, the hunched intellect straightens up and takes in the sweep of the board, cacophony subsides, and the instruments mesh into unison [p. 94].

For action to merge with awareness to such an extent, the activity must be feasible. Flow seems to occur only when persons face tasks that are within their ability to perform. This is why one experiences flow most often in activities which have clearly established rules for action, such as rituals, games, or participatory art forms like the dance.

Here are a few quotes from our interviews with people engaged in flow-producing activities. Their words illustrate more clearly what the merging of action and awareness means in different cases. An outstanding chess-player:

The game is a struggle, and the concentration is like breathing—you never think of it. The roof could fall in and if it missed you, you would be unaware of it.

A basketball player from a state champion high-school team:

The only thing that really goes through my mind is winning the game . . . I really don't have to think, though. When I am playing it just comes to me. It's a good feeling. Everything is working out—working smooth.

And one of his team-mates:

When I get hot in a game . . . Like I said, you don't think about it at all. If you step back and think about why you are so hot all of a sudden you get creamed.

Centering of attention

The merging of action and awareness is made possible by a centering of attention on a limited stimulus field. To insure that people will concentrate on their actions, potentially intruding stimuli must be kept out of attention. Some writers have called this process a "narrowing of consciousness," a "giving up the past and the future (Maslow, 1971, pp. 63-65)." One respondent, a university science professor who climbs rocks, phrased it as follows:

When I start on a climb, it is as if my memory input has been cut off. All I can remember is the last thirty seconds, and all I can think ahead is the next five minutes.

The same experience is reported by dancers:

I get a feeling that I don't get anywhere else . . . I have more confidence in myself than at any other time. Maybe an effort to forget my problems. Dance is like therapy. If I am troubled about something I leave it out the door as I go in (the dance studio).

And by composers—in this case a woman composer of modern music:

I am really quite oblivious to my surroundings after I really get going. I think that the phone could ring, and the doorbell could ring, or the house burn down, or something like that . . . when I start working I really do shut out the world. Once I stop I can let it back in again.

In games, the rules define what the relevant stimuli are, and exclude everything else as irrelevant. But rules alone are not always enough to get a person involved with the game. Hence the structure of games provides motivational elements which will draw the player into play. Perhaps the simplest of these inducements is competition. The addition of a competitive element to a game usually insures the undivided attention of a player who would not be motivated otherwise. When being "beaten" is one of the possible outcomes of an activity, the actor is pressured to attend to it more closely. Another alternative is to add the possibility of material gains. It is usually easier to sustain flow in simple games, such as poker, when gambling is added to the rules. But the payoff is rarely the goal of a gambler. As Dostoevski (1961) clearly observed about his own compulsion, "The main thing is the play itself, I swear that greed for money has nothing to do with it, although heaven knows I am sorely in need of money." Finally there are play activities which rely on physical danger to produce centering of attention, and hence flow. Such is rock climbing, where one is forced to ignore all distracting stimuli by the knowledge that survival is dependent on complete concentration.

The addition of spurious motivational elements to a flow activity (competition, gain, danger), make it also more vulnerable to intrusions from "outside reality." Playing for money may increase concentration on the game, but paradoxically one can also be more easily distracted from play by the fear of losing. A Samurai swordsman concerned about winning will be beaten by his opponent who is not thus distracted. Ideally, flow is the result of pure involvement, without any consideration about results. In practice, however, most people need some inducement to participate in flow activities, at least at the beginning, before they learn to be sensitive to intrinsic rewards.

Loss of Ego

Most writers who have described experiences similar to what here is called "flow," mention an element variously described as "loss of ego," "self-forgetfulness," "loss of self-consciousness," and even "transcendence of individuality" and "fusion with the world" (Maslow, 1971, p. 65-70).

When an activity involves the person completely with its demands for action, "self-ish" considerations become irrelevant. The concept of self (Mead, 1934) or ego (Freud, 1927) has traditionally been that of an intrapsychic mechanism which mediates between the needs of the organism, and the social demands placed upon it.

A primary function of the self is to integrate one person's actions with that of others, and hence it is a prerequisite for social life (Berger & Luckmann, 1967). Activities which allow flow to occur (i.e., games, rituals, art, etc.), however, usually do not require any negotiation. Since they are based on freely accepted rules, the player does not need to use a self to get along in the activity. As long as all the participants follow the same rules, there is no need to negotiate roles. The participants need no self to bargain with about what should or should not be done. As long as the rules are respected, a flow situation is a social system with no deviance. This is possible only in activites in which reality is simplified to the point that is understandable, definable, and manageable. Such is typically the case in religious ritual, artistic performances, and in games.

Self-forgetfulness does *not* mean, however, that in flow a person loses touch with his or her own physical reality. In some flow activities, perhaps in most, one becomes more intensely aware of internal processes. This obviously occurs in yoga and many religious rituals. Climbers report a great increase of kinesthetic sensations, a sudden awareness of ordinarily unconscious muscular movements. Chess players are very aware of the working of their own minds during games. What is usually lost in flow is not the awareness of one's body or of one's functions, but only the *self-construct,* the intermediary which one learns to interpose between stimulus and response.

The same experience is reported by people involved in creative activities. An outstanding composer has this to say about how he feels when he is writing music:

You yourself are in an ecstatic state to such a point that you feel as though you almost don't exist. I've experienced this time and time again. My hand seems devoid of myself, and I have nothing to do with what is happening. I just sit there watching it in a state of awe and wonderment. And it just flows out by itself.

Or in chess:

Time passes a hundred times faster. In this sense, it resembles the dream state. A whole story can unfold in seconds, it seems. Your body is nonexistent—but actually your heart pumps like mad to supply the brain . . . .

Control of Action and Environment

A person in flow is in control of his actions and of the environment. While involved in the activity, this feeling of control is modified by the "ego-less" state of the actor. Rather than an active awareness of mastery, it is more a condition of not being worried by the possibility of lack of control. But later, in thinking back on the experience, a person will usually feel that for the duration of the flow episode his skills were adequate to meeting environmental demands, and this reflection might become an important component of a positive self-concept.

A dancer expresses well this paradoxical feeling of being in control and being merged with the environment at the same time:

If I have enough space, I am in control. I feel I can radiate an energy into the atmosphere. It's not always necessary that another human being be there to catch that energy. I can dance for walls, I can dance for floors . . . I don't know if its usually a control of the atmosphere. I become one with the atmosphere.

In nonflow states, such a feeling of control is difficult to sustain for any length of time. There are too many imponderables. Personal relationships, career obstacles, health problems—not to mention death and taxes—are always to a certain extent beyond control.

Even where the sense of control comes from defeating another person, the player often sees it as a victory over his or her own limitations, rather than over the opponent. A basketball player:

I feel in control. Sure I've practiced and have a good feeling for the shots I can make . . . I don't feel in control of the other player—even if he's bad and I know where to beat him. It's me and not him that I'm working on.

Flow experiences occur in activities where one can cope, at least theoretically, with all the demands for action. In a chess game, for instance, everything is potentially controllable. A player need never fear that the opponent's move will produce any threats except those allowed by the rules.

The feeling of control and the resulting absence of worry are present even in flow situations where "objectively" the dangers to the actor seem very real. The famous British rock climber, Chris Bonington, describes the experience very well:

At the start of any big climb I feel afraid, dread the discomfort and danger I shall have to undergo. It's like standing on the edge of a cold swimming-pool trying to nerve yourself to take the plunge; yet once in, it's not nearly as bad as you have feared; *in fact it's enjoyable . . . . Once I start climbing, all my misgivings are forgotten.* The very harshness of the surrounding, the treacherous layer of verglas covering every hold, even the high-pitched whine of falling stones, all help build up tension and excitement that are ingredients of mountaineering [Unsworth, 1969; italics added].

Although the dangers in rock climbing and similar activities are real, they are finite and hence predictable and manageable; a person can work up to mastering them. Practically every climber says that driving a car is more dangerous than the incredible acrobatic feats on the rock; and in a sense it may be true, since in driving, the elements outside one's control are more numerous and dangerous than in climbing. In any case, a sense of control is definitely one of the most important components of the flow experience, whether an "objective" assessment justifies such feeling or not.

Demands for Action and Clear Feedback

Another quality of the experience is that it usually contains coherent, noncontradictory demands for action, and provides clear unambiguous feedback to a person's actions. These components of flow, like the preceeding ones, are made possible by limiting awareness to a restricted field of possibilities. In the artificially reduced reality of a flow episode it is clear what is "good" and what is "bad." Goals and means are logically ordered. A person is not expected to do incompatible things, as in real life. He or she knows what the results of various possible actions will be.

But in flow, one does not stop to evaluate the feedback—action and reaction have become so well practiced as to be automatic. The person is too concerned with the experience to reflect on it. Here is the clear account of a basketball player:

I play my best games almost by accident. I go out and play on the court and I can tell if I'm shooting o.k. or if I'm not—so I know if I'm playing good or like shit—but if I'm having a super game I can't tell until after the game . . . guys make fun of me because I can lose track of the score and I'll ask Russell what the score is and he'll tell me and sometimes it breaks people up—they think "That kid must be real dumb."

In other words, the flow experience differs from awareness in everyday reality because it contains ordered rules which make action and the evaluation of action automatic and hence unproblematic. When contradictory actions are made possible (as for instance when cheating is introduced into a game), the self reappears again to negotiate between the conflicting definitions of what needs to be done, and the flow is interrupted.

Autotelic Nature of Flow

A final characteristic of the flow experience is its "autotelic" nature. In other words, it appears to need no goals or rewards external to itself. Practically every writer who has dealt with play has remarked on the autotelic nature of this activity (e.g., Callois, 1958; Huizinga, 1950; Piaget, 1951, 1965). In The *Gita*, Lord Krishna instructs Arjuna to live his whole life according to this principle: "Let the motive be in the deed, and not in the event. Be not one whose motive for action is the hope of reward [2.47]."

A young poet who is also a seasoned climber, describes the autotelic experience in words that would be difficult to improve on:

The mystique of rock climbing is climbing; you get to the top of the rock glad it's over but really wish it would go forever. The justification of climbing is climbing like the justification of poetry is writing; you don't conquer anything except things in yourself . . . the act of writing justifies poetry. Climbing is the same; recognizing that you are a flow. The purpose of the flow is to keep on flowing, not looking for a peak or utopia but staying in the flow. It is not a moving up but a continuous flowing; you move up only to keep the flow going. There is no possible reason for climbing except the climbing itself; is is a self-communication.

The various elements of the flow experience are inextricably linked together and dependent on each other. By limiting the stimulus field, a flow activity allows people to concentrate their actions and ignore distractions. As a result, they feel in potential control of the environment. Because the flow activity has clear and noncontradictory rules, people performing it can temporarily forget their identity and its problems. The result of all these conditions is that one finds the process intrinsically rewarding.

REFERENCES

ABRAHAMS, G. *The chess mind.* London: Penguin, 1960.

ATTNEAVE, R. *Applications of information theory to psychology.* New York: Henry Hold, 1959.

BEACH, F. A. Current concepts of play in animals. *American Naturalist,* 1945, **79,**523-541.

BEKOFF, M. The development of social interaction, play, and metacommunication in mammals: An ethological perspective. *Quarterly Review of Biology,* 1972, **47** (4), 412-434.

BERGER, P., & LUCKMANN, T. *The social construction of reality,* Garden City, New York: Doubleday, 1967.

BERLYNE, D.E. *Conflict, arousal and curiosity.* New York: McGraw-Hill, 1960.

BERLYNE, D. E. Curiosity and exploration. *Science.* 1966, **153,** 25-33.

BHAGAVAD GITA, Juan Mascaro (Trans.), Harmondsworth: Penguin, 1962.

BROWN, N. O. *Life against death.* Middleton, Conn.: Wesleyan University Press, 1959.

CALLOIS, R. *Les jeaux et les hommes.* Paris: Gallimard, 1958.

CSIKSZENTMIHALYI, M., & BENNETT, S. H. An exploratory model of play. *American Anthropologist,* 1971, 73 (1), 45-58.

DE CHARMS, R. *Personal causation.* New York: Academic Press, 1968.

DEREN, M. *Divine horseman.* London: Thames and Hudson, 1953.

DILLON, J. T. *Approaches to the study of problem-finding behavior.* Unpublished manuscript, The University of Chicago, 1972.

DOSTOEVSKI, F. M. *Letters.* New York: Horizon, 1961.

EIBI-EIBESFELDT, I. *Ethology: The biology of behavior.* New York: Holt, Rinehart and Winston, 1970.

ELIADE, M. *Yoga: Immortality and freedom.* Princeton: Princeton University Press, 1969.

ERIKSON, E. H. *Childhood and society.* New York: Norton, 1950.

FAGEN, R. Selective and evolutionary aspects of animal play. *The American Naturalist,* 1974, **108,** 850-858.

FREUD, S. *The ego and the id.* London: Allen and Unwin, 1927.

GETZELS, J. W., & CSIKSZENTMIHALYI, M. Creative problem-finding: A longitudinal study with artists. Unpublished Manuscript, The University of Chicago, 1974.

GHISELIN, B. (Ed.). *The creative process.* New York: Mentor, 1952.

HERRIGEE, E. *Zen in the art of archery.* New York: Pantheon, 1953.

HUIZINGA, J. *Homo ludens.* Boston: Beacon Press, 1950.

JEWELL, P. A. & LOIZOS, C. Play, exploration and territoriality in mammals. *Symposia of the Zoological Society,* London, 1966, **18.**

KENYON, G. S. Six scales for assessing attitude toward physical activity. In W. P. Morgan (Ed.). *Contemporary readings in sport psychology.* Springfield, Illinois: Thomas, 1970.

LASKI, M. *Ecstasy: A study of some secular and religious experiences,* Bloomington, Ind.: Indiana University Press, 1962.

MACKAY, D. H. *Information, mechanism and meaning.* Cambridge: MIT Press, 1969.

MASLOW, A. *Toward a psychology of being.* Princeton, New Jersey: Van Nostrand, 1962.

MASLOW, A. Humanistic science and transcendent experiences. *Journal of Humanistic Psychology,* 1965, 5 (2), 219-227.

MASLOW, A. *The farther reaches of human nature.* New York: Viking, 1971.

MEAD, G. H. *Mind, self, and society.* Chicago: The University of Chicago Press, 1934.

MOLTMAN, J. *Theology of play.* New York: Harper and Row, 1972.

MONTMASSON, J. M. *Invention and the unconscious.* New York: Harcourt, Brace, 1932.

MURPHY, M. *Gold and the kingdom.* New York: Viking, 1972.

NARANJO, C., & ORNSTEIN, R. E. *On the psychology of meditation.* New York: Viking, 1971.

PIAGET, J. *Play, dreams and imitation in childhood.* New York: Norton, 1951.

PIAGET, J. *The moral judgment of the child.* New York: The Free Press, 1965.

RAHNER, H. *Man at play.* New York: Herder and Herder, 1967.

ROBERTS, J. M., ARTH, M. S., & BUSH, R. Games in culture. *American Anthropologist,* 1959, **61,** 597-605.

ROBERTS, J. M., & SUTTON-SMITH, B. Child training and game involvement. *Ethnology,* 1962, **1** (2), 166-185.

ROBERTS, J. M., & SUTTON-SMITH, B. Cross-cultural correlates of games of chance. *Behavior Science Notes,* 1966, **3,** 131-144.

SARTRE, J. P. *Being and nothingness.* New York: Philosophical Library, 1956.

SCHILLER, C. F. *Essays aesthetical and philosophical.* London: Bell, 1884.

STEINER, G. Fields of force, *The New Yorker,* Oct. 28, 1972, 42-117.

SUTTON-SMITH, B. Play, games, and controls. In J. P. Scott & S. F. Scott, (Eds.), *Social control and social change.* Chicago: The University of Chicago Press, 1971.

TURNER, V. *The ritual process.* Chicago: Aldine, 1969.

UNSWORTH, W. *North face.* London: Hutchinson, 1969.

WORSLEY, P. *The trumpet shall sound.* New York: Schocken, 1968.

I can't abide by the dictum that play is bad and seriousness is laudable. (Bach's) scherzos are not serious, yet he is sincere all the same. Cubs and pups are playing. But could they learn to hunt and live without such games?

FRITZ PERLS

SLEEP AND DREAMS

Tiredness is a natural "low." Psychiatrist Ernest Hartmann notes there are two different kinds of tiredness: physical fatigue after hard exertion, and the tiredness that comes after emotional stress. Of the two, simple physical tiredness is the more pleasant; we can still feel relaxed and mentally alert. Mental tiredness, on the other hand, leaves us tense, cranky, and uncomfortable; we regress in our thoughts and deeds to childish ways of dealing with the world, we have little mental energy for serious thinking, and our attention drifts off easily.

Each night during sleep, we go through a repeated cycle of roughly ninety minutes during which we enter different states of sleep. The most familiar of these, dreaming, is but one of several distinct sleep stages, each with its own pattern of brain activity, physical arousal, and awareness—or lack thereof. Sleep researcher William Dement explains how he monitors these stages of sleep and what their distinguishing features are.

You know what your dreams are like, but what about the dreams other people have? Wilse B. Webb reviews the research on the contents of dreams, and finds that most are disappointingly commonplace. We generally remember our more fascinating and exciting dreams and forget the mundane ones. This selective recall has given us a distorted picture of dream contents. Although it is true that we sometimes may have dreams of deep personal or symbolic meaning, most dreams are simply not so dramatic. The dreams we remember, says Webb, "are more coherent, sexier, and generally more interesting" than those collected at random in the sleep laboratory.

Dreams can tell us much about our waking selves, if we will give their messages the attention they deserve, says psychologist Calvin Hall. Modern civilization, however, is so biased toward rational, waking awareness that it has discounted the wisdom of dreams. In other cultures, such as among the Senoi of Malaya, dreams are given a special importance as messages about how people are getting along with each other. Dreams tell us how we see ourselves, others, and the world, and reveal our hidden impulses, driving forces, and unresolved conflicts. The dream is a doorway to the unconscious, mapping a psychological region normally inaccessible to us in waking consciousness. Hall pleads that we take our dreams more seriously, as a source of insight into, and solution of, life's dilemmas.

The Psychology of Tiredness

E. L. Hartmann

By tiredness I do not mean the fatigue after exercise, from which one recovers merely by lying down without sleeping, but the tiredness at the end of a day, apparently reversible only by sleep. One approach to the functions of sleep is to examine carefully the state of tiredness and to determine what characteristics or structures of the mind appear to wear out during the day and to need restoration by sleep. It is perfectly obvious both from our own subjective experience and from observation of other persons, especially children, that considerable changes in psychological functioning are produced by tiredness, and these are what we shall examine here.

What I will discuss here is based on experience with patients in psychotherapy and psychoanalysis, several hundred interviews with normal and abnormal sleepers in various sleep studies, observation of children, and introspection. The chief problem lies in attempting to extricate constant themes from the changing, variegated clinical material, for the effects of tiredness clearly depend to a great extent on the background mental characteristics of the person, as well as on his social and physical environment.

Nonetheless, it appears to me that two patterns or "syndromes" of tiredness can be identified (see Table I). They are seldom present in pure form, and not everyone reports both types, but a large number of individuals, when they stop to think about it, can pick out these two very different characteristic sorts of tiredness in themselves. One is the tiredness that comes after a day of purely physical activity, such as a day of skiing or physical work. This could be called physical tiredness or simple tiredness and is associated usually with a relaxed feeling in the musculature, including the facial and head muscles, and very seldom with any tightness or headaches. It is usually described affectively as either pleasant or neutral and is not associated with any characteristic psychic changes: people find it difficult to say that their mental functioning was altered in this kind of tiredness. In children my impression is that this physical tiredness is associated with relaxation and with rapid sleep onset without fuss or bother.

The second kind of tiredness, which we might call mental tiredness, is reported more frequently after a long day of intellectual or emotional and intellectual work. This

TABLE 1 TWO KINDS OF TIREDNESS, REQUIRING SLEEP

	Tiredness I	Tiredness 2
Rough Designation	"Physical"	"Mental"
Typically Follows	A day of physical activity, sport, or mixed physical-intellectual activity without worry or anxiety	A day of emotional stress or a day of hard, not entirely pleasant, intellectual work or intellectual plus emotional work
Muscles	Usually relaxed	Often tense
Physical Symptoms	None	Sometimes headache, eye strain, or cramped or tense feelings in various muscles
Affective Tone	Neutral or pleasant	unpleasant
Sleep Onset	Rapid, easy	Sometimes slow, difficult
Mental Changes (Adult)	No definite changes	Discomfort, irritability, anger, lack of energy, inability to concentrate, loss of social adaptiveness, loss of ability for careful patterning or long term planning
Mental Changes (Children	No definite changes	Regression, loss of super-ego, emergence of naked anger or hostility, temper tantrums, "too tired to get to sleep"
Metapsychological Formulation	No change	Wearing out of the most recently developed or most subtle ego mechanisms, wearing out of secondary process, emergence of drive and impulses, especially anger
Hypothesized Relationship to Sleep	Represents a "need" for SWS	Represents a "need" for "D

tiredness, with which most of us are all too familiar, is often accompanied by tension or tightness of the muscles, especially muscles of the face and head; and it is usually described with a negative tone—it is unpleasant or at best neutral. It sometimes has the paradoxical effect of making it hard to fall asleep. Associated with this sort of tiredness is an obvious lack of energy or unwillingness to try anything new; irritability and anger are also prominent. One feels uncomfortable and on edge in social interactions and wants to be left alone in an undemanding situation. One tends to read easy material and to lapse into wish-fulfilling daydreams.

The exact effects obviously vary with the individual's personality structure. In some persons with a tendency toward depression, increasing depression is characteristic of tiredness, and they may even go to sleep to avoid depression. For others (especially certain patients with sleep-onset insomnia) the great problem in becoming tired is the feeling of losing control, losing one's normal ways of dealing with sexual and especially aggressive impulses.

This second sort of tiredness clearly involves alterations in psychic functions, a tiring of the psychic apparatus; but I believe that not every aspect of mental functioning tires equally. In cognitive fields this tiredness expresses itself as a difficulty in concentration, especially in sustained attentive thinking, and also as a defect in exclusion of extraneous or unwanted stimuli.

In children there are clear evidences of ego regression. As the day wears on to evening there is a striking inability to control impulses and wishes. The child becomes more of a baby as he becomes tired. For instance, a four-year-old boy who has learned perfectly that hitting his younger sister when he is angry at her is not tolerable and has learned to displace and to sublimate his impulse, nonetheless reverts to simply hitting her when he is extremely tired. Also, when small children are very tired, there are frequent instances of verbal perseveration—using the same phrases to make the same demands over and over again. This is perhaps a regression to one of the earliest psychic tendencies—the repetition compulsion. The general impression both in children and adults is that more subtle and more recently developed ego mechanisms are the ones which tire most easily.

From the economic point of view mental tiredness means that less psychic energy is available for higher-level activities, such as directed conscious attention; and there is a greater mobility of cathexes. Secondary-process functioning tires especially, sometimes allowing primary process to emerge. In the conflict-free sphere lowered energy shows up as poor attention and decreased activity-directed energy.

From the dynamic point of view there is a weakening in the ego defense mechanisms for dealing with drives and with reality, and a regression to earlier "easier" mechanisms. The forms this regression takes vary with the characteristics of the individual.

In the normal individual the ego maintains a smooth balance, hopefully not requiring too much energy, between the demands of the external world and the demands of its own drives. When very tired, a small child often, and the

adult sometimes, will be taken over by his more primitive wishes and desires: I want this, I want that, I want what I want, and so on. The adult's aggression often takes over during extreme tiredness and overrides generally well-learned social amenities. On the other hand, in the adult, in whom the demands of reality are sometimes extremely strong, the balance often tips the other way in extreme tiredness, so that rather than feeling overwhelmed by one's drives, one feels entirely overwhelmed by the outside world, by the amount of work needed to be done, by external demands, and so on. It is the balance which appears to be lacking.

Although nothing can be proved conclusively from the evidence presented here, the implications for function are clear. We have delineated psychologically two kinds of tiredness which, in turn, suggests two restorative functions—one relatively simple and physical, the other involving restoration of subtle adaptive ego functions, which can also be seen as feedback guidance processes. I suggest that the first, relatively simple, "physical tiredness" represents a need for slow wave sleep (stages 3-4), while the second, more complex, "mental tiredness" represents a need for D-sleep. In the normal course of events a night's sleep fills both of these needs. Sleep basically has a restitutive or restorative function, in accordance with our commonsense notion. Sleep is required by all persons and by all mammals, and apparently there are separable requirements for the two major states of sleep.

FUNCTIONS OF S-SLEEP

Let me consider first what we have discovered about possible functions of S-sleep. From what has gone before it is likely that slow-wave sleep (SWS), the deeper and probably most intensive part of S-sleep, has a physically restorative function, which is more necessary after exercise or when catabolism has been increased. One could consider SWS an anabolic phase of sleep. Although the increased requirements for SWS may be produced by states of general body tiredness or increased catabolism, the increased synthetic processes probably occur especially in the brain. It is brain electrophysiology that dramatically differentiates SWS from relaxed wakefulness, and I also believe SWS plays an additional preparatory role for the functions of D (deep sleep) in the brain.

FUNCTIONS OF D-SLEEP (D)

Functions of D have been discussed in more detail; these appear clearly to involve the central nervous system and to be more complex than the functions of S. From the studies of sleep deprivation and the studies of tiredness we have concluded that sleep, and probably D-sleep specifically, may have a restorative function with respect to systems of focused attention (especially the ability to focus on one item while ignoring others); systems involving the ability to maintain an optimistic mood, energy, and self-confidence; and systems involving processes of emotional adaptation to the physical and social environment.

From the studies of long, short, and variable sleepers we have concluded that sleep, especially D-sleep, is needed in larger quantities after days of stress, worry, or intense new learning, especially if the learning is in itself somewhat stressful. D-sleep thus may have a role in consolidating learning or memory, but there is a strong hint that stress is important and that more D is needed when there have been emotionally involving changes during the day. In other words, those who require more sleep are not so much persons who have learned a lot of new facts during the day, but rather persons who have disrupted their usual ways of doing things, who have, often stressfully, reprogrammed themselves during their waking hours. Thus sleep and D-sleep may have a role in consolidating or reconnecting these important alterations made during the day. Thinking of psychodynamic concepts in somewhat too literal a sense, one can almost see psychic structures, when they are tried out in new ways (at times of stress), rubbing against each other and producing friction and then requiring increased restoration by sleep; while these same mechanisms when they are functioning smoothly, can handle a great deal of input without requiring much sleep for restoration.

Two Kinds of Sleep

William Dement

HOW SLEEP IS MEASURED

In order to identify and classify sleep, it is necessary to record the electrical activity of three systems: the brain, the eyes, and the muscles. These systems are monitored simultaneously by an instrument called the polygraph, which allows measurements to be made continuously throughout the night without disturbing the sleeping subject. Tiny electrodes attached to the scalp and face of the subject convey signals to the polygraph where they are recorded on moving chart paper by pens that move up and down automatically in response to changes in electrical potentials.

The up-and-down movement of the pens and the lateral movement of the paper produces a pattern of waves. These waves are meaningless scribbles to the uninformed observer, but if they are recorded in a standard and conventional manner, a night of sleep can be interpreted accurately by an knowledgeable researcher. In somewhat the manner of the experienced surfer watching ocean waves, the sleep researcher looks for changes in form and frequency of brain waves.

The record of brain activity is called *electroencephalogram* or EEG. The polygraph records the voltage fluctuations between two points on the scalp or, in the case of animals, within the brain itself. The record of eye movements is called an *electrooculogram* or EOG. The eyes are like tiny batteries with a difference of electrical potential between the cornea and the retina. Changes of the electrical field are recorded as transorbital potential differences whenever the eyes move. The record of muscle activity is called an *electromyogram* (EMG). It shows the electrical potentials generated in the muscle fibers.

In routine studies of nocturnal sleep, the subject arrives at the laboratory about an hour before his usual bedtime. He prepares for bed by going through the same bedtime ritual he is accustomed to at home, while the experimenter checks the equipment. When the subject is ready for bed, the experimenter begins the routine application of electrodes. All of this must be completed, and fail-safe, before the subject goes to sleep so it will not be necessary to make adjustments in the middle of the night and therefore disturb the normal sleep pattern. In certain subjects or patients, these recordings are continued around-the-clock for many days, and the subject essentially lives in the laboratory.

After a final equipment check, the experimenter wishes the subject a good night's sleep, turns off the light, and closes the door as he departs. By the time the subject awakens in the morning—to be greeted by a sleepy-eyed experimenter—nearly one thousand feet of chart paper or magnetic tape will have been traced with a record of brain waves, eye movements, and muscle activity. Although the subject may experience minor discomfort from the electrodes taped to his face, there is no pain involved in sleep recording, and at no time is any current flowing from the polygraph to the subject.

THE DISCOVERY OF REM SLEEP

Every day every human being—every mammal, in fact—experiences two kinds of sleep that alternate rhythmically throughout the entire sleep period. These two kinds of sleep are as different from each other as sleep is from wakefulness. If there is a cat or a dog in your household, chances are you have observed the two states of sleep many times. At one moment the sleeping animal seems to be lifeless except for its regular breathing. Then the breathing becomes irregular, paws and whiskers begin to twitch, lips and tongue begin to move—and someone says, "Oh, look at Rover! He's *dreaming!*"

The discovery of the two kinds of sleep occurred almost accidentally at the University of Chicago. In 1952 Dr. Kleitman became interested in the slow rolling eye movements that accompany sleep onset and decided to look for these eye movements throughout the night to determine whether they were related to the depth or quality of sleep. Kleitman gave the assignment of watching eye movements to one of his graduate students in the department of physiology, Eugene Aserinsky.

The young student soon noticed an entirely new kind of eye movement. At certain times during the night, the eyes began to dart about furiously beneath the closed lids. These unexpected episodes were startlingly different from the familiar slow, pendular movements that were the original object of the study.

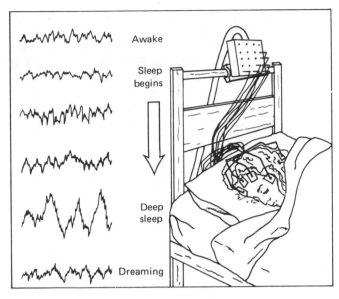

Typical EEGs from subjects in different states ranging from alert wakefulness to dreaming.

Over the years, many people have asked me, "How can you see the eye moving when the lids are closed?" As a matter of fact, it is very easy to see eye movements when the eyes are closed. Have someone do it and see for yourself. However, Aserinsky was using the polygraph to monitor the subject, and the eye movements were actually discovered on the chart paper. It was not until he directly observed these movements in sleeping subjects that he could believe the spectacular inked-out deviations. It would be difficult today to understand how skeptical we were. These eye movements, which had all the attributes of waking eye movements, had absolutely no business appearing in sleep. In those days, sleep was conceived of as a state of neural depression or inhibition—quiescence, rest. It was definitely not a condition in which the brain could be generating highly coordinated eye movements that were, in many instances, faster and sharper than the subject could execute while awake.

Of course, the change in all our concepts of sleep didn't occur overnight. Having joined the research effort at this point as a sophomore medical student under Kleitman, I began to record the electroencephalograph and other physiological variables, along with eye movement activity. Since I didn't know what to expect, I kept my eyes glued to the moving chart paper all night long. After many nights, certain definite relationships were discernible in the enormous amounts of data. Rapid eye movements were always accompanied by very distinctive brain wave patterns, a change in breathing, and other striking departures from the normal, quiet sleep pattern. In addition, what we now call the basic ninety-minute sleep pattern began to emerge from the night-to-night variability.

As more and more physiological changes were discovered and described, we realized that sleep was *not* a quiet resting state that continued without variance as long as the subject was fortunate enough to remain asleep. No. For the first time we realized what has probably been true of man's sleep since he crawled out of the primordial slime. Man has *two* kinds of sleep. His nocturnal solitude contains two entirely different phenomena.

REM AND NREM SLEEP

I coined the term "REM" (for rapid-eye-movement) sleep to define the phenomenon my colleagues and I had observed. The other kind of sleep eventually acquired the name "NREM" (pronounced non-REM) sleep.

Most of the changes typically associated with falling asleep are the consequence of reclining and relaxing. Cardiac and respiratory rates will decrease, body temperature will fall, blood pressure will decline, and metabolic activity will drop. If we continue to lie still and relax, we may fall asleep without the occurrence of any further changes.

The NREM state is often called "quiet sleep" because of the slow, regular breathing, the general absence of body movement, and the slow, regular brain activity shown in the EEG. It is important to remember that the body is not paralyzed during NREM sleep; it *can* move, but it *does not* move because the brain doesn't order it to move. The sleeper has lost contact with his environment. There is a shut-down of perception because the five senses are no longer gathering information and communicating stimuli to the brain. When gross body movements (such as rolling over) occur during NREM, the EEG suggests a transient intrusion of wakefulness—yet the individual may not be responsive at the time, nor recall having moved if subsequently awakened. In one respect the term "quiet sleep" is a misnomer: it is during NREM sleep that snoring occurs.

REM sleep, which has been called "active sleep," is an entirely different state of existence. At the onset of REM sleep, the sleeper's body is still immobile, but we can see small, convulsive twitches of his face and fingertips. His snoring ceases, and his breathing becomes irregular—very fast, then slow—he may even appear to stop breathing for several seconds. Under the eyelids the corneal bulges of his eyes dart around, back and forth. If we gently pull back the eyelids, the subject seems to be actually looking at something. Cerebral blood flow and brain temperature soar to new heights, but the large muscles of the body are completely paralyzed; arms, legs, and trunk cannot move. Throbbing penile erections occur in adult—and newborn—males.

There is some speculation that REM sleep is not really sleep at all, but a state in which the subject is awake, but paralyzed and hallucinating.

All of the short-lived events or bursts of activity that occur *within* the periods of REM sleep—individual eye movements, muscle twitches, and so forth—are collectively called phasic activity. This includes short-lived contractions of the middle ear muscles that occur in sleep only during the REM state. These contractions are identical with middle ear muscle activity seen in wakefulness as a response to various intensities and pitches of sound. In the cat, researchers may have located the primary phasic activity—the one that triggers all the others. It is an electrical event called the PGO spike. The acronym stands for pons, geniculate bodies, and occipital cortex—areas of the brain where the electrical spike is recorded during REM periods. Although it has so far been impossible in humans to get recordings from the depth of the brain, Rechtschaffen has discovered, in both humans and cats, a REM phasic activity that may be closely associated with PGO spikes. This event, known as phasic integrated potential (PIP), is a sharp shift in electrical potential recorded from the muscles surrounding the eyes.

All of these discoveries are helping to bring the mystery of REM sleep—and maybe even the fantasy of dreams—out of the shadowy dusk of speculation and into the clear bright light of observable phenomena. Sometimes it seems a shame, to anyone who believes that mystery and fantasy enrich our lives. Nonetheless, a researcher is obliged to state the facts—to describe phenomena in terms of what we know. Speaking in such a strict manner with regard to REM sleep, I can only say: "It's there. It looks the way I've described it." We just don't know yet, despite twenty years of intensive research, *why* it's there. In many ways, REM periods resemble epileptic seizures. Perhaps they are equally useful.

COURSE OF EVENTS DURING THE NIGHT

Frequently associated with the reverie of sleep onset is a feeling of floating or falling, which often terminates abruptly in a jerk returning us to wakefulness. Such starts, called myoclonias, generally occur only during the first five mintues of sleep and are a normal occurrence, seemingly more prevalent in "nervous" people. On some occasions the myoclonia may be an arousal response to a very weak, insignificant external stimulus.

Even with an EEG reading it is impossible to pinpoint the exact instant of sleep onset. The essential difference between wakefulness and sleep is the loss of awareness. Sleep onset occurs at the exact instant when a meaningful stimulus fails to elicit its accustomed response. (This does not mean that no response whatsoever can be obtained. A stimulus of sufficient magnitude or significance, such as a loud noise or the soft calling of one's name, elicits a very definite response: arousal.)

A dramatic illustration of the nature of sleep onset has been obtained in the laboratory through the use of visual stimuli. A sleepy subject lies in bed with his eyes taped open (which can be achieved, believe it or not, with relatively little discomfort). A very bright strobe light is placed about six inches in front of his face and is flashed into his eyes at the rate of about once every second or two. A microswitch is taped to his finger, which he is instructed to press every time he sees a flash. A simple task. How can he possibly avoid seeing the flash? The subject will press and press. Suddenly he stops. If we immediately ask why, he will be surprised. The light exploded right into his widely open eyes, yet he was totally unaware. In one second, he was awake, seeing, hearing, responding—in the very next second, he was functionally blind and asleep.

At the moment when visual perception ceases, the eyes begin to drift slowly from side to side either synchronously or asynchronously. This slow rolling of the eyes is one of the most reliable signs of the onset of sleep. The first sleep of the night is always NREM sleep, which must progress through its various stages before the first REM period occurs. Along with the slowly rolling eye movements, we see a gradual transition in the pattern of EEG waves from the characteristic rhythm of wakefulness to the NREM Stage I configuration.

What follows is a progressive descent from Stage I into other stages of NREM sleep. The term "descent" is meant to imply a progression along the depth-of-sleep continuum as sleep becomes deeper and deeper, the sleeper becomes more remote from the environment, and increasingly more potent stimuli are necessary to cause arousal.

Each new stage is announced by its own characteristic pattern in the EEG. After only a few minutes of Stage I, the onset of Stage 2 is established by the appearance of spindling and K complexes. Several minutes later the slow delta waves of Stage 3 become apparent. After about ten minutes of this stage, the delta activity becomes more and more predominant and signals the presence of Stage 4. At this point it is extremely difficult to awaken the sleeper. A child in this stage of sleep is virtually unreachable and may take several minutes to return to full awareness if he can be aroused at all. It is during this period that sleeptalking, sleepwalking, night terrors, and bed-wetting are initiated in young children.

In Stage 4, thirty or forty minutes following sleep onset, a series of body movements heralds the start of a re-ascent through the stages of NREM sleep. Approximately seventy or eighty minutes from the onset of sleep the Stage I EEG pattern occurs again. But now there are sawtooth waves in the EEG, rapid eye movements in the EOG, a suppression of activity in the EMG, and a host of other physiological changes. The first REM period has begun. It will last about ten minutes.

Throughout the night this cyclic variation between NREM and REM sleep continues. The NREM-REM cycle varies from seventy to 110 minutes but averages around ninety minutes. In the early part of the night, sleep is dominated by the NREM state, particularly Stages 3 and 4, but as the night wears on, REM sleep periods become progressively longer, sometimes as long as sixty minutes, and Stage 2 represents the only NREM interruption.

An adult who sleeps seven and one-half hours each night generally spends one and one-half to two hours in REM sleep. Since people who are awakened during REM periods usually recall a dream, it can be said that we dream roughly every ninety minutes all night long. After offering us several short episodes early in the night, the brain may produce an hour-long "feature film."

The Nature of Dreams

Wilse B. Webb

Before we begin a discussion of dreams it would be wise for us to know, with a little more certainty than most of us have, just what a dream is like. Since most of us have had dreams of our own this may seem a little strange, but think about it. Although we know our own dreams we certainly cannot directly experience someone else's. All we directly know about dreams is the nature of our own. But are these like the dreams of others? Frequently I am asked a question like, "Do people dream in color?" I often reply by saying, "Do you?" This is usually most unsatisfactory. The questioner, more often than not, looks puzzled or annoyed and may well say, "I was asking about dreams, not me."

What we know about dreams in general, then, is what other people tell us about their dreams. If we happen to be psychoanalysts we have heard a large number of dreams. Most of us, however, know about others' dreams from casual reports ("Hey, I had this funny dream last night") or highly selective ones ("Man, I had this dream I can't forget"). Our other primary sources are visualizations or descriptions of dreams which make some particular point about clairvoyance, psychodynamics, or enhance some movie, poem, or story theme. In short, we know very little about those night-to-night occurrences that make up the full dream world.

The first problem in knowing the dreams of others is that we can never actually see them and must accept a description of them. This bridge between the dream and our knowing is made of words, and words are often hard to come by. The following is an actual transcript of a laboratory dream report.

S: Yes. Yes, I can hear you. Go ahead.

E: Was anything going through your mind?

S: No, I really just, uh, I was dreaming about . . . let me see, a group of college boys walking down the lane, in the lane, in the uh, in the park, singing, and they were outside there in the distance, and there was a group of girls and all, dressed in white sitting on the park benches, uh . . . carrying flowers, I think. Um, it was dark and they were covering, uh, they were wearing white gloves, I remember long, you know, long white gloves . . . and there was, uh, let's see . . . I'm trying to think of the details . . . lots of flowers in the park. Yellow ones, I think, Regular flowers.

E: Did you recognize anybody in the dream?

S: Uh, no. There's nobody I could recognize.

E: Were you in the dream?

S: No, I wasn't. I couldn't particularly single out anybody that I could recognize in the dream. . . . I had to make a special effort to retain the . . . you know, it disappears after a very few seconds, if I don't make a constant effort to retain it.

E: Were there any feelings connected with it?

S: No. I, uh, I guess you might say I was a passive observer of the scene. I has no feelings either way of what was going on. It had been going on maybe a few mintues, I guess, then I woke up. At the beginning, sometime earlier, it had something to do about insects, uh, bees. I was catching bees. Somebody was catching bees and letting them go on flowers, you know, pollinating the flowers, and uh . . . and uh, uh, I don't know.

(H. Witkins and H. Lewis, "Presleep Experience and Dreams," in *Experimental Studies of Dreaming,* eds. H. Witkins and H. Lewis [New York: Random House, 1967], pp. 164-65.)

Here is a second one from a young librarian:

I was in the library and I was filing cards, and I came to some letter between 'a' and 'c.' I was filing some, I think it was Burma, some country, and just as I put that in, there was some scene of some woman who was sent to look for a little girl who was lost, and she was sent to Burma. They thought the little girl was going there for some reason. This was sort of like a dramatization of what I was doing. I mean I was filing, and then this scene took place, right at the same time. In the setting it was sort of like you'd imagined it, but I had a feeling that it was really happening. (David Foulkes, "Theories of Dream Formation and Recent Studies of Dream Consciousness," *Psychological Bulletin,* vol. 62, 1964, 244-45.)

There are many aspects of these "raw materials" of dreams. I will point up a few of them. They are very different in clarity and coherence of recall. We can guess that the first dream may not have even been retained as a dream "in real life;" at best, there might have been a vague recall of having had a dream about "being in a park." Second, note the shifting participant roles. In the first dream there was a shift from being an observer to an earlier active role of catching bees. In the second dream there was a dramatic shift from filing cards to "some woman" to "they" who "thought." Most particularly, note that though strange in many ways, the dreams were populated with real and imaginable events and people: college boys, white gloves, bees, flowers, file cards, Burma, a little girl. While much of the dreams were "as if," they were also composed of "as."

Remember that these dream reports were very close to their sources. A second problem of knowing dreams lies in the recall of the recall. What we finally hear of a dream is very likely to be different from the original dream. Again and again studies have shown that reports of "home dreams" occurring outside the laboratory are very different from those reported in the laboratory. The "home" dreams are more coherent, sexier, and generally more interesting than those reported in the laboratory. Certainly some of this may be due to a difference in the dreams themselves. Laboratory dreams are essentially "random" samples while home dreams are usually final-awakening dreams. Much of the difference is likely to stem from the recall process itself. Freud used the term "secondary elaboration" to describe the pressures toward rationality and the repression which works to modify the original recall. Then there is simply the matter of what we remember and whether we try to remember. In our examples we may well have received no report at all from the first dream and our second dream would have probably been something like "I dreamed about a little girl who was lost" or "I dreamed about a little girl who was kidnapped and taken to Burma."

Given these limitations, what are the dreams of "people" like? Fortunately, we have two reports which have extensively described and categorized dream content "non-interpretively." One set was composed of 1,000 "home" dreams of college students collected from dream logs by Dr. Calvin Hall,[1] and one set was composed of 650 laboratory dreams collected by Dr. Fred Snyder.[2] In describing dreams I have drawn heavily from the latter study, since its results are likely to be closer to the "raw" dream itself; I have used the Hall study to elaborate, confirm, and occasionally disagree with the laboratory reports.

The most striking conclusion of both studes is that dreams do not conform to the common assumption that they are generally bizarre, highly unusual, and emotion-laden. Snyder says "Our data . . . entirely conforms to this [Hall's] conclusion that the outstanding feature of dream settings is their commonplaceness." Snyder reports that in only 20 percent of the dreams was the setting not clear, and three-fourths of these dreams were very short reports. In only 4 percent of the dreams was the setting exotic or unusual and less than 1 percent of the settings were classifiable as "fantastic." In the remaining dreams the scenes were familiar, identifiable, or most reasonable.

Dreams are not lonely. In 95 percent of the dreams analyzed by Hall another person beside the dreamer was present, and in 35 percent more than one other person was present. More than half the people were recognizable and familiar to the dreamer. Animals appeared occasionally but

[1] Calvin S. Hall and R. L. Van de Castle, *The Content Analysis of Dreams* (New York: Appleton-Century-Crofts, 1966).

[2] Fred Snyder, "The Phenomenology of Dreaming," in *The Psycho-dynamic Implications of the Physiolgical Studies on Dreams,* eds. Leo Madow and Laurence H. Snow (Springfield, Ill. and Charles C. Thomas, 1970).

only one "monster" appeared in the 1,000 dreams. Notables such as movie stars, sports figures, or politicians were quite rare.

There is a great deal of activity, but this activity is surprisingly unstrenuous. Some 38 percent of the activity involves talking, listening, looking, or thinking. Another 32 percent consists of going from one place to another—walking or riding (but seldom floating). Only about one-fourth of the dreams were about physical activities, and these were mostly recreational. Here dreams do indeed differ from real life in that we seldom find the dreamer working at routine daily tasks of typing or cleaning or repairing or doing manual labor.

Dreams often have dramatic themes. We can categorize these along various dimensions. Dreams of misfortune and failure are more frequent than ones dealing with good fortune and success; their respective precentages were 46 and 17 percent in the Hall sample. There was evidence of aggression in 47 percent of the dreams and friendly encounters in 38 percent. As a special form of friendliness (or aggression) overt sexual behavior was quite rare. In the Snyder study only 6 of the 620 dreams contained overt sexual acts; in the 1,000 dreams analyzed by Hall only 76 displayed sexual behavior and these included sexual fantasies, overtures, kissing, and "petting." There were only 25 incidences of sexual intercourse.

Emotionality within dreams is remarkably bland even in the face of occasionally highly dramatic events. Snyder writes about his experience with this dimension of dreams.

I am particularly unsatisfied with our ability to assess the emotional dimension of our dream descriptions. It did not seem difficult at first, for unwittingly we were frequently inferring what would have been the appropriate emotion under the circumstances described. Then we began to encounter reports in which the subject emphatically disavowed any such feelings. For instance, a waiter in a restaurant was making erotic advances to the dreamer's sister, resulting in a fist fight; but he specifically denied any accompanying feelings of anger. The fight just seemed like a necessary social amenity. After a few such instances we started all over again, tabulating emotions only when they were defintely identified by the reporter, and none were identified in more than two-thirds of the narratives.

Of the emotions identified in dreams, unpleasant ones were most prominent. Fear and anxiety were associated with more than one-third of the dream emotions, followed closely by anger.

These reports accord well with my own observation of dreams. On the whole the reports are relatable to the real world. To use Snyder's analogy drawn from art, they are "representational" rather than "surrealistic," with occasional forays into "impressionism." They are populated by real people in real settings performing and acting in patterns of recognizable behavior.

Where, then, does the impression of strangeness, which is certainly a characteristic of dreaming, come from? I would say from three primary sources: 1) A loosened temporal and spatial world, 2) Loosened attentional controls and 3) Less critical evaluations.

The dream world has many aspects of fantasy or imagination. In the dream all things are possible in a physical sense. Time and matter are not bound by their physical properties. Time does not flow inexorably forward and matter is not bound by gravity. The past and the future may have reality in the present, the dead may live, and I can ice skate in Burma. Scenes in dreams may change with remarkable rapidity or awesome slowness. I may be in a park in one instance and a laboratory in the next or, indeed, I can be in parts of both at the same time.

The way I attend to the world when I am awake is selective and purposeful. In reality as I walk through the park I may be attending to my destination, or to the potential of being mugged, or to a pretty girl. I am unlikely to attend to yellow gloves or hidden elbows. If I am filing cards I attend to them and not to a woman in Burma. In my dreams I may attend to minute details, or thoughts in a fashion that seems little dominated by particular purposes or the demands of the surround.

Above all, I am not critical in my dreams. I do not say, "That is not possible" or "Don't believe this" or "How puzzling." Rather, I accept what is there even though the event is physically impossible or even disgusting or frightening.

In summary, dreams do have their strange qualities. However, when their components are placed under the microscope of objective analysis, the particular elements of the dream turn out to be remarkably prosaic.

The Meaning of Dreams

Calvin Hall

Let us try to weave the fabric of man's mind out of the threads which have been spun from his dreams. These dreams, bear in mind, are not the consciously contrived daydreams of waking fancy but the unconsciously fashioned night dreams of sleep. During sleep the mind expresses itself in pictures. A dream is defined, therefore, as a sequence of pictures or images which embody the ideas or conceptions of the dreamer. The goal of dream interpretation is to discover the meaning of a dream by translating images into ideas. When this task is accomplished the mind of man is exposed to public view and becomes an object of scientific study. In the last analysis dreams interest us only because they enable us to extend our knowledge of man. They tell us things about man that would be difficult to learn by any other means except by the specialized methods used in the treatment of disturbed people. Since these methods are not convenient to use in the study of a large cross-section of normal people, it devolves upon dreams to help us solve the riddle of man.

The function of dreaming is to reveal what is in the person's mind, not to conceal it. Dreams may appear enigmatic because they contain symbols, but these symbols are nothing more than pictorial metaphors, and like the verbal metaphors of waking life their intention is to clarify rather than to obscure thought. What is the difference between a person awake exclaiming, "He's a majestic individual," and a person asleep conjuring up the image of a king? There is no difference except in the medium of expression. The verbal metaphor expressed by the adjective "majestic" and the dream image of a king represent the same conception.

What is enigmatic about dreams is that the roots from which they grow are often buried below the surface of the conscious mind. The conscious mind is the mind which is known to us and whose contents we can talk about if we choose to. For the most part the conscious mind is filled with externals. Our awareness is an awareness of things and people and of our own bodies. We think about objective reality as it appears to us through our senses. Awake we live in a world of events and happenings so that the record of consciousness resembles nothing so much as the daily newspaper. We even persuade ourselves that if we can't talk about something it doesn't exist, or, to reverse the rule, if we can talk about it it does exist. So it comes about that the layer of the mind which represents the public world of objective reality is assumed to be the whole of the mind.

In view of this narrow conception of the mind man is bound to be puzzled by his dreams and is forced to invent fantastic explanations to account for them. If one judges the mind to encompass only the familiar thoughts of waking life, then it follows that dreams must be foreign matter which are put into the heads of sleeping persons by ancestors or gods or devils. If one prefers a less supernatural explanation he can console himself with the theory that dreams are sound and fury, signifying nothing.

There are two reasons why dreams seem to be mysterious. The first reason is that the mind of the sleeping person makes use of a relatively unfamiliar medium of expression. Most people when they are awake do not draw pictures of their ideas. They use words. Consequently they get little or no practice in expressing themselves pictorially, or in interpreting the meaning and significance of picture. Since thinking in pictures is an unusual and unfamiliar language, it is difficult for most people to make much sense out of their dreams. If we were taught to understand the meaning of pictures as we are taught to understand the meaning of language this reason for the mystery of dreams would be abolished.

Even if by some miracle we were to become educated to the interpretation of pictures, dreams would still be unintelligible to an untrained person because they concern themselves largely with the private world of the mind, a world which lies below the surface of consciousness. Of this world the average person has very little knowledge. Hints of its existence are furnished by a consciousness of vague apprehensions and anxieties, of moods and forebodings, of restlessness and uneasiness, and of doubts and ambiguities. Like the vapors that arise from the deeper recesses of a volcanic mountain, the private regions of the mind spew forth a few visible emblems of their existence. These emblems may disturb man but he rarely of his own initiative tries to explore the regions from which these disturbances emanate. It is only within very recent times that people have made serious and systematic attempts to chart the territory of the whole mind. Chief of these explorers was Freud.

What are the contents of the mind as revealed in dreams? First, there is a system which contains the person's self-conceptions. These conceptions answer the question, How do I see myself? The self-conceptions of the unconscious mind often bear little resemblance to the self-deceptions of consciousness. We may fool ourselves with trumped-up and distorted self-portraits in waking life but sleep is no friend to embellishment and illusion. Dreams are the mirror of the self.

Then there is a group of interconnected systems which embrace the person's conceptions of other people. These conceptions answer for others what the self-conceptions answer for the self. They too are often at variance with one's conscious thoughts. "You say you love your husband? Let me see your dreams."

A third system contains the conceptions of the world, what the Germans call *Weltanschauung,* a word meaning "world outlook." These conceptions attempt to personalize an impersonal world. They animate the inanimate by attributing human qualities to it. To the optimist the world is a cheerful place, while to the pessimist the same world is a cheerless place.

A fourth system consists of the conceptions of one's impulses or driving forces, the ways and means by which they are to be gratified, the obstacles which stand in the way of their fulfillment, and the penalties which are exacted when the rules governing the control of the impulses are broken.

In the fifth system of conceptions are located the conflicts. This system also has a number of intercommunicating subsystems. A conflict consists of opposing conceptions which war with one another for dominance. These inward struggles generate tensions and anxieties in the conscious mind. The person feels miserable without knowing why, or he attributes his worries to the wrong causes. Dreams are a faithful pictorial record of these inner conflicts and the dreamer's attempts to resolve them.

The minds of most, if not all, human beings are occupied with five major conflicts at some time during their lives. The first of these conflicts is the conceptual struggle which a child goes through in trying to define his feelings toward his mother and father and their feelings toward him. He is pushed this way and that way by the opposing forces of love, fear and hate, and he seeks constantly to find a solution which will compose his mental turbulence. Although this conflict begins in early childhood, it maintains a stubborn hold over the mind for many years thereafter and there is even some question as to whether it ever does relax its grip completely during one's lifetime. At best this conflict probably terminates in an uneasy armistice, and may be renewed whenever the conditions are favorable. Certainly it appears to be a motivating force in the dreams of people, both young and old.

The second conflict, which is not unrelated to the first one, consists of the opposing ideas of freedom and security. This conflict also originates in childhood but reaches its climax during the late teens and early twenties. It also perseverates and may be regarded as a permanent fixture of the mind, since it is hardly likely that a person will ever obtain complete freedom or complete security, or be satisfied if he could.

These first two conflicts arise out of man's long period of immaturity during which he is a dependent member of a family group. The third conflict grows out of the androgynous nature of man as a biological entity. By nature he is both male and female, although one or the other is the dominant physical expression and is used to classify him as man or woman. The typing of individuals on the basis of distinguishing physical structures does not do away with man's inherent bisexuality. In fact the implicit denial of bisexuality which is accomplished by making a sharp division of people into two sexes aggravates the condition, because it encourages the setting up of different standards of conduct for men and women. Men are expected to act in masculine ways and women in feminine ways according to the standards of a particular society. When a man behaves like a woman or a woman like a man, he runs the risk of incurring contemptuous ridicule from his associates. Since bisexuality is the biological norm and unisexuality is the social norm, it is easily understandable why man is tormented by conflicting conceptions regarding his sex role. Both sides of his nature require satisfaction, yet society sanctions the development of only one side of his nature. Of course, many people are clever enough to find ways of outwitting the demands of society, while there are those who just ignore them, but in either case arriving at a solution involves a certain amount of stress and strain. Moreover, as dreams so clearly show, the conscious resolution of a conflict is more apparent than real since conflicts persist unconsciously even though they may have been put out of mind.

The moral conflict is essentially a conflict between biology and sociology. That is to say it is a conflict between man's animal nature and the culture's expectations regarding his conduct. As an animal, man is equipped to preserve his life by destroying his enemies and to perpetuate himself by cohabiting with a member of the opposite sex. As a socialized being, man possesses a conscience which places a stamp of approval or disapproval upon his actions. The conscience is nothing more or less than a special conceptual system which contains the person's ideas of right and wrong. These conceptions are learned through experience with the prevailing standards of the society in which the person lives.

The impulses of man come into conflict with his moral conceptions because fighting and cohabitating, except as their expression is provided for by the rules of society, are deemed to be improper modes of conduct. Morality is largely taken up with condemning sex and aggression, nor is the condemnation limited to their behavioral manifestation but also extends to their expression in thought and fancy. Since man can hardly hope to eradicate from his mind conceptions of impulses which are such an integral part of his being, and since he has a conscience imposed upon him long before he has acquired enough sagacity to integrate biological demands with sociological expectations, it follows that the moral conflict will be a constant source of trouble to him. Man may deceive himself into thinking he has fused biology with sociology when all he has really done is to repress one or the other out of immediate awareness. Dreams cut through man's conscious pretensions and show us that the moral conflict is a very provocative force in the private world of the mind.

Finally, there is that most profound of all human conflicts, the opposing vectors of life and death. In this conflict sociology plays no role. It is purely a biological drama of conflicting biological modes, the constructive, synthesizing and assimilating processes of anabolism versus the destructive, disintegrative and decomposing processes of catabolism. Anabolism or life builds to more and more complex form, catabolism or death decomposes complex forms into simpler ones. Although man is not directly aware of these biological processes unless they express themselves in easily discernible forms, as in the extremes of sickness and health, they do provide him with a constant flow of unconscious conceptions. Because of the biological tensions between anabolism and catabolism, he conceives of himself as striving to live when the anabolic vector is ascendant and as striving to die when the catabolic vector is ascendant. Our mind reflects these inner energy changes of the body as surely as they reflect the outer energy changes of the world. Indeed it is possible that the inner world always speaks with more authority than the outer world does, that sociology is ever the servant of biology. In any event the analysis of dreams gives meaning to that paradoxical assertion in the *Book of Common Prayer,* "In the midst of life we are in death."

These then are the underformings of the mind as they crop out in dreams. The foundations of the mind consist of an intricate network of conceptual systems which develop out of man's nature as a biological energy system and his status as a receptacle of culture.

Now let us address ourselves to a question that must be in the mind of every reader. What bearing do these conceptual underformings have upon the actions of a person? Do the innermost thoughts in the labyrinth of the mind make their effects known in behavior? What is the connection, if any, between the unconscious and man's conduct?

The answer which is favored by observation and experiment is that the unconscious exercises a considerable selective influence on one's behavior. Given a wide range of behavior possibilities, the particular mode of action which is adopted is dictated by the conceptual systems of the person. His conduct like his dreams is a manifestation of inner mental states, or as Emerson said, "The event is the actualizing of thought." Deeds and dreams are both in a sense metaphors or symbols of the mind. For example, if a young man conceives of older men as enemies and if he thinks that the way to cope with them is to be submissive, these ideas will be embodied in his behavior. He will be deferential to his father, to male teachers, to bosses and to other older men who enter his life. What appears to be a habitual mode of conduct is, in this case, merely the expression of a persistent set of conceptions which direct his behavior in a consistent way. His deference symbolizes an idea of which he may be totally unaware.

Another young man may harbor the idea of rebellion against older men, in which case his behavior will be characterized by rebelliousness. This conception may be acted out in a variety of ways. A boy wrecks his father's car and it is found that this is an unconscious act of aggression against the father. A student refuses to learn because he hates the teacher. Workers rebel against the boss by going out on strike. Criminals and other antisocial persons may regulate their whole lives in accordance with the idea of rebellion.

Or consider the contrasting world views of two people who supposedly live in the same world. One of them conceives of the world as a friendly place. In his relations with people, he is friendly, co-operative, helpful and courteous. The other conceives of the world as a hostile place. In his interpersonal conduct he is unfriendly, competitive, selfish and unmannerly. Let these two people meet and they understand one another as little as though they came from different planets. They cannot communicate with one another because their conceptual systems are so different.

Take a young man whose dreams reveal that he has contrasting conceptions of women. Guided by the conception that women are pure, sublimated beings, his conduct, we would predict, would be characterized by tenderness and thoughtfulness. Guided by the other conception that women are aggressively sexual, his behavior would be crude and thoughtless. Now suppose that this lad was observed by one person when the first conception was directing his behavior and by another person when the second conception was in control. Do you suppose that the descriptions given by these two observers would coincide? Not at all. To all intents and purposes, the two observers might as well have been describing two different people.

If one adopts the view that man's behavior is determined to a great extent by ideas which reside in the basements and attics of the mind, a good deal of behavior which we find puzzling makes sense. Why, for example, do we instinctively dislike some people when we first meet them? May it not be because the person we meet reminds us unwittingly of another person? The resemblance may be nothing more than a wrinkle under the eyes, a slight distention of the nostrils, an almost invisible curl of the lips, or an inclination of the head, but it is enough to reinstate the same feeling of antagonism toward the new person that we feel toward the other individual.

Nothing happens by chance. A person dreams that he is hurt in an accident and we discover by analyzing the dream that he is punishing himself for a misdeed. Why then should we be surprised to find that a person who hurts himself in waking life is acting out an idea of atonement? Is not an event always an actualizing of an unconscious thought?

We all know why an old maid looks under the bed at night. Are not many of our fears based upon the same principle, that what is on our mind might come true? We warn a person who is handling a sharp knife to be careful. Before warning him have we not had an image of his being cut, so that the warning serves to prevent *our* idea from being actualized in *his* behavior?

A person cannot do anything without expressing some aspect of his personal ideology. The clothes he selects, the books he reads, the hobbies he cultivates, the entertainment he seeks, the candidates he votes for—in every department of life man reacts selectively to his world in terms of his conceptual systems. Even such a simple task as estimating the size of coins bears the imprint of one's personal convictions. Poor children, who value money more highly than rich children do, actually think coins are larger than they really are. In a similar vein, people who are hungry have more thoughts of food, talk about food and see more food objects in their environment than do people who are not hungry. The extreme case is that of hallucinations, in which a person is under the influence of such a strong idea that he builds the world in the image of that idea.

It is clear from these many examples that man's conduct is the visible embodiment of his conceptions, that behavior is the shadowing forth of deeply recessed mental states. During sleep, when the mind turns in upon itself, these recesses are explored and charted in the shape of dreams. Dreams, in effect, provide us with maps of regions which are inaccessible in waking consciousness. With these maps we are better able to follow the course of man's behavior, to understand why he selects one road rather than another, to anticipate the difficulties and obstacles he will encounter, and to predict his destinations.

In looking back over what we have written it strikes us that we have presented a rather gloomy picture of man. We have talked a great deal about his conflicts and anxieties, his perplexities and predicaments, and scarcely at all about man's joys and accomplishment. In a sense this is not our fault since we have let the dreams of man fashion their own picture of him. Our role has been that of interpreter, not creator. We have tried to put in everything about man that we have found in his dreams, without distorting, exaggerating or concealing the actual picture.

The fact of the matter is that dreams do not have much to say about the joys and accomplishments of man. Nor is this to be accounted for by the kind of people whose dreams have been studied. Our informants are not neurotic individuals. They are not social misfits or psychiatric patients. They are, on the whole, an accomplished, capable group of people who have had more than their share of successes and gratifications in life. As a group they are probably pretty much like the readers of this article.

Dreams of successful achievement are rare because our accomplishments do not provide the mind with energy and tension. An accomplishment represents a reduction of tension, and without tension there is no thinking and no dreaming. Since we only dream when there is a problem to dream about it follows that our dreams are more concerned with the complexities of life than with its simplicities. In fact when we run across a dream series which is replete with simple wish fulfillment we suspect that the dreamer is indulging in magical thinking. He is evading his problems instead of facing them.

There is a positive side to this depressing dream picture of man. After all, man cannot solve his problems unless he recognizes them for what they are and then tries to think his way through to rational solutions. Nothing is to be gained and a lot may be lost by glossing over the very real contradictions which exist in man. We certainly cannot cause these contradictions to disappear by drugging our minds with sentimental moonshine and happy endings.

Throughout history man has displayed considerable creativity in mastering problems of existence and in discovering the secrets of the physical world. By using his intelligence he has made the world a more comfortable place in which to live. The accomplishments of science and technology are among the most notable achievements of the human mind. Nor has man ever quailed for long before the immensity of the problems facing him. Goaded on by insatiable curiosity, man has penetrated deeper and deeper into the nature of the material environment.

When he is asleep and dreaming his mind is occupied with other kinds of problems than those of the external world. Dreams attempt to solve the inner problems of the person himself. Dreaming like all thinking is essentially a creative process, and not a soporific one as daydreaming is. Dreams are the products of good hard thought and it is too bad that man ignores them as he does.

We suggest that man begin to pay attention to his dreams and that he learn to use them as the starting point for additional creative thinking about his personal problems. If he would give as much thought to himself during the day as he does during the night, man might deepen his self-knowledge to the point where he could master his conflicts instead of being mastered by them. For it is only by being completely self-conscious that man can be rational and wise in all of his undertakings.

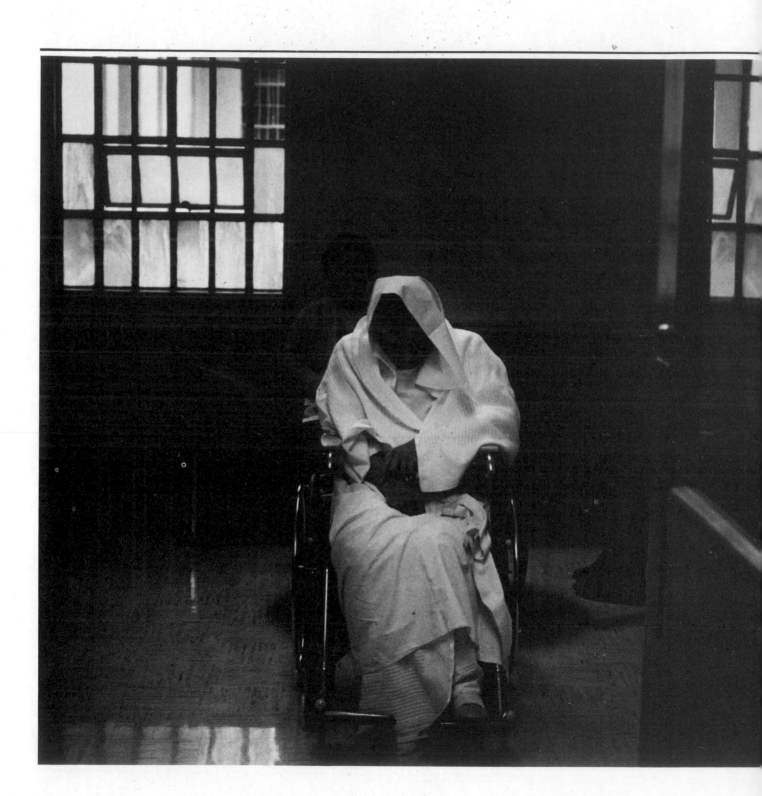

ALTERED STATES OF CONSCIOUSNESS

Out of the total range of states the human nervous system potentially allows us to experience, we actually enter a range of states drastically narrowed by our upbringing. What is normal for one culture—say, the everyday trance anthropologists report among Balinese—can be rare or nonexistent for people in another culture. Each of us has a typical range of states of consciousness; the range of states any one person normally experiences can be quite different from another person's normal range. When we break through this normal range of experience, we enter an altered state of consciousness.

THE NATURE OF ALTERED STATES

Charles Tart defines some basic terms in the study of consciousness. Within a person's normal range there are innumerable *discrete* states of consciousness, each noticeably different from all others. Fatigue, excitement, sexual arousal, rage, and fear are all discrete states of consciousness, each unique as an experience and as a pattern of brain arousal. Such discrete states are within normal bounds; when a shift in consciousness overleaps the normal limits of consciousness, it is an *altered* state. But normality is relative. For that reason, strictly speaking, an altered state is any shift in consciousness away from an ordinary, *baseline* state of consciousness. If a person's waking state is the baseline, then sleep, dreams, drunkenness, and meditative absorption are all altered states.

When researchers investigate states of consciousness they look for the most rigorous criteria to define the boundaries of various states. People have always known that the dream state is radically different from waking, but only with the discovery in the 1950s of rapid eye movement during dreaming have researchers been able to find the hard index of dreaming that let them comfortably speak of it as a distinct state. This research strategy, called "convergent operations," defines a state's boundaries by bringing together a person's reports of a state with what researchers can observe of the behavior and bodily reactions. Psychologist Ernest Hilgard suggests that this same approach can be fruitfully applied to the study of hypnotic trance, as well as the whole range of altered states.

Many discrete states of consciousness are brought about by a change in the brain's arousal level as it swings through the spectrum from deep sleep through meditative states to normal busy alertness, then beyond through hyperactive agitation to an arousal peak of ecstacy. At each discrete level the brain processes information differently, perceives uniquely, and has its own set of characteristic memories. Alcohol gives us the most common example of what Roland Fischer calls "state-specific knowledge," where the sober person cannot recall what he did the night before while drunk, until he again becomes drunk and the memories flood in.

The Systems Approach to States of Consciousness

Charles T. Tart

Our ordinary state of consciousness is not something natural or given, but a highly complex construction, a specialized tool for coping with our environment and the people in it, a tool that is useful for doing some things but not very useful, and even dangerous, for doing other things. As we look at consciousness closely, we see that it can be analyzed into many parts. Yet these parts function together in a pattern: they form a system. While the components of consciousness can be studied in isolation, they exist as parts of a complex system, consciousness, and can be fully understood only when we see this function in the overall system. Similarly, understanding the complexity of consciousness requires seeing it as a system and understanding the parts. For this reason, I refer to my approach to states of consciousness as a systems approach.

To understand the constructed system we call a state of consciousness, we begin with some theoretical postulates based on human experience. The first postulate is the existence of a basic awareness. Because some volitional control of the focus of awareness is possible, we generally refer to it as *attention/awareness*. We must also recognize the existnece of *self-awareness,* the awareness of being aware.

Further basic postulates deal with *structures,* those relatively permanent structures/functions/subsystems of the mind/brain that act on information to transform it in various ways. Arithmetical skills, for example, constitute a (set of related) structure(s). The structures of particular interest to us are those that require some amount of attention/awareness to activate them. Attention/awareness acts as *psychological energy* in this sense. Most techniques for controlling the mind are ways of deploying attention/ awareness energy and other kinds of energies so as to activate desired structures (traits, skills, attitudes) and deactivate undesired structures.

Psychological structures have individual characteristics that limit and shape the ways in which they can interact with one another. Thus the possibilities of any system built of psychological structures are shaped and limited both by the deployment of attention/awareness and other energies and by the characteristics of the structures comprising the system. The human biocomputer, in other words, has a large but limited number of possible modes of functioning.

Because we are creatures with a certain kind of body and nervous system, a large number of human potentials are in principle available to us. But each of us is born into a particular culture that selects and develops a small number of these potentials, rejects other, and is ignorant of many. The small number of experiential potentials selected by our culture, plus some random factors, constitute the structural elements from which our ordinary state of consciousness is constructed. We are at once the beneficiaries and the victims of our culture's particular selection. The possibility of tapping and developing latent potentials, which lie outside the cultural norm, by entering an altered state of consciousness, by temporarily *restructuring* consciousness, is the basis of the great interest in such states.

The terms *state of consciousness* and *altered state of consciousness* have come to be used too loosely, to mean whatever is on one's mind at the moment. The new term *discrete state of consciousness* (d-SoC) is proposed for greater precision. A d-SoC is a unique, dynamic pattern or configuration of psychological structures, an active system of psychological subsystems. Although the component structures/subsystems show some variation within a d-SoC, the overall pattern, the overall system properties remain recognizably the same. If, as you sit reading, you think, "I am dreaming," instead of "I am awake," you have changed a small cognitive element in your consciousness but not affected at all the basic pattern we call your waking state. In spite of subsystem variation and environmental variation, a d-SoC is stabilized by a number of processes so that it retains its identity and function. By analogy, an automobile remains an automobile whether on a road or in a garage (environment change), whether you change the brand of spark plugs or the color of the seat covers (internal variation).

Examples of d-SoC's are the ordinary waking state, nondreaming sleep, dreaming sleep, hypnosis, alcohol intoxication, marijuana intoxication, and meditative states.

A *discrete altered state of consciousness* (d-ASC) refers to a d-SoC that is different from some *baseline state of consciousness* (b-SoC). Usually the ordinary state is taken as the baseline state. A d-ASC is a new system with unique properties of its own, a restructuring of consciousness. *Altered* is intended as a purely descriptive term, carrying no values.

Our current knowledge of human consciousness and d-SoC is highly fragmented and chaotic. The main purpose of the systems approach presented here is organizational: it allows us to relate what were formerly disparate bits of data and supplies numerous methodological consequences for guiding future research. It makes the general prediction that the number of d-SoCs available to human beings is definitely limited, although we do not yet know those limits. It further provides a paradigm for making more specific predictions to sharpen our knowledge of the structures and subsystems that make up human consciousness.

There are enormously important individual differences in the structure of d-SoCs. If we map the experiential space in which two people function, one person may show two discrete, separated clusters of experiential functioning (two d-SoCs), while the other may show continuous functioning throughout both regions and the connecting regions of experiential space. The first person must make a special effort to travel from one region of experiential space (one d-SoC) to the other; the second makes no special effort and does not experience the contrast of pattern and structure differences associated with the two regions (the two d-SoCs). Thus what is a special *state* of consciousness for one person may be an everyday experience for another. Great confusion results if we do not watch for these differences: unfortunately, many widely used experimental procedures are not sensitive to these individual differences.

Induction of a d-ASC involves two basic operations that, if successful, lead to the d-ASC from the b-SoC. First we apply *disrupting forces* to the b-SoC—psychological and/or physiological actions that disrupt the stabilization processes discussed above either by interfering with them or by withdrawing attention/awareness energy or other kinds of energies from them. Because a d-SoC is a complex system, with multiple stabilization processes operating simultaneously, induction may not work. A psychedelic drug, for example, may not produce a d-ASC because psychological stabilization processes hold the b-SoC stable in spite of the disrupting action of the drug on a physiological level.

If induction is proceeding successfully, the disrupting forces push various structures/subsystems to their limits of stable functioning and then beyond, destroying the integrity of the system and disrupting the stability of the b-SoC as a system. Then, in the second part of the induction process, we apply *patterning forces* during this transitional, disorganized period—psychological and/or physiological actions that pattern structures/subsystems into a new system, the desired d-ASC. The new system, the d-ASC, must develop its own stabilization processes if it is to last.

Deinduction, return to the b-SoC, is the same process as induction. The d-ASC is disrupted, a transitional period occurs, and the b-SoC is reconstructed by patterning forces. The subject transits back to his customary region of experiential space.

Psychedelic drugs like marijuana or LSD do not have invariant psychological effects, even though much mis-guided research assumes they do. In the present approach, such drugs are disrupting and patterning forces whose effects occur in combination with other psychological factors, all mediated by the operating d-SoC. Consider the so-called reverse tolerance effect of marijuana that allows new users to consume very large quantities of the drug with no feeling of being stoned (in a d-ASC), but later to use much smaller quantities of marijuana to achieve the d-ASC. This is not paradoxical in the systems approach, even though it is paradoxical in the standard pharmacological approach. The physiological action of the marijuana is not sufficient to disrupt the ordinary d-SoC until additional psychological factors disrupt enough of the stabilization processes of the b-SoC to allow transition to the d-ASC. These additional psychological forces are usually "a little help from my friends," the instructions for deployment of attention/awareness energy given by experienced users who know what functioning in the d-ASC of marijuana intoxication is like. These instructions also serve as patterning forces to shape the d-ASC, to teach the new user how to employ the physiological effects of the drug to form a new system of consciousness.

The systems approach can also be applied within the ordinary d-SoC to deal with *identity states,* those rapid shifts in the central core of a person's identity and concerns that are overlooked for many reasons, and emotional states. Similarly the systems approach indicates that latent human potential can be developed and used in various d-ASCs, so that learning to shift into the d-ASC appropriate for dealing with a particular problem is part of psychological growth. At the opposite extreme, certain kinds of psychopathology, such as multiple personality, can be treated as d-ASCs.

One of the most important consequences of the systems approach is the deduction that we need to develop *state-specific sciences.* Insofar as a "normal" d-SoC is a semi-arbitrary way of structuring consciousness, a way that loses some human potentials while developing others, the sciences we have developed are one-state sciences. They are limited in important ways. Our ordinary sciences have been very successful in dealing with the physical world, but not very successful in dealing with particularly human psychological problems. If we apply scientific method to developing sciences within various d-ASCs, we can evolve sciences based on radically different perceptions, logics, and communications, and so gain new views complementary to our current ones.

The search for new views, new ways of coping, through the experience of d-ASCs is hardly limited to science. It is a major basis for our culture's romance with drugs, meditation, Eastern religions, and the like. But infatuation with a new view, a new d-SoC, tends to make us forget that *any* d-SoC is a limited construction. There is a price to be paid for everything we get. It is vital for us to develop sciences of this powerful, life-changing area of d-ASCs if we are to optimize benefits from the growing use of them and avoid the dangers of ignorant or superstitious tampering with the basic structure of consciousness.

Altered States of Awareness

Ernest R. Hilgard

WAKING AS A COMPLEX STATE

By a normal waking state we mean one in which we can report accurately what is happening in the environment about us and can use this information to control our behavior. We do not do these things well when we are asleep, or drugged, or delirious. Under those other conditions most of us are willing to say that someone is in an altered state, even though the borderlines are hard to define.

A little reflection will show us that the waking state itself is far from simple. When we carry on a conversation, we are simultaneously listening and formulating a reply, and even while replying we are thinking of our next maneuver. Thus we are not doing just one thing at a time, and how many things we can do at once, and how well we do them, pose problems for experimental study. This is the kind of thing that sets the functionalist to work; subjective observation has set him some problems that he hopes he can solve by objective methods. His preference for operationism does not make him deny the problems. He performs experiments on listening to more than one conversation at a time, on one message to one ear and another to the other, on reciting aloud what is coming in over earphones, with informative results (10). It takes a little effort to remain alert, even when we are not very tired, and to avoid vacant staring we do a good deal of squirming about, chewing of pencils, lighting a pipe, adjusting clothing, or talking merely to eliminate silence. My point here, as against those who deny "states," is that I see no reason to deny that being awake is a state, even though it is hard to give it a fully satisfactory definition.

SLEEPING AND DREAMING AS ALTERED STATES

With the discovery of the rapid eye movement state of sleep (the REM state) and another state of sleep, defined negatively as non-rapid eye movement (the NREM state), we now understand quite well that there are at least three states where before we thought there were only two. That is the sleep state is divided (in addition to several levels of depth) into two quite distinct states with different properties. But I should like to point out something here: it did not take electroencephalographic (EEG) studies to tell us that there were two states, such as waking and sleeping,

even though it was sometimes hard to tell when a person was asleep (or merely playing possum). If he was trustworthy, he would tell you when he was simulating sleep, although sometimes, when really asleep, he might deny having been asleep. It is important to remember this when we come to the discussion of hypnosis, for the dismissal of hypnosis as a state because we don't know its physiology would be like dismissing sleep as a state *before* we knew its physiology. Lack of perfect correlation and ill defined border conditions do not prevent useful experiments from reaching satisfactory inferences through convergent operations (15).

Fortunately, the study of sleep and dreaming has advanced greatly since the discovery of REM sleep by Aserinsky and Kleitman (1), and the questions of "state" are essentially now empirical ones. Stoyva and Kamiya (47) have made a very useful contribution to the discussion of a strategy for the study of consciousness by citing in some detail the recent history of research on sleeping and dreaming. Extending the notion of convergent operations, they have shown how useful the interchange has been between the physiological indicators (chiefly, but not exclusively, EEG and REM) and dream recall. There would be no way of knowing whether the eye movements were related to dreaming except by asking the subject. At the same time there is no certainty with respect to the subject's reported dream content. Only by exercising ingenuity in relating the two kinds of data (physiological response and verbal report) can the true state of affairs be inferred. Some of the work of Kamiya (cited in 29) on the operant control of the EEG alpha rhythms is referred to as a further illustration of the usefulness of combining objective measures with verbal reports. Under the conditions in which the alpha is "on," the subject commonly reports that he is relaxed and not experiencing visual imagery: he usually finds long periods of time in continuous alpha to be quite pleasant (35).

Our "inventory" of states now adds up to the three-fold cycle of waking, REM, and NREM, through which everyone goes every day, and now another set (alpha and non-alpha) through which people also go, but which they can learn to control in the laboratory, or in certain kinds of exercises, as under a Zen master.

If one wishes to argue that sleep is not a state, I have no quarrel with that, because then the argument is not over fact but over words. If sleep is not a state, then hypnosis is not a state either. But if sleep *is* a state, which I suppose most of us would accept, then maybe hypnosis is a state, too. Let us see where we are on empirical grounds.

Suppose we apply to sleep the same critical attacks that have been made on hypnosis. First, it is very difficult to define sleep; as Kleitman (26) pointed out, it is usually defined negatively as the opposite of wakefulness. It is hard to distinguish it from coma, for example, except by some sort of operational definition: you can be aroused from sleep, but not from coma. (This departs from a "state" definition and hence can be used to argue against sleep as a state.) Or suppose you build some sort of behavioral test for sleep, such as what the person tells you when you wake him up ("I must have been asleep, because I didn't hear you come in"), whether or not he reports a dream, or some more "objective" measures such as whether or not he snores or how loud a bell it takes to rouse him. These would not work out too badly, but they would be subject to the same criticisms as those leveled against hypnotic scales. For one thing, any of these measures can be "faked." A person can imitate snoring, even though he is not asleep; he can report a dream when he had none. Therefore, we do better to abandon the notion of "sleep," write the word in quotation marks, and stick to the input-output measures that we use in experiments concerned with the phenomena associated with a person who is lying in bed at night with his eyes closed.

Those who might wish to save sleep as a state, but still reject hypnosis, have another line of argument. Because of the EEG we now have a physiological definition of sleep and hence are on much more secure ground when we study, for example, the question of whether or not sleep-learning is possible. This is a good argument, but it does not completely escape the circularity that the EEG measures of depth of sleep can only be validated by behavioral measures. It turns out, in fact, that is is more difficult to be aroused from stage 1 than from "deeper" stages, if REMs are occurring in stage 1. This evidence comes not from physiology but from behavior, although, to the extent that there are lawful correlates, everything remains in order. It would be a great help to the researcher on hypnosis if there were physiological indicators such as the EEG in sleep, to help define more precisely what condition the subject is in. The search for such indicators, as illustrated by our use of the blood pressure measure in relation to pain, is valid and should be pressed. But the question I am raising is this: would we have denied sleep as a "state" before the EEG measures were available? I think not. Perhaps hypnosis research lags behind sleep research by a decade or two. Hence I do not believe that the absence of clear physiological correlates of hypnosis is crucial in the answer to the question of whether or not it represents a state.

The temptation to use state as a cause or an explanation is another matter. Even though snoring and dreams typically occur during sleep, it does not help very much to say that sleep causes them, for of course it is possible to sleep without snoring or dreaming. Still it does no harm to point out that their presence is *more likely* during sleep. This is an empirical question, and similar empirical questions arise in relation to hypnosis: is typical hypnotic behavior more likely when the conditions have been favorable for entering a hypothesized hypnotic state? The empirical answer is not as easy as might be supposed. In one of our investigations concerned with this problem we found that it was necessary to use careful designs to demonstrate rather small increments as a result of hypnotic induction (21). As Tart and I pointed out, the experimental design must take into account the following considerations: 1) many nonhypnotizable people are not going to change following attempted induction; 2) some highly susceptible subjects do not require induction to enter hypnosis and yield all the phenomena, and hence they do not change between waking suggestion and hypnosis; 3) the argument for change with induction therefore rests on a minority of subjects who respond only slightly to waking suggestion but are very responsive to suggestion after induction procedures. Under these circumstances, small groups of unselected subjects are quite likely to lead to no statistical difference attributable to induction, especially if extraneous demands toward increasing voluntary compliance are added in the nonhypnotic condition. While our conditions, favorable to detecting small changes, led to the conclusion that the effects of induction could be demonstrated, the matter is still subject to some empirical controversy (6). Although the question of the effects of induction continues to be of interest, it is not crucial to the question whether or not some subjects can enter a state of hypnosis. That has to be determined on more subtle grounds, using converging operations which will doubtless include subjective report, overt behavior, and physiological indicators.

Suppose the results turn out that there are phenomena associated with the hypnotic state that are not as likely when the subject is not in that state. It is possible to accept all of this without making the state of hypnosis the cause of the behavior, any more than sleep causes snoring or dreams.

Note also that the use of a classificatory rubric does not require that there be no differentiation within that rubric. Thus sleep turns out not to be one state but at least two (REM and NREM). This does not negate a differentiation between sleep and waking: both the REM subject and NREM subject are still asleep. I doubt if there will turn out to be just one state of hypnosis; subjects capable of deep relaxation under hypnosis are also capable of alert hyperactivity, and only careful study will reveal what it is that they have in common physiologically. But there is no harm in still defining the area of experimental study as that of hypnosis, just as the student of REM and NREM sleep still studies sleep.

It would be possible to go on to the definition of other kinds of altered states of awareness, such as those engendered by fever or by drugs. These cover a wide range from stupor to ecstasy. All the arguments over states as descriptive and as explanatory apply here as well. The work of Schachter and Singer (41) shows how careful we have to be before we assign emotional states on the basis on the kind of drug ingested. This does not require us to argue that emotion is a myth.

REFERENCES

1. ASERINSKY, E., and KLEITMAN, N. Regularly occurring periods of eye mobility, and concomitant phenomena, during sleep. Science, *118:* 273-274, 1953.
2. BANDURA, A., and WALTERS, R. *Social Learning and Personality Development.* Holt, Rinehart, and Winston, New York, 1963.
3. BARBER, T. S. "Hypnosis" as a causal variable in present-day psychology: A critical analysis, Psychol. Rep., *14:* 839-942, 1964.
4. BARBER, R. X. Hypnotic phenomena: A critique of experimental methods. In Gordon, J. E., ed. *Handbook of Clinical and Experimental Hypnosis,* pp. 444-480. Macmillan, New York, 1967.
5. BARBER, T. X. Reply to Conn and Conn's "Discussion of Barber's 'Hypnosis as a causal variable. . .' " Int. J. Clin. Exp. Hypn., *15:* 111-117, 1967.
6. BARBER, T. X., and CALVERLEY, D. C. Toward a theory of "hypnotic" behavior: Replication and extension of experiments by Barber and co-workers (1962-65) and Hilgard and Tart (1966). Int. J. Clin. Exp. Hypn., *16:* 179-195, 1968.
7. BARBER, T. X., and HAHN, K. W., JR. Physiological and subjective responses to pain-producing stimulation under hypnotically suggested and waking-imagined "analgesia." J. Abnorm. Soc. Psychol., *65:* 411-418, 1962.
8. BARRON, F. *Creativity and Personal Freedom.* Van Nostrand, New York, 1968.
9. BOWERS, K. Hypnotic behavior: The differentiation of trance and demand characteristic variable. J. Abnorm. Psychol., *71:* 42-51, 1966.
10. BROADBENT, D. E. *Perception and Communication,* Pergamon, New York, 1958.
11. BUGENTAL, J. F. The challenge that is man. J. Humanistic Psychol., *7:* 1-9, 1967.
12. CHAVES, J. F. Hypnosis reconceptualized: An overview of Barber's theoretical and empirical work, Psychol. Rep., *23:* 587-608, 1968.
13. DEWEY, J. The reflex are concept in psychology. Psychol. Rev., *3:* 357-370, 1896.
14. GALANTER, E., and GERSTENHABER, M. On thought: The extrinsic theory, Psychol. Rev., *63:* 218-227, 1956.
15. GARNER, W. R., HAKE, H. W., and ERIKSEN, C. W. Operationism and the concept of perception. Psychol. Rev., *63:* 145-159, 1956.
16. GILL, M. M., and BRENMAN, M. *Hypnosis and Related States.* International Universities Press, New York, 1959.
17. HILGARD, E. R. Pain as a puzzle for psychology and physiology. Amer. Psychol., *24:* 103-113, 1969.
18. HILGARD, E. R. A quantitative study of pain and its reduction through hypnotic suggestion. Proc. Nat. Aead. Sci. U.S.A., *57:* 1581-1586, 1967.
19. HILGARD, E. R. *Theories of Learning,* 1st ed. Appleton-Century-Crofts, New York, 1948.
20. HILGARD, E. R., COOPER, L. M., LENOX, J., MORGAN, A. H., and VOEVODSKY, J. The use of pain-state reports in the study of hypnotic analgesia to the pain of ice water. J. Nerv. Ment. Dis., *144:* 506-513, 1967.
21. HILGARD, E. R., and TART, C. T. Responsiveness to suggestion following waking and imagination instructions and following induction of hypnosis, J. Abnorm. Psychol., *71:* 196-208, 1966.
22. HILGARD, J. R. *Personality and Hypnosis: A Study of Imaginative Involvements.* University of Chicago Press, in press.
23. HINES, E. A., and BROWN, G. E. A standard stimulus for measuring vasomotor reactions; Its application in the study of hypertension. Proe. Staff Meetings Mayo Clin., *7:* 332, 1932.
24. HOLT, R. R. Imagery: The return of the ostracized. Amer. Psychol., *19:* 254-264, 1964.
25. JAMES, W. *Principles of Psychology,* vols. 1 and 2. Holt, New York, 1890.
26. KLEITMAN. N. *Sleep and Wakefulness,* rev. ed. University of Chicago Press, Chicago, 1963.
27. KUBIE, L. S., and MARGOLIN, S. The process of hypnotism and the nature of the hypnotic state. Amer. J. Psychiat., *100:* 611-622, 1944.
28. LEWIS, T., PICKERING, G. W., and ROTHSCHILD, P. Observations upon muscular pain in intermittent claudication. Heart, *15:* 359-383, 1931.
29. LUCE, G. G., and SEGAL, J. *Sleep.* Coward-McCann, New York, 1966.
30. MASLOW, A. H. *Toward a Psychology of Being,* Van Nostrand, Princeton, N.J., 1962.
31. McClelland, D. C. The psychology of mental content reconsidered. Psychol. Rev., *62:* 297-302, 1955.
32. MILLER, G. A., GALANTER, E., and Pribram, K. H. *Plans and the Structure of Behavior.* Holt-Dryden, New York, 1960.
33. MISCHEL, W. *Personality and Assessment.* Wiley, New York, 1968.
34. MURPHY, G. *Human Potentialities.* Basic Books, New York, 1958.
35. NOWLIS, D. The control of EEG alpha through auditory feedback and the associated mental activity. Unpublished manuscript, 1968.
36. ORNE, M. T. Hypnosis, motivation, and compliance. Amer. J. Psychiat., *122:* 721-726, 1966.
37. OTTO, H. A., ed. *Human Potentialities: The Challenge and the Promise.* Warren H. Green, St. Louis, 1967.
38. SARBIN, T. R. The concept of hallucination. J. Personality, *35:* 359-380, 1967.
39. SARBIN, T. R. Ontology recapitulates philology: The mythic nature of anxiety. Amer. Psychol., *23:* 411-418. 1968.
40. SARBIN, T. R., and ANDERSEN, M. L. Role-theoretical analysis of hypnotic behavior. In Gordon, J. E., ed. *Handbook of Clinical and Experimental Hypnosis,* pp. 319-324. Macmillan, New York, 1967.
41. SCHACHTER, S., and SINGER, J. E. Cognitive, social, and physiological determinants of emotional state. Psychol. Rev., *69:* 379-399, 1962.
42. SEVERIN, F. T. ed. *Humanistic Viewpoints in Psychology.* McGraw-Hill, New York, 1965.
43. SHOR, R. E. Physiological effects of painful stimulation during hypnotic analgesia under conditions designed to minimize anxiety. Int. J. Clin. Exp. Hypn., *10:* 183-202, 1962.
44. SKINNER, B. F. *Verbal Behavior.* Appleton-Century-Crofts, New York, 1957.
45. SMITH, G. M., LAWRENCE, D. E., MARKOWITZ, R. A., MOSTELLER, F., and BEECHER, H. K. An experimental pain method sensitive to morphine in man: The submaximum effort tourniquet technique. J. Pharmacol. Exp. Ther., *154:* 324-332, 1966.
46. STEVENS, S. S. Matching functions between loudness and ten other continua. Percept. Psychophysics, *1:* 5-8, 1966.
47. STOYVA, J., and KAMIYA, J. Electrophysiological studies of dreaming as the prototype of a new strategy in the study of consciousness. Psychol. Rev., *75:* 192-205, 1968.
48. THURSTONE, L. L. The stimulus-response fallacy in psychology. Psychol. Rev., *30:* 354-369, 1923.
49. WOLF, S., and HARDY, J. D. Studies on pain: Observations on pain due to local cooling and on factors involved in the "cold pressor" effect. J. Clin. Invest., *20:* 521-533, 1941.

State-Bound Knowledge

Roland Fischer

In the film *City Lights,* Charlie Chaplin saves a drunken millionaire from an attempted suicide and becomes his friend. When sober, the millionaire has no memory of Charlie. But he soon gets drunk and again spots Charlie, treats him like a long-lost friend, and takes him home to his mansion. Sober the next morning, the millionaire forgets Charlie is his invited guest and has the butler throw him out.

Charlie's story illustrates an amnesia between states of mind that most of us may have experienced. Like the drunken millionaire, we may forget on a sober morning what we did or said at a party the night before. Or the memory of a relaxing vacation fades as we slide back into the frenetic pace of a working day. In both cases, our experience is state-bound, i.e., tied to a particular state of consciousness. The reality of the event is most vivid in the state it was first experienced, and less so in other states.

States of consciousness depend on the level of arousal in both brain and body. The level fluctuates greatly during the day. When we are anxious or excited, the brain speeds up its rate of information processing—that is, how it organizes and reacts to what it takes in through the senses. At the same time, the body quickens its autonomic activity, speeding up heart rate, sweat levels, and other systems. When we relax, these rates slow down.

The brain processes and stores information differently at each level of arousal. The same event is very different in our perception, depending on whether we are calm, in a panic, or in between. Our memory of events, I believe, is distributed over a variety of arousal states. Each bit of knowledge is bound to, and most easily retrieved at, a particular level of arousal. The greater the difference between these states, the more difficult it is to recall in one state specifics learned in another.

Lost access. The difficulty in remembering events that occurred in another state of arousal has long posed a problem in court cases. Witnesses to violent crimes, for example, often produce vague or incorrect testimony because of amnesia between states. Witnessing a robbery, rape, or murder can put a person into a state of extreme arousal. When the witness later tries to recall the crime in court, he is no longer aroused and do does not have free access to his memory of the crime. The closer the states of arousal are, the easier it is to remember from one to the other. I have developed a diagram of arousal states. It helps us see which states are near each other, and which deviate most from our normal waking state.

Beyond normal busy alertness, the person moves through more intense levels of sensitivity, creativity, and then anxiety. Then come conditions of hyperarousal, which include manic or acute schizophrenic episodes. Catatonia, oddly enough, is the height of schizophrenic brain arousal. The catatonic sits frozen because his brain is racing so fast he cannot keep up with his thoughts to make a move. Going further, there is the arousal peak of the mystic's ecstasy.

The rebound phenomenon. In the opposite direction, arousal sinks beyond simple relation into the tranquillity of Zen meditation, where the mind is in a quiet state of alertness. In deeper meditation, body and mind become progressively more quiescent as concentration becomes more focused. At first, the person's attention focuses on a single object. Later the mind seems to merge with the object; there are no other thoughts whatever. Finally, the mind, though alert, is without a single thought, not even the original point of focus. Paradoxically, low and high arousal states meet at this extreme, because of the phenomenon psychophsiologists know as "rebound."

In rebound, a biological system pushed to the limits of stillness or of aroused excitation will snap back to the opposite pole of arousal. An infant breathless and red from tantrum, for example, suddenly drops off to sleep. Rebound seems to be a built-in safety mechanism that protects our bodies from the adverse effects of extreme arousal. At the height of increasing arousal, as in the mystic's ecstasy, intense brain activity suddenly gives way to a quiet state of deep calm. Or, in the opposite case, low arousal of deep meditation surges into the ecstatic awakening of kundalini Yoga. Either way, the extremes of high and low arousal connect through rebound.

Conscious awareness seems to come from the combination of our state of arousal and the symbol or lables we connect with that state. In the normal arousal range, there is flexibility in the interpretations we attach to arousal levels. Stanley Schachter, a psychologist at Columbia University, has shown that people experience the same arousal state as either pleasure or anger, depending on the cues provided by their surrounding. When volunteers Schachter injected with adrenalin were with a happy, joking stooge, they reported feeling pleasantly aroused; when other volunteers given the same injection were with a hostile stooge they felt angry. In both situations the physiological arousal was the same, but the person's interpretations of the physical effects of the drug varied with the situation.

Tea-soaked cake.   As a person approaches the extremes of high or low arousal, he has fewer labels available for interpreting his state. At the most extreme levels, there is a virtual loss of freedom in interpretation, since meaning is only meaningful at that level of arousal at which it is experienced. The enraptured mystic and entranced meditator have few words with which to label their altered state. Only the creative mystic has no difficulty describing his transcendental experience. Creativity is the ability to recollect thoughts or images experienced at a variety of arousal levels. For this reason mystics have always had difficulty describing transcendental experiences.

Since experience is the product of both arousal and the symbol or label for that level of arousal, the full memory of an experience can be triggered either by duplicating the original level or by evoking some symbol of it. A famous example is Proust in *Swann's Way,* when he tastes a tea-soaked cake like those of his childhood and is instantly flooded with a stream of early memories. One of the oldest descriptions of the symbolic triggering of a state-bound memory comes from the Spaniard Juan Luis Vives, who wrote in 1538, "When I was a boy in Valencia, I was ill of a fever; while my taste was deranged I ate cherries; for many years afterwards, whenever I tasted the fruit I not only recalled the fever, but also seemed to experience it again."

T. S. Eliot consciously used symbols to evoke arousal states. In his theory of the "objective correlative," he proposed that the poet elicits specific emotions in his audience by his use of symbols. In a set of objects, a situation, or a chain of events, the poet creates a formula for evoking a particular emotion. I extend Eliot's idea to all the arts. Specific emotions can be evoked by a melody or image as well as by a flow of words. We feel very different about the calm placidity of a Constable landscape, the sensual richness of Rousseau's plush jungles, and the tortured faces of Munch's portraits. Each of these visual images triggers a specific emotional state.

Partial amnesia.   The other route to re-experiencing the state-bound past is through duplicating the arousal level of the previous experience. One therapist says that when he uses sodium amytal ("truth serum") as part of psychotherapy, his patient picks up his narrative each time exactly where he left off at the close of the previous session.

Alcohol is the most common route to an altered state, and provides the best documentation of state-bound memory. Research headed by Herbert Weingartner at the National Institute of Mental Health in Bethesda may explain the erratic actions of Charlie Chaplin's drunken millionaire. Weingartner's team wondered if we don't remember things in different ways when we are drunk or sober, so that a partial amnesia exists between these states. They had volunteers learn a list of 10 words, then asked them to recite the words when they were either in the same

state as when they learned them or in the opposite state. Recall was best when a volunteer was in the same state as when he learned the words, whether drunk or sober. This partial amnesia between states means that people do not necessarily remember events better when sober than when drunk. They remember best when in the same state as when the original event occurred. Other studies have shown that this rule of thumb also holds for altered states induced by amphetamines, barbiturates, and marijuana.

Weingartner's study of state-bound memory suggests a general principle for increasing our memory of things. We should reenter the state we were in during the original moment. This principle may explain why psychoanalysts since Freud have had their patients lie on a couch and free-associate as they search back to childhood's traumas and triumphs. The reverie of the free-associating patient produces a slowed brain-wave rhythm, like that of children when they are awake and alert. By slowing their brain waves to the rate of a child's, patients in analysis may increase their chances of recalling events from childhood.

I carry the same-state, better-memory rule a step further. Since some degree of anmesia exists between our normal everyday state and other states of increased or decreased arousal, it may be that when is called the "subconscious" is but another name for this amnesia. Instead of there being just one subconscious, therefore, there are as many layers as there are arousal levels. These many layers remind me of a captain with girl friends in several ports, each unaware of the existence of the others, and each existing for him from visit to visit—that is, from state to state.

Some of us can travel on the continuum of increasing and decreasing arousal more easily than other. I have identified the kind of person who moves most freely between arousal levels. I used a simple test in which a person copies a 28-word text four times on separate sheets of paper, and then computes the differences among the four sheets in the area covered by his handwriting. If the handwriting area varies greatly from sheet to sheet, the writer is likely to vary his behavior and perception often. This simple index of variability, we found, predicts the intensity of changes the person will experience on a psychedelic drug like psilocybin; the more variation his writing shows, the more intense his trip will be.

About one third of the population falls into the variable category, but only about one third of these can be easily hypnotized. The variability of this one-ninth of the population seems to indicate fluidity within mental states that allows them to flashback, that is, re-experience an altered state rather than simply remember it. For these people, movies, novels, and the like may be especially gripping, and the moods they evoke particularly real.

The richness of our daily experience is not limited to what we see and hear. Our lives are enriched also by the range of internal states from which we witness the seen and heard. In the words of Octavio Paz, "Memory is not that which we remember, but that which remembers us. Memory is a present that never stops passing."

DRUG-INDUCED ALTERED STATES

The direct relationship between states of consciousness and changes in the brain is most obvious with drug-induced states. Every drug that changes brain chemistry induces a distinctive state of consciousness. The hashish "high" is quite different from the amphetamine "high," and both differ from alcohol intoxication. Psychopharmocologist Murray Jarvik outlines the major brain-changing drugs, and what we know of the state they bring about. Someday in the future, Jarvik conjectures, it should be possible to detail a behavioral profile for every brain-changing drug.

Novelist Aldous Huxley, an early explorer in the effects of psychedelic drugs, describes his first voyage into the mescaline state. The changes for Huxley were not revolutionary—no hallucinations, no earth-shaking revelations. But his perceptions underwent an intensification so that the ordinary took on a dimension of profundity, colors became translucent, reality fluid. Reflecting on his experience, Huxley was reminded of the idea that the perceptual system of the brain is primarily a reducing valve, screening out most of the multitudinous bits of information our senses receive so that the brain can find some order and make sense of the world. Mescaline, he felt, swept away these screens, admitting him to perceive "Mind at Large," the richness of the world that in our ordinary state we cannot afford to experience if we are to survive.

The effects of another kind of drug, amphetamine, are very different from the pleasant changes Huxley describes under mescaline. "Speed-freaks," chronic abusers of amphetamines, begin to think and act like paranoid schizophrenics. For this reason researcher Solomon Snyder conjectures that "speed" offers the best chemical model of schizophrenia, producing in the user brain changes akin to those the paranoid undergoes during an acute psychosis. The effects of speed on the brain are to make brain cells fire with much more rapidity than normal. The particular brain tracts affected seem to account for the unique pattern of euphoria, hyperalertness, repetitive actions, hyperactivity and sleeplessness that combine to flavor the user's state of consciousness.

The Psychopharmacological Revolution

Murray E. Jarvik

One hot August evening in 1955, Helen Burney sat listlessly on her bed in the violent ward of the large Texas hospital where she had been confined for the past four months. During most of that unhappy time, Helen had been highly vocal, abusive, and overactive. Only the day before she had tried to strike a ward aide, but immediately several burly attendants had grabbed her, roughly tying her into a straitjacket and pinioning her arms against her chest. But today Helen's behavior was very different. Her incessant talking and shouting had stopped; all day long she spoke only when spoken to; most of the time she lay on her bed with her eyes half closed, moving little, and looking rather pale. However, she was unusually cooperative with the nursing personnel, got out of bed when told to, and went to the dining room without resisting. What had happened to bring about this remarkable change?

That morning she had received an injection of a new synthetic drug, chlorpromazine, which had been discovered a few years earlier in France. On the same day thousands of mental patients throughout the world were receiving the same drug, many of them for the first time. News of the drug's usefulness had spread rapidly in the preceding months, and it was being tried in mental hospitals throughout the world. Few of those taking or administering the drug realized that they were participating in a revolution in psychiatric treatment. In fact, many psychiatrists felt that this drug would be no more effective in treating schizophrenia than the other drugs which had previously been tried with little success. But they were wrong—and luckily, too—for there was little else they could offer the masses of impoverished patients who clogged the mental institutions all over the world. Soon it would be difficult to find a psychotic patient who was not receiving a drug of some kind for the treatment of his illness. The era of clinical psychopharmacology had begun, and the new drugs were hailed as the first real breakthrough in the treatment of one of man's most serious and mysterious afflictions—psychosis.

Until it was discovered that drugs could help the severely disturbed, almost the only recourse in the management of such patients was physical restraint. Philippe Pinel, the famous French psychiatrist, campaigning for humane treatment of the insane at the end of the 18th century, freed the inmates of the grim Bicetre mental hospital from their iron chains. Unfortunately, other physical restraints had to be substituted when patients became assaultive or destructive, and though the padded cell and the camisole, or straitjacket, may have been softer than chains, they allowed no greater freedom. Not until the mid-1950s did drugs finally promise total emancipation from physical restraint for most patients. Despite the fears of some psychiatrists, psychologists, and social workers that the social and psychological factors contributing to mental illness would be ignored, the use of psychopharmaceuticals radically improved the treatment of the mentally ill within and without the hospital. Indeed, only with their use has it been possible for some families to be held together, for some individuals to be gainfully employed, and for some patients to be reached by psychotherapy.

Since 1955, psychopharmacology has burgeoned as an important scientific discipline in its own right. In the past 15 years, many new chemical agents have been developed for the treatment of each major category of mental illness. These drugs include phenothiazines, rauwolfia alkaloids, butyrophenones, propanediol and benzodiazepine compounds, monoamine oxidase (MAO) inhibitors, dibenzazepine derivatives, and many more. They have been found useful in the treatment of psychoses, neuroses, and depressions. Even autistic behavior, psychopathy, sexual deviation, and mental retardation have been attacked with drugs, but clinical psychopharmacologists feel that the surface has only been scratched in these areas. The search continues, though presently on a smaller scale than in the past, for more effective agents.

FOLK-PSYCHOPHARMACOLOGY

Although as a fullfledged scientific discipline psychopharmacology is less than 15 years old, the psychological effects of drugs have piqued the curiosity of occasional researchers for almost a hundred years. Indeed, it is surprising that interest was so slow in developing, for man's empirical knowledge of the effects of drugs on behavior is both ancient and widespread.

The records of mankind, going back thousands of years, are filled with anecdotal and clinical reports of the psychological action of drugs obtained from plants. Though we can be sure that most of these folk remedies were merely placebos, a few have demonstrable medicinal properties and are still in use today. The cuneiform tablets of ancient Assyria contain numerous references to medicinal preparations with psychological effects. For more than 5000 years, the Chinese have used the herb Ma Huang (yellow astringent), which contains the potent stimulant, ephedrine, and in the earliest writings of China, Egypt, and the Middle East there are references to the influence of various drugs on behavior.

In the first century before Christ, the Roman poet Horace wrote lyrically of the psychological effects of **alcohol**: "What wonders does not wine! It discloses secrets; ratifies and confirms our hopes; thrusts the coward forth to battle; eases the anxious mind of its burthern; instructs in arts. Whom has not a cheerful glass made eloquent! Whom not quite free and easy from pinching poverty!" And "In vino veritas" was already a familiar Roman adage when it was cited by Pliny.

Opium, an effective folk remedy, is mentioned in the Ebers papyrus, and Homer tells us that Helen of Troy took a "sorrow-easing drug" obtained from Egypt—probably opium. Although the analgesic and sedative properties of opium were extensively described in classical literature, little was said about its addictive properties until Thomas de Quincy hinted at them, early in the 19th century, in his *Confessions of an English Opium Eater.* And while the chemical isolation of morphine and the invention of the hypodermic needle, in the middle of the 19th century, made profound addiction truly feasible, morphine is still considered by many physicians the most essential drug they use—"God's own remedy."

Morphine and its derivatives and analogs (for example, heroin) are self-administered by countless thousands of people throughout the world, although in many countries, especially in the West, such use is illegal. The practice persists, nevertheless, perhaps for the reasons given by the French poet, Jean Cocteau, who was himself an addict: "Everything that we do in life, including love, is done in an express train traveling towards death. To smoke opium is to leave the train while in motion; it is to be interested in something other than life and death."

Like morphine, **cocaine** is another vegetable product discovered by primitive man. It is clearly not a placebo, and its use is illegal. The Indians of Peru have chewed coca leaves for centuries, and still do, to relieve hunger, fatigue, and the general burdens of a miserable life. The alkaloid cocaine was isolated in 1859, and its systematic use was not only practiced but advocated by such respected figures as Sigmund Freud and William Halsted, as well as by the legendary Sherlock Holmes. It is highly doubtful that the continued use of cocaine produces a physiological dependence. Today, cocaine-taking is relativley uncommon in the northern hemisphere.

On the other hand, an ancient drug which remains exceedingly popular, though its medical uses today are nil, is **marijuana**, the dried leaves of the hemp plant *Cannabis sativa.* Cannabis is so ubiquitous, and grows so easily, that its widespread use is not surprising. Marco Polo is credited with bringing the "Green Goddess" to the Occident, although Herodotus tells us that the Scythians inhaled the vapor, obtained by heating hemp seeds on redhot stones, and then "shouted for joy." To this day, cannabis is almost always smoked; this allows its active ingredients to be absorbed into the pulmonary blood circulation and, avoiding the liver, to be promptly carried to the brain. Similarly, the active ingredients of opium and tobacco are are usually self-administered by inhalation of the vapors from heated plant products.

Hashish, derived from cannabis, and smoked, chewed, or drunk, has been widely used for centuries throughout the Middle East. The Arabic term for a devotee of hashish is "hashshash;" from the plural, "hashshashin," comes the English word "assassin," for at the time of the Crusades, the Hashshashin were a fanatical secret Moslem sect who terrorized the Christians by swift and secret murder, after having taken hashish to give themselves courage. Richard Burton, the famous traveler, adventurer, and writer, described his experiences with hashish during a pilgrimage to Mecca at the end of the 19th century. About 50 years earlier, Moreau de Tours Suggested that physicians should take hashish in order to experience mental illness and thereby understand it better. Claude Bernard, the great French physiologist, is said to have declared that "hashish is the curare of the mind." Today we know a great deal about the mode of action of curare and almost nothing about that of hashish, but Bernard suggested a working hypothesis. Perhaps cannabis, like curare, blocks some vital neuro-humor in the brain.

Quantitative, objective studies of cannabis are rare, even today. However, a recent report by Carlini indicates that cannabis facilitates maze-learning in rats. In the absence of comparative studies, it is difficult to say how cannabis resembles or differs from other drugs; anecdotal reports suggest that it resembles lysergic acid diethylamide (LSD).

Another drug with a long history of use is **mescaline** or **peyote**, which the Aztecs are credited with having used five centuries ago, and which has been and still is used by certain Indians of Central America and the Southwest United States. Its effects resemble those of marijuana and LSD; they have also been compared with those of **psilocybin**, a drug which the Aztecs derived from a psychotogenic mushroom they called "teonanacatl," or "God's flesh."

THE CHEMICAL ERA

Until the 19th century, the only drugs known to affect behavior were those derived from plants and long familiar to mankind. With advances in chemistry during the first half of the 19th century, however, the general anesthetics, including nitrous oxide, diethyl ether, and chloroform were discovered and brought into widespread use; and by the time Emil Kraepelin began his psychopharmacological investigations in the 1880's, a few new sedatives, including the bromides and chloral hydrate, were available.

Nitrous oxide, an artificially prepared inhalation anesthetic, was investigated by Sir Humphrey Davy, who described its effects thus in 1799: "I lost all connections with external things; trains of vivid images rapidly passed through my mind and even connected with words in such a manner as to produce perceptions perfectly novel. I existed in a world of newly connected and newly modified ideas."

Inhaling nitrous oxide soon became a favorite student diversion, and enterprising showmen charged admission for public demonstrations of its effects; the popular interest in this gas reminds one very much of the current preoccupation with LSD. But though nitrous oxide was beguiling to thrill seekers, it never became as popular as LSD, perhaps because the gas is difficult to transport. Although **diethyl ether** was originally prepared in 1543 by Valerius Cordus when he distilled alcohol with sulfuric acid, its potential as an anesthetic remained unknown for 300 years until Crawford Long and William Morton first used it clinically in the 1840s. Ether parties subsequently became popular among students, although the drug's extreme flammability probably discouraged more widespread and persisting popular use. **Chloroform** was introduced about the same time as ether, but its toxic effects upon the heart, recognized almost immediately, discouraged its nonmedical use. It was not known for many years that the liver, also, is severely damaged by this drug.

Chloral hydrate, a powerful sleep-producing drug, was introduced into medicine in 1869 but has been generally ignored by experimental psychologists—though not by the underworld where, in the form of "knockout drops" mixed with alcohol, it has been the active ingredient of the "Mickey Finn." **Paraldehyde**, first used in 1882, has similarly been eschewed by psychological investigators, perhaps because of its extremely unpleasant odor; nevertheless, it has been used extensively for many years in mental institutions for producing temporary narcosis in dangerously violent patients, especially those with delirium tremens from alcohol withdrawal.

Bromides, particularly potassium bromide, slowly gained popularity during the 19th century to the point where millions of people were taking them as sedatives. Unlike the barbiturates, however, the bromides produce psychoses involving delirium, delusions, hallucinations, as well as a variety of neurological and dermatological disturbances. For a time, chronic toxicity resulting from continued use of these compounds became a leading cause of admission to mental hospitals. Bromide is still a common ingredient in headache remedies, "nerve tonics." and over-the-counter sleeping medications.

THE ANTIPSYCHOTIC DRUGS

With the antipsychotic drugs, as happens more often than is supposed, use preceded research. The ancient preparation, Indian snakeroot powder, mentioned more than 2500 years ago in the Hindu Ayurvedic writings, deserves at least as much credit for ushering in the era of clinical psychopharmacology as does the modern synthetic drug, chlorpromazine. According to the ancient doctrine of signs, since the roots of the plant *Rauwolfia serpentina* were snakelike, they were administered for snakebite. Snakeroot was also used for insomnia and insanity—quite rational uses, in view of modern findings—as well as for epilepsy and dysentery which it actually aggravates, and for a host of other conditions for which its value is questionable.

The first scientific intimation that Indian snakeroot might be useful in mental illness came in 1931 when Sen and Bose published an article in the *Indian Medical World* entitled *"Rauwolfia serpentina*, a new Indian drug for insanity and high blood pressure." But this suggestion was not confirmed for almost a quarter of a century. Rauwolfia began to attract the attention of the Western world only in 1949, when Rustom Valkil advocated it for hypertension, and the Swiss pharmaceutical firm, Ciba, subsequently isolated the active ingredient which they named **reserpine**. In 1953 a Boston physician, Robert Wilkins, confirmed that reserpine was effective in the treatment of hypertension, and a year later a New York psychiatrist, Nathan Kline, announced that he had found reserpine useful in the treatment of psychotic disorders. Soon numerous psychiatrists in other parts of the world corroborated Kline's results, and the use of reserpine spread with amazing speed. When Frederick Yonkman at Ciba used the term "tranquilizing" to describe the calming effect of reserpine, the word "tranquilizer" entered all modern languages to designate a drug which quiets hyperactive or anxious patients.

The subsequent clinical history of reserpine is a strange one. Reserpine and chlorpromazine were twin heralds of the dawn of psychopharmacological treatment, but the popularity of reserpine in the treatment of mental disease has dwindled until today, a decade and a half later, its use has been practically abandoned for such therapy while chlorpromazine is still the leading antipsychotic drug. Yet there are many studies which attest to the efficacy of rauwolfia and its derivatives in the treatment of psychiatric disorders; probably its tendency to produce depression was one of the chief reasons for its near demise. Furthermore, chlorpromazine has spawned scores of offspring-phenothiazines, widely used for the mentally ill.

Like reserpine, **chlorpromazine's** usefulness as an antipsychotic drug was discovered more or less by accident. In the early 1950s the French surgeon, Henri Laborit, introduced chlorpromazine into clinical anesthesia as a successor to promethazine, known to be a sedative antihistamine capable of heightening the effect of other drugs. It was noticed that chlorpromazine reduced anxiety in surgical patients and enabled them to face their ordeal with indifference. This led to its trial with agitated psychotics, whom it calmed with dramatic effectiveness. In 1954 the drug was released commercially in North America by Smith, Kline and French as an antiemetic, but shortly thereafter it was tried with psychiatric patients. Large-scale controlled studies by the United States Veterans Administration and by the Psychopharmacology Service Center of the National Institute of Mental Health showed chlorpromazine and the related phenothiazines to be useful in the treatment of acute schizophrenia. Other studies show that phenothiazines help discharged mental patients to stay out of the hospital. A drug with ubiquitous actions on all body systems, chlorpromazine has been used in the treatment of anxiety and tension, depression, mental retardation, senility, drug addiction, pain, nausea and vomiting, and spasticity. Since its mechanisms of action are still not known, it is difficult to delimit the validity of these applications.

ANTI-ANXIETY DRUGS

Anxiety is such a common experience that everyone reading this article has a subjective understanding of the term. It may be defined as an unpleasant state associated with a threatening situation, and is closely allied to fear. Sedative hypnotic drugs including alcohol, barbiturates, bromides, and chloral hydrate, have frequently been employed for the treatment of anxiety. In 1955 a number of new drugs with properties common to the sedative hypnotics were introduced for the treatment of anxiety, but the most successful of these, by far, was **meprobamate**, popularly known as Miltown or Equanil. Many of the arguments concerning the uniqueness of meprobamate revolve around its similarity or dissimilarity to the barbiturates. But since the properties of the various barbiturates differ from one another, it is not easy to compare the whole class to meprobamate. All, however, tend to produce sleep when used in large doses, to produce effects reported as pleasant, and to produce convulsive seizures as a consequence of sudden withdrawal after the prolonged administration of large doses. Giving meprobamate to a patient suffering from neurotic anxiety is not quite the same as inserting a nail into a broken bone to hold it together, or giving insulin to a diabetic. In giving meprobamate, we are employing a drug with a poorly defined action to treat a poorly defined condition. But the condition is widespread, important, and demands action, and the drug seems to help.

In any case, meprobamate's standing as the most popular tranquilizer was soon usurped by **chlordiazepoxide** (Librium). This compound strongly resembles meprobamate and the barbiturates, but there do appear to be differences which the experimentalist can measure. For example, Leonard Cook and Roger Kelleher recently reported an experiment in which rats could postpone a punishing shock by pressing a lever. Cook and Kelleher found that at some doses chlordiazepoxide will produce an increase in the rate of lever pressing whereas meprobamate does not. Also it has been shown with a Lashley jumping stand that rats will sometimes become "fixated" if the discrimination problem is made insoluble. Chlordiazepoxide seems to eliminate this fixated behavior whereas meprobamate does not. The possible differences in the behavioral effects of sedative hypnotic drugs have not yet been fully explored, and the study of these differences should tell us a great deal about the drugs themselves.

ANTI-DEPRESSION DRUGS

While depression, at least in a mild form, is an experience perhaps as common as anxiety, it can also constitute a severe disease (formerly called melancholia) which frequently leads to suicide. Psychiatrists are far from unanimous in their definitions of this complicated entity, but during the past decade they have found two classes of drugs helpful in combatting it—the **monoamine oxidase (MAO) inhibitors**, and their successors, the **dibenzazepine** compounds. As with reserpine and chlorpromazine, their usefulness as antidepressants was discovered by accident when iproniazid (a MAO inhibitor) was given to tubercular patients and found to elevate their mood, and when imipramine (a dibenzazepine derivative related to chlorpromazine) was found to relieve depressed psychotics.

In attempting to understand the etiology of depression, it is ironic that biochemists have not hesitated to rush in where experimental psychologists fear to tread. What has emerged, based on a combination of clinical observations and animal studies, is the *catecholamine theory* of depression. Broadly interpreted, the theory says that a state of well-being is maintained by continuous adrenergic stimulation of certain receptors in the brain by catecholamines like norepinephrine and dopamine (hormones produced in the brain). For example, reserpine's so-called tranquilizing effect—indifference to surrounding, lack of appetite, and apparent lassitude—is attributed to depletion of catecholamines. Another compound, alphamethyltyrosine, which decreases the synthesis of catecholamines, has been found to produce "depression" in animals. On the other hand, some compounds have been found which produce an increase in the level of brain catecholamines. Administration of MAO inhibitors, which inactivate MAO and thus prevent catecholamine from being destroyed, produce increased levels of catecholamines and greater alertness, activity, and degree of electrical self-stimulation (in animals implanted with electrodes in "reward" areas of the brain). Administering the precursors of catecholamines—for example, dihydroxyphenylalanine (DOPA)—or MAO inhibitors, will prevent or reverse the depression caused by reserpine. The dibenzazepine compounds, typified by **imipramine**

(Tofranil), do not change the level of brain catecholamines in animals, yet they are effective antidepressants. However, the mode of action of these compounds may be compatible with the theory. Studies show that the catecholamine level in the brain is reduced, not only by enzymatic destruction, (for example, by MAO), but also by reabsorption of the catecholamines into the neurons. It has been hypothesized that the dibenzazepine compounds potentiate the action of normally present catecholamines by preventing this reabsorption.

LSD

LSD shares the responsibility with reserpine and chlorpromazine for ushering in the psychopharmacology era. Albert Hofmann's accidental discovery of this substance at Sandoz Pharmaceuticals in Basel, Switzerland in 1943 is now well known. LSD is a semi-synthetic compound of plant origin, a derivative of ergot (a fungus which infects rye). Although its effects are similar to those of marijuana and mescaline, its outstanding characteristic is its extreme potency, and its ability to produce bizarre mental states picturesquely described by Humphrey Osmond as psychedelic or "mind-expanding." The ability of LSD to block 5-hydroxytryptamine (another amine resembling the catecholamines in some respects, abbreviated 5HT) and thus to change brain levels of 5HT, has excited interest. More recently Maimon Cohen has reported the frightening finding that LSD can damage chromosomes. The role of LSD in producing a psychotic state has not been established. Despite thousands of papers dealing with this substance, we have very little idea of what LSD does, and we don't know how it does it. It is unfortunate that legal restrictions and the manufacturers' understandable diffidence make this fascinating chemical inaccessible for research.

There is something in the use or action of pscyhotogenic or "hallucinogenic" drugs which appeals to certain towering if unconventional figures in literature and the arts. From the time of Toulouse-Lautrec throug the era of the expatriates (Gertrude Steain, James Joyce, Ernest Hemingway), bohemian Paris was not exactly abstemious nor did it restrict itself to alcohol for thrills or new sensations. Though the virtues of illicit drugs do not appear in paid advertisements in the public press, nevertheless very talented "copywriters" have turned out flowing testimonials to promote the use of these drugs. Thomas de Quincey and Samuel Coleridge, at the beginning of the 19th century, recommended opium, and Paolo Mantegazza in 1859 gave highly colored accounts of the beatific effects of coca. Freud also approved of cocaine and advised his fiancee to take it. Charles Baudelaire, called the "De Quincey of hashish," was supported by Arthur Rimbaud and Paul Verlaine in acclaiming the beneficence of this drug; more recently Aldous Huxley declared that the "doors of perception" could be opened by mescaline and LSD. Many jazz, swing, bop, and other musicians claim that marijuana and other stimulant drugs enhance their playing or composing.

Whether drugs truly enhance creativity is a moot point. Artists, poets, scientists, and inventors will testify that LSD or marijuana or amphetamine inspired them to produce works of value, but controlled experiments to test these claims are lacking. Who would not like to find a magic drug that would turn an ugly frog into a handsome prince, or a Cinderella into a princess? Drugs can sometimes seem to have magic powers, but they do not ordinarily instill beauty, wisdom, and virtue into the taker. Yet estrogens can change a skinny adolescent girl into a beauty queen and, if one can extrapolate from cases of precocious puberty (or infant Hercules), super-androgens must be responsbile for Clark Kent's transformation into Superman.

Drugs do change our perception of the world, and when this perception becomes unbearable, as in terminal cancer, drug use is clearly justified. The question is whether it is justified for the relief of unhappiness, dissatisfaction, or boredom. The religious uses of wine and peyote for sacramental purposes have, in part, inspired Timothy Leary to found a new religion, The League for Spiritual Discovery (LSD), which advocates the use of LSD and other so-called psychedelic drugs. The legal difficulties of this organization have spurred city, state, and federal legislative and enforcement bodies to enter the field of psychopharmacology in order to control the distribution and use of behavior-affecting drugs. But the government is trying to make rules about substances which are still poorly understood, and it rests with psychopharmacologists to clarify the action of pschotogenic drugs so that such rules can be made on a more rational basis.

THE BIRTH OF SCIENTIFIC PSYCHOPHARMACOLOGY

Without the spur of clinical success, it is doubtful that basic research in the effects of drugs on behavior could have advanced very rapidly. During the first half of the 20th century, drugs were seldom used in the treatment of mental illness, since morphine, cocaine, barbiturates, and other sedative hypnotics had already been tried and proven generally ineffective. Other more physical approaches to therapy, including hydrotherapy, occupational therapy, and psychosurgery had been employed with varying results. Only electroconvulsive shock (ECS) seemed to be very successful, but its administration required considerable skill. Psychiatrists depended chiefly, therefore, on psychological methods (primarily communicative interactions) which, unfortunately, were usually inefficient and ineffective for the majority of severely psychotic individuals.

Experimental psychologists showed only an intermittent and desultory interest in the effects of drugs on behavior. A handful of drugs had already been investigated, but the results were of very little interest to the most influential psychologists who were busy, in the 1930's and 1940's, building their own psychological systems or attacking rival systems.

In fact, however, psychopharmacology had already been born more than half a century earlier. In 1879 the first laboratory of experimental psychology had been established at Leipzig by Wilhelm Wundt. One of Wundt's most famous students was Emil Kraepelin, sometimes called the father of modern psychiatry because he invented a widely used system for classifying mental disorders. Kraepelin might also be called the father of scientific psychopharmacology, for he applied Wundt's new experimental methods to investigate the influence of drugs on psychological functions. Kraepelin studied pharmacology at Tartu in Estonia, then a center of research in this field. During his stay there he demonstrated that alcohol, morphine, and other drugs impair reaction time and the mental processes involved in associational learning. It is an ironic coincidence that Kraepelin was interested in the two areas which finally coalesced 75 years later—basic, quantitative, experimental psychopharmacology, and the treatment of mental disease.

Though psychopharmacology had little scientific status at the beginning of the 20th century, Kraepelin's early work was continued by a few psychologists who studied the effects of alcohol, caffeine, cocaine, strychnine, and nicotine. In 1908 the Englishman, W. H. R. Rivers, reported on the influence of drugs on fatigue; in 1915 the Americans, Raymond Dodge and Francis Benedict, and Harry Hollingsworth (1912, 1924) examined the effects of drugs on motor and mental efficiency. In 1924 even Clark Hull, one of the most influential psychologists of the mid-20th century, studied the effect of pipe smoking and coffee drinking on mental efficiency, before he turned his attention to building theoretical systems.

Psychopharmacological research was spurred in the 1930's and 1940's by the imminence and advent of World War II, which aroused military interest in the applications of drugs, particularly the amphetamines, and concern about the psychological consequences of anoxia, i.e., severe oxygen deficiency. Both allied and German soldiers were given amphetamines to combat sleeplessness and fatigue; these drugs were found to diminish fatigue, but whether they could raise performance above normal levels was an open question which is still not fully answered. Insufficient supply of oxygen to the brain was shown to adversely affect reasoning, memory, and sensory functioning; for example, it renders the subject less sensitive to visual stimuli, and prolongs the time needed for the eyes to adapt to the dark. Such impairment was particularly serious in military pilots for whom the loss of judgment and sensory function resulting from lack of oxygen at high altitudes could be disastrous.

More recently a number of factors have converged to make psychopharmacology a popular field for research. During the mid-1950's, Europe and the United States were

prospering, and governmental support for health services and medical research began to expand at an unprecedented rate. Spurred by therapeutic success and the possibilities of large profits, and as yet unencumbered by severe governmental restrictions concerning drug safety and efficacy, pharmaceutical companies were eager to discover new drugs prescribable to millions of waiting patients. Support for research on new psychotherapeutic drugs became big business. In addition, the Psychopharmacology Service Center, established within the National Institute of Mental Health, contributed millions of dollars for research on the psychological effects of drugs.

With the rise of psychopharmacology, clinical psychologists immediately began to devise methods, such as rating scales and questionnaires, to evaluate the effects of the new drug therapies. However, some of the psychotherapeutic achievements credited to the action of drugs may also be attributed to reforms in mental hospitals and better programs of community mental hygiene.

PSYCHOLOGICAL METHODS IN PSYCHOPHARMACOLOGICAL RESEARCH

To screen out potentially useful drugs and characterize their action, psychopharmacologists have used a variety of procedures in studies carried out with rats and mice. Measures of spontaneous motor activity are widely employed, as are other observational and rating techniques. Among the most favored procedures are those based on operant conditioning, because they are objective, automatic, generally quite reliable, and permit extended investigation of a single animal. The chief apparatus is the Skinner box, a cage containing a lever-pressing mechanism. Depending on the experimental conditions, depression of this level can produce either a positive reinforcement (food) or a negative reinforcement (electrical shock). Some investigators feel that the schedule, and not the kind or amount of reinforcement, determines a particular drug susceptibility. Some schedules require that the animal respond quickly, or slowly, or in certain patterns, in order to obtain food or avoid shock. On the other hand, even before the phenothiazines and reserpine appeared on the market, it was shown that these drugs seemed to selectively impair conditioned responses controlled by aversive consequences (that is, punishing shock) but had less effect upon unconditioned responses. It appears that the strength of the stimulus and the nature of the motor response required are vital factors determining the relative susceptibility to different drugs.

Many psychopharmacologists not trained in the Skinnerian approach use discrimination boxes and mazes to study the effects of drugs, and a number also use classical conditioning procedures; maze-learning was used in a recent study which demonstrated that analeptics (such as strychnine) facilitate learning. Similarly, work on the amnesia produced by intracerebral antibiotics was based on results obtained with mazes and shuttleboxes. Even single-trial learning procedures are being increasingly used to study the effects of drugs. Psychological research has not yet reached a point at which any one method of measuring behavior can be considered superior to any other.

CHEMISTRY AND THE BRAIN

Psychologists have subdivided behavior in different ways, but they are in general agreement about certain broad categories of functions. If different psychological functions depend upon discrete chemical substances, then we might expect to find specificity of drug action—that is, that certain drugs selectively affect certain functions. If the localization of psychological functions involves a grosser type of organization—if it depends, say, on complex neural connections—then we would not necessarily expect to find such specific relations between drug action and psychological function.

Certain sensory structures are clearly chemically coded. Taste and smell receptors obviously are and respond to specific drugs. Sodium dehydrochlorate and saccharin, even when injected into an antecubital vein, respectively produce a characteristic bitter or sweet taste on reaching the tongue and are used for measuring blood circulation time. Streptomycin and dihydrostreptomycin selectively, though not exclusively, attack the eighth nerve; visual effects are produced by santonin, digitalis, and LSD. Haptic sensations are said to be produced by cocaine ("cocaine bug"), but there is no good evidence that somesthetic sensory pathways are selectively affected by any chemical substance. Histamine and polypeptides, such as substance P or bradykinin, will at times produce itch or pain, and hint that sensory chemical specificty is a possibility.

Motor structures are also chemically coded and enable curariform drugs to have a selective paralyzing action. Similarly, autonomic ganglia can be affected selectively by different drugs and the vast field of peripheral neuropharmacology rests on such specificty.

We are beginning to learn how the central nervous system is organized neuropharmacologically. Histochemical, radioautographic, and fluorescent techniques are making such mapping possible. For example, it is known that the central nervous system pathways which control motivational mechanisms such as hunger, thirst, and sex, are susceptible to cholinergic, adrenergic, and hormonal substances. Further mapping of this kind is bound to result in better understanding of the relationship between drug action and functional localization in the central nervous system.

One can inhibit activity with a wide variety of depressant drugs or activate animals with stimulant drugs. No simple role can be ascribed to acetylcholine, norepinephrine, or 5-hydroxytryptamine (serotonin) in the control of behavior. What part, if any, these substances play in learning is even more mysterious. Some theorists have proposed an inhibitory cholinergic system balanced by an excitatory adrenergic system, and the facts seem to fit thus far. Of course, the brain is full of all species of chemicals which are waiting to be investigated by psychologists. Nucleic acids and particularly ribonucleic acid (RNA) have been assigned a special role in learning by some, but evidence is conflicting. Proteins seem a more likely candidate, and such inhibitors of protein synthesis as puromycin and cyclohexamide do interfere with both memory and learning. The production of retrograde amnesia and the post-trial facilitation of learning by drugs provide evidence for a consolidation process. But the experiments are difficult to perform, and many unspecified sources of variability will have to be identified before general mechanisms can be revealed.

THE FUTURE OF PSYCHOPHARMACOLOGY

Ever since Loewenhoek's invention of the microscope, scientists have tended to believe that in the "ultra-fine structure" of an organism lie the explanations for its functioning. Hence it is not surprising that attempts to explain drug action are couched in terms of chemical binding to specific molecular receptors. However, behavior can no more be seen in a test tube full of brain homogenate, than can the theme of a mosaic be determined from an analysis of its stones. The Gestalt principle that the whole is something more than the sum of its parts is not always recognized by physical scientists who tend to be very analytical, to look at "parts" in their approach to explanation. The psychologist has an increasingly important role to play in psychopharmacology, for he must determine whether the particular sedative, antidepressant, psychotogenic, or facilitating drug which the biochemists and neurophysiologists want to study, really has the behavioral properties they think it does.

In the future it should be possible to say in what ways each important psychopharmaceutical influences behavior, and thus to characterize it by a behavioral profile, just as we can now describe a chemical in terms of its chromatographic pattern. Ultimately, it ought to be possible to look at the chemical structure of any new drug and predict whether it will be useful as an antipsychotic, and antifatigue agent, an appetite stimulant, and so forth. By the same token, the physiological determinants of behavior will be so well worked out that we will understand why a drug which causes alertness also depresses hunger, or why one that causes difficulty in doing arithmetic also causes peculiar sensations in the skin. One can envisage the day when drugs may be employed not only to treat pathological conditions (reduce pain, suffering, agitation, and anxiety), but also to enhance the normal state of man—increase pleasure, facilitate learning and memory, reduce jealousy and aggressiveness. Hopefully such pharmacological developments will come about as an accompaniment of, and not as a substitute for, a more ideal society.

The Doors of Perception

Aldous Huxley

From what I had read of the mescaline experience I was convinced in advance that the drug would admit me, at least for a few hours, into the kind of inner world described by Blake and AE. But what I had expected did not happen. I had expected to lie with my eyes shut, looking at visions of many-colored geometries, of animated architectures, rich with gems and fabulously lovely, of landscapes with heroic figures, of symbolic dramas trembling perpetually on the verge of the ultimate revelation. But I had not reckoned, it was evident, with the idosyncrasies of my mental make-up, the facts of my temperament, training and habits.

I am and, for as long as I can remember, I have always been a poor visualizer. Words, even the pregnant words of poets, do not evoke pictures in my mind. No hypnagogic visions greet me on the verge of sleep. When I recall something, the memory does not present itself to me as a vividly seen event or object. By an effort of the will, I can evoke a not very vivid image of what happened yesterday afternoon, of how the Lungarno used to look before the bridges were destroyed, of the Bayswater Road when the only buses were green and tiny and drawn by aged horses at three and a half miles an hour. But such images have little substance and absolutely no autonomous life of their own. They stand ı real, perceived objects in the same relation as Homer's ghosts stood to the men of flesh and blood, who came to visit them in the shades. Only when I have a high temperature do my mental images come to independent life. To those in whom the faculty of visualization is strong my inner world must seem curiously drab, limited and uninteresting. This was the world—a poor thing but my own—which I expected to see transformed into something completely unlike itself.

The change which actually took place in that world was in no sense revolutionary. Half an hour after swallowing the drug I became aware of a slow dance of golden lights. A little later there were sumptuous red surfaces swelling and expanding from bright nodes of energy that vibrated with a continuously changing, patterned life. At another time the closing of my eyes revealed a complex of gray structures, within which pale bluish spheres kept emerging into intense solidity and, having emerged, would slide noiselessly upwards, out of sight. But at no time were there faces or forms of men or animals. I saw no landscapes, no enormous spaces, no magical growth and metamorphosis of buildings, nothing remotely like a drama or a parable. The other world to which mescaline admitted me was not the world of visions; it existed out there, in what I could see with my eyes open. The great change was in the realm of objective fact. What had happened to my subjective universe was relatively unimportant.

I took my pill at eleven. An hour and a half later, I was sitting in my study, looking intently at a small glass vase. The vase contained only three flowers—a fullblown Belle of Portugal rose, shell pink with a hint at every petal's base of a hotter, flamier hue; a large magenta and cream-colored carnation; and, pale purple at the end of its broken stalk, the bold heraldic blossom of an iris. Fortuitous and provisional, the little nosegay broke all the rules of traditional good taste. At breakfast that morning I had been struck by the lively dissonance of its colors. But that was no longer the point. I was not looking now at an unusual flower arrangement. I was seeing what Adam had seen on the morning of his creation—the miracle, moment by moment, of naked existence.

"Is it agreeable?" somebody asked. (During this part of the experiment, all conversations were recorded on a dictating machine, and it has been possible for me to refresh my memory of what was said.)

"Neither agreeable nor disagreeable," I answered, "It just *is.*"

Istigkeit—wasn't that the word Meister Eckhart liked to use? "Is-ness." The Being of Platonic philosophy—except that Plato seems to have made the enormous, the grotesque mistake of separating Being from becoming and identifying it with the mathematical abstraction of the Idea. He could never, poor fellow, have seen a bunch of flowers shining with their own inner light and all but quivering under the pressure of the significance with which they were charged; could never have perceived that what rose and iris and carnation so intensely signified was nothing more, and nothing less, than what they were—a transience that was yet eternal life, a perpetual perishing that was at the same time pure Being, a bundle of minute, unique particulars in which, by some unspeakable and yet self-evident paradox, was to be seen the divine source of all existence.

I continued to look at the flowers, and in their living light I seemed to detect the qualitative equivalent of breathing—but of a breathing without returns to a starting point, with no recurrent ebbs but only a repeated flow from beauty to heightened beauty, from deeper to ever deeper meaning. Words like "grace" and "transfiguration" came to my mind, and this, of course, was what, among other things, they stood for. My eyes traveled from the rose to the carnation, and from that feathery incandescence to the smooth scrolls of sentient amethyst which were the iris. The Beatific Vision, *Sat Chit Ananda,* Being-Awareness-Bliss—for the first time I understood, not on the verbal level, not by inchoate hints or at a distance, but precisely and completely what those prodigious syllables referred to. And then I remembered a passage I had read in one of Suzuki's essays. "What is the Dharma-Body of the Buddha?" ("The Dharma-Body of the Buddha" is another way of saying Mind, Suchness, the Void, the Godhead.) The question is asked in a Zen monastery by an earnest and bewildered novice. And with the prompt irrelevance of one of the Marx Brothers, the Master answers, "The hedge at the bottom of the garden." And the man who realizes this truth," the novice dubiously inquires, "What, may I ask, is he?" Groucho gives him a whack over the shoulders with his staff and answers, "A golden-haired lion."

It had been, when I read it, only a vaguely pregnant piece of nonsense. Now it was all as clear as day, as evident as Euclid. Of course the Dharma-Body of the Buddha was the hedge at the bottom of the garden. At the same time, and no less obviously it was these flowers, it was anything that I—or rather the blessed Not-I, released for a moment from my throttling embrace—cared to look at. The books, for example, with which my study walls were lined. Like the flowers, they flowed, when I looked at them, with brighter colors, a profounder significance. Red books, like rubies; emerald books; books bound in white jade; books of agate; of aquamarine, or yellow topaz; lapis lazuli books whose color was so intense, so intrinsically meaningful, that they seemed to be on the point of leaving the shelves to thrust themselves more insistently on my attention.

"What about spatial relationships?" the investigator inquired, as I was looking at the books.

It was difficult to answer. True, the perspective looked rather odd, and the walls of the room no longer seemed to meet in right angles. But these were not the really important facts. The really important facts were that spatial relationships had ceased to matter very much and that my mind was perceiving the world in terms of other than spatial categories. At ordinary times the eye concerns itself with such problems as *Where—How far?—How situated in relation to what?* In the mescalin experience the implied questions to which the eye responds are of another order. Place and distance cease to be of much interest. The mind does its perceiving in terms of intensity of existence, profundity of significance, relationships within a pattern. I saw the books, but was not at all concerned with their positions in space. What I noticed, what impressed itself upon my mind was the fact that all of them glowed with living light and that in some the glory was more manifest than in others. In this context position and the three dimensions were beside the point. Not, of course, that the category of space had been abolished. When I got up and walked about, I could do so quite normally, without misjudging the whereabouts of objects. Space was still there; but it had lost its predominance. The mind was primarily concerned, not with measures and locations, but with being and meaning.

And along with indifference to space there went an even more complete indifference to time.

"There seems to be plenty of it," was all I would answer, when the investigator asked me to say what I felt about time.

Plenty of it, but exactly how much was entirely irrelevant. I could, of course, have looked at my watch; but my watch, I knew, was in another universe. My actual experience had been, was still, of an indefinite duration or alternatively of a perpetual present made up of one continually changing apocalypse.

From the books the investigator directed my attention to the furniture. A small typing table stood in the center of the room; beyond it, from my point of view, was a wicker chair and beyond that a desk. The three pieces formed an intricate pattern of horizontals, uprights and diagonals—a pattern all the more interesting for not being interpreted in terms of spatial relationships. Table, chair and desk came together in a composition that was like something by Braque or Juan Gris, a still life recognizably related to the objective world, but rendered without depth, without any attempt at photographic realism. I was looking at my furniture, not as the utilitarian who has to sit on chairs, to write at desks and tables, and not as the cameraman or scientific recorder, but as the pure aesthete whose concern is only with forms and their relationships within the field of vision or the picture space. But as I looked, this purely aesthetic, Cubist's-eye view gave place to what I can only describe as the sacramental vision of reality. I was back where I had been when I was looking at the flower—back in a world where everything shone with the Inner Light, and was infinite in its significance. The legs, for example, of that chair—how miraculous their tubularity, how supernatural their polished smoothness! I spent several minutes—or was it several centuries?—not merely gazing at those bamboo legs, but actually *being* them—or rather being myself in them; or, to be still more accurate (for "I" was not involved in the case, nor in a certain sense were "they") being my Not-self in the Not-self which was the chair.

Reflecting on my expérience, I find myself agreeing with the eminent Cambrige philosopher, Dr. C. D. Broad, "that we should do well to consider much more seriously than we have hitherto been inclined to do the type of theory which Bergson put forward in connection with memory and sense perception. The suggestion is that the function of the brain and nervous system and sense organs is in the main *eliminative* and not productive. Each person is at each moment capable of remembering all that has ever happened to him and of perceiving everything that is happening everywhere in the universe. The function of the brain and nervous system is to protect us from being overwhelmed and confused by this mass of largely useless and irrelevant knowledge, by shutting out most of what we should otherwise perceive or remember at any moment, and leaving only that very small and special selection which is likely to be practically useful." According to such a theory, each one of us is potentially Mind at Large. But in so far as we are animals, our business is at all costs to survive. To make biological survival possible, Mind at Large has to be funneled through the reducing valve of the brain and nervous system. What comes out at the other end is a measly trickle of the kind of consciousness which will help us to stay alive on the surface of this particular planet. To formulate and express the contents of this reduced awareness, man has invented and endlessly elaborated those symbol-systems and implicit philosophies which we call languages. Every individual is at once the beneficiary and the victim of the linguistic tradition into which he has been born—the beneficiary inasmuch as language gives access to the accumulated records of other people's experience, the victim in so far as it confirms him in the belief that reduced awareness is the only awareness and as it bedevils his sense of reality, so that he is all too apt to take his concepts for data, his words for actual thing. That which, in the language of religion, is called "this world" is the universe of reduced awareness, expressed, and, as it were, petrified by language. The various "other words," with which human being erratically make contact are so many elements in the totality of the awareness belonging to Mind at Large. Most people, most of the time, know only what comes through the reducing valve and is consecrated as genuinely real by the local language. Certain persons, however, seem to be born with a kind of by-pass that circumvents the reducing valve. In others temporary by-passes may be acquired either spontaneously, or as the result of deliberate "spiritual exercises," or through hypnosis, or by means of drugs. Through these permanent or temporary by-passes there flows, not indeed the perception "of everything that is happening everywhere in the universe" (for the by-pass does not abolish the reducing valve, which still excludes the total content of Mind at Large), but something more than, and above all something different from, the carefully selected utilitarian material which our narrowed, individual minds regard as a complete or at least sufficient, picture of reality.

The brain is provided with a number of enzyme systems which serve to co-ordinate its workings. Some of these enzymes regulate the supply of glucose to the brain cells. Mescalin inhibits the production of these enzymes and thus lowers the amount of glucose available to an organ that is in constant need of sugar. When mescalin reduces the brain's normal ration of sugar what happens? Too few cases have been observed, and therefore a comprehensive answer cannot yet be given. But what happens to the majority of the few who have taken mescalin under supervision can be summarized as follows.

(1)   The ability to remember and to "think straight" is little if at all reduced. (Listening to the recordings of my conversation under the influence of the drug, I cannot discover that I was then any stupider than I am at ordinary times.)

(2)   Visual impressions are greatly intensified and the eye recovers some of the perceptual innocence of childhood, when the sensum was not immediately and automatically subordinated to the concept. Interest in space is diminished and interest in time falls almost to zero.

(3)   Though the intellect remains unimpaired and though perception is enormously improved, the will suffers a profound change for the worse. The mescalin taker sees no reason for doing anything in particular and finds most of the causes for which, at ordinary times, he was prepared to act and suffer, profoundly uninteresting. He can't be bothered with them, for the good reason that he has better things to think about.

(4)   These better things may be experienced (as I experienced them) "out there," or "in here," or in both worlds, the inner and the outer, simultaneously or successively. That they *are* better seems to be self-evident to all mescalin takers who come to the drug with a sound liver and an untroubled mind.

These effects of mescalin are the sort of effects you could expect to follow the administration of a drug having the power to impair the efficiency of the cerebral reducing valve. When the brain runs out of sugar, the undernourished ego grows weak, can't be bothered to undertake the necessary chores, and loses all interest in those spatial and temporal relationships which mean so much to an organism bent on getting on in the world. As Mind at Large seeps past the no longer watertight valve, all kinds of biologically useless things start to happen. In some cases there may be extra-sensory perceptions. Other persons discover a world of visionary beauty. To others again is revealed the glory, the infinite value and meaningfulness of naked existence, of the given, unconceptualized event. In the final stage of egolessness there is an "obscure knowledge" that All is in all—that All is actually each. This is as near, I take it, as a finite mind can every come to "perceiving everything this is happening everywhere in the universe."

The True Speed Trip: Schizophrenia

Solomon H. Snyder

The patient has just been admitted to the hospital emergency room, so violent that it took three strong men to bring him in.

From relatives and from bits of the patient's incoherent ramblings, the admitting psychiatrist begins piecing together an account. Yesterday John felt that others were looking at him in a peculiar way. He had walked the streets all night and spent this morning looking for gold in the gravel paths of the city park. This afternoon he heard voices talking about him. Hostile, secretive persons were looking at him; he was sure they were planning to kill him.

In an interview, the psychiatrist concludes that John suffers from auditory hallucinations and that he has delusions of persecution, and volatile, inappropriate emotion. The diagnosis is simple: an obvious case of paranoid schizophrenia.

But there is a hooker. John is not schizophrenic at all. After a few hours his wife arrives at the hospital and tells the psychiatrist that John has been injecting methamphetamine into his veins for the past three months. John is a speed-freak, an amphetamine addict, and is suffing the principal hazard of the habit.

Key. For years researchers have been trying to find a chemcial key to schizophrenia. The first quest is for a drug that will make normal persons act, temporarily, in the peculiar ways that schizophrenic patients act. Such a drug could provide an important lead to the causes of schizophrenia. And if the drug also will make animals behave schizophrenically, investigators will be able to manipulate schizophrenia in their laboratories. They can explore how environmental, chemical and genetic factors influence schizophrenic behavior, and they can investigate a wealth of possible cures. A growing number of scientists believe that this approach is likely to pay off in the search for a cure for schizophrenia.

Amphetamine offers promise to be this key drug, because it produces patients like John who can trick even experienced clinicians into erroneous diagnoses of schizophrenia. But other chemicals also are under serious study in the search. LSD is the best known psychotomimetic—psychosis-mimicking—drug; LSD, mescalin, psilocybin and other drugs produce effects similar to psychosis. Alcohol is

another; an alcoholic in withdrawal undergoes delirium tremens—d.t.s.—an agitated state fraught with frequent, frightening hallucinations. And many drunks have heard nonexistent voices and seen occasional elephants of unusual colors. Marijuana and its concentrate, hashish, taken in sufficient quantity, can produce hallucinations. And the United States Army, with somewhat different motives, has investigated several highly secret chemicals related to atropine, minute doses of which produce a delirious, psychoticlike state.

Daze. Most of these drugs yield only imperfect approximations of schizophrenia: drugged patients usually become disoriented and confused—often they cannot say who they are, where they are, or what time of day it is, or what month. The true schizophrenic patient, on the other hand, is likely to be well oriented as to person, place and time. Most drug-produced disorientation resembles the symptoms of brain damage—from accident, stroke, brain tumor, vitamin deficiency, or hormonal imbalance—more than it resembles schizophrenia. Amphetamines provide a much better chemical analog to schizophrenia—speed-freaks are invariably well oriented, perhaps even more when they are under the influence than when they are not drugged.

After recovering from a psychotic episode, an amphetamine user usually retains a detailed memory of the whole experience, as do most patients recovering from schizophrenia. By contrast, the other drugs—possibly excepting the psychedelic—deaden the mental faculties so that a patient may have partial or total amnesia that covers the episode.

See. Another important difference is that in drug-induced psychosis, hallucinations or perceptual distortions are primarily visual; in true schizophrenia they are almost always auditory.

When a schizophrenic patient does report visual hallucinations, it is usually during the early stages, after an acute onset. This was true in the cases of amphetamine psychosis reported by Phillip H. Connell in London: visual hallucinations occurred primarily in patients whose psychoses developed acutely after a few large doses of amphetamine. The patients who had escalated dosage gradually over several months tended to have mostly auditory hallucinations. Another telling link is that the drug therapy most effective for schizophrenia is the one that is most effective for amphetamine psychosis. A barbiturate or sedative may be helpful for a number of drug states, but phenothiazine tranquilizers are uniquely effective in amphetamine psychosis and schizophrenia.

For all of these reasons, it appears that amphetamine psychosis is the best chemical model of true schizophrenia, at least of the paranoid type.

Pills.   The average patient with amphetamine psychosis started taking the drug in pill form. Most pills on the market contain five or 10 milligrams of active drug, and are called pep pills or diet pills, depending on the user's purpose. Tolerance for amphetamine builds up rapidly; the pill-popping addict must take more and more pills at shorter and shorter intervals to reach the same high—sometimes more than 100 pills a day. But the typical amphetamine addict tires of pills quickly and begins mainlining: he injects the drug directly into his veins, with perhaps 100 or 200 milligrams of methamphetamine—crystal—in each injection, or hit.

Even before he withdraws the needle he feels an intense buzzing euphoria, called a rush, that users sometimes liken to an orgasm of the whole body. After this, the addict will be elated and hyperactive for several hours, with no desire for food. He may eventaully shoot up every three or four hours, on a five- or six-day run, until he crashes, exhausted, to sleep for two to four days. He awakens with a ravenous hunger; after he has eaten as much as he can hold, he goes into profound depression, he seeks the only known cure: more amphetamine.

F.B.I.   Signs of amphetamine psychosis first develop while the speed-freak is under the influence of the drug (they are thus unlike delirium tremens, a withdrawal psychosis). The harbinger is vague fear and suspicion—*What was that? I heard something. Is somebody trying to get me?* Soon the paranoia centers around a specific delusion—for example, that the FBI is out to get him. An amphetamine party may begin with everyone very elated and talkative, and may end with each person stationed silently at a window, peeking through the curtains for signs of the police.

Acting on his delusions, the speed-freak may become violent—*to get them before they get me.* It is in this sense that the slogan "Speed Kills" is most accurate: more persons die from senseless and brutal violence associated with amphetamine delusions than from overdoses of the drug itself.

Bag.   Another unique feature of amphetamine psychosis is compulsive, stereotyped behavior that the victim repeats hour after hour, apparently without fatigue or boredom. A woman sorted out her handbog over and over for several hours. A man at a table constantly rearranged his knife and spoon. A teenager counted cornflakes all evening. While a

user is busy at this major repetitive behavior, he may also grind his teeth, lick his lips, or constantly shift his eyes from side to side.

Drugged laboratory animals behave similarly. Under small doses of amphetamine, they become hyperactive and vigilant; with greater doses, they develop repetitive, stereotyped behavior. And Roy Pickens and his colleagues have found that when laboratory rats can dose themselves with amphetamines by pressing a bar, they follow a pattern of intake and abstinence, run and crash, that is similar to the pattern of the human amphetamine user.

Why.   Some theorists believe that lack of sleep may cause amphetamine psychosis, not any ingredient of the drug itself. We know that often persons who go without sleep for long periods develop bizarre, psychotic-like behavior. Others speculate that amphetamine's overstimulation of the senses brings on the psychosis. Still others argue that the intense emotional arousal in the amphetamine experience simply triggers a latent psychosis that any stress could have provoked.

The best way to resolve these questions was to produce amphetamine psychosis in human being—deliberately drive people crazy—and carefully follow the sequence of events.

The first person to essay such an experiment was a physician, John Griffith at Vanderbilt University. He recruited four men in their late 20s and early 30s who already were amphetamine addicts but who had never shown signs of amphetamine psychosis, or any tendencies toward schizophrenia. They were all mildly to moderately psychopathic, a condition that is readily distinguishable from schizophrenia. Griffith relentlessly dosed each man with dextroamphetamine—10 milligrams, orally, every hour of the day and night—until he developed signs of amphetamine psychosis. Griffith carefully monitored each man's physiological and psychological symptoms throughout the experiment.

Cling.   Each man exhibited unequivocal psychosis within two to five days, and the psychotic symptoms followed the same sequence in each. After the first doses of amphetamine he showed the usual euphoria, excitement and hyperactivity. During this time he was lucid, in good contact with his surroundings, normally boyish and warm. But by the fifth or sixth dose, he had changed: he became quiet, depressed, uninterested in amusement—a hypochondriac who clung dependently to Griffith.

This pattern was not ordinary amphetamine behavior, probably because the subjects were tested in solitude in a controlled hospital environment. On his own, an amphetamine addict would probably increase his dosage before such symptoms developed, and social variable undoubtedly would color the experience. For example, his interactions with other amphetamine users probably would keep him hyperactive longer than Griffith's subjects were.

Signs.   The first patient developed psychotic signs after about 24 hours; the last after 120 hours (five days). In each case the subject began peculiar behavior about eight hours before the explicit psychotic symptoms appeared. He became taciturn, and refused to talk about his thoughts or feelings. He asked guarded questions about the room, the experiment, or unusual noises, but backed off if anyone asked why he wanted the information. In retrospect, the patients recalled that it was at about this time that paranoid ideas first entered their minds. For a while they could recognize that the ideas were unfounded, chemical delusions—familiar and expected side-effects of the drug. Later the ideas were not so easy to dismiss.

The florid psychosis commenced abruptly in each man. After being stony-faced and silent for about eight hours, he began discussing his thoughts openly and sharply, though he remained cold and aloof. His paranoid ideas became more elaborate and organized, and he believed them. One man believed he was the target of rays from a "giant oscillator." Another maintained that his wife planned to kill him. Strikingly unlike patients with other forms of drug-psychosis, these subjects could not be comforted easily and they were not at all suggestible. The psychosis dissipated within eight hours of the drug cut-off in three of the subjects; the fourth remained somewhat paranoid for another three days.

Out.   Griffith's experiment answers some questions about possible alternative explanations of drug-induced psychosis. First of all, the psychosis can not be attributed simply to sleep deprivation, because two of the men became psychotic after losing only one night's sleep, which alone is not long enough to produce psychotic symptoms.

Nor can the psychosis be attributed to intense stimulation and arousal—the men never appeared to be overstimulated—in fact, after the first few hours they all appeared to be depressed.

Griffith also was careful to rule out pre-drug personality as a significant factor; he selected subjects who had never shown schizophrenic tendencies either in a drugged state or undrugged.

Order.   The amphetamine psychosis that Griffith observed is a good imitation of schizophrenia, probably the best of the drug-induced states. But it isn't perfect; there are differences, the most salient being that Griffith's subjects showed no signs of formal, schizophrenic thought disorder. This is the bizarre mental process that produces crazy associations and meandering, contradictory, hard-to-follow speech. Other researchers confirm Griffith's finding: amphetamine addicts rarely display thought disorder.

This lack would seem to destroy any systematic analogy between amphetamine psychosis and schizophrenia, for many psychiatrists consider thought disorder to be the vital element of schizophrenia. But the issue is not so simple. Doctrinaire diagnosis aside, thought disorder does not invariably accompany schizophrenia. Acute schizophrenics show much less thought disorder than chronic schizophrenics do; and paranoid schizophrenics, with their tight and ordered delusional systems, may show no thought disorder at all. In this connection it is encouraging to note that the amphetamine psychosis usually is both acute and paranoid, and thus resembles the types of schizophrenia with least thought disorder.

Brain.   From Griffith's research and from clinical experience, it seems safe to say that large doses of amphetamines will almost invariably produce psychosis similar to acute, paranoid schizophrenia. The clinical picture is not identical to schizophrenia, however, perhaps because amphetamine's grabbag of side-effects (arousal, sleeplessness, loss of appetite, stereotyped behavior, etc.) may complicate matters. To find out which components of the amphetamine experience are most responsible for the psychosis, we must study the brain to find how nerves, tissues and brain chemicals respond when amphetamine is added to the system.

An obvious clue is that the chemical structure of amphetamine closely resembles the structures of dopamine and norepinephrine, two chemicals that occur naturally in the brain. Dopamine and norepinephrine are found at the brain's synapses, the points at which branches of one neuron come close to, but do not quite touch, the sensitive portions of another neuron.

Fire.   When a nerve impulse in a neuron reaches a synapse, it triggers the release of chemicals—dopamine or norepinephrine, among others—out of the nerve endings. These wash up against the next neuron and trigger it to renew the nerve impulse and send it on its way to the next neuron link in the chain.

It is through these brain chemicals that one neuron thus communicates with the next, and this neuronal conversation underlies all information-processing, thoughts, plans, and perceptions in the brain. Whether the neurotransmitter is dopamine, norepinephrine or some other chemical, it must be inactivated after it has done its job. Otherwise it would continue to stimulate the second neuron and make it continue firing. Some transmitters are inactivated by other chemicals that neutralize them. Dopamine and norepinephrine are inactivated by being transported back into the nerve endings that released them. Julius Axelrod, who discovereed this mechanism, called it "reuptake," and won a Nobel Prize in 1970 for his discovery.

One of the ways amphetamine enters the picture is by inhibiting the reuptake mechanism: small pools of used dopamine or norepinephrine build up at the synapses, thereby causing nerves that are sensitive to dopamine and norepinephrine to fire erratically, repeatedly, and without stimulation from other neurons. The resulting behavior depends on whether the stimulated nerves are in dopamine pathways or norepinephrine pathways.

Image. Which pathways are responsible for which symptoms? We get help in answering this question because amphetamine can be broken down into two mirror-image forms that have different effects on behavior and on the brain's transmitter chemicals. One type rotates polarized light to the right, and is called dextroamphetamine; the left-handed form is levoamphetamine, borrowing *dextro* from Latin to indicate *right* and *levo* to indicate *left*.

It has long been known that dextroamphetamine is by far the more potent of the two forms in stimulating the central nervous system. Smith, Kline & French puts out a pill form of dextroamphetamine, under the trade name Dexedrine.

Joseph Coyle, Kenneth Taylor and I have found that dextroamphetamine is 10 times more powerful than levoamphetamine in inhibiting the reuptake mechanism in norepinephrine nerves. When dextroamphetamine is present in a system, there will be more norepinephrine at brain synapses, the nerves triggered by norepinephrine will fire more often than usual, and the behaviors that are governed by these norepinephrine tracts will be exaggerated. And all of these effects will be dramatically more pronounced with dextroamphetamine than they are with levoamphetamine.

In dopamine tracts, on the other hand, dextroamphetamine and levoamphetamine tend to be equally effective: dextroamphetamine produces a slightly greater pileup of dopamine at the synapses than levoamphetamine does, but the difference is nowhere near the order of 10 to one. This suggests that if a given symptom of amphetamine intake appears about as often with dextroamphetamine as with levoamphetamine, that behavior is probably mediated by the dopamine neurons. If a behavior occurs much more readily with dextroamphetamine than with levoamphetamine, the behavior probably is governed by tracts of norepinephrine neurons.

Rats. Kenneth Taylor and I recently studied two typical amphetamine effects—motor activity and stereotyped behavior—in laboratory rats. With relatively small doses the animals appeared to be exicted, running about their cages furiously, and this effect was exactly 10 times more pronounced under dextroamphetamine than it was under levoamphetamine. This perfectly parallels the 10-fold advantage that dextroamphetamine has in producing excess norepinephrine, and it strongly suggests that the central-stimulant and heightened-activity effects are probably produced when amphetamine comes in contact with the norepinephrine neurons of the brain.

With somewhat larger doses of amphetamine, animals begin stereotyped behavior similar to the compulsive repetitive behavior of speed-freaks. Rats tend to stay in one corner of the cage, to sniff and lick repeatedly, and to gnaw incessantly on any available ojbect, such as the bars of the cage. We found that the two forms of amphetamine were fairly close in their ability to produce stereotyped gnawing in rats. This suggests that the brain's dopamine tracts are responsible for repetitious, stereotyped behavior in amphetamine users. Other investigators have reached the same conclusion by showing that, when dopamine areas of the rat brain are cut out, amphetamine does not produce stereotyped behavior as readily as it usually does.

After hearing about our successful experiments with animals, Burton Angrist and Samuel Gershon at New York University asked the next logical question: how do dextroamphetamine and levoamphetamine compare in producing amphetamine psychosis in human being? They studied three former amphetamine addicts, volunteers, putting them through the 10-milligram-per-hour regimen that Griffith followed. Each subject went through three separate sessions; once with levoamphetamine, and once with a mixture of the two.

Both drugs and the mix produced psychosis in each man and none was markedly more powerful than any other. (Dextroamphetamine was slightly faster than the other preparations, levoamphetamine was the slowest, and the mixture, as might be expected, was intermediate.)

Maps. This finding suggests that amphetamine psychosis is produced by excessive activity in the dopamine tracts of the brain, while such other amphetamine affects as hyperactivity and euphoria originate in the norepinephrine tracts. With a chemical stain developed by a group of Swedish researchers, it has recently become possible to map dopamine and norepinephrine pathways through the brain. We have learned, for example, that some prominent dopamine tracts end in areas of the brain's limbic system that regulate a variety of emotional behaviors. The largest dopamine tract has become famous in its own right: it leads to an area that coordinates body movements, and if the tract is damaged so that there is a deficiency of dopamine, the patient is likely to suffer from Parkinson's disease. L-dopa, the drug that is converted to dopamine in the brain, has been hailed as a miraculous treatment for Parkinson's disease.

The major norepinephrine tracts start in the brain stem and ascend through the medial forebrain bundle—the pleasure center. Animals will work very hard to get electrical stimulation in this area, which likely has an important role in the euphoric high of amphetamine use. The norepinephrine tracts also extend into other parts of the hypothalamus, perhaps into the so-called satiety center which, when stimulated, makes a food-deprived animal stop eating.

Several pharmacologists have found that phenothiazine tranquilizers produce improvements in schizophrenic patients by blocking the dopamine receptors in the brain. This fits nicely with our idea that amphetamine produces psychosis by increasing the amount of dopamine around dopamine-sensitive cells. Phenothiazine alleviates symptoms by working in the opposite direction: it makes the dopamine-sensitive neurons less sensitive.

Systems.   Amphetamine-induced psychosis seems to be the best available chemical imitation of schizophrenia. But there remains one nagging difficulty: the amphetamine illness resembles paranoid schizophrenia, not catatonic schizophrenia, undifferentiated schizophrenia, or other forms of the disorder. I don't think this means that paranoid schizophrenia is a different disease from other types. I think that if amphetamine were to act solely on dopamine neurons and had no effect on norephinephrine neurons, the result might be the classic, undifferentiated form of schizophrenia, or a form with characteristics determined only by the personality of the patient. But norepinephrine stimulation adds another set of symptoms to the clinical picture—hyperactivity, sleeplessness, and loss of appetite. The alerting effect may make the patient try to find an intellectual framework for the strange feelings that come over him. He searches for explanations and meanings, and this leads to the elaborate system of delusions that is the essence of paranoia. In short, the basic amphetamine psychosis may arise through the brain's dopamine mechanisms, but the specific paranoid solution comes from the contribution of norepinephrine systems.

Investigators are now trying to improve upon amphetamine, to find a drug that will stimulate dopamine systems but not norepinephrine systems. If my reasoning is accurate, such a drug would produce a pure schizophrenia indistinguishable from the disorder that is observed in mental-hospital wards. The drug would be a boon. It would give specific direction to the search for the cause of natural schizophrenia, and would allow investigators to manipulate schizophrenic symptoms in the laboratory and study, in animals, a vast range of possible cures.

PSYCHOTIC STATES

The inner world of the schizophrenic is vividly portrayed by Norma MacDonald, a Canadian nurse who became psychotic and later recovered. There are many sub-types of schizophrenia, each with its own characteristic alterations in consciousness; although Ms. MacDonald's exact diagnosis is unknown, from her description it was not the paranoid type that amphetamine users mimic. Her description of an "exaggerated awareness" where dormant parts of her brain "awoke" and ordinary experiences took on a new dimension of special meaningfulness sound very much like Huxley's experience with mescaline. But the hellish nature of Ms. MacDonald's experience, her panicked disorientation and anxiety, set it apart from Huxley's pleasant drug trip. Even so, after her recovery Ms. MacDonald found she felt a special kinship with those who had taken LSD, for their voyages into altered states made them more understanding of her own involuntary plunge into the nightmare state of the schizophrenic.

The dynamics of the schizophrenic's world are revealed through the garbled speech of the psychotic. The confused and nonsensical word salad is a hallmark of schizophrenia, and one of the sure indicators that this is the right diagnosis. Using new computer techniques and advances in psycholinguistic theory, psychologist Brendan Maher undertook a searching analysis of the structure of schizophrenic speech. He discovered that schizophrenics find it difficult to focus their attention, so that they are easily distracted by stimuli others tune out. As they speak, associations to words or ideas in their sentences that normal people screen out flood in to their awareness and intrude in their utterances. Thus, their mad speech betokens an underlying attentional spasticity.

The value cultures place on an altered state even so frightening as an acute psychosis is by no means universally negative. Psychologist Julian Silverman has culled the anthropological literature to demonstrate that among certain peoples an acute psychosis is regarded as an ennobling experience, one which sets a person apart and qualifies him to become a shaman. It is precisly the unnerving aspects of the psychotic state—the loss of contact with reality, hallucinations, narrowing of attention and confusion— that give the shaman power when he recovers. His culture supports him while he undergoes this altered state, and holds the post-psychotic shaman in high regard because he has confronted and overcome the dangers of a different reality. During his practice as a shaman he will need to enter and return from this or similar states; the psychotic episode is a necessary qualification for the healer's art.

Living with Schizophrenia

Norma MacDonald

It seems unlikely that I will be able to say anything understandable about schizophrenia, because as a sufferer I've never felt certain, to begin with, that I am living with schizophrenia. Until an informed friend asked me to write an article on schizophrenia, I didn't know I'd ever had it, though, eleven years ago, I spent ten months in a mental hospital being psychoanalyzed and prepared for rehabilitation. Recently I spent three years studying psychiatric nursing, and often wondered what my own diagnosis might have been. I had all the symptoms of manic-depressive psychosis, paranoia, or even a character disorder coupled with neurosis. I still don't know whether I really had schizophrenia, what type of schizophrenia I had, and I don't think I want to know. It would be entirely irrelevant. I've had to adjust to this strange upsetting personality and I've learned to cope with some facets of it while others are still baffling me. Labelling it with a name wouldn't be of any use and might complicate things more by setting up a number of expectations.

I know that I spent an unhappy childhood and a tragic adolescence, and that until a complete mental collapse occurred when I was 24, I lived through a series of emotional upheavals, depressions, abrupt changes of mind and plan, severe asthma, and a great many minor ailments like colds, fevers, influenza, and general fatigue, which left me little energy for sports or social life. Worst of all, I lived with constant fear and inhibition, making it impossible for me to make friends unless they were younger or in some respect inferior, or unless they were so extroverted they could take me under their social wings and brighten my life a little. Intellectual pursuits were my only strength, and fear of failing at these kept me in a state of continual anxiety. I achieved some success at art.

I knew vaguely that something was wrong with me, and while studying first-year psychology at college I began to find symptoms within myself of serious mental disorder. Friends just laughed at the idea, but I was beginning to feel cheated. It appeared that life for others wasn't all frustration, loneliness, depression, and disillusionment. My father had been in a mental hospital since I was four years of age, I hadn't seen him for many years, and I lived in secret dread that it might be hereditary. My mother wouldn't talk about him because it upset her. I was an only child, with no one else to talk to.

After that year at college I returned to school-teaching for a year, and then attended a radio academy in Toronto to answer a life-long urge to learn about acting. Life on a shoe-string in a situation tense with the threat of competition worked things up to a crisis. When the illness finally hit me with all its force, I spent months of living hell in Toronto before my mother realized that something was wrong and flew down to take me home and put me in a hospital. During those months my mind convinced me completely of intense feelings of other people toward me—feelings of love, hate, indifference, spite, friendship. These certainties were groundless and led me into dreadful relationships with people. My physical health was low and I worked fitfully at a job which left nothing but an irritating sense of failure. My sick leave piled up until I was going to have practically no pay cheque. I could eat and sleep very little because of voices telling me I mustn't. I was "forced" by voices to walk miles and miles about the city until my feet were blistered and bleeding, and then I was persuaded to do an increasing number of senseless things. Still no let-up in the vicious thoughts that tortured my imagination. Visual and tactile hallucinations came to enliven the auditory ones. Though I fought the idea of hospital restrictions desperately, I experienced a sense of relief as well, knowing that I might be afforded some protection from the nameless threats outside in the world.

There has been so much written about acute schizophrenic illnesses, and there is so much material available on delusions and hallucinations, that I won't go further into those. What I do want to explain, if I can, is the exaggerated state of awareness in which I lived before, during, and after my acute illness. At first it was as if parts of my brain "awoke" which had been dormant, and I became interested in a wide assortment of people, events, places, and ideas which normally would make no impression on me. Not knowing that I was ill, I made no attempt to understand what was happening, but felt that there was some overwhelming significance in all this, produced either by God or Satan, and I felt that I was duty-bound to ponder on each of these new interests, and the more I pondered the worse it became. The walk of a stranger on the street could be a "sign" to me which I must interpret. Every face in the windows of a passing streetcar would be engraved on my mind, all of them concentrating on me and trying to pass me some sort of message. Now, many years later, I can appreciate what had happened. Each of us is capable of coping with a large number of stimuli, invading our being through any one of the senses. We could hear every sound within earshot and see every object, line, and colour within the field of vision, and so on. It's obvious that we would be incapable of carrying on any of our daily activities if even one-hundredth of all these available stimuli invaded us at once. So the mind must have a filter which functions without our conscious thought, sorting stimuli and allowing only those which are relevant to the situation in hand to disturb consciousness. And this filter must be working at maximum efficiency at all times, particularly when we require a high degree of concentration. What had happened to me in Toronto was a breakdown in the filter, and a hodge-podge of unrelated stimuli were distracting me from things which should have had my undivided attention.

New significance in people and places was not particularly unpleasant, though it got badly in the way of my work, but the significance of the real or imagined *feelings* of people was very painful. To feel that the stranger passing on the street knows your innermost soul is disconcerting. I was sure that the girl in the office on my right was jealous of me. I felt that the girl in the office on my left wanted to be my friend but I made her feel depressed. It's quite likely that these impressions were valid, but the intensity with which I felt them made the air fairly crackle when the stenographers in question came into my office. Work in a situation like that is too difficult to be endured at all. I withdrew farther and farther, but I became more and more aware of the city around me. The real or imagined poverty and real or imagined unhappiness of hundreds of people I would never meet burdened my soul, and I felt martyred. In this state, delusions can very easily take root and begin to grow. I reached a stage where almost my entire world consisted of tortured contemplation of things which brought pain and unutterable depression. My brain, after a short time, became sore with a real physical soreness, as if it had been rubbed with sandpaper until it was raw. It felt like a bleeding sponge. Meaningful distractions from the real world, such as the need to carry on a conversation with a friend, sometimes brought welcome relief from the pain and depression, but not always. By the time I was admitted to a hospital I had reached a stage of "wakefulness" when the brilliance of light on a window sill or the colour of blue in the sky would be so important it could make me cry. I had very little ability to sort the relevant from the irrelevant. The filter had broken down. Completely unrelated events became intricately connected in my mind.

There are some highlights to the months spent in mental hospital, times when I grasped ideas that led to a new world of light. One was the realization that I was sick and could get well—this I recall was promoted by a "sane" fellow inmate who suffered from nothing more than alcoholism. I also learned that there wasn't necessarily a definite connection between my father's illness and mine,

and that it's possible for a person to deal with fate. I gained a bit of confidence, made a few friends, began to appreciate social life, and started to cope with some adult ideas, such as the individual's responsibility to society, and an individual's right to be herself and to develop her own interests and abilities without the constant need to please mother or daddy or the best friend.

These turning points were merely beginnings, not a cure. It has taken years of living to ingrain slowly a few of them deeper into my being. At first it was all a matter of fighting depression, loneliness, and the threat of suicide. It meant fighting an urge to flee back to the security of the hospital at the expense of all my thin veneer of confidence and self-reliance. It meant a long struggle to find friends I could trust and learning where not to trust. It became clear in time that one of my worst faults was inability to judge human beings or to know what to expect from them. Trial and error and an increasing reliance on my own intuition changed and sharpened this concept until in later years I was often complimented on my superior understanding of human beings and their behaviour. This makes me smile sometimes, because in spite of insight gained through self-analysis, occasionally I still make an error in judgment, and when I do it's a big one.

During my years as a psychiatric nurse I have realized that I am not likely ever to know if my problems are shared by other schizophrenics or not, for the acutely ill are as much of a puzzle to me as they are to staff who have never known the illness. So incapable of communication, the schizophrenic cannot seem to make any of his needs or wishes clear. Sometimes a flash of intuition has led me into what seems to be an unusually keen insight into one patient's problems and behaviour, but this experience is rare. It is not unlikely that in a day or so a staff member who has no organic experience of schizophrenia will exhibit an equally keen intuitive flash about the same patient, or another one. I'm not speaking here of the realm of feelings, for I'm quite sure that I can empathize with many patients more easily than a staff member who hasn't shared our experiences. Their fears and disturbances are familiar territory to me. I've been there. But when it comes to understanding what goes on in the patient's mind to cause the moods, then anyone's guess is as good as mine. I have almost reached the conclusion that there is no common meeting ground for schizophrenics, whether acutely ill or recovered. Schizophrenia seems to consist of explorations in fathomless worlds of unreality, sometimes controlled and channelled into creative thought. At best it seems to lead to deep introspection.

I am almost convinced that natural instinct could lead a schizophrenic to a cure, when tempered with common sense and a learned ability to test reality. It is another interesting paradox. Living with this illness is a matter of blancing opposites which are enormously incompatible.

A psychiatrist at our hospital jolted me severely by asking, "Why do you try so hard to be normal?" I began to see that in schizophrenia I had much more than a handicap—I had a tool and a potential. This sort of mind, controlled and used, has a far-reaching imaginative power, a sharp instinctual awareness, and the ability to understand a wide span of emotional and intellectual experiences. Perhaps in 10 or 20 more years I will be able to control it much better than I do now, and then perhaps it will be more use to me. As it is I have written an enormous book full of the most intimate stories of the conflicts that have raged in my mind through the years of convalescence, and the attempts to bring each problem into focus. Perhaps in time I will be able to form the book into something which makes sense to people. So far few of my conclusions seem to be practical.

Simplest of all is perhaps the knowledge that this illness rests very definitely upon physical factors. When I was in hospital the doctors told me that if I hoped to remain well I *must* have three square meals, my necessary nutrients, and at least eight hours' sleep nightly. Lapses have proven to me that they were absolutely right. I know that by going without food for a day or two or by missing sleep two or three nights in a row I could (and do) lapse into a state where dreams worry my mind at night, fatigue sets in, voices begin to pester me, and suspicion of the motives of even my best friends rises up to turn my life into a living hell. To have to carry on at my work and social life in this state is dangerous. I can almost feel the filter breaking down, the old soreness pulling and tightening at my brain. Soon every stimulus will have to be interpreted at once. My environment will start to close in on me. I will become irritable and inefficient. The menstrual cycle has considerable influence on this state of mind, and so do various kinds of fatigue. Lack of sleep and a day's work overcharged with pressing activities are the most obvious causes of tiredness, but there is nothing more tiring than ennui. Repetition of boring social events, boring old topics of conversation, dull routine jobs—these are excessively fatiguing. Noises can be tiring too, and colours. I am fond of blue, but I recoil in horror at the thought of living in a blue room, and an apartment painted deep rose seems to have contributed strangely to a crisis through which my illness passed about five years ago. I suspect that climate influences my health, for both my major illness and the crisis of which I spoke occurred in Ontario during the hot and humid summer months, and while in Trinidad recently I began to feel depressed in the same way, growing concerned with negative more than positive aspects of society, and beginning to feel that old pull of "fate." I was glad that my stay wouldn't be long enough to prove that climate would bring about an acute illness, but I was back on my cool dry and high prairies about two hours when my mind cleared and I felt as if a load had been taken from my head. At a 2000-foot elevation, in actual fact a load had been taken from my head! I feel young, carefree and gay at Field, B. C. Pressure does seem to have a definite influence upon mood.

In my campaign to keep healthy, I have had to spend fortunes on food, because of my belief that instinct would tell me what to eat when I needed it. Sometimes a chocolate, an orange, or a steak is all that is needed to restore my mind to a state where suspicions vanish and life begins to look livable again. I have had to move from rooming houses and apartments when healthier neighbors couldn't see why five or six hours' sleep wasn't sufficient to keep anyone in good health. I have often felt insecure in jobs because of the sick leave I need. Often the sick leave is necessary because of utter exhaustion; because I have had to listen to a party next door until one or two a.m. I have no inner resources to cope with such emergency situation. A day or two lying quietly in bed and living on soup or a light diet seems to restore the delicate physical balance and allow a slow revival of mental powers. Job situations which might reduce me to tears and tantrums and lead even to aggressive behaviour and rehospitalization one day, may be well within my control after a day of complete rest. For years I have had to ask for time off every eight to twelve weeks, simply stating that I am "sick" and having to exaggerate symptoms of a cold or a touch of stomach upset for an excuse. I dream of a day when I can say, "I am mentally sick and I need a day in bed." It seems to me a very valid reason, since years of experience have proven the necessity for it. But I can just imagine what would happen if I told the truth!

Walking was made for conditioning and regenerating both mind and body, for it seems to work off emotion and aid the troubled mind to sort itself, at the same time affording exercise and working up an appetite. The lack of places to walk in our country horrifies me. Almost everything about the modern world bothers the sick part of me: escalators, automobiles, stop lights, neon signs, noise, speed, tension—I could list hundreds of them. A half hour in Idlewild Airport in New York, while tired and hungry, reduced me to tears! So did a single afternoon at a telephone switchboard. But it is unrealistic for the schizophrenic to expect a return to the simplicity of pastoral life in today's world, and unrealistic to imagine that the urge to learn and change would be satisfied to live that way if it got the chance. It is realistic to try to learn to cope with the hectic scientific devices, one by one, and master them just as threatening situations in human relationship must be mastered. So far, walking is not illegal, there is housekeeping to do and a person can cook if she is lucky enough to find a room where it is permitted. I have always found that knitting and sewing are reasonably cheap occupations and the routine procedures have often helped me to grasp and hold fleeting ideas and aided my mind in rearranging itself. I can concentrate on an activity for many hours when I find it necessary, and find interruptions very threatening. If I am not in the "mood," I find such activities painful and frustrating. My ability to settle to reading also depends upon mood. Through the years I have learned to master these moods more and more, and they are no longer my absolute rulers, but experience has shown me that it is pointless to master them completely. Just as instinct has often guided me in matters of eating and working and playing, so it seems to guide me in matters of hobbies. Without this reliance on natural cycles of creative activities which have made my life meaningful would be possible. I feel that, left to its own devices, my mind can work out its own cure. The only danger lies in letting instinct get away on reason. Another problem in balance.

One of the most encouraging things which has happened to me in recent years was the discovery that I could talk to normal people who had had the experience of taking mescaline or lysergic acid, and they would accept the thing I told them about my adventures in mind without asking stupid questions or withdrawing into a safe, smug world of disbelief. Schizophrenia is a lonely illness, and friends are of great importance. I have needed true friends to help me to believe in myself when I doubted my own mind, to encourage me with their praise, jolt me out of unrealistic ideas with their honesty, and to teach me by their example how to work and play. The discovery of LSD by those who work in the field of psychiatry has widened my circle of friends.

Living with schizophrenia can be living in hell, because it sets one so far apart from the trend of life followed by the majority of persons today, but seen from another angle it can be really living, for it seems to thrive on art and education, it seems to lead to a deeper understanding of people and liking for people, and it's an exacting life, like being an explorer in a territory where no one else has ever been. I am often glad that illness caused my mind to "awaken" 11 years ago, but there are other times when I almost wish that it would go back to sleep. For it is a constant threat. A breakdown in physical health, too much pressure, too many responsibilities taken on because they sound interesting to the "well" side of me, and I could be plunged back into the valley. Am I to live in a chair on a basement ward of a mental hospital, forced to endure a meaningless existence because people don't know how important freedom is to survival, or am I to move ahead to find a place in the modern world outside hospital walls? It's like being on a swing.

When this fear arises I have to think, "What if I am thrown from the swing? It doesn't matter. I am playing about in the void. See, the mind can act as its own control. Find the balance again. Get back to that delicate psychological homoeostasis that keeps your feet on the ground and your head in the clouds. That way a schizophrenic can live."

The Shattered Language of Schizophrenia

Brendan A. Maher

Somewhere is a hospital ward a patient writes: *"The subterfuge and the mistaken planned substitutions for that demanded American action can produce nothing but the general results of negative contention and the impractical results of careless applications, the natural results of misplacement, of mistaken purpose and unrighteous position, the impractical serviceabilities of unnecessary contradictions. For answers to this dilemma, consult Webster."* The document is never sent to anyone; it is addressed to no one; and perhaps intended for no reader.

Another patient, miles away, writes: *"I am of I-Building in B.. State Hospial. With my nostrils clogged and Winter here, I chanced to be reading the magazine that Mentholatum advertised from. Kindly send it to me at the hospital. Send it to me Joseph Nemo in care of Joseph Nemo and me who answers by the name of Joseph Nemo and will care for it myself. Thanks everlasting and Merry New Year to Mentholatum Company for my nose for my nose for my nose for my nose for my nose."*

Yet another writes: *"Now to eat if one cannot the other can—and if we cant the girseau Q. C. Washpots prizebloom capacities—turning out—replaced by the head patterns my own capacities—I was not very kind to them. Q. C. Washpots under-patterned against—bred to pattern. Animal sequestration capacities and animal sequestired capacities under leash—and animal secretions. . ."**

Experienced clinicians, when called upon to diagnose the writers of language like this, agree closely with each other (80 percent of the time or more). The diagnosis: schizophrenia. Nearly every textbook on psychopathology presents similar examples, and nobody seems to have much difficulty in finding appropriate samples. It would seem obvious that there must be a well-established and explicit definition of what characteristics language must possess to be called schizophrenic. But when we ask clinicians to tell us exactly what specific features of an individual language sample led them to decide that the writer was schizophrenic, it turns out that they aren't exactly sure. Instead of explicit description, the expert comment is likely to be: "It has that schizophrenic flavor" or "It is the confusion of thought that convinces me."

Impressionistic descriptions abound. The language is described as *circumlocutious, repetitive, incoherent,* suffering from an *interpenetration of ideas, excessively concrete, regressed,* and the like. Doubtless, all of these descriptions have merit as clinical characterizations of the language. Unfortunately, they are quite imprecise, and they give us no adequate basis for developing theoretical accounts of the origin of schizophrenic language. This is, of course, hardly surprising. Quantitative studies of language have been notoriously laborious to undertake. However, two recent developments in behavioral sciences have combined to change the situation quite significantly. The first of these is the development of language-analysis programs for computer use, and the second is the increasing sophistication of psycholinguistics as a framework for the study of applied problems in the psychology of language.

Before turning to look at the consequences of these developments, we should glance at the kinds of hypotheses that have already been advanced to account for schizophrenic language. The first of these might be termed the *Cipher Hypothesis.* In its simplest form this says that the patient is trying to communicate something to a listener (actual or potential) but is afraid to say what he means in plain language. He is somewhat in the same straits as the normal individual faced with the problem of conveying, let us say, some very bad news to a listener. Rather than come right out and tell someone directly that a family member is dying, the informant may become circumlucutious and perhaps so oblique that his message simple does not make sense at all.

In the case of the schizophrenic patient, however, it is assumed that the motives which drive him to disguise his message may be largely unconscious—that he could not put the message into plain language if he tried. Where the normal person is trying to spare the feelings of the listener by his distortions and evasions, the patient purportedly is sparing his own feelings by the use of similar techniques. This analogy can be stretched a little further. Just as the normal speaker is caught in a dilemma—the necessity to convey the message and the pressure to avoid conveying it too roughly—so the patient is caught in a conflict between the necessity of expressing himself on important personal topics and the imperative need to avoid being aware of his own real meanings. Thus, so the Cipher Hypothesis maintains, it is possible in principle to decipher the patient's message—provided one can crack the code. This hypothesis assumes, of course, that there really is a message.

Obviously, the Cipher Hypothesis owes its genesis to psychoanalytic theory. In essence, it is identical with

*These quotations are taken from "The Neurology of Psychotic Speech" by McDonald Critchley

Freud's interpretation of the relationship between manifest and latent dream content. Unfortunately, from a research point of view, this hypothesis suffers from the weakness of being very hard to disprove. No two patients are assumed to have the same code, and so the translation of schizophrenic language into a normal communication requires a detailed analysis of the case history of the individual writer. As the code that is discovered for any one case cannot be validated against any other case, the hypothesis rests its claim to acceptance upon its intrinsic plausibility *vis-a-vis* the facts of the life history of the patient. But plausible interpretations of a patient's language may reflect the creative (or emphathetic) imagination of the clinician, rather than a valid discovery of an underlying process governing the patient's utterances.

One more or less necessary deduction from the Cipher Hypothesis is that language should become most disorganized when the topic under discussion is one of personal significance, and less disorganized when the topic is neutral. To date, no adequate test of this deduction has been reported. In the absence of this or other independent tests of the Cipher Hypothesis, it must be regarded for the time being as, at best, an interesting speculation.

A second explanation has been that the patient's communications are confusing and garbled precisely because he wishes to *avoid* communicating with other people. This hypothesis, which we shall call the *Avoidance Hypothesis,* interprets the disordered language as a response that is maintained and strengthened by its effectiveness in keeping other people away. Presumably, the normal listener becomes frustrated or bored with such a speaker and simply goes away, leaving the schizophrenic in the solitude he seeks. This theory rests, in turn, upon the assumption that the patient finds personal interactions threatening. We might expect that casual interactions—such as chatting about the weather—are relatively unthreatening and do not provoke avoidant disorder in language. The language disturbance should become more evident when the threat of personal involvement arises.

At this level, the Avoidance Hypothesis cannot be distinguished from the Cipher Hypothesis. The main difference between the two is that the Avoidance Hypothesis is concerned with a *dimension* of incomprehensibility and does not imply that the incomprehensible can be unscrambled. Both of these hypotheses have their attractions.

"For answers to this dilemma, consult Webster," wrote the first patient we have quoted. Is he just playing a word game with an imaginary reader or is there a meaning to his message? We might remark on the similarity of the prefix in many of the words he uses: *subterfuge, substitution; unrighteous, unnecessary; mistaken, misplacement; contention, contradiction.* His message might, indeed, sound like a random sampling from a dictionary.

Or did the dictionarylike nature of the "message" only occur to the patient himself toward the end—and

hence the closing remark? In any event, the sample seems to fit plausibly into the notion that some kind of enciphering was going on between the patient's basic "message" and the language that he wrote.

Our third sample of schizophrenic language, on the other hand, seems to be absolutely incomprehensible. Fragments of phrases, neologisms ("girseau") and repetitions—*sequestration* and *sequestired*—combine into a jumble that seems to defy understanding. It is hard to believe that there might be a message in disguise here, or even that the language was uttered with any wish to communicate.

Although both hypotheses can be made to seem plausible, they are intrinsically unsatisfying to the psychopathologist. They do not deal with the most fascinating problem of schizophrenic language: why does a particular patient utter the particular words that he does, rather than some other jumbled-up sequence?

Some beginnings of an answer to this question have begun to emerge. Years ago, Eugen Bleuler commented on the presence of *interfering associations* in schizophrenic language. He suggested that the difficulty for the patient was that ideas associated with the content of his message somehow intruded into the message and thus distorted it. A patient of his, whom he had seen walking around the hospital grounds with her father and son, was asked who her visitors were. "The father, son and Holy Ghost," she replied. These words have a strong mutual association as a single phrase and although the last item, "Holy Ghost," was probably not meant as part of her message, it intruded because of its strong associative links with other units in the message.

Bleuler also noticed the difficulty that patients seemed to have in *understanding* a pun, despite their tendency to talk in punning fashion. A patient asked about her relationships with people at home says, "I have many ties with my home! My father wears them around his collar." The pun on the word *tie* was unintentional, hence humorless.

Against the background of this general hypothesis of interfering associations, my students and I began investigations of schizophrenic language some years ago in Harvard's Laboratory of Social Relations. Our first concern was with the original question of definition. What must language contain to be labeled schizophrenic? Our work began with a plea to over 200 hospitals for examples of patients' writings—whether the patients were schizophrenic or not. Colleaguial response was rather overwhelming, and we amassed a very large number of letters, documents, diaries and simple messages written in almost every state of the Union. (Many of these were inappropriate to our purposes. A carton load of documents in Spanish from a Texas hospital, some brief obscenities scribbled on matchcovers and dropped daily onto the desk of a colleague in a St. Louis hospital and other similar items were eliminated, of course.)

From this mass, we selected a set of documents that were legible, long enough to include several consecutive sentences—and written in English. These texts were then read by a panel of clinicians. Each text was judged independently, and then was classified as *schizophrenic language* or *normal language.* (We obtained typical inter-judge agreements of around 80 per cent.) At this juncture we did not know whether the writers of the letters had been diagnosed as schizophrenic or not. Our concern was with the characteristics of the language—and with the clinicians' reactions to it.

Our two sets of texts then were submitted for computer analysis with the aid of the *General Inquirer* program. This program codes and categorizes language in terms of content, and also provides a summary of grammatical features of the language. Out of this analysis, we developed some empirical rules (or a guide on how to write a document that a clinician will judge schizophrenic). Two of the most reliable rules were:

1. Write about politics, religion or science. Letters dealing with global social issues of this kind are highly likely to be regarded as schizophrenic by clinicians.

2. Write more *objects* than *subjects* in sentences. Typical sentences consist of enumerations of classes of objects in a form illustrated in our second and third examples above: "send it to me, Joseph Nemo, in care of Joseph Nemo and me who answers by the name of Joseph Nemo"; or "I fancy chocolate eclairs, chocolate eclairs, doenuts." Or in chains of associations at the end of a sentence. When, for example, a woman patient writes: "I like coffee, cream, cows, Elizabeth Taylor," the associational links between each word and the one following seem obvious.

This kind of associative chaining already had been described clinically by Bleuler; hence it was hardly surprising that the computer should find it to be a reliable discriminator in our document samples. What began to interest us, however, was the fact that these associations interfere most readily at the end of a sentence. Why not chains of subjects or chains of verbs, and why not at the beginning or middle of a sentence? Furthermore, why is this kind of interference found clearly in some schizophrenic patients and yet never occurs at all in others?

For some time it has become increasingly apparent that, in schizophrenia, *attention* is greatly disrupted. It is hard for a patient to remain focused on any one stimulus for any length of time. He is unable to "tune out" or ignore other surrounding stimuli. These distract him; they enter consciousness at full strength and not in an attenuated fashion as they do with the normal person. Reports by the patients themselves make the point dramatically:

"Things are coming in too fast. I lose my grip of it and get lost. I am attending to everything at once and as a result I do not really attend to anything."

"Everything seems to grip my attention, although I am not particularly interested in anything. I am speaking to you just now but I can hear noises going on next door and in the corridor. I find it difficult to concentrate on what I am saying to you."

"I cannot seem to think or even put any plans together. I cannot see the picture. I get the book out and read the story but the activities and the story all just do not jar me into action."

Experimental tasks that require close attention, tasks that call for fast reactions to sudden stimuli, or any continuous monitoring of a changing stimulus field are almost invariably done poorly by schizophrenics. Sorting tasks, where the subject must organize objects or words into conceptual groups, are progressively more difficult for the schizophrenic if irrelevant or puzzling factors appear in the material.

We may regard the focusing of attention as a process whereby we effectively inhibit attention to everything but certain relevant stimuli in the environment. As attention lapses, we find ourselves being aware of various irrelevant stimuli—the inhibitory mechanism has failed temporarily.

It is possible that an analogous set of events takes place when we produce a complex sequence of language. Attention may be greater or lesser at some points in a language sequence than at others. The end of a sentence—the period point—may be particularly vulnerable to momentary attentional lapses: one thought has been successfully completed, but the next one may not yet have been formed into utterable shape. Within a single sentence itself, there may be other points of comparative vulnerability, though not perhaps as marked as at the sentence ending.

Uttering a sentence without disruption is an extremely skilled performance, but one that most of us acquire so early in life that we are unaware of its remarkable complexity. (However, we become more aware of how difficult it is to "make sense" when we are extremely tired, or ripped out of sleep by the telephone, or distraught, or drunk.)

Single words have strong associational bonds with other words—as the classic technique of word association indicates. We know that the word "black" will elicit the response "white" almost instantaneously from the majority of people. The associational bond between black and white is clearly very strong. Strong as it is, it will not be allowed to dominate consciousness when one is uttering a sentence such as "I am thinking about buying a black car." Our successful sentences come from the successful, sequential inhibition of all interfering associations that individual words in the sentence might generate. Just as successful visual attention involves tuning out irrelevant visual material, so successful utterance may involve tuning out irrelevant verbal static.

By the same token, disordered attention should lead to an increasing likelihood that this kind of interference will not be inhibited, but will actually intrude into language utterance. Its most probable point of intrusion is wherever attention is normally lowest.

"Portmanteau" words or puns provide unusually good occasions for disruptive intrusions. Consider, for example, the word "stock." This word has several possible meanings, each of them with its own set of associations. Financial associations might be *Wall Street, bonds, dividend,* etc. Agricultural associations might include *cattle, barn* and *farm;* theatrical associations might be *summer, company* and the like. Webster's Third International Dictionary gives 42 different definitions of the word *stock,* many of them archaic or unusual, but many of them common. If one set of meanings intrudes into a sentence that is clearly built around another set of meanings, the effect is a pun, and an accompanying digression or cross-current in surface content. The sentences—"I have many ties with my home. My father wears them around his collar,"—seem to skip, like a stone on a lake, from *ties* (bonds) to *home* to *father* to *ties* (neckties). On the surface, this is a witty statement, but the speaker had no idea of what was really going on inside or underneath the form of words. The statement was therefore unwitting and hence unwitty.

Loren Chapman and his associates, in work at Southern Illinois University, demonstrated that schizophrenics as a group are more open to interference from the most common meaning of a punning word. When we use a word like *stock* as a stimulus for word association, we discover that most normal respondents give financial associations first, and may find it difficult to respond when asked to "give associations to another meaning." Associations to the other meaning are weaker or less prepotent, and only emerge under special instructional sets. Chapman's work suggests that if the plan of a sentence calls for the use of a weaker meaning, the schizophrenic runs some risk that associational intrusions will interfere and actually produce a punning effect.

On the other hand, if the plan of a sentence involves the stronger meaning, then there may be no intrusion of associations. And if associations do intrude, these intrusions will appear relevant to the sentence and will not strike the listener as strange. Which meanings will be strong or weak will depend to some extent upon the culture from which the patient comes. (Personal experience may of course produce uniquely strong or weak associations in individual cases.) However, Chapman was able to predict correctly the direction of errors for schizophrenic patients as a group on the basis of estimates of strength obtained from normal respondents. Thus, some patients may have personal idiosyncracies, but the associations that interrupt the schizophrenic are generally the same as those that are strong for the population at large.

A parallel investigation I conducted at the University of Copenhagen included a study of the language of Danish schizophrenics. I observed the same general effect: patients were liable to interference from strong meanings of double-meaning words. English is a language, of course, that is unusually rich in puns, homonyms, cognates and indeed a whole lexicon of verbal trickery. But it seems plausible to suppose that in any language in which double-meaning words are to be found, this kind of schizophrenic disturbance may be found.

From these observations we can begin to piece together a picture of what happens when schizophrenic intrusions occur in a sentence that started out more or less normally. Where a punning word occurs at a vulnerable point, the sequence becomes disrupted and rapidly disintegrates into associative chaining until it terminates.

We may look at schizophrenic utterances as the end result of a combination of two factors: the vulnerability of sentence structure to attentional lapses, and the inability of patients to inhibit associational intrusions, particularly at these lapse points. From this point of view, the problem of language is direclty related to the other attentional difficulties which the schizophrenic has; he is handicapped in making language work clearly, just as he is at any other task that requires sustained attention. The emotional significance of what the schizophrenic plans to say may have little or no bearing on when an intrusion occurs, or what it seems to mean. Any sentence with vulnerable points in its syntactic or semantic structure may result in confusion, whether the topic is of great psychological importance or has to do with a patient's harmless liking for chocolate eclairs and doughnuts.

Serious and sustained difficulties in the maintenance of attention suggest a biological defect. Peter Venables at the University of London has suggested swimming or unfocusable attention in schizophrenia may be connected with low thresholds of physiological arousal—stimuli can be very weak and yet trigger strong physiological reactions. This low arousal theshold is found mostly in acute, rather than chronic, schizophrenia.

Evidence from studies of a variety of attentional tasks supports this interpretation. Additional and intriguing evidence was obtained by one of my students, Dr. Joy Rice at the University of Wisconsin. Using electrochemical (galvanic) changes in the skin as a measure, she found that schizophrenic patients who were most responsive to noise stimulation were also the patients who showed the most difficulty in dealing with the meaning of punning sentences. The magnitude of galvanic skin response to external stimulation is presumably greatest in patients with low initial arousal levels (and hence the most receptivity to external stimulation). Rice's data may therefore support the notion that verbal associational interference is part and parcel of a total syndrome of which biological control of attention is a crucial central focus.

Recent research into the effects of LSD has shown that it is people with low initial arousal systems who have the "good trips"; the most cursory glance at literary biography will reveal an extraordinary number of poets and writers who were "sensitive," "neurasthenic," and so on. Which leads me to a sort of Parthian speculation.

Look again at the samples quoted in the beginning of this article. What you see there, I think, is the literary imagination gone mad, if I may use so unclinical a term here. The first sample, had it come from the pen of someone whose brain we trusted, might almost be a crude parody of ponderous political tracts or socio-economo-political gobbledygook of one sort or another. In the second, the fragment, "With my nostrils clogged and Winter here," is really not bad, and one wouldn't be terribly surprised to find it occurring in, say, the *Cantos* of Ezra Pound. The kind of wordplay indulged in throughout the third quote is not essentially different technically from that employed by the later James Joyce, or by the John Lennon of *In his own write.*

What is lacking from these samples, so far as we can tell, is context and control and the critical, or pattern-imposing, intelligence. It would seem, therefore, that the mental substrata in which certain kinds of poetry are born probably are associative in a more or less schizophrenic way. (In the case of poets like Dylan Thomas or Hart Crane, of course, these substrata had to be blasted open by liquor.) The intelligence that shapes, cuts, edits, revises and erases is fed by many conscious sources, most of them cultural; but the wellsprings seem to be, as poets have been telling us for centuries, sort of divine and sort of mad.

Shamans and Acute Schizophrenia

Julian Silverman

This paper presents an analysis of the behaviors of shamans with certain personality traits in primitive cultures and of certain schizophrenic individuals in our own.

Implicit in this formulation is the following basic assumption: the often noted overt similarities between the psychotic-like behaviors of marginally adjusted shamans and of acute schizophrenics reflect even more basic identities in the cognitive processes that generate these behaviors.

It is important first to define what is meant here by the terms "shaman" and "schizophrenic." A detailed statement should serve to avoid some of the conceptual entanglements that repeatedly arise in this area.

SHAMANISM

In order to avoid the pitfalls of previous disagreement, and to highlight the likenesses and differences between shamans and schizophrenics, *this discussion will be primarily concerned with those inspirational medicine men who communicate directly with the spirits and who exhibit the most blatant forms of psychotic-like behaviors.* These include grossly nonreality-oriented ideation, abnormal perceptual experiences, profound emotional upheavals, and bizarre mannerisms. Shamans exhibiting such behaviors are often accorded great prestige, and the belief in their powers is total. For in many a primitive society where the conditions of daily life are harsh, relationships with the environment are closely bound up with the cosmic forces controlling life; the spiritual contacts of the shaman constitute a primary means of sustenance in such a society by their alleviation of the anxieties and fears of its members. Shamanism in all its forms absorbs all that is unpredictable and morally indeterminate (Nadel 1958). When during a "performance" a shaman becomes hysterical in his spirit possession, the members of the group anticipate that they will soon be visited by powerful spirits able to divine their vital problems. When he transports himself to the spirit world to divine or cure, his "returning" pronouncements are received respectfully and obediently.

SCHIZOPHRENIA

Schizophrenia is a general label covering a heterogeneous group of syndromes. Among the prominent clinical features of this group of disorders are: (a) an unmistakable change in personality; (b) autism—nonreality-oriented ideation; (c) "disturbances" of perception; (d) "disturbances" of thinking; (e) profound emotional upheavals; (f) bizarre forms of behavior. In accord with recent perceptual and cognitive research in this area (Silverman 1964b, 1967) and with earlier clinical observations (Sullivan 1953a, Langfeldt 1956), two important restrictions are placed upon the use of the term "schizophrenia" in this paper. The first deals with the distinction between "process" and "reactive" categories of schizophrenics. In the former, the prepsychotic personality is typically more poorly integrated than it is in the latter, there is a continuous and prolonged development of schizophrenic symptoms, and prognosis is poor. More common in the "process" group . . . "is the congeries of signs and symptoms pertaining to an organic, degenerative disease usually of insidious development" (Sullivan 1953a:148). In the "reactive" schizophrenia category, on the other hand, the prepsychotic personality is better integrated, the onset of the disorder rapid, and the clinical picture stormy. For this schizophrenic, "it is primarily a disorder of living. . . . The person concerned becomes schizophrenic—as one episode in his career among others—for situational reasons and more or less abruptly" (Sullivan 1953a:149). This latter schizophrenic condition is the one that will be considered here.

In the paranoid schizophrenic type, the psychotic adjustment is quite different: ". . . the patient, caught up in the spread of meaning, magic, and transcendental force, suddenly 'understands' it all as the work of some other concrete person or persons" (Sullivan 1953a:135). His focus of attention is thereafter primarily upon environmental events and people. In laboratory studies of sensory-perceptual responsiveness, this type of schizophrenic is characteristically overtly responsive to unfamiliar stimulation, extensively scans the environment, especially in the early throes of the paranoid resolution, and evidences a tendency to augment the experienced intensity of environmental input (Silverman 1964b, 1967). It is as if the paranoid schizophrenic, unable to comprehend or tolerate the stark terrors of his inner world, prematurely redirects his attention to the outside world. In this type of abortive crisis solution, the inner chaos is not, so to speak, worked through *or* is not capable of being worked through. Since the working through of the innerworld experience turns out to be a primary concern in this paper (both for the shaman and for the schizophrenic), the paranoid schizophrenic resolution is considered to be an incomplete one and the essential, nonparanoid schizophrenic form is therefore regarded as more comparable to that of the shaman, the *"healed"* madman."

THE THEORETICAL MODEL—AN OVERVIEW

The underlying premise of this paper asserts that both the pathological and the shamanistic types of behaviors and cognition under consideration here are the result of a specific ordering of psychological events. The essential difference between the two lies in the degree of cultural acceptance of the individual's psychological resolution of a life crisis. Thus the same behaviors that are viewed in our society as psychiatric symptoms may, in certain other societies, be effectively channeled by the prevailing institutional structure or may perform a given function in relation to the total culture. The necessary and sufficient sequence of events leading to either a psychotic or a shamanistic resolution is conceptualized in terms of the following five stages:

1. The Precondition: Fear; Feelings of Impotence and Failure; Guilt. Clinical and anthropological writings indicate that both the extreme type of shamanistic call and the schizophrenic experience often have as a primary condition the evoking of intense feelings of fear, psychological impotence, failure, and guilt *and consequent seriously damaged self-esteem.* These feelings are the result of inadequate or incompetent behaviors in life situations that are culturally acknowledged as crucially important.

2. Preoccupation; Isolation; Estrangement. The intensity of these feelings becomes the primary source of concern for the preshaman or preschizophrenic, and intense self-absorption results in his becoming increasingly divorced from "social reality." This second phase is characterized by a marked preoccupation with one's personal situation and a psychological state of isolation and estrangement.

3. Narrowing of Attention; Self-Initiated Sensory Deprivation. Prolonged self-absorption of the above sort results in the constriction of the *ordinary* field of attention. The intensity of the emotional experience serves to enhance attentional constriction. This altered psychological state brings

about changes in perceptual and ideational figure-ground relationships (or "cognitive structures") that are vitally important to one's internal representation of reality. Sustained constriction of the field of attention under these conditions also results in a state of self-initiated sensory deprivation, with consequent inevitable difficulty in the differentiation between phantasy and nonphantasy, between hallucination and perception.

4. The Fusing of Higher and Lower Referential Processes. The progressive dedifferentiation of the representations of one's environment and of oneself that occurs under conditions of prolonged constriction of the field of attention and self-initiated sensory deprivation considerably modifies one's perceptual and conceptual experience. The already unstable and weakened "psychological self" is disorganized by this drastically altered environment and is innundated by lower order referential processes such as occur in dreams or reverie. Owing to the depths of the emotional stirring that triggered the whole process, the world comes to be experienced as filled with superpowerful forces and profound but unimaginable meanings.

5. Cognitive Reorganization. The psychological resolution of such a state may take any one of a variety of forms and any one of a number of content patterns, but each resolution invariably involves a reorganized set of perceptions and conceptions in which the structure of reality is "something else." However, the new symbolization of reality is not dependent upon the sequence of necessary and sufficient conditions elaborated above, but rather upon the contingencies of existence, which are different for each man in his own milieu.

Much of what follows is concerned with a more elaborate consideration of each of these five stages.

Stage 1. The Precondition: Fear; Feelings of Impotence and Failure; Guilt

In those areas of an individual's life where chance and circumstance play a prominent part and where he is unable to bring his environment under his direct control, contact is sought with various supernatural forces that are assumed to exercise that control. The ideas concerning causality that are generated by this approach to a "condition of psychological impotence" are most often considered as purely personal and as nonreal by "high" cultural standards. On the other hand, in those aspects of his life in which he is able to exercise control, he is not nearly so motivated to seek supernatural contact. Furthermore, in time of crisis, when a person is face to face with the issues of life and death, with success and utter failure, attention also becomes focused on such cosmic problems as why he is in the world and that of his relationship with the forces upon which he feels dependent.

An individual diagnosed as psychotic in our culture exhibits and experiences nothing that is specifically different from what is manifested by any other human being who has been oversensitized by *extreme* and *prolonged* threat. It is suggested that what is encountered in various stages of schizophrenia and in the forms of shamanism under consideration here—the odd, awe-inspiring, terror-provoking feelings of vastness and littleness, the strange comprehending of things and events—begins with a subjective evaluation of oneself as being incapable of exercising any effective control over a current life situation. Clinicians have often noted that schizophrenics give evidence of having had some unsolved or traumatic problem prior to the disorder that arouses a strong emotional reaction. Invariably this problem involves a feeling of personal inadequacy occurring in an already hypersensitive and often introverted person (Boisen 1936, 1942, 1947; Sullivan 1953a, 1956; Kaplan 1964). The inability to solve the problem or to extricate oneself from the situation gives rise to an intolerable sense of inner disharmony and frustration—a feeling of impotence in being unable to master the disturbance. This inability to cope with one's world may give rise also to a strong sense of guilt (e.g., I must be wicked if this state of affairs exists).

Comparable psychological conditions have been recorded among prospective shamans (Bogoras 1909; Benedict 1934; Linton 1956; Eliade 1958, 1964).

As one reads accounts of the "making of shamans," one finds that there take place certain uniform, or almost uniform, experiences. For example, the shaman as a child usually shows marked introvert tendencies. When these inclinations become manifest, they are encouraged by society. The budding shaman often wanders off and spends a long time by himself. He is rather antisocial in his attitudes and is very frequently seized by mysterious illnesses of one sort or another [Linton 1956:124].

To people of more mature age [among the Chukchee], the shamanistic call may come during some great misfortune, dangerous and protracted illness, sudden loss of family or property, etc. Then the person, having no other sources, turns to the spirits and claims their assistance [Borgoras 1909:421].

It is also considered perfectly natural that a young boy should try to call the spirits. . . . In the same way a number of Chukchee tales tell of young orphans, despised and oppressed by all their neighbors, who call to the spirits and with their assistance become strong men and powerful shamans [Borgas 1909:424].

. . . the shamanic vocation often implies a crisis so deep that it sometimes borders on madness. And since the youth cannot become a shaman until he has resolved this crisis, it plays the role of a mystical initiation [Eliade 1958:89].

Devereux (1961) has viewed this choice of the shaman's way of life as a less risky resolution of a life crisis than a "choice," by one living in the same society, of neurosis or psychosis. The preshaman is thought to be able to manage such an adjustment because he is insufficiently acculturated. While Devereux's notions of what is and what is not acculturation are quite different from this author's, our basic orientations are in accord: shamanism is regarded as a total psychological adjustment to a condition of extreme threat, in which one is provided with an alternative to more drastic (i.e., culturally less acceptable) forms of deviancy. By "extreme threat" is meant that psychological state in which one perceives oneself as being unable (a) to attain what are culturally acknowledged as the basic satisfactions or (b) to solve the culturally defined basic problems of existence. In this condition, one invariably experiences a sense of personal failure and inadequacy. Any subsequent deviant behaviors that occur because of this psychological state will inevitably bear the influence of the culture in which they emerge.

Wallace conceives of the process of becoming a shaman as an instance of "mazeway resynthesis." This term refers to the sudden reorganization of one's mode of structuring the world in an attempt to make sense of a highly anxiety-provoking environment. It thereby serves a highly therapeutic function. The therapeutic value of the shamanistic inspiration experience, however,

depends both on the resources of the individual and on the support his effort is given by the community. The culture enters into the process here, rather evidently, by imposing certain evaluations on the content of such experiences as well as on their form. . . . The existing cultural milieu can act as a support or a hindrance to the mazeway resynthesis process by facilitating or suppressing the institutionalization of behavior patterns and beliefs conceived in the course of such experinces [Wallace 1961:192].

Stage 2. Preoccupation; Isolation; Estrangement

Both the schizophrenic's experience and the shaman's "answering the call" begin with a marked preoccupation with their personal situations and with emotions so intense that they are carried, as it were, into another world. This experience comes about in an abrupt and obscure manner. Often, the experience is activated by various omens, such as participating in or seeing a certain event take place, having a dream, finding an object of some peculiar form, etc. "Each of these omens has in itself nothing extraordinary but derives its significance from its mystical recognizance in the mind of the person to whose notice it is brought" (Borgoras 1909:418). The consequent self-absorption results in longer and longer breaks in the normal process of communication and social interaction. An outstanding characteristic is the sense of isolation and estrangement, which makes social interaction progressively more difficult.

To feel oneself cut off from those with whom one seeks identification is death. . . . It appears to be just as important for an individual to feel himself part of the social organism as for a cell to be a functioning unit in the body to which it belongs [Boisen 1936:150].

This observation is consistent with Sullivan's (1953a, 1956) and others' (e.g., Perry 1962) comments on the schizophrenic experience. It is also consistent with the work of Eliade (1958, 1964), who, in summarizing studies of shamanism the world over (e.g., in Africa, Australia, North America, Siberia), notes the very common belief among shamans in their own deaths and mystical transfigurations occurring just prior to taking on their new identities.

During this period of intense personal preoccupation one tends to become absorbed in a narrow circle of ideas. In most cases this is accompanied by a loss of sleep carried to the point where the boundaries between sleep and waking are lost. Sullivan, in his discussion of the individual in the early throes of the schizophrenic state, writes: "His awareness is now that of a twilight state between waking and dreaming: his facial expression is that of absorption in ecstatic inner experiences, and his behavior is peculiar to the degree that he no longer eats or sleeps, or tends to any of the routines of life" (1953a:133). Highly similar kinds of experiences among budding shamans have been reported by field workers in many primitive cultures, for example, among the Sedang Moi, the South African Bantu, the Eskimos of the Arctic, in Indonesia, in Siberia (Bogoras 1909; Ackerknecht 1943; Eliade 1958, 1964). Clinical and anthropological observations also suggest that a kind of autohypnotic state is common under these conditions (Borgoras 1909; Benedict 1934; Boisen 1936; Roheim 1952; Eliade 1958, 1964; Kaplan 1964). The principle behind the induction of autohypnosis is one of perceptual fixation, and some of its behavioral manifestations are apparent in the pathological staring of schizophrenics and novice shamans or in the total attentiveness of certain shamans to their frenzied, prolonged drum beating or whistling.

Stage 3. Narrowing of Attention; Self-Initiated Sensory Deprivation

There is impressive experimental evidence suggesting that prolonged perceptual fixation may readily lead to two highly significant kinds of alterations in one's characteristic manner of experiencing the world. The first has to do with changes in attention and is well illustrated by the laboratory research of Piaget (1950), Gardner *et al.* (1959), and their collaborators. They have presented experimental evidence indicating that persons who fixate upon stimulus patterns (e.g., illusions, size judgments) to an excessive degree show more distortion or inaccuracy than those who vary their attention to the different aspects of the stimulus field. It is suggested here that the altered perceptions and cognitions of the schizophrenic and budding shaman evolve out of (a) their constriction of the range of stimulus input to which they are responsive and (b) their intense absorption with a *narrow* circle of ideas. The latter most often are either newly acquired or are accentuated through physical illness or self-evaluated failure and impotence. This extreme mode of narrowing attention changes both sensory and ideational figureground relationships and hence the cognitive structural relationships acquired over the course of psychological development.

The main point being emphasized here is that the abnormal behaviors of the schizophrenic and the shaman are the result of a specific psychological process. This process involves extreme "styles" of attention deployment, marked withdrawal from ordinary kinds of activities, and, simultaneously, a marked reduction in meaningful sensory (i.e., perceptual) input.

Stage 4. The Fusing of Higher and Lower Referential Processes

What we discover in the self-system of a person undergoing schizophrenic change or schizophrenic processes is . . . in its simplest form, an extremely fear marked puzzlement, consisting of the use of rather generalized and anything but exquisitely refined referential processes in an attempt to cope with what is essentially a failure at being human—a failure at being anything that one could respect as worth being [Sullivan 1956:184-185].

The crises facing preshamans and preschizophrenics on their brinks of chaos may be viewed as revolving around a severely damaged conception of self (Sullivan 1953a, Wallace 1961: 183-184 [quoted above], Perry 1962). From this perspective their mental abnormalities are regarded as the *result* of a desperate attempt at redefinition of a personally meaningful and adequate self-concept. Since these redefinitions are intrinsically related to personal conceptions of "what reality is" (Mullahy 1953, Sullivan 1953b), *the fragmentation of one's self-concept in the course of redefinition also implies a fragmentation of reality as it has been culturally elaborated by and for the individual.*

What follows then is the eruption into the field of attention of a flood of archaic imagery and attendant lower-order referential processes such as occur in dreams or reverie (e.g., association of ideas by contiguity or *pars pro toto* condensation, displacement). Ideas surge through with peculiar vividness as though from an outside source. The fact that they are entirely different from anything previously experienced lends support to the assumption that they have come from the realm of the supernatural. One feels oneself to be swelling among the mysterious and the uncanny. Ideas of world catastrophe, of cosmic importance, and of mission abound. Words, thoughts, and *dreams* can easily be seen to reside in external objects. Causal relationships are perceived against a background of magic and animism. Everything is now capable of being related to everything else in terms of a mental orientation that is grossly subjective. New ideas, crowded in upon the anxious individual, are experienced as real thing. Reality becomes something else. Chaos prevails.

Eliade writes:

The total crisis of the future shaman, sometimes leading to complete disintegration of the personality and to madness, can be valuated not only as an initiatory death, but also as a symbolic return to the precosmogonic chaos, to the amorphous and indescribable state that precedes any cosmogony . . . [1958:89].

Sullivan describes a comparable state in the schizophrenic:

The experience which the patient undergoes is of the most awesome, universal character; he seems to be living in the midst of struggle between personified cosmic forces of good and evil, surrounded by animistically enlivened natural objects which are engaged in ominous performances that it is terribly necessary—and impossible—to understand . . . [1953a:151-152].

It is at this point that consideration of the cognitive/affective experiences of the schizophrenic and of the shaman need to be given within separate frames of reference. Whereas the initial shamanistic experience is most often highly valued and rewarded in primitive society, no such institutional supports are available for the schizophrenic in modern society. The social role of the shaman has legitimated within it free access to lower referential processes. For the schizophrenic, the absence of such culturally acceptable and appropriate referential guides only has the effect of intensifying his suffering over and above the original anxieties. There are simply too few acceptable or realistically valid concepts available with which to label these unusual felings and beliefs. It is not surprising then that guilt—the internalization of negative feelings regarding nonadherence to societal standards—in intensified where social standards of behavior prohibit such types of life-crisis resolutions.

Note here also that these crisis resolutions are grossly aberrant and inaccurate ones only in cultures maintaining definitions of "reality" that are different from ours. Thus, for example, when a beetle or a small louse is found in the wilderness and "shown" to be of a supernatural kind, as in several Chukchee myths, who among the Chukchee will argue that the possessor does not thereby acquire immense shamanistic power? These revelations clearly serve their adaptive ends not by providing an accurate translation of reality (for what is reality except what a culture states it to be), but rather by effecting what Klein (1958) has called a "workable fit" between personal need and personal perception and the demands of the environment. If reality-testing, as a theoretical construct, is to have any sensible usage in psychosociocultural theory, then it must refer only to the effective coordination between the properties of things and a given culture's various concepts and perceptions of these properties.

Stage 5. Cognitive Reorganization

The mental and emotional reorganization that the shaman undergoes in the course of his life occurs according to a more or less accepted pattern—that is, once it has been set in motion by the shamanistic call and once enough shamanistic "inspiration" has been gathered. Even in the trance the individual holds to the rules and expectations of his culture (Benedict 1934).

The high regard in which the shaman is held stems principally from the fact that

he has succeeded in integrating into consciousness a considerable number of experiences that, for the profane world, are reserved for dreams, madness, or post-mortem states. The shamans and mystics of primitive societies are considered—and rightly—to be superior beings; their magicoreligious powers also find expression in an extension of their mental capacities. The shaman is the man who *knows* and *remembers,* that is, who understands the mysteries of life and death. . . . He is not solely an ecstatic but also a contemplative . . . [Eliade 1958:102].

The degree of prestige acquired by the shaman also depends in part upon the successful outcome of his pronouncements and mystical performances. He must therefore be capable of a rather high degree of flexibility in the sense of being able to attend to the needs of both his "clients" in the physical world and his "spirits" in the other world. Often the shaman's ritual tricks, performed during his trancelike ecstasy states, require an extraordinary amount of physical and psychological control. Also, he must be continually able to "enter" and "return" from the far-flung reaches of the cosmos. Thus it appears that many of his remarkable feats of skill require as a precondition a significantly altered psychic state. Similar kinds of ritualistic behavior when performed by a person in a schizophrenic state lead to absolutely nothing at all that has cultural significance, other than as verification of his insanity. (Such feats of physical dexterity—of balancing and ritualistic dance—have been repeatedly noted in the past among catatonic schizophrenics, e.g., Sullivan 1956.)

In contrast to the shaman, the chances of the schizophrenic achieving a successful readaptation are comparatively small. For the crisis solutions of the schizophrenic are totally invalid ones in the eyes of the great majority of his peers. Thus, somewhere along the way he must resolve the additional problem of whether his new insights are "better" or "worse" than the more culturally appropriate ones. Where his life situation is essentially lacking in constructive premorbid factors with no apparent consensually valid solutions in sight—where there is little to come back to—then the prognosis for a prolonged "return" is poor (Boisen 1936).

The essential difference between the psychosocial environments of the schizophrenic and the shaman lies in the pervasiveness of the anxiety that complicates each of their lives. The emotional supports and the modes of collective solutions of the basic problems of existence available to the shaman greatly alleviate the strain of an otherwise excruciatingly painful existence. Such supports are all too often completely unavailable to the schizophrenic in our culture.

REFERENCES

ABSE, D. W. 1959 Hysteria. *In* The American handbook of psychiatry, vol. 1. S. Arieti, ed. New York, Basic Books.

ACKERKNECHT, E. H. 1943 Psychopathology, primitive medicine, and primitive culture. Bulletin of History of Medicine 14:30-67.

ADLER, G. 1948 Studies in analytic psychology. New York, Norton.

BARENDREGT, J. T., and F. VAN REE 1961 Prediction of the nature of reaction to LSD 25. *In* Psychological studies I, Research in diagnostics. J. T. Barendregt, ed. The Hague, Mouton.

BENEDICT, R. 1934 Patterns of culture. Boston, Houghton Mifflin.

BOGORAS, W. 1909 The Chukchee, Memoirs of the American Museum of Natural History, Vol. XL. New York, Leiden.

BOISEN, A. 1936 The exploration of the inner world. New York, Harper. 1942 The form and content of schizophrenic thinking. Psychiatry 5:23-33. 1947 Onset in acute schizophrenia. Psychiatry 10:159-166.

BOURKE, J. G. 1892 The medicine men of the Apache. BAE-R, p. 460.

BRODY, E. B. 1964 Some conceptual and methodological issues involved in research in society, culture and mental illness. Journal of Nervous and Mental Disease 139:62-74.

DEVEREUX, G. 1956 Normal and abnormal: the key problem of psychiatric anthropology. *In* Some uses of anthropology: theoretical and applied. J. B. Casagrande and T. Gladwin, eds. Washington, Anthropological Society of Washington. 1961 Mohave ethnopsychiatry and suicide: the psychiatric knowledge and the psychic disturbances of an Indian tribe, Washington, Smithsonian Institution.

ELIADE, M. 1958 Birth and rebirth, New York, Harper. 1964 Shamanism: archaic techniques of ecstacy. New York, Pantheon.

FREEDMAN, S. J., H. U. GRUNEBAUM, and M. GREENBLATT. 1961 Perceptual and cognitive changes in sensory deprivation. *In* Harvard Medical School symposium on sensory deprivation. P. Solomon *et al.,* eds. Cambridge, Harvard University Press.

GARDNER, R. W., P. S. HOLZMAN, G. S. KLEIN, H. B. LINTON, and D. P. SPENCE 1959 Cognitive control: a study of individual consistencies in cognitive behavior. Psychological Issues, No. 4.

HALLOWELL, A. I. 1942 The role of conjuring in Salteaux society. Philadelphia, University of Pennsylvania Press.

KAPLAN, B., Ed. 1964 The inner world of mental illness. New York, Harper and Row.

KLEIN, G. S. 1958 Cognitive control and motivation. *In* The assessment of human motives. G. Lindzey, ed. New York, Rinehart.

KROEBER, A. L. 1952 The nature of culture. Chicago, University of Chicago Press.

KURAMOCHI, H., and R. TAKAHASHI. 1964 Psychopathology of LSD intoxication. Archives of General Psychiatry 11:151-161.

LANGFELDT, G. 1956 The prognosis in schizophrenia. Acta Psychiatrica Scandinavia, Suppl. 110.

LINTON, R. 1956 Culture and mental disorders. Springfield, Ill., C C Thomas.

LOER, E. M. 1929 Shaman and seer. American Anthropologist 31: 60-84.

LOWIE, R. H. 1954 Indians of the plains. New York, McGraw-Hill.

McFANN, H. H., and C. E. GREEN. 1962 U.S. Army Leadership Human Research Unit. Quarterly Research Report, January-March, Presidio of Monterey, California.

MACIVER, R. M. 1942 Social causation. Boston, Ginn & Company. Quoted from 1964 edition, New York, Harper Torchbooks.

MCREYNOLDS, P. 1960 Anxiety, perception and schizophrenia. *In* Etiology of schizophrenia. D. Jackson, ed. New York, Basic Books.

MULLAHY, P. 1953 The theory of interpersonal relations and the evolution of personality. *In* Conceptions of modern psychiatry. H. S. Sullivan, ed. New York, W. W. Norton.

NADEL, S. F. 1958 A study of shamanism in the Nuba Mountains. *In* Reader in comparative religion. W. A. Lessa and E. Vogt, eds. New York, Row, Peterson & Co.

OPLER, M. K. 1959 Culture and mental health. New York, Macmillan.

PERRY, J. W. 1962 Reconstitutive process in the psychopathology of the self. Annals of the New York Academy of Sciences 96:853-876.

PIAGET, J. 1950 The psychology of intelligence. London, Routledge and Kegan Paul.

RAPAPORT, D. 1960 On the psychoanalytic theory of motivation. *In* The Nebraska symposium on motivation. M. R. Jones, ed. Lincoln, University of Nebraska Press.

RINDER, I.D. 1964 New directions and an old problem: the definition of normality. Psychiatry 27:107-115.

ROHEIM, G. 1952 The gates of the dream. New York, International Universities Press.

SILVERMAN, J. 1964a The scanning control mechanism and "cognitive filtering" in paranoid and nonparanoid schizophrenia. Journal of Consulting Psychology 28:385-393. 1964b The problem of attention in research and theory in schizophrenia. Psychological Review 71:352-379. 1967 Variations in cognitive control and psychophysiological defense in the schizophrenias. Psychosomatic Medicine. In press.

SOLOMON, P., P. E. KUBZANSKY, P. H. LEIDERMAN, J. H. MENDELSOHN, R. TRUMBULL, and D. WEXLER, Eds. 1961 Harvard Medical School symposium on sensory deprivation, Cambridge, Harvard University Press.

SPENCER, B., and F. J. GILLEN. 1899 The native tribes of Central Australia. New York, Macmillan.

SULLIVAN, H. S. 1953a Conceptions of modern psychiatry. New York, Norton. 1953b The interpersonal theory of psychiatry. New York, Norton. 1956 Clinical studies in psychiatry. New York, Norton.

WALLACE, A. F. C. 1961 Culture and personality, New York Random House.

SECTION 4

THE SELF-REGULATION OF CONSCIOUSNESS

An adverse result of the stresses our society forces on us is excessive arousal of the "fight-or-flight" response, a discrete state marked by physiological excitation, increased alertness, and, often, anxiety. This stress response is the cause of a range of psychosomatic and neurotic disorders. Meditation, cardiologist Herbert Benson reports, produces a discrete state, which he dubs "the relaxation response," that is the exact opposite of stress arousal. Although historically meditation has been part of a total program of spiritual development, anyone can use the relaxation response as an antidote to stress.

More serious pursuit of meditation can take a person beyond the threshold of simple discrete states of consciousness like the relaxation response, and plunge him into a variety of altered states. Psychologist Daniel Goleman summarizes an ancient Buddhist manual for meditators that gives detailed instructions on the attentional training required to enter various meditative altered states. If the meditator hones his attention to a single fine point, he can enter a blissful trance state that can then be refined to varying degrees of subtlety. If he follows another attentional tactic, adopting a neutral "witness" posture toward his stream of awareness, he will undergo a different progression of altered states that finally culminates in "nirvana," the complete cessation of all experience whatsoever.

While meditation has been the time-honored Eastern approach to altering consciousness, the West is developing its own avenues. Biofeedback allows a person to control the workings of the brain and body to an extent previously thought impossible by physiologists. Gerald Jonas explains how a biofeedback device can tell a person exactly what changes are occurring in the bodily process it taps, giving information about processes such as brain waves, blood pressure, or muscle tension that otherwise could never be known. With this information the person can use hit-or-miss learning to control the process itself. Biofeedback thus opens a new avenue to wresting control of one's bodily processes, and, conceivably, consciousness.

The most dramatic use of biofeedback to alter consciousness thus far has been in teaching people to control their brain waves. Biofeedback pioneer Thomas Budzynski uses biofeedback to teach people to stabilize in the "twilight" state most of us pass through just as we are dozing off to sleep. Awareness during the twilight state is dreamlike, sometimes hallucinatory, and focused inward; brain waves during this state are dominantly in the very slow, rhythmic theta range. By giving people feedback whenever their brainwaves are in the theta range, Budzynski shows them how to prolong the twilight state for much longer than they normally could. While in this state, people have greater access to creative insights, are deeply relaxed, and can reprogram deep-seated psychological attitudes.

The Relaxation Response

Herbert Benson
Jamie B. Kotch
Karen D. Crassweller
Martha M. Greenwood

In the past decade, there has been a growing interest in nonpharmacologic, self-induced altered states of consciousness because of the alleged benefits of better mental and physical health and an increased ability to deal with tension and stress. Many believe that altered states of consciousness represent a normal and natural human desire (Brecher 1972). Indeed, mood-altering by man has been historically documented in many cultures throughout the world. One such altered state of consciousness has been attained through practices such as meditative prayer, found in virtually all religions, through cultic meditational techniques such as Transcendental Meditation (TM) and Yoga, as well as through secular practices such as autogenic therapy and hypnosis (Benson 1975; Benson, Beary, and Carol 1974).

Despite the diversity of these practices, there appears to be a common denominator. Subjective and objective data exist which support the hypothesis that a physiologic response, recently termed the *relaxation response,* underlies an altered state of consciousness (Benson, Beary, and Carol 1974). The elicitation of the relaxation response results in physiologic changes which are thought to characterize an integrated hypothalamic response (Wallace and Benson 1972; Wallace et al. 1971). These physiologic changes are consistent with generalized decreased sympathetic nervous system activity. Uniform and signficant decreases have been observed in oxygen consumption and carbon dioxide elimination with no change in respiratory quotient. In addition, there is a simultaneous lowering of heart and respiratory rates and a marked decrease in arterial blood lactate concentration. The electroencephalogram shows intensification of slow alpha-wave activity with occasional theta waves. The physiologic changes of the relaxation response are distinctly different from those observed during quiet sitting or sleep and characterize a wakeful hypometabolic state.

Physiologic changes similar to those constituting the relaxation response were initially termed the *trophotropic response* by Hess (1957). He electrically stimulated one hypothalamic area of the cat brain and induced physiologic changes like those later noted during the elicitation of the relaxation response in man. These physiologic changes are opposite to those of a response originally described by Cannon in 1914, which he termed the *emergency reaction*—popularly called the *fight-or-flight response.* The physiology of the fight-or-flight response, correspondingly, consists of generalized increased sympathetic nervous system activity and includes increased catecholamine production with associated increases in blood pressure, heart and respiratory rates, and skeletal muscle blood flow (Abrahams et al. 1960; Cannon 1914). The relaxation response appears to be a basic bodily response that may have significance in countering overactivity of the sympathetic nervous system in man and other animals (Hess 1957). This article will describe both subjective and objective data that demonstrate the existence and usefulness of the relaxation response.

THE SUBJECTIVE EXPERIENCE

Many of the subjective experiences associated with the elicitation of the relaxation response consitute an altered state of consciousness. These subjective experiences have been described as peace of mind, feeling at ease with the world, and a sense of well-being. Other descriptions have been of an ecstatic, clairvoyant, beautiful, and totally relaxing experience (Dean 1970).

The concept of altered states of consciousness, in general, has been somewhat unacceptable to Western man. As Robert Ornstein asserts in *The Psychology of Consciousness* (1972), the Western "impersonal, objective scientific approach, with its exclusive emphasis on logic and analysis makes it difficult for most of us even to conceive of a psychology which could be based on the existence of another intuitive gestalt mode of thought." The ultimate aim of practices or techniques used to attain this state has varied—union with God, transcendence from the physical, and inner awareness of one's self. This is not to be interpreted as viewing religion or philosophy in a mechanistic manner, since the purpose of any of these exercises corresponds to the philosophy or religion in which it is used. Moreover, no one technique can claim uniqueness. William James (1958) expresses this view: "To find religion is only one out of many ways of reaching unity; and the process of remedying inner discord is a general psychological process."

Despite the diversity of descriptions of these experiences, however, striking similarities between the techniques used to achieve this altered state strongly suggest the existence of a common physiologic basis, which is hypothesized to be the relaxation response. Further, it appears that this altered state of consciousness has been experienced by man throughout all ages in both Eastern and Western cultures. Four elements seem to be integral to these varied practices and are necessary to evoke the relaxation response: a quiet environment; decreased muscle tone; a mental device, i.e. a sound, word, or phrase repeated silently or audibly; and a passive attitude.

Meditative practices that may bring forth the relaxation response have been an important part of Indian culture for thousands of years. Age-old practices of Yoga strive for "union" of the self with a supreme being or principle. Yogic meditation often invovles concentration on a single point to exclude all thoughts that are associated with everyday life (Benson, Beary, and Carol 1974; Eliade 1958). Yoga has evolved into techniques that often place more emphasis upon the physical aspects of achieving an altered state of consciousness. Essential to these forms of Yoga are appropriate posture to enhance concentration and regulation of respiration (Benson 1975; Benson, Beary, and Carol 1974).

One of the meditative practices of Zen Buddhism, Zazen, employs a Yogic technique of coupling respiration with counting to ten—one on inhaling, two on exhaling, and so on. With time, one stops counting and simply "follows the breath" (Johnston 1971) in order to achieve a state of no thought, no feeling, to be completely "in nothing" (Ishiguro 1964). Similar experiences have been described in many other Eastern practices, including the Japanese and Chinese religions of Shintoism and Taoism, and Sufism, an Islamic mystical tradition.

In the East, these meditational techniques, which are hypothesized to elicit the relaxation response, were extensively developed and became a major element in religion and everyday life. In the Western world, however, practice of various meditative techniques that are thought to bring forth the relaxation response was limited primarily to religious traditions. Many Christian writers, including St. Augustine and Martin Luther, wrote descriptions of prayers, often called contemplative exercises, which could be used to transcend the mundane world in order to realize a union with God. One example is the following set of instructions given by Gregory of Sinai in the fourteenth century for the "Prayer of the Heart," or "The Prayer of Jesus," a repetitive prayer of early Christian origin:

Sit down alone and in silence. Lower your head, shut your eyes, breathe out gently, and imagine yourself looking into your own heart. Carry your mind, i.e., your thoughts, from your head to your heart. As you breathe out, say "Lord Jesus Christ, have mercy on me." Say it moving your lips gently, or simply say it in your mind. Try to put all other thoughts aside. Be calm, be patient and repeat the process very frequently [French 1968].

In the Judaic literature one also finds portrayals of contemplative or meditative exercises. Again, the ultimate purpose is union with God. One of the early forms of mysticism in Judaism is Merkabolism, which dates back to approximately the first century B.C. The meditative exercises of Merkabolism included placing one's head between one's knees, whispering hymns, and repeating the name of a magic emblem. Repetition of the magic emblem would chase away distractions and cause the "demons and hostile angels to flight" (Scholem 1967).

Meditative practices may also be found outside of a religious context, and many descriptions of transcendent experiences appear in the secular literature. Tennyson experienced visions of ecstasy that were the foundation of his deepest beliefs of the "unity of all thing, the reality of the unseen, and the persistence of life" (Spurgeon 1970). For him, transcendence was achieved through the repetition of his own name!

Throughout history many techniques or practices that are similar in nature have been used to achieve an altered state of consciousness. It is proposed that the relaxation response underlies many of the subjective experiences of this altered state. The recently documented physiologic effects of these various practices reflect the commonality of these experiences and thus of the relaxation response.

A SIMPLE NONCULTIC TECHNIQUE

Incorporating the four elements common to a multitude of historical techniques, a simple noncultic technique was developed in our laboratory. Use of the technique results in the same physiologic changes that our laboratory first noted using TM as a model. The instructions for this noncultic technique are the following:

1. Sit quietly in a comfortable position and close your eyes.

2. Deeply relax all your muscles, beginning at your feet and progressing up to your face. Keep them deeply relaxed.

3. Breathe through your nose. Become aware of your breathing. As you breathe out, say the word *one* silently to yourself. For example, breathe in . . . out, *one;* in . . . out, *one;* etc. Continue for 20 minutes. You may open your eyes to check the time, but do not use an alarm. When you finish, sit quietly for several minutes at first with closed eyes and later with opened eyes.

4. Do not worry about whether you are successful in achieving a deep level of relaxation. Maintain a passive attitude and permit relaxation to occur at its own pace. Expect other thought. When these distracting thoughts occur, ignore them by thinking "Oh well" and continue repeating "one." With practice the response should come with little effort. Practice

the technique once or twice daily, but not within two hours after any meal, since the digestive processes seem to interfere with the subjective changes.

In an investigation by Beary and Benson (1974), 17 naive subjects were taught this relaxation technique immediately prior to being studied. Oxygen consumption, carbon dioxide elimination, and respiratory rate were analyzed during the testing session. Samples of expired air were processed continuously throughout the experiment, thus enabling more accurate data collection than that afforded by a system of random sampling. Comparison of the results revealed no statistically significant differences between the values of the three control periods, during which the subjects say quietly and read material selected for its neutral emotional content. During the practice of the noncultic relaxation technique, oxygen consumption decreased by 13% (p < 0.01) and carbon dioxide elimination by 12% (p < 0.01), with no change in respiratory quotient. Respiratory rate also decreased (p < 0.01) Sitting quietly with eyes closed did not produce these decreases in O_2 consumption, CO_2 elimination, or respiratory rate. The results indicate that simply sitting quietly with eyes closed fails to induce the essentially hypometabolic elements of the relaxation response evidenced during the practice of the noncultic relaxation technique.

These results parallel those yielded by an earlier study, conducted in 1968 (Wallace and Benson 1972; Wallace et al. 1971), which indicated that a consistent wakeful hypometabolic state accompanies the practice of TM. This technique, derived from the Vedic tradition of India and adapted to Western life (Wallace et al. 1971), requires learning a systematic method of perceiving a "suitable" sound or thought (the mantra) without attempting to concentrate specifically upon that sound or thought. The data revealed pronounced and consistent physiologic changes during the practice of TM. The respiratory changes consisted of a 16% decrease in O_2 consumption, a 15% decrease in CO^2 elimination, and a respiratory rate lowered by two breaths per minute.

Another investigation, by Benson, Steinert, Greenwood, et al. (1975), using TM was conducted employing a more sophisticated methodology but retaining the experimental design of the earlier TM investigation. Continuous measurement, however, as opposed to intermittent sampling, of O_2 consumption, CO_2 elimination, and heart rate, enabled the calculation of the mean value for each discrete period as well as for selected intervals during these periods. Results demonstrated a 5% decrease in O_2 consumption and a 6% decrease in CO_2 elimination for the entire meditation period. The discrepancy between these values and the substantially higher percentages (16% and 15% for O_2 and CO_2, respectively) observed in the previous study may be attributable to the revision in methodology. The less striking results obtained in the later TM study may reflect a difference between the sampling method employed in the first study and that of the second investigation.

THERAPEUTIC USEFULNESS

Humans, like other animals, react in a predictable way to stressful situations (Gutmann and Benson 1971). When we are faced with situations that require behavioral adjustment, an involuntary response, the fight-or-flight response, is activated. It is associated with increased sympathetic nervous system activity and thus with increases in blood pressure, heart rate, respiratory rate, skeletal muscle blood flow, and metabolism, preparing, speaking teleologically, for conflict or escape. The continual stresses of contemporary living, however, have led to the excessive elicitation of the fight-or-flight response. Further, within the constructs of our society, the behavioral features of this response, running or fighting, are often inappropriate. Indeed, the *excessive* and *inappropriate* arousal of the fight-or-flight response with its corresponding sympathetic nervous system activation may have a role in the pathogenesis and exacerbation of several disorders. Regular elicitation of the relaxation response may be of preventive and therapeutic value in diseases in which increased sympathetic nervous system activity is implicated.

Several longitudinal investigations have demonstrated that the regular elicitation of the relaxation response lowers blood pressure in both pharmacologically treated and untreated hypertensive subjects (Benson et al. 1974a,b; Datey et al. 1969; Patel 1973, 1975; Stone and DeLeo 1976). In an early investigation done by our laboratory, would-be initiates of TM who were also hypertensive, volunteered to participate in the study (Benson et al. 1974a,b). Baseline measurements of blood pressure were taken weekly, for approximately six weeks, after which the subjects were taught to bring forth the relaxation response through the practice of TM. Of the 36 patients included in the study, 22 received no medication during the investigation and 14 remained on unaltered antihypertensive medications during both the control and experimental periods. In the 22 nonmedicated subjects, control blood pressures averaging 146.5 mm Hg systolic and 94.6 mm Hg diastolic decreased significantly to 139.5 mm Hg systolic (p < 0.001) and 90.8 mm Hg diastolic (p < 0.002) after the regular elicitation of the relaxation response through the practice of TM. In the 14 patients who maintained constant antihypertensive medications, mean control blook pressures of 145.6 mm Hg systolic and 91.9 mm Hg diastolic dropped significantly to 135.0 mm Hg systolic (p < 0.01) and 87.0 mm Hg diastolic (p < 0.05) post-intervention.

Several other researchers report similar findings. Datey and co-workers (1969) noted decreases in both systolic and diastolic blood pressures in 47 hypertensive patients who evoked the relaxation response through the practice of another Yogic technique, called *Shavasan*. In this study, subjects served as their own controls. Information regarding the length of the pre-intervention control period and the number of control blood-pressure measurements made, however, was not reported.

In two well-controlled longitudinal investigations, Patel (1973, 1975) combined Yogic relaxation with biofeedback techniques in the treatment of 20 patients with hypertension. The average systolic blood pressure in these subjects was reduced by 20.4± 11.4 mm Hg, which mean diastolic pressure was reduced by 14.2 ± 7.5 mm Hg (p < 0.001). A hypertensive control group matched for age and sex was employed. Length of testing sessions, number of attendances, and the procedure for measuring the blood pressure of the control group were identical to those of the treatment group. Control patients were not given instruction in the relaxation technique, however, but simply were asked to rest on a couch. No significant changes in blood pressure occurred in the control group.

Further substantiation of the usefulness of the relaxation response in the treatment of hypertension has come from Stone and DeLeo (1976), who obtained significant decreases in systolic and diastolic blood pressures using a Buddhist meditation exercise. The control group, which received no psychotherapeutic intervention, was matched for blood pressure, age, and race, and exhibited virtually no change in systolic and diastolic pressures.

A more recent example of the clinical usefulness of the relaxation response is that of reducing the number of premature ventricular contractions (PVCs) (Benson, Alexander, and Feldman 1975). Participating in a study were 11 nonmedicated ambulatory patients who had proven ischemic heart disease for at least one year's duration, with documented relatively stable PVCs. Frequent PVCs are correlated with an increased mortality in such patients (Desai et al. 1973; Tominaga et al. 1973). The frequency of the PVCs was measured over 48 consecutive hours, after which the subject was taught to elicit the relaxation response by using the noncultic technique described above. After four weeks of regularly practicing the relaxation technique and recording their frequency of practice, the patients returned to repeat the two days of monitoring.

A reduced frequency of PVCs was observed in 8 of the 11 patients. Before the intervention, the PVCs per hour per patient for the total group had averaged 151.5 for the entire monitoring session. Four weeks after the intervention was instituted, the average PVCs per hour per patient dropped to 131.7. The reduction of PVCs was even more marked during sleep. Initially, the number of PVCs per hour per patient during sleeping hours averaged 125.5, while after four weeks of regular elicitation of the relaxation response, the PVCs during sleep decreased to 87.9 (p < 0.05). When the PVCs were expressed per 1,000 heartbeats per patient for the entire group, there was a significant decrease during sleeping hours from 29.0 to 21.1 (p < 0.05).

The results suggest that the regular elicitation of the relaxation response with its hypothesized decreased sympathetic nervous system activity may have been the mechanism by which PVCs were reduced. This finding is consistent with that of Lown and his co-workers (1976),

who, in a recent case study, reported that a patient was able to abolish his arrhythmias by meditation. These results were attributed to lessened sympathetic tone (Lown et al. 1973), although others (Weiss et al. 1975) implicate increased parasympathetic activity as a mechanism for the reduction of PVCs.

In another longitudinal study, the use of the relaxation response as treatment for vascular headache was investigated (Benson, Klemchuk, and Graham 1974). All patients chosen for the study had long histories of severe vascular headaches (migraine and cluster), for which they had received pharmacologic therapy with little relief of symptoms. After one to three months of recording the severity of their headaches and the type and amount of antiheadache medications used, the subjects were taught to bring forth the relaxation response through the practice of TM. Data from at least four months indicated that the twice-daily elicitation of the relaxation response using TM has limited value in the therapy of severe migraine and cluster headaches. Three of the 17 migraine patients experienced a significant decrease in headache severity during the experimental period as compared to the premeditation, control period, while one patient experienced a significantly greater severity. Thirteen of the 17 migraine patients reported essentially no change. Of the four subjects who suffered severe, incapacitating cluster headache before starting the study, one subject underwent a remarkable clinical recovery that lasted for several years.

Claims had been made that the elicitation of the relaxation response through TM may alleviate drug abuse, so an investigation was undertaken by our laboratory to test this hypothesis (Benson and Wallace 1972). Approximately 1,800 people who had practiced TM for an average of 20 months completed a questionnaire that assessed their usage of marijuana, LSD, other hallucinogens, narcotics, amphetamines, and barbiturates. The questionnaires indicated that, after starting the practice of TM, there was a marked decrease in the number of drug abusers for all drug categories. For example, 78% of the population had used marijuana prior to practicing the TM technique; after 21 months of meditation, only 12% continued to use the drug, thus constituting a 66% decrease in the number using marijuana. The decrease in the number who used LSD was even more marked: after regularly practicing TM for 22 months, 97% of LSD users had given up the drug. Significant decreases in the use of other hallucinogens, amphetamines, narcotics, and barbiturates were also reported. In addition, most subjects had decreased or stopped engaging in drug-selling activity and changed their attitudes in the direction of discouraging others from abusing drugs. The magnitude of these changes increased with the length of time TM was practices.

This drug-abuse study had weaknesses, however. First, since all the subjects were active meditators prior to entering the study, the number of people who had originally started meditation and then stopped only to return to drugs is not known. In addition, all the subjects were future teachers of TM and therefore biased in favor of the technique. Last, the study was limited, owing to its retrospective design, in that data was based on personal recall.

To deal with these limitations and biases, we carried out a long-term study in collaboration with Maynard W. Shelly, of the University of Kansas (Benson et al. unpulb.). Junior-year students at selected high schools in Massachusetts and Michigan anonymously completed questionnaires assessing their drug-abuse habits. Pairs of high schools were matched with respect to their size and their geographic proximity. Programs of TM were introduced in half of the matched high schools; the others, serving as controls, were offered no introductory courses. Of approximately 460 students who were offered the option of learning TM, only 6 (1.3%) started meditation and practiced it regularly. These few meditators, however, did use fewer drugs, which confirmed the previous finding. The data from this study suggest that TM was unacceptable as a nonchemical alternative to drugs for these high school students. It would appear that this mode of bringing forth the relaxation response did not fulfill the basic motivations behind youthful drug abuse.

•••

The relaxation response has been defined as an integrated hypothalamic reaction resulting in generalized decreased sympathetic nervous system activity and has proved to be a useful therapeutic intervention. The efficacy of the relaxation response has been shown for medicated and nonmedicated hypertensive patients, for patients with premature ventricular contractions, and for some patients suffering from severe migraine or cluster headaches. The relaxation response, as a nonpharmacologic modality, may thus be of considerable therapeutic and perhaps preventive value to the many individuals faced with situations in which excessive sympathetic nervous system activity is present and undesirable.

REFERENCES

ABRAHAMS, V. C., S. M. HILTON, and A. W. ZBROZYNA. 1960. Active muscle vasodilatation produced by stimulation of the brain stem: Its significance in the defense reaction. *J. Physiol.* 154:491-513.

BEARY, J. F., and H. BENSON. 1974 A simple psychophysiologic technique which elicits the hypometabolic changes of the relaxation response. *Psychosom. Med.* 36:115-20.

BENSON, H. 1975. *The Relaxation Response.* William Morrow.

BENSON, H., S. ALEXANDER, and E. L. FELDMAN. 1975 Decreased premature ventricular contractions through use of the relaxation response in patients with stable ischemic heart disease. *Lancet* 2:380-82.

BENSON, H., J. F. BEARY, and M. P. CAROL. 1974 The relaxation response. *Psychiatry* 37: 37-46.

BENSON, H., H. P. KLEMCHUK, and J. R. GRAHAM. 1974 The usefulness of the relaxation response in the therapy of headache. *Headache* 14:49-52.

BENSON, H., J. B. KOTCH, and M. W. SHELLY. A prospective study of drug abuse in high school students and the unacceptability of Transcendental Meditation as an alternative. Submitted for publication.

BENSON, H., B. A. ROSNER, B. R. MARZETTA, et al. 1974a. Decreased blood pressure in borderline hypertensive subjects who practiced meditation. *J. Chronic Dis.* 27:163-69.

BENSON, H., B. A. ROSNER, B. R. MARZETTA, et al. 1974b. Decreased blood pressure in pharmacologically treated hypertensive patients who regularly elicited the relaxation response. *Lancet* 1:289-91.

BENSON, H., R. F. STEINERT, M. M. GREENWOOD, et al. 1975. Continuous measurement of O_2 consumption and CO_2 elimination during a wakeful hypometabolic state. *J. Human Stress* 1:37-44.

BENSON, H., and R. K. WALLACE. 1972. Decreased drug abuse with Transcendental Meditation—a study of 1,862 subjects. In *Drug Abuse Proc. of the Int. Conf.,* ed. C. J. D. Zarafonetis, pp. 369-76. Lea and Febiger.

BRECHER, E. M., and editors of *Consumer Reports.* 1972. *Licit and Illicit Drugs.* Consumers Union.

CANNON, W. B. 1914. The emergency function of the adrenal medulla in pain and the major emotions. *Am. J. Physiol.* 33:356-72.

DATEY, K. K., S. N. DESHMUKH, C. P. DALVI, et at. 1969. "Shavasan"; A yogic exercise in the management of hypertension. *Angiology* 20:325-33.

DEAN, S. R. 1970. Is there an ultraconscious beyond the unconscious? *Can. Psychiatr. Assoc. J.* 15:57-61.

DESAI, D., P. I. Hershberg, and S. ALEXANDER. 1973. Clinical significance of ventricular premature beats in an out-patient population. *Chest* 64:564.

ELIADE, M. 1958. *Yoga: Immortality and Freedom.* Trans. W. R. Trask. London: Routledge and Kegan Paul.

FRENCH, R. M., trans. 1968. *The Way of a Pilgrim.* Seabury Press.

GUTMANN, M. C., and H. BENSON. 1971. Interaction of environmental factors and systemic arterial blood pressure: A review. *Medicine* 50:543-53.

HESS, W. R. 1957. *The Functional Organization of the Diencephalon.* Grune and Stratton.

ISHIGURO, H. 1964. *The Scientific Truth of Zen.* Tokyo: Zenrigaku Society.

JAMES, W. 1958. *The Varieties of Religious Experience.* New American Library.

JOHNSTON, W. 1971. *Christian Zen.* Harper and Row.

LOWN, B., J. V. TEMTE, P. REICH, et al. 1976. Basis for recurring ventricular fibrillation in the absence of coronary heart disease and its managment. *N. E. J. Med.* 294:623-29.

LOWN, B., M. TYKOCINSKI, A. GARFEIN, et al. 1973. Sleep and ventricular premature beats. *Circulation* 48:691.

ORNSTEIN, R. E. 1972. *The Psychology of Consciousness.* W. H. Freeman.

PATEL, D. H. 1973. Yoga and biofeedback in the managment of hypertension. *Lancet* 2: 1053-55.

PATEL, C. H. 1975. Twelve-month follow-up of yoga and biofeedback in the management of hypertension. *Lancet* 1:62-64.

SCHOLEM, G. G. 1967. *Jewish Mysticism.* Schocken Books.

SPURGEON, C. F. E. 1970. *Mysticism in English Literature.* Kennikat Press.

STONE, R. A., and J. DELEO. 1976. Psychotherapeutic control of hypertension. *N. Engl. J. Med.* 294:80-84.

TOMINAGA, S., H. BLACKBURN and the Coronary Drug Project Research Group. 1973. Prognostic importance of premature beats following myocardial infarction. *J.A.M.A.* 223:1116.

WALLACE, R. K., and H. BENSON. 1972. The physiology of meditation. *Sci. Am.* 226: 84-90.

WALLACE, R. K., H. BENSON, and A. F. WILSON. 1971. A wakeful hypometabolic physiologic state. *Am. J. Physiol.* 221:795-99.

WEISS, T., G. W. LATTIN, and K. ENGELMAN. 1975. Vagally mediated suppression of premature ventricular contractions in man. *Am. Heart J.* 89-700.

A Map of Inner Space

Daniel Goleman

The classical Buddhist *Abhidhamma* is probably the broadest and most detailed traditional psychology of states of consciousness. In the fifth century A.D., the monk Buddhaghosa summarized the portion of Abhidhamma about meditation into the *Visuddhimagga,* the "Path to Purification." Buddhaghosa explains that the ultimate "purification" should be strictly understood as *nibbana* (sanskrit: *nirvana),* which is an altered state of consciousness.

The Visuddhimagga describes the specific ways the meditator trains his attention and the landmarks he encounters in traversing the meditative path to the nirvanic state. It ends with the psychological consequences for the meditator of his experience of nirvana.

The Visuddhimagga is a traditional recipe book for meditation, but it does not necessarily tell us about the specific practices of contemporary Theravadan Buddhists. The progression it describes is an ideal type and as such need not conform to the experiences of any given person. But experienced meditators will most certainly recognize familiar landmarks here and there.

THE PATH OF CONCENTRATION

At the outset, the meditator's focus wanders from the object of meditation. As he notices he has wandered, he returns his awareness to the proper focus. His one-pointedness is occasional, coming in fits and starts. His mind oscillates between the object of meditation and distracting thoughts, feelings, and sensations. The first landmark in concentration comes when the meditator's mind is unaffected both by outer distractions, such as nearby sounds, and by the turbulence of his own assorted thoughts and feelings. Although sounds are heard, and his thoughts and feelings are noticed, they do not disturb the meditator.

In the next stage, his mind focuses on the object for prolonged periods. The meditator gets better at repeatedly returning his mind to the object as it wanders. His ability to return his attention gradually increases as the meditator sees the ill results of distractions (e.g., agitation) and feels the advantages of a calm one-pointedness. As this happens, the meditator is able to overcome mental habits antagonistic to

calm collectedness, such as boredom due to hunger for novelty. By now, the meditator's mind can remain undistracted for long periods. In the early stages of meditation, there is a tension between concentration of the object of meditation and distracting thoughts. The main distractions are sensual desires; ill will, despair, and anger; sloth and torpor; agitation and worry; and doubt and skepticism. With much practice, a moment comes when these hindrances are wholly subdued.

This is the first noteworthy attainment in concentrative meditation; because it is the state verging on full absorption, it is called "access" concentration. The meditator is still open to his senses and remains aware of surrounding noises and his body's feelings. The meditation subject is a dominant thought but does not yet fully occupy the mind. At this access level, strong feelings of zest or rapture emerge, along with happiness, pleasure, and equanimity. There is also fleeting attention to the meditation subject as though striking at it, or more sustained focus on it, repeatedly noting it. Sometimes there are luminous shapes or flashes of bright light, especially if the meditation subject is a kasina or respiration. There may also be a sensation of lightness, as though the body were floating in the air.

Visionary experiences can occur on the threshold of this level. Visions can be frightening—an image of oneself as a corpse, for example, or the form of a threatening and terrifying beast—or quite benign, such as the figure of a benevolent deity or a Buddha. Meditative visions are quite vivid; the Visuddhimagga says they are as realistic as talking to a guest who comes on a visit. Timid or anxious persons who have a terrifying vision, it is warned, can be driven mad. Another danger to the meditator is becoming enraptured by beatific visions and so halting further progress by making them the goal of one's meditation, failing to further strengthen concentration. The meditator's goal is beyond visions.

Full Absorptions or Jhana

By continually focusing on the object of meditation, there comes the first moment marking a total break with normal consciousness. This is full absorption, or *jhana.* The mind suddenly seems to sink into the object and remains fixed in it. Hindering thoughts cease totally. There is neither sensory perception nor the usual awareness of one's body; bodily pain cannot be felt. Apart from the initial and sustained attention to the primary object, consciousness is dominated by rapture, bliss, and one-pointedness. These are the mental factors that, when in simultaneous ascendance, constitute jhana.

The first taste of jhana lasts but a single moment, but with continued efforts, the jhanic state can be held for longer and longer intervals. Until the jhana is mastered, it is unstable and can be easily lost. Full mastery comes when the meditator can attain jhana whenever, wherever, as soon as, and for as long as he wishes.

In the course of meditation, one-pointedness becomes more and more intensified. Becoming even more one-pointed after mastery of the first jhana requires eliminating initial and repeated returning of the mind to the meditation object. After emerging from the jhanic state, these attentional processes seem gross in comparison to the other more subtle mental factors of jhana. To go beyond these kinds of attention, the meditator enters the first jhana by focusing on the primary object. But then he frees the mind of any thought of the object by instead turning the mind toward rapture, bliss, and one-pointedness. This level of absorption is more subtle and stable than the first. The meditator's mind is now totally free of any verbal thoughts, even that of the original primary object. To go still deeper, the meditator masters the second jhana as he did the first. Then, when he emerges from the second jhana, he sees that rapture—a form of excitement—is gross compared to bliss and one-pointedness. He attains the third level of jhana by again contemplating the primary object and abandoning first thoughts of the object, then rapture. In the third level of absorption, there is a feeling of equanimity toward even the highest rapture. This even-mindedness emerges with the fading away of rapture. This jhana is extremely subtle, and without this newly emergent equanimity, the meditator's mind would be pulled back to rapture.

To go deeper still, the meditator has to abandon all forms of mental pleasure. He has to give up all those mental states that might oppose more total stillness, even bliss and rapture. With the total cessation of bliss, equanimity and one-pointedness gain their full strength. In the fourth jhana, feelings of bodily pleasure are fully abandoned; feelings of pain ceased at the first jhana. There is not a single sensation or thought. The meditator's mind at this extremely subtle level rests with one-pointedness in equanimity.

The next step in concentration culminates in the four states called "formless." The first four jhanas are attained by concentration on a material form or some concept derived therefrom. But the meditator attains the formless states by passing beyond all perception of form. To enter the first four jhanas, the meditator had to empty his mind of mental factors. To enter each successive formless jhana, the meditator substitutes progressively more subtle objects

of concentration. All the formless jhanas share the mental factors of one-pointedness and equanimity, but at each level these factors are more refined. Concentration approaches imperturbability. The meditator cannot be disturbed but emerges after a self-determined time limit set before entering this state.

The meditator reaches the first formless absorption and the fifth jhana by entering the fourth jhana. Mentally extending the limits to the largest extent imaginable, his attention is then turned toward the space occupied by it. With this infinite space as the object of contemplation and with the full maturity of equanimity and one-pointedness, the meditator's mind now abides in a sphere in which all perceptions of form have ceased.

Once the fifth jhana is mastered, the meditator goes still deeper by first achieving an awareness of infinite space and then turning his attention to that infinite awareness. In this way, the thought of infinite space is abandoned, while objectless infinite awareness remains. This marks the sixth jhana. Having mastered the sixth, the meditator obtains the seventh jhana by first entering the sixth and then turning his awareness to the nonexistence of infinite consciousness. Thus, the seventh jhana is absorption with no-thing-ness, or the void, as its object. That is, the meditator's mind takes as its object the awareness of absence of any object.

Mastering this seventh jhana, the meditator can then review it and find any perception at all a disadvantage, its absence being more sublime. So motivated, the meditator attains the eighth jhana by first entering the seventh. He then turns his attention to the aspect of peacefulness and away from perception of the void. The delicacy of this is suggested by the stipulation that there must be no hint of desire to attain this peacefulness or to avoid perception of no-thing-ness. Attending to the peacefulness, he reaches an ultrasubtle state in which there are only residual mental processes. There is no gross perception here at all: This is a state of "no perception." There *is* ultrasubtle perception: thus, "not nonperception." The eighth jhana, therefore, is called the "sphere of neither perception nor nonperception." No mental states are decisively present. Their residuals remain, though they are nearly absent. This state approaches the ultimate limits of perception.

THE PATH OF INSIGHT

The Visuddhimagga sees mastery of the jhanas and tasting their sublime bliss as of secondary importance to pañña, discriminating wisdom. Jhana mastery is part of a fully rounded training, but its advantages for the meditator are in making his mind wieldy and pliable, so speeding his training in pañña. Indeed, the deeper jhanas are sometimes referred to in Pali, the language of the Visudhimagga, as "concentration games," the play of well-advanced meditators. But the crux of his training is a path that need not include the jhanas. This path begins with mindfulness (*satipatthana*), proceed thorough insight (*vipassana*), and ends in nirvana.

Mindfulness

The first phase, mindfulness, entails breaking through stereotyped perception. Our natural tendency is to become habituated to the world around us, no longer to notice the familiar. We also substitute abstract names or preconceptions for the raw evidence of our senses. In mindfulness, the meditator methodically faces the bare facts of his experience, seeing each event as though occurring for the first time. He does this by continuous attention to the first phase of perception, when his mind is *receptive* rather than reactive. He restricts his attention to the bare notice of his senses and thoughts. He attends to these as they arise in any of the five senses or in his mind, which, in the Visuddhimagga, constitutes a sixth sense. While attending to his sense impressions, the meditator keeps reaction simply to registering whatever he observes. If any further comment, judgment, or reflection arises in the meditator's mind, these are themselves made the focus of bare attention. They are neither repudiated nor pursued but simply dismissed after being noted.

There are four kinds of mindfulness, identical in function but different in focus. Mindfulness can focus on the body, on feelings, on the mind, or on mind objects. Any one of these serves as a fixed point for bare attention to the stream of consciousness. In mindfulness of the body, the meditator attends to each moment of his bodily activity, such as his posture and the movements of his limbs. The meditator notes his body's motion and position regardless of what he does. The aims of his act are disregarded; the focus is on the bodily act itself. In mindfulness of feeling, the meditator focuses on his internal sensations, disregarding whether they are pleasant or unpleasant. He simply notes all his internal feelings as they come to his attention. Some feelings are the first reaction to messages from the senses, some are physical feelings accompanying psychological states, some are by-products of biological processes. Whatever the source, the feeling itself is registered.

In mindfulness of mental states, the meditator focuses on each state as it comes to awareness. Whatever mood, mode of thought, or psychological state presents itself, he simply registers it as such. If, for instance, there is anger at a disturbing noise, at that moment he simply notes "anger." The fourth technique, mindfulness of mind objects, is virtually the same as the one just described save for the level at which the mind's workings are observed. Rather than noting the quality of mental states as they arise, the meditator notes the attentional objects that occupy those states, for example, "disturbing noise." As each thought arises, the meditator notes it in terms of a detailed schema for classifying mental content. The broadest category on this list labels all thoughts as either hindrances to or helps toward enlightenment.

Any of these techniques of mindfulness will break through the illusions of continuity and reasonableness that sustain our mental life. In mindfulness, the meditator begins to witness the random units of mind stuff from which his reality is built. From these observations emerge a series of realizations about the nature of the mind. With these realizations, mindfulness matures into insight. The practice of insight begins at the point when mindfulness continues without lag. In insight meditation, awareness fixes on its object so that the contemplating mind and its object arise together in unbroken succession. This point marks the beginning of a chain of insights—mind knowing itself—ending in the nirvanic state.

The first realization in sight is that the phenomena contemplated are distinct from mind contemplating them: Within the mind, the faculty whereby mind witnesses its own workings is different from the workings it witnesses. The meditator knows awareness is distinct from the objects it takes, but this knowledge is not at the verbal level as it is expressed here. Rather, the meditator knows this and each ensuing realization in his direct experience. He may have no words for his realizations; he understands but cannot necessarily state that understanding.

Continuing his practice of insight, after the meditator has realized the separate nature of awareness and its objects, he can, with further insight, gain a clear understanding that these dual processes are devoid of self. He sees that they arise as effects of their respective causes, not as the result of direction by any individual agent. Each moment of awareness goes according to its own nature, regardless of "one's will." It becomes certain to the meditator that nowhere in the mind can any abiding entity be detected. This is direct experience of the Buddhist doctrine of *anatta,* literally "not self," that all phenomena have no indwelling personality. This includes even "one's self." The meditator sees his past and future life as merely a conditioned cause-effect process.

Continuing to practice insight, the meditator finds that his witnessing mind and its objects come and go at a frequency beyond his ken. Hee sees his whole field of awareness in continual flux. The meditator realizes that his world of reality is renewed every mind moment in an endless chain. With this realization, he knows the truth of impermanence (Pali: *anicca*) in the depths of his being.

Finding that these phenomena arise and pass away at every moment, the meditator comes to see them as neither pleasant nor reliable. Disenchantment sets in: What is constantly changing cannot be the basis for any lasting satisfaction. As the meditator realizes his private reality to be devoid of self and ever changing, he is led to a state of detachment from his world of experience. From this detached perspective, the impermanent and impersonal qualities of his mind lead him to see it as a source of suffering (Pali: *dukkha*).

Pseudonirvana

The meditator then continues without any further reflections. After these realizations, the meditator begins to see clearly the beginning and end of each successive moment of awareness. With this clarity of perception, there may occur:

- the vision of a *brilliant light* or luminous form;

- *rapturous feelings* that cause goose flesh, tremor in the limbs, the sensation of levitation, and the other attributes of rapture;

- *tranquility* in mind and body, making them light, plastic, and wieldy;

- *devotional feelings* toward and faith in the meditation teacher, the Buddha, his teachings—including the method of insight itself—and the sangha, accompanied by joyous confidence in the virtues of meditation and the desire to advise friends and relatives to practice it;

- *vigor* in meditating, with a steady energy neither too lax nor too tense;

- sublime *happiness* suffusing the meditator's body, an unprecedented bliss that seems never-ending and motivates him to tell others of this extraordinary experience;

- *quick and clear perception* of each moment of awareness: noticing is keen, strong, and lucid, and the characteristics of impermanence, nonself, and unsatisfactoriness are clearly understood at once;

- *strong mindfulness* so the meditator effortlessly notices every successive moment of awareness; mindfulness gains a momentum of its own;

- *equanimity* toward whatever comes into awareness: No matter what comes into his mind, the meditator maintains a detached neutrality;

- a subtle *attachment* to the lights and other factors listed here and pleasure in their contemplation.

The meditator is often elated at the emergence of these ten signs and may speak of them thinking he has attained enlightenment and finished the task of meditation. Even if he does not think they mark his liberation, he may pause to bask in their enjoyment. For this reason, this stage, called "Knowledge of Arising and Passing Away," is subtitled in the Visuddhimagga "The Ten Corruptions of Insight." It is a pseudonirvana.

As this pseudonirvana gradually diminishes, the meditator's perception of each moment of awareness becomes clearer. He can make increasingly fine discrimination of successive moments until his perception is flawless. As his perception quickens, the ending of each moment of awareness is more clearly perceived than its arising. Finally, the meditator perceives each moment only as it vanishes. He experiences contemplating mind and its object as vanishing in pairs at every moment. The meditator's world of reality is in a constant state of dissolution. A dreadful realization flows from this; the mind becomes gripped with fear. All his thoughts seem fearsome. He sees becoming, that is, thoughts coming into being, as a source of terror. To the meditator everything that enters his awareness—even what might once have been very pleasant—now seems oppressive.

Feeling this misery in all phenomena, the meditator becomes entirely disgusted with them. Though he continues with the practice of insight, his mind is dominated by feelings of discontent and listlessness toward all its own contents. Even the thought of the happiest sort of life or the most desirable objects seem unattractive and boring. He becomes absolutely dispassionate and adverse toward the multitude of mental stuff—to any kind of becoming, destiny, or state of consciousness.

Between the moments of noticing, it occurs to the meditator that only in the ceasing of all mental processes is relief possible. Now his mind no longer fastens on to its contents, and the meditator desires to escape from the suffering due to these phenomena. Painful feelings may flood his body, and he may no longer be able to remian long in one posture. The comfortless nature of mind stuff becomes more evident than ever; the desire for deliverance from it emerges at the root of his being.

Now the meditator's contemplation proceeds automatically, without special effort, as if borne onward of itself. Feelings of dread, despair, and misery cease. Body pains are absent entirely. The meditator's mind has abandoned both dread and delight. An exceedingly sublime clarity of mind and a pervasive equanimity emerge. The meditator need make no further deliberate effort; noticing continues in a steady flow for hours without his tiring. His meditation has its own momentum, and insight becomes especially quick.

Insight is now on the verge of its culmination; the meditator's noticing of each moment of awareness is keen, strong, and lucid. The meditator instantly knows each moment to be impermanent, painful, or without self as he sees its dissolution. He sees all mental phenomena as limited and circumscribed, devoid of desirability, or alien. His detachment from them is at a peak. His noticing no longer enters into or settles down on any phenomena at all. At this moment, a consciousness arises that takes as its object the "signless, no-occurrence, no-formation": *nirvana.* Awareness of all physical and mental phenomena ceases entirely.

This moment of penetration of nirvana does not, in its first attainment, last even for a second. Immediately following this, the "fruition" moment occurs, when the meditator's mind reflects on the experience of nirvana just past. That experience is a cognitive shock of deepest psychological consequence. Because it is of a realm beyond that of the common-sense reality from which our language is generated, nirvana is a "supramundane reality," describable only in terms of what it is not. Nirvana has no phenomenology, no experiential characteristics. It is the unconditioned state.

The word "nirvana" derives from the negative prefix "nir" and the root "vana," to burn, a metaphorical expression for the extinction of motives for becoming. In nirvana, desire, attachment, and self-interest are burned out. Decisive behavior changes follow from this state of consciousness, and the full realization of nirvana actuates a permanent alteration of the meditator's consciousness per se. With the meditator's realization of nirvana, aspects of his ego and of his normal consciousness are abandoned, never to arise again.

The path of insight differs significantly from the path of concentration on this point: Nirvana destroys "defiling" aspects of mental states—hatred, greed, delusion, etc.—whereas jhana merely suppresses them. The fruit of nirvana for the meditator is effortless moral purity; in fact, purity becomes his only possible behavior. Jhana smothers the meditator's defilements, but their seeds remain latent in his personality as potentialities. On his emergence from the jhanic state, impure acts again become possible as appropriate trigger situations arise. To attain effortless purity, the meditator's egoism must "die," that is, all of his desires originating from self-interest must cease to control his behavior.

After insight has culminated in the nirvanic state, the meditator's mind remains free of certain motivations and psychological states, which no longer arise. On full maturation of insight, his purity is perfected. By then, he will have utterly given up the potential for impure acts. What was in the early stages effortful for the meditator becomes a self-maintaining state in which attitudes of purity are effortless, choiceless by-products of the state itself.

These different paths mark two extremes in exploring and controlling the mind. A meditator who could marshal enough one-pointedness to attain the formless jhanas might easily enter the nirvanic state should he choose to turn his powerful concentration to watching his own mind. Conversely, a meditator who had entered the nirvanic state might well be so indifferent to hindrances and distractions that, should he choose to focus on a single object of awareness, he would readily enter and proceed through the jhanic levels. Those who traverse these distinctly different paths to their summits, then, may no longer belong solely to one but to both. With full mastery of either samadhi or insight, the other is readily attainable. At their end, the distinction between meditation avenues melts.

Biofeedback

Gerald Jonas

The first attempts to teach human beings to modify "autonomic" functions with the help of feedback signals came in the early 1960s. The results of these experiments were highly controversial. The functions being monitored—heart rate, blood pressure, skin resistance to electricity—seemed to shift in the desired direction during training. But the changes were quite small—on the order of a few beats per minute or a few millimeters of mercury—and critics argued that such changes could easily have been produced by skeletal and respiratory maneuvers that had no longterm medical significance. To rule out this possibility, the researchers devised more and more rigorous experimental controls, but the critics were not satisfied. In the face of such unremitting skepticism, few scientists cared to test their theories in a genuine clinical situation. When Neal Miller and his co-workers announced that their curarized rats were learning to control a variety of visceral functions, biofeedback research with human subjects suddenly became more respectable, and the possibility that sick people might someday benefit from biofeedback training no longer seemed so preposterous.

One of the most persistent and ingenious researchers in this field is Barnard Engel, a psychologist now affiliated with the Baltimore City Hospitals and the National Institute of Child Health and Human Development. Engel has worked out a method of training subjects to speed up or slow down the heart, and he has applied it to the treatment of cardiac arrhythmias—irregularities in the normal pumping rhythm of the heart which, in severe cases, may lead to sudden death. One common arrhythmia is characterized by premature contractions of the left ventricle, the chamber that forces freshly oxygenated blood into the arterial system. In a normal heart, the left ventricle expands and contracts about once a second. In a premature ventricular contraction (PVC), it closes too soon; this may happen as often as thirty times a minute. Some patients are conscious of the irregularity; they say that it feels as if the heart were "skipping a beat." But most people with PVCs do not feel anything unusual, even after their condition has been diagnosed by a physician.

In 1970 Engel and a colleague, Dr. Theodore Weiss, attempted to teach eight patients with PVCs to stabilize their heart rhythm. The training process was long and demanding. Each patient received about fifty training sessions, with as many as three sessions scheduled per day. The average session lasted eighty minutes. During this time the patient lay on a hospital bed in a quiet room with standard EKG electrodes taped to his chest. The signals generated by his beating heart were transmitted to an electrocardiograph connected to a feedback display panel with three colored lights—green, red, and yellow. The green and red lights served as cues for the patient: when the green light came on, he was supposed to make his heart beat faster; when the red light came on, he was supposed to slow his heart down. The yellow light was the "reinforcer" or reward light; it came on whenever the patient was responding correctly to the other cues. Through this feedback system, the patient could be kept informed about changes in his heart rate on a beat-by-beat basis. Once he had demonstrated the ability to speed up or slow down his heart on cue, he was given the new task of maintaining his heart rate within a predetermined range. As long as he succeeded, the yellow light remained on, signifying a job well done. If the number of beats per minute fell on either side of the acceptable range, the yellow light went off and the appropriate cue light came on. During this stage of training the display panel was programed to flash a special signal—a red light followed immediately by a green light—whenever a PVC occurred. By tagging each premature contraction in this manner, Engel and Weiss hoped to draw the patient's attention to the faint but distinctive sensations that accompany an abnormal beat. In the final stage of training, the patient was gradually weaned from all external feedback. Instead of being available continuously, the colored lights were inoperative every other minute, then three minutes out of every four, then seven minutes out of every eight. After that the patient was on his own. Presumably, he had learned to sense his PVCs through internal cues, and to bring his heart back to its normal pumping rhythm whenever something went wrong.

According to Engel and Weiss, five of the eight patients did learn to control their PVCs to some extent during the study. The most successful trainee was a middle-aged woman with very frequent PVCs and a long history of heart disease. During training, her PVCs virtually disappeared. Follow-up examinations indicated that irregular beats were still quite rare three years later; the drugs she had formerly taken to control her arrhythmia were no longer necessary, and she had had no further heart trouble.

The researchers asked the five successful patients to describe exactly what they did to stabilize their heart rates. Some said that they could stop their PVCs by slowing down the heart; others said that speeding it up was more effective. To make the heart beat slower, one patient said that she thought about swinging back and forth on a swing; another simply lay still and stared at the red light. To make the heart beat faster, one patient thought about "bouncing a rubber ball;" another imagined that she was arguing with her children or running down a dark street. The middle-aged woman mentioned above said that as soon as she sensed a PVC she "thought about relaxing," which some-how *speeded* up her heart and stabilized it.

The lack of consistency in these answers came as no surprise to Engel. Like Miller and other biofeedback researchers, he believes that what a person says he is doing to control his glands and internal organs may have no relation to what his nervous system is actually doing. From all the physiological evidence, Engel suspects that his trainees learned to stabilize their heart rhythm by directly modifying the firing rate of the vagus nerve. Whether or not their conscious use of mental imagery helped the heart patients achieve more precise control is anybody's guess. One patient showed a more stable heart rate after training, even though he had never learned to tell when a PVC was occurring. On the other hand, two of Engel's subjects learned to correct serious arrhythmias only after they came to realize what a normal heartbeat felt like. These patients were so accustomed to the sensations produced by a malfunctioning heart that they were actually frightened by a sequence of regular beats, which they took as a sign that something was wrong. Once their misconceptions were cleared up, both made rapid progress.

"Sick headaches" are probably the most common of all psychosomatic complaints. Doctors recognize two basic kinds: migraines and tension headaches. The causes of migraine attacks are not fully understood, but the pain seems to be associated with excessive blood flow in the scalp region (*not* in the brain tissue itself); the pain of tension headaches comes from a chronic contraction of the skeletal muscles in the forehead and neck. Although such headaches do not kill anyone, the suffering they cause and the work days lost as a consequence make them a major health problem by any standard. Recently two separate teams of researchers have shown that biofeedback training can help people moderate or even suppress severe headache pain.

Improbable as it may sound, migraine sufferers have learned to turn off the pain in their head by warming up their hands "from the inside." This strange treatment was discovered more or less by accident at the Menninger Foundation in Topeka, Kansas, a few years ago. A group of Menninger scientists—psychologists Elmer E. Green and E. Dale Waters and internist Joseph D. Sargent—had been engaged in a far-ranging research program into unconventional methods of bodily control.

Green and his colleagues decided to see if they could combine biofeedback instrumentation with a self-hypnotic technique known as autogenic training. This form of mental and physical therapy was developed in the early 1900s by a German psychiatrist named Johannes Schultz, who was interested in both hypnosis and yoga. The basis of autogenic training—which is widely used in European clinics—is a series of verbal formulas that the subject repeats to himself to induce a state of deep relaxation. Among the phrases recommended by Schultz and his followers are: "I feel quite quiet . . . I am beginning to feel quite relaxed . . . . . . my feet feel heavy and relaxed, my solar plexus and the whole central portion of my body feel relaxed and quiet . . . my arms and hands are heavy and warm . . . my hands are warm . . . warmth is flowing into my hands, they are warm, warm . . ."

In adapting this technique to their own purposes, the Menninger scientists attached temperature-sensing devices to the hands of volunteer subjects, so that while the subjects were practicing their hand-warming exercises, the slightest increase in skin temperature would be immediately displayed on an easy-to-read meter. This would reward their initial effort and presumably spur them on to greater success. Purely by chance, one of the first subjects recruited for the pilot study in "autogenic feedback training" was a Kansas housewife who suffered from migraines. During a training session at the lab, this woman had a migraine attack. The researchers allowed her to sit quietly in a dark room, but they did not unhook her from the recording equipment, and a few minutes later Green was astonished to see the temperature meter jump 10 degrees, indicating a tremendous surge of blood into the hands. On questioning the woman, he found that her headache had vanished at just that moment.

Following up this lead, Green, Walters, and Sargent launched an experiment in which seventy migraine sufferers were given autogenic feedback training. More than two-thirds of these subjects ended up with warmer hands and fewer headaches. No one has explained exactly why the treatment works, but there is some evidence that the blood vessels in the head and the hands are on opposite sides of a cardiovascular seesaw. When the vessels in the hands contract, the vessels in the head dilate (as in a migraine attack), and when the balance is restored, the headache goes away. Normal hand temperature is around 90 degrees. On the first day of training, the migraine patients often arrived at the laboratory with hand temperatures around 70 degrees. Many of them learned to raise this temperature 15 or 20 degrees in a single session. They were then given portable temperature meters and told to continue practic-ing their autogenic exercises at home. Those subjects who managed to keep their hand temperatures close to normal—as measured in weekly check-ups at the lab—had fewer headaches, and when headaches did occur, they were able to moderate them. (Simply putting on gloves or holding one's hands over a fire will not help; the warming must come from the inside with a change in blood flow.)

Some of the successful subjects reported that their headache control was becoming more and more automatic as time went by. Green cites the case history of one woman, a computer programer, whose migraines were invariably preceded by what doctors call an aura. Her particular aura was an olfactory hallucination; before each attack she became aware of a strong ammonia-like smell. Early in her training the woman discovered that if she went home as soon as she sensed the aura, lay down on her bed, and practiced her warmth-and-relaxation exercises for an hour, the headache would go away before it became very painful. After a few months of training, she found that it was enough if she just sat down in her private office and did her exercises for fifteen mintues. Now, whenever she senses the aura, she simply gives the mental command, "Go back down, blood!" Presumably, her brain and body do the rest, because the headache passes and she is able to go on working.

Just as there is no theoretical limit to the involuntary functions that can be brought under control through biofeedback training, the same techniques can be used to *increase* the individual's control over skeletal muscles that are normally thought of as completely voluntary. For example, most people can wrinkle and unwrinkle their brows at will by contracting and relaxing the frontalis muscle in the forehead. But this muscle can also tighten up gradually—so gradually in fact that the individual is not aware that anything is happening. Unfortunately, the result of this constant muscular tension is impossible to ignore—a painful headache that may last weeks and even months. Even when people with tension headaches are told the cause of their trouble, they cannot simply relax their frontalis muscles, any more than a person can simply "will" away a painful leg cramp. But two psychologists at the University of Colorado Medical Center, Johann Stoyva and Thomas Budzynski, have demonstrated that the frontalis can be coaxed into relaxing with feedback from an electromyograph (EMG) machine, which records the electrical activity in skeletal muscle tissue.

What Stoyva and Budzynski did in the lab was to convert the EMG signals from the frontalis into a continuous chatter of click sounds. These clicks increased in frequency as muscular tension increased—so that the subject could literally hear how tight his forehead was. The subject's job was to slow down the clicks by progressively relaxing his frontalis muscle. Of the six subjects who went through biofeedback training in the laboratory and who diligently practiced relaxation at home, four showed significant improvement; they learned to recognize the warning signs of muscle tension and to turn off most of their headaches. An objective measure of their success was the fact that they were able to get through an average day with much less pain-killing medication than they had previously required. A year and a half later three of the subjects reported that the frequency and severity of their headaches had remained at a relatively low level. Two control groups of six subjects each, who were systematically exposed to various aspects of the experimental situation but who did not receive actual EMG feedback training, showed no significant improvement.

Since some part of the brain is involved in the regulation of every bodily function, the ultimate in biofeedback would be reliable information on the constantly changing electrical activity within specific brain structures. If this information were available, it would no longer be necessary to monitor muscles, organs, and glands throughout the body; the instructor could simply reinforce the appearance of EEG patterns that are known to accompany desired patterns of behavior. The problem, as with alpha-wave training, is to find a close correlation between specific brain waves and specific behavior. Alpha waves are easy enough to monitor (with the right equipment), but predicting how behavior will change as a result of alpha-wave training is not so easy. Similarly, even if one knows that the hypothalamus plays a major role in regulating hunger, it may be extremely difficult to detect momentary fluctuations in the hunger drive—as Neal Miller and his co-workers found out. The most dramatic medical application of EEG feedback training so far was reported in 1972 by psychologist Maurice B. Sterman of the Veterans Administration Hospital in Sepulveda, California.

To begin with, Sterman and his associates identified a particular pattern of electrical activity in the sensorimotor cortex—the part of the brain that controls movements of the skeletal muscles. This pattern, which has been labeled the sensorimotor rhythm (SMR), seems to be associated with muscular quietude. Subjects produce SMR waves when they are awake but completely motionless. (The sensorimotor rhythm, which originates in a specific region of the brain, should not be confused with the alpha rhythm, which is recorded over a much wider area.) The SMR was first discovered in cats. Sterman found that hungry cats with implanted electrodes could easily be trained to increase their SMR production if they were given food only when that pattern appeared in their electroencephalographic records. Instead of pawing around their cages looking for food, these trained animals would sit like statues, inhibiting all skeletal muscle activity until they were fed. Other experiments revealed that the cats who had been trained to produce a lot of SMR also became unusually resistant to drug-induced convulsions. This gave Sterman the idea of training epileptics, whose repeated seizures are thought to result from a breakdown of those components in the nervous system that normally inhibit muscular activity.

Preliminary tests on three epileptic patients have been highly encouraging. Standard feedback devices—lights, bells, pictures projected on a screen—were used to let the patients know when they were producing the right kind of brain wave. Once the patients had learned to increase their SMR production in the laboratory, their epileptic seizures became less frequent. In one case, that of a six-year-old boy, the results of the training were astonishing. The boy had been suffering as many as twenty-five seizures a week despite massive medication. When brought to the laboratory by his parents, he was so drugged and disordered that Sterman doubted his ability to comprehend even the simplest instructions. Yet after half a year of training the young patient had remained free of seizures for four months, and he was able to lead a relatively normal life on a much lower dosage of anticonvulsive drugs.

Perhaps because biofeedback research lends itself so easily to commercial exploitation, scientists in the field go to great lengths to avoid premature claims of success. Many of the pilot studies have been published in *Psychosomatic Medicine,* a journal whose editor, Dr. Morton F. Feiser, urges extreme caution in interpreting the results. With the exception of the tension-headache study, the research so far lacks the necessary controls to rule out placebo effects and other artifacts. Yet Reiser adds, "This is the way science always progresses, one small step at a time."

Biofeedback and the Twilight States of Consciousness

Thomas Budzynski

For a brief time as we lie in bed at night, neither fully awake nor yet asleep, we pass through a twilight mental zone that Arthur Koestler has described as a state of reverie. Many people associate this drowsy stage with hallucinatory images, more fleeting and disjointed than dreams, and compare it to the viewing of a speeded-up, jerky series of photographic slides. A host of artists and scientists have credited the imagery of this twilight state with creative solutions and inspiration for their work. Koestler once tried to describe the process: "The temporary relinquishing of conscious controls liberates the mind from certain constraints which are necessary to maintain the disciplined routines of thought but may become an impediment to the creative leap," he wrote. "At the same time, other types of ideation on more primitive levels of mental organization are brought into activity."

We are now beginning to understand that during this brief somnolent state, people not only may have creative insights but may also be more in touch with the unconscious in general. They are hypersuggestible and capable of learning certain things more efficiently and painlessly than during the day, when logical and analytical faculties are in control. There is even evidence that the suspension of critical judgment associated with the usually dominant left hemisphere of the brain may allow the nondominant right side of the brain, with its more intuitive and emotional processes, to take over.

My colleagues and I at the University of Colorado Medical Center and at the Biofeedback Institute of Denver have found that people can make use of the twilight zone for many kinds of learning. We have found, for example, that it may help some people who have trouble assimilating certain kinds of information: students who have mental blocks for subjects such as foreign languages; fat people who are unable to comply with suggestions to eat properly; prejudiced people who find it hard to believe anything a member of a minority group says. Resistances, biases, prejudices, emotional blocks are a few of the terms used to describe this inability to absorb certain kinds of information. By presenting carefully prepared material during the twilight state, these assimilation blocks can be at least partially eliminated.

The twilight state, I believe, opens a kind of pipeline to the unconscious, to the nonrational half of our brain that we usually ignore. If we learn to open the pipeline at will, rather than by chance, perhaps we can resolve some of the conflicts between the conscious and unconscious mind—conflicts that create problems in many areas of our lives. The difficulty is that most people do not stay in this transitional period for long. As an indiviudal falls asleep, he goes from a relaxed alpha brain-wave pattern, accompanied by slow, rolling eye movements, to the disappearance of alpha and its replacement by slower, small-amplitude theta waves of 4-7 Hz (cycles per second)—all within roughly five to 10 minutes.

With my colleagues Johann Stoyva, Kirk Peffer, and Pola Sittenfeld, I taught subjects to maintain a twilight state in the laboratory. We used an electromyograph (EMG), which trains them to reduce tension in forehead muscles through biofeedback. By learning to relax those muscles, they decrease cortical and autonomic arousal as well. Once they learn to produce theta brain waves, they can be trained to maintain the theta pattern indefinitely with a device called a Twilight Learner.

Developed with the aid of John Picchiottino, an engineering consultant, the unit enables a trainee to maintain a twilight state as information from a cassette tape recorder is presented to him. Sensors placed on the trainee's scalp pick up the tiny brain-wave signals. When the trainee produces the theta pattern characteristic of the twilight state, the signal automatically turns on the tape recorder. As long as he produces theta, the tape recorder runs. If his brain waves change to alpha or beta, indicating an increase in alertness and a marshaling of critical cognitive faculties, the recorder shuts off.

The Twilight Learner increases the volume of the tape message if theta increases in amplitude and/or decreases in frequency—a change that indicates a person is moving toward deeper sleep. When this happens, the increased volume gently nudges the trainee back into twilight sleep. Beginning trainees often find themselves oscillating between an alert alpha pattern and a sleep theta pattern. With more experience they learn to stay almost totally within theta.

We have used the Twilight Learner to treat a variety of problems. One client was a graduate student who had failed a Spanish-language exam and was so anxious about taking it a second time that he was unable to study at all. Therapist Kirk Peffer and the client made a Spanish-English tape which included suggestions that the client would be able to study effectively and remember the material. After hearing the tape 12 times under twilight-state conditions, the student was able to study without anxiety and passed the exam easily.

The Twilight Learner can also be valuable in psychotherapy. Of course, there is a risk in generalizing about individual cases, because success may be due to circumstances in the client's life that have nothing to do with the treatment itself. Moreover, we don't know how long-lasting are the effects on those who have seemingly been "cured" of their symptoms.

Still, the results are surprising. One man who had trouble asserting himself or saying no to anyone had tried conventional therapy for three years without success. There was dramatic improvement following five weekly sessions of twilight learning. The machine was used to produce a theta state and accompanying imagery. One of the images was a vivid memory of a confrontation which occurred when, as a young boy, he had refused one of his father's requests and had been harshly punished.

The therapist and client discussed the image and then designed a cassette tape, which the client recorded in his own voice. It dealt with the relation of his current problems to the early experience with his father, and suggested that he had the right to refuse unreasonable requests. The client gradually seemed to become more assertive and reported that he was able to deal more effectively with authority figures.

Another client was suffering from extreme anxiety associated with his wife's request for a divorce and her threats of suicide. He had earlier conquered a drinking problem, but the new strain was too much and he started drinking again. We designed a tape to help alter the irrational thoughts that were contributing to his severe guilt feelings. Three twilight-learning sessions helped reduce his guilt and anxiety, lessened an insomnia problem, and helped him control his drinking.

Whether or not our treatments offer permanent relief, we believe they open up remarkable possibilities. Work being done elsewhere in the country confirms the potential of such techniques in psychotherapy. For instance, Dr. Ian Wickramasekera, a psychobiologist in Peoria, Illinois, has also achieved notable results in preparing people to accept suggestions for positive change through recreating the twilight state in the laboratory.

Earlier research in Eastern Europe—prior to the development of biofeedback techniques—suggests how the twilight state may be used as a learning tool. For example, the Russian tutorial method known as "hypnopedia" uses repetition of material over several days or weeks. While the student is awake, he is given a mental set or expectancy that he will absorb the material during sleep. Evidence from hypnopedic studies suggests that the lighter sleep stages produce greater learning. As sleep deepens, the brain's

processing of auditory material changes and makes it difficult for the sleep learner to assimilate complex verbal material.

The Bulgarian scientist Georgi Lozanov has students in his "suggestopedia" program relax in comfortable chairs and focus their attention on classical music. The information to be learned is presented by an instructor who modulates her voice according to the tempo of the music. Students are told to focus on the music, not the voice. Lozanov reports that this type of learning is both qualitatively and quantitatively different from what occurs in the normal waking state. He claims that suggestopedic learning is more intuitive and holistic and that information is retained longer than under alert conditions.

In the United States, Elizabeth Philipov of Pepperdine University has adapted Lozanov's technique to teach Cyrillic languages to English-speaking students. In 120 hours of training, the students learning Bulgarian assimilated 1,800 new words on the average and were then able to use them in reading, writing, and speaking. A study comparing this method with traditional language instruction showed the suggestopedic students were more proficient with only one-third study time.

Three researchers at the Menninger Foundation have been studying the relationship between the twilight state and creativity. Through biofeedback, Alyce and Elmer Green along with Dale Walters were the first to closely examine the association between a theta state and creativity. In one experiment, they recorded the brain-wave patterns of a physics professor, a psychiatrist, and a psychologist, as each deliberately produced a special state he associated with creative thoughts. The brain-wave patterns of two of them showed high percentages of the theta waves (4-7 Hz); both reported their customary hallucinatory images as they reached the special state. The third subject showed a slowing of alpha frequency from 9.5 to 8.3 Hz and reported that he had attained a mind-quieting, imageless state but did not quite reach the creative state.

As may be obvious by now, the twilight state resembles in many ways other altered states of consciousness, including drug trips, hypnosis, meditation techniques, faith healing, and primitive religious rituals. All involve an extreme state of mental arousal, with the participants, flying high or feeling somnolent, becoming excited or approaching the drowsy state. All change people in some way—often dramatically. What do they have in common and why don't they work all the time? For some speculative answers to these questions, we looked at a relatively new field of research, brain lateralization.

Researchers have learned a great deal in the last 10 years about how the brain's two cortical hemispheres function. The left hemisphere is dominant in nearly all right-handed people and about two-thirds of the left-handers. It controls the characteristics generally ascribed to consciousness and high-order functioning, and is the seat of our reasoning faculties.

Each hemisphere gathers in essentially the same sensory information, but handles it in a different way, much as if two different computer programs were being used. The left hemisphere codes the information into verbal form and uses logical, analytical processing to arrive at a "reasonable" conclusion. The right, nondominant hemisphere performs a holistic or Gestalt synthesis, arriving at a conclusion based more on nonverbal input, without using deductive reasoning.

This ability to reach two conclusions is useful for the most part since it is theoretically possible for a person to act upon the superior solution, achieving better results than if just one choice were available. Unfortunately, there is also the danger of conflict between the two solutions. When this occurs, the dominant hemisphere will usually win out, but what happens to the conflicting idea or attitude? Perhaps these subjugated "programs" remain in storage to plague the individual in subtle ways not easily accessible to the verbal, conscious hemisphere. Perhaps these conflicts produce both psychological and physiological malfunction, such as the psychotic break of the schizophrenic, and mass murder of innocent individuals by a boy who was "always quiet and shy and never hurt anyone."

Freud believed that repressed memories and action tendencies influence our everyday behavior even though we are not consciously aware of their power. It may be that brain-lateralization research points to a physiological basis for Freud's theories—with the unconscious residing in the nondominant side of the brain. The dominant hemisphere appears to function effectively over a smaller range of cortical arousal than does the nondominant side, perhaps because its functions—analysis, abstraction, logic—are more complex. The dominant hemisphere controls thinking most of the time. But when individuals get excited or frightened, the right hemisphere takes over. People "don't think straight," and they do things that later, when they calm down, surprise or dismay them.

The same switch happens at the other end of the arousal scale—for instance, when someone is very fatigued or in the twilight state. The dominant hemisphere stops functioning efficiently, while the other side keeps plugging along. Without the normal censorship of the dominant hemisphere, the other is free to accept and act upon suggestions or commands made under these conditions. Less critical by design, the nondominant side is more likely to attempt to implement the command even though it may be nonsensical.

This can happen at normal arousal levels, too, in unusual situations. If, for example, a world-famous mathematician tells you that two plus two does not equal four, you may believe him, at least for a moment. Or, if a world-renowned healer or a famous Philippine psychic surgeon "lays on his hands," you may be "cured" even though you are not in a high or a low arousal state. The "embedded-suggestion" technique of Milton Erickson, the great hypnotist, is another example of this effect.

What these situations have in common is a suspension of critical judgment and the acceptance of an illogical message. There seems to be an interruption or overloading of dominant-hemisphere functioning and a relatively uncritical absorption of material presented to the nondominant hemisphere. I qualify this statement because even the nondominant hemisphere has some protective defenses. We need to know more about these unconscious resistances as well as more efficient ways of communicating with the right brain.

The right hemisphere prefers visual communication to verbal, but recent research indicates that the nondominant side can absorb more verbal material than had been thought, if it is presented properly. From research with aphasics—people who have lost speech skills because of stroke or other injury to the dominant hemisphere—we know that using concrete rather than abstract words improves comprehension. It also helps if the words are spoken slowly. And, strangest of all, singing helps aphasics: they understand better if sentences are sung to them, and they are able to express thoughts more easily by singing the words themselves.

Apparently the right hemisphere processes verbal material better if it is coded in rhythm or emotion. When someone speaks in a monotone, only the verbal, dominant hemisphere is activated. If the speaker adds intonation, the nonverbal side starts to pay attention. The right hemisphere's language is not the logical content of *what* is said, but the emotions conveyed by *how* it is said. Lecturers, preachers, and politicians who are famous for their oratory know intuitively what to do with their voices to generate emotion and thereby persuade their audiences.

Based on this theory, my colleagues and I have developed another way to reach the nondominant hemisphere (in this case, without biofeedback). Since we want to suspend critical screening by the left hemisphere, we overload it with some meaningless task which the nondominant side does not care to process, leaving it free to do other things. The other thing in this case is listening to a message carefully prepared for the right brain.

I discovered that repeating out loud a fast sequence of random numbers presented by a tape recorder made it impossible to consciously hear another tape recorded message being played at the same time. To enhance the effect, the random numbers are played at a slightly higher volume level in the right ear (more of what a person hears in their right ear goes to the left hemisphere, and vice versa). The message intended for the right hemisphere is played at a lower volume, but still audibly, in the left ear. If someone listens for and repeats the fast sequence of numbers, he hears very little of the other message.

We tested these techniques on 20 men and women who were interested in weight control, using a tape with 10 weight-control suggestions. It also contained one suggestion that had nothing to do with weight loss: "The back of your neck will itch." When the 20 people repeated the random numbers as a group—sounding like some jet-age mantra—12 of them scratched.

Afterward, I asked if anyone heard a suggestion that did not concern weight control. Two of the people said they had heard the scratch suggestion; neither of them had scratched. A few days later, a woman told me that when she reached for a second helping of food, she heard a voice in her head say, "You will eat only one helping . . . 37, 96 . . . ."

We have also prepared tapes to help people stop smoking. The technique is simple, but the wording and intonation of the material is crucial. I believe that as we learn more about communicating with the nonverbal hemisphere, we will find important applications for its use not only in psychotherapy but also in sports, the arts, and education. Perhaps we are only rediscovering abilities we once possessed before speech and logic came to dominate our behavior. It is exciting to consider that we may be learning again to talk to the long-neglected half of our brain.

SECTION 5

HYPNOSIS, DISSOCIATION, AND TRANCE

Like meditation and biofeedback, hypnosis can open the way for a person to enter a wide range of discrete states of consciousness, or, more rarely, altered states. As Ernest Hilgard points out, researchers have not been able to specify as yet any generally accepted objective criterion for the hypnotic trance. Indeed, the specifics of hypnotic trance vary greatly, depending on the particular suggestion given. Nevertheless, skilled clinicians are said to be able to recognize when a person is in a trance, despite the fact that there are no specific brain wave or bodily changes necessarily present. Deep trance during self-hypnosis—a rarified and little-studied state—may resemble the meditative trance.

Some people seem naturally capable of sliding into a hypnotic trance, others cannot be hypnotized at all. Psychologist Kenneth Bowers shows that a key ability that allows one to be hypnotized is the capacity to "dissociate," to screen from conscious awareness information or events that may still register out-of-awareness. Phenomena as diverse as sleep-learning and unconscious hearing while under anesthetic may offer clues to the ability to dissociate, a trait which marks the good hypnotic subject from the poor one.

Psychiatrist Milton Erickson, an eminent clinical hypnotist, reports a dramatic incident that illustrates Bowers' view of the role of dissociation in hypnosis. A medical student studying with Erickson uses self-hypnosis to retrieve a totally repressed traumatic event from his childhood. Under hypnosis he vividly relives the event, although he has no conscious awareness of recalling it until after its unfolding is complete. By reliving the trauma, the medical student is able to free himself from the neurotic effects it was having on his life. In this case, hypnosis proved an effective gateway to the unconscious and a quick therapy.

The Hypnotic State

Ernest R. Hilgard

THE HYPNOTIC STATE

After a subject has agreed to participate in hypnosis and has been hypnotized according to any of the several methods, he perceives that some changes have taken place, partly as a response to the suggestions that have been given in the induction, such as relaxation of his muscles, drowsiness and other subtle changes that are part of the total experience for him. If asked to do so, he finds it easy to assign a numerical value to indicate his degree of hypnotic depth or involvement. This feeling of being hypnotized, being in some kind of changed condition or state, makes him ready to accept the suggestions of the hypnotist to produce the specific responses that are called for, such as muscular movements or inhibitions, hallucinations, and so on. Hence the first task is to examine some of the alterations that are associated with the hypnotic state before turning to the manner in which the subject responds to specific suggestions.

A subject who, after hypnotic induction, feels himself more relaxed than he has ever felt before, has a right to attribute this to hypnosis. If he has other feelings such as a special sense of detachment from the environment, these have become part of his description of the hypnotic state.

The hypnotist also observes a number of consequences of successful hypnotic induction in addition to noting the success with which the subject follows his suggestions.

The following have been noted among the kinds of behavior giving rise to a conception of hypnosis as an altered state:

1. Increased suggestibility. This characteristic of hypnosis has been so much emphasized that, since Bernheim, many have defined hypnosis according to the changes in suggestibility that it produces. Although these changes can be demonstrated, alone they provide a very limited characterization of the total alterations that hypnosis produces.

2. Enhanced imagery and imagination, including the availability of visual memories from the past. The prominence of imagery, spontaneous as well as instructed, and its correlations with hypnotic susceptibility give it a high place in describing what happens in hypnosis. Visual images from the past, including those from childhood, are familiar in age regression. Imagination and memory are necessarily closely related, for the elements of something imagined must be something previously experienced in some form and retained in memory.

3. Subsidence of the planning function. The hypnotized subject loses initiative and lacks the desire to make and carry out plans of his own; he appears to have turned over much of this to the hypnotist. The change from the normal controls is relative only, for the hypnotic subject retains the *ability* to initiate or terminate action, or, within a task assigned by the hypnotist he can exercise initiative. For example, if told to deliver a political speech he can improvise one of his own choosing; what is impressive is that without encouragement he has little desire to do so. The avoidance of initiative is illustrated by statements such as this from one of our subjects: "Once I was going to swallow, but decided it wasn't worth the effort. At one point I was trying to decide if my legs were crossed, but I couldn't tell, and didn't quite have the initiative to move to find out."

4. Reduction in reality testing. Reality distortions of all kinds, including acceptance of falsified memories, changes in one's own personality, modification of the rate at which time seems to pass, doubling of a person seated at the table, absence of heads or feet of people observed to be walking around the room, inappropriate naming—these and many other distortions of reality that would normally be readily detected and corrected can be accepted without criticism in the hypnotic state. This fact has led Orne to speak of *trance logic*, denoting this peculiar acceptance of what would normally be found incompatible.

Other aspects might be mentioned, such as the prominence of amnesia and some alterations in the attentive functions, but those mentioned suffice to indicate how the subject has enough evidence to convince himself that he is hypnotized and how the experimenter-hypnotist can recognize that he is.

ALERT HYPNOSIS AND THE PROBLEM OF A SINGLE HYPNOTIC STATE

The subject knows when he is hypnotized because of changes that he perceives in himself, but some of these changes are produced by the specific suggestions that he received in the induction, and the state might have been different if other suggestions had been given. This possibility of more than one state raises a problem for those who may wish to define hypnosis as a unique kind of state, with appropriate physiological correlates. It is known that hypnotic states can be produced without any suggestions of relaxation; thus to characterize hypnosis as a deeply relaxed state is to limit it unnecessarily. It did not take laboratory experiments to discover this, for the trance states of the whirling dervishes or the dancing Balinese are just as real as the states of those who achieve trance states by quiet meditation, and all may resemble hypnosis.

An active-alert hypnosis can be produced in the laboratory without any suggestions of relaxation or sleep. Even if induction has been of the relaxation-sleep type, the state itself can readily be converted to an active one. There are, then, these two chief ways of producing the active state; to begin with the more usual relaxation method and convert it, or to begin directly with an active-alert induction.

In the first method the usual induction stressing relaxation and employing the metaphor of sleep may lead the person into the familiar kind of hypnotic condition. Then, at the suggestion of the hypnotist, the subject can alert himself without destroying his sense of being hypnotized. The stage hypnotists have made such a procedure widely familiar. They usually induce hypnosis in conventional ways but soon have their subjects dancing about or crowing like roosters. Strenuous activity is not incompatible with conventional hypnosis as studied in the experimental laboratory. Hypnotized subjects who are given suggestions to perform at their maximum in learning tasks or strength tasks are more successful if the subject, while hypnotized, is first alerted and then given added suggestions that he is strong or able.

The second method of inducing alert hypnosis is to begin immediately with an alert induction. It is not necessary to detach the subject from his usual reality orientation to the environment by reducing proprioceptive or visual feedback. Essentially the same results can be accomplished by telling him that he feels more alert, that he is less fatigued by exertion, that the surroundings seem brighter. In an experiment along these lines Ludwig and Lyle produced a hyperalert state in their hypnotized subjects, driving them to a kind of frenzy that they found unpleasant. In a later experiment in our laboratory, Eva Banyai demonstrated that an active induction, carried out without going to extremes, led to responses to scaled items on the Stanford Hypnotic Susceptibility Scales essentially similar to those following the more usual relaxed or passive induction. The method was to seat the subject on a stationary laboratory bicycle (a bicycle ergometer, in laboratory parlance) and to have the subject pedal continuously against a load that felt like actual rapid riding. The subject's eyes were open, and the riding led to increased breathing and perspiration, as expected. However, the subject received suggestions that the pedaling would not seem difficult and would be without discomfort, that the room would seem bright, and that alertness would be increased as the pedaling went on. The induction was, in fact, modeled after that used in the usual test, but where drowsiness had ordinarily been suggested, alertness was substituted, and where relaxation had been suggested, increased effort was substituted. Although there were naturally some different descriptions of such a trance and the usual one, the fact of an altered condition was reported by the same subjects who reported a change in the relaxed induction. Control experiments showed that the active induction increased hypnotic responsiveness over the waking condition; thus more was involved than waking suggestion while on the bicycle.

Once it is recognized that the usual relaxed hypnotic state can be converted to strenuous participative activity by suggestion or that the more strenuous state can be produced directly, the contrast between the two is between induction procedures rather than between unique hypnotic states. Both types of induction produce enough changes for the subject to identify that some massive changes have taken place (if he is hypnotically responsive), and these changes have a common influence on responsiveness to suggestions. The alternative inductions will modify the aspects of the hypnotic state according to which the subject defines his involvement and will doubtless alter the accompanying physiological changes; the modifications of control systems that result have enough in common to define the effects of either induction as hypnosis.

DEEP HYPNOSIS AND ITS CHARACTERISTICS

Hypnotic responsiveness and hypnotic depth are related in that the more hypnotizable person can experience greater depth of hypnosis. Responsiveness and depth are not the same thing, however, because a responsive person can experience hypnosis at greater or lesser degrees of depth and has no difficulty in assigning numerical values to the depth as he perceives it. To obtain a more complete picture of the massive dissociations possible in hypnosis, it is essential to work with the highly responsive persons as described here and to permit them to experience hypnosis at depths beyond those usually attained.

The concept of depth of hypnosis, like depth of sleep, is a convenient metaphor. The metaphor is an ancient one and is carried also by the word profound, with the root meaning of near the bottom (Latin, *pro fundus)*. The psychologies deriving from Freud are often called depth psychologies. The notion of exploring the depths of personality goes back at least to a fragment from Heraclitus (ca. 500 B.C.):

You could not discover the depths of the psyche, even if you traveled every road to do so; such is the depth of its meaning.

The metaphor of depth is very compelling, but it is only a metaphor; care must be taken not to embody it with our own values. In hypnosis it means only the pervasiveness of the changes from the normal condition and can as well be described as degree of involvement or immersion in the hypnotic experience.

Depth cannot be described solely by the responsiveness to suggestions as these are scored in tests of hypnosis; at greater depths, responses to suggestion, instead of being enhanced, may disappear entirely. When deep hypnosis is involved, the best measures are numerical estimates made by the subject on his own scale. This is equivalent to magnitude estimation as used in psychophysics and is very satisfactory. As in psychophysical experiments, very little practice is required for the subject to learn to assign self-consistent numbers for his subjectively experienced depth. If he uses a number between 5 and 10 to define his depth when he is capable of meeting the usual demands made on a hypnotized subject, he may assign numbers as high as 50 or 100 or even higher as he goes still deeper.

To achieve great depth it is necessary to select a responsive subject and permit him to increase his depth over time, either by repeated and prolonged suggestions by the hypnotist or by extensive self-hypnosis.

Charles Tart had experimented for some time with self-report scales of hypnotic depth before conducting his experiment on great depth. His case of William represents the deep hypnosis experiences of a subject who scored within a point of the maximum of the Profile Scales, hence in the upper 1 or 2% of hypnotic responsiveness. He had been hypnotized 18 times previously for various purposes, often with an emphasis on depth. Although extreme depth had not been stressed, on his scale William usually gave reports of 40 or 50, with amnesia experienced at 30. He had never gone beyond 60.

A session was undertaken in which he agreed to attempt to go much deeper than he had gone before. He was instructed that at each 10-point interval on a depth continuum he should remain at that depth as the experimenter had him describe what he was experiencing.

His reports of changes at the depths more commonly studied in the laboratory repeat the familiar: an early relaxation, a fairly normal awareness of the experimenter, although he may become a little distant, an increase in peacefulness, a gradual withdrawal from the environment. Beginning at a level of about 50 on this scale, however, distortions of consciousness occur that have some similarity to the reports of mystical experiences. The experimenter's voice becomes impersonal, the passage of time becomes meaningless, the body seems to be left behind, a new sense of infinite potentiality emerges, ultimately reaching the sense of oneness with the universe. These reports from this single subject are intriguing enough to indicate that the full potential of hypnosis may not be explored in most of the experiments or in clinical applications that rely on demonstrable changes in behavior brought about by the hypnotic interaction.

One feature of William's account that is interesting in relation to dissociation is the intrusion, in the earlier stages of the now deeper hypnosis, of the experience that some part of him is amused by his participation in these consciousness-alerting activities. This sudden intrusion of a critical observing part amused by the turn of events began about 50, was first reported clearly at 70, and then dropped out at 90 and was no longer mentioned. A hint of a hidden observer is implied.

In our studies of deep hypnosis in a few pilot subjects who were not as experienced in hypnosis as William, many similar experiences have been reported. Our method has been to select moderately high subjects (not necessarily those classified as virtuosos), to hypnotize them, and then to invite them to experience deeper hypnosis without repeated suggestions from the hypnotist. They are to report their depth on a numerical scale from time to time, but there is little questioning of the experience while it is occurring. A protective suggestion is given that, if a subject should happen to lose contact with the hypnotist's voice at a deeper stage, his depth can be lightened by the hypnotist's hand placed on the shoulder, and he will then be back in communnication with the hypnotist. We recognize that there is an implied suggestion here that such a state may be reached, and we have not yet performed the necessary control experiments to determine the role of the subject's expectations and his interpretation of the experimenter's demands.

Our arbitrary scale starts somewhat lower than Tart's, for our subjects have assigned a depth of about 8 or 10, in most cases, to the established hypnotic state in which they experience analgesia and amnesia, can perform automatic writing, and so on. However, they go on to much deeper states by themselves. Those who have lost contact with the experimenter as evidenced by no longer replying to requests for a depth report have done so typically at a depth of about 50. They may then continue to depths they later report to have been 80 or 90. After the experimenter places his hand on the shoulder to reduce the depth and inquires about the current hypnotic depth, he asks what the deepest depth had been. This completes the deep hypnosis part of the experiment, and the subject is told that he will remember his experiences when aroused from hypnosis and will be able to talk about them. A thorough inquiry then follows.

Observations frequently include a loss of any connection with the body, a failure of time to have any meaning, the pleasantness of the experience, and some reports characteristic of mystical experiences—a sense of oneness, a feeling of having acquired some knowledge that is not communicable. What the subject reports is colored by his nonhypnotic experiences of meditation, perhaps of familiarity with Gestalt therapy, sometimes evident in the vocabularies used to describe the experiences, such as the nonlinearity of the experiences or their Gestalt qualities. The method is more like meditation than ordinary hypnosis in that the experimenter is so much less intrusive; in hypnosis the subject commonly waits for what the experimenter is going to ask him to do; in self-deepening, the deepening is his own affair, and the depth reports are quite automatic. Tart reports William as saying that the appropriate number to describe his state just popped into his mind. He had no idea how these numbers were generated, and it was reported that he did not "understand" them. Our subjects confirmed this nature of the numerical reports of depth.

The experiments just described have not gone into the question of prolonged hypnosis, and little evidence is available. Erickson gave his account of deep hypnosis, leading to what he described as a *plenary* trance, in which the subject becomes essentially inert or stuporous. His discussions are generally quite informal; therefore, comparison with the deep state produced in the laboratory studies is not possible. However, it may be noted that the primary symptom Erickson emphasized was losing contact with the body; restoration sometimes came as a shock, and he warned that care should be taken to restore the normal condition slowly as a precaution against this. Although responses to the hypnotist came more slowly in the deep trance, his subject, according to Erickson, did not in fact lose contact.

Because hypnosis is usually studied at much lighter levels of involvement, it is more often described according to the characteristic responses to the hypnotist's suggestions. The studies of deep hypnosis indicate that these specific responses may not occur in the context of massive dissociations characterizing the more involved hypnotic condition.

Hypnosis and Dissociation

Kenneth Bowers

Consider first of all the person who is sound asleep. Ordinarily, we think of such a person as oblivious to his or her surroundings, but a little reflection clearly shows that this is far from the truth. Everyone has had the experience of being awakened by an alarm clock or a baby's cry that must have been "heard" while asleep in order to disturb slumber effectively. Less common, perhaps, are people who talk in their sleep, and who can even respond appropriately to questions put to them by an amused roommate or spouse. Such dialogues are not consciously experienced by the "sleep talker." Then there is the undeniable fact that most adults do not fall out of bed at night. It is my (somewhat hazy) impression that our success in this regard results from unconsciously reconnoitering the bed's boundary by an extension of the arms and legs; when the edge of the bed is thus located, the next major body movement is directed away from it. The ability of the sleeping subject to negotiate the hazards of the bed's edge is of course a mere shadow of the sleepwalker's successful avoidance of reality hazards in his path (Kales *et al.*, 1966).

The point of these examples is to remind the reader that the sleeping subject, although "unconscious" by ordinary waking standards, is very much in touch with some aspects of reality. Or, to put my point somewhat more forcefully, these examples establish the fact that various reality features can be effectively registered in the nervous system without being consciously perceived (see, for example, Dixon, 1971; Smith and Groen, 1974; MacKay, 1973; Lewis, 1970.) As we have already seen, the possibility for "registration without perception" seems to be of fundamental importance for trance logic, which permits a deeply hypnotized subject to successfully avoid the negatively hallucinated chair that he does not consciously see. In a similar fashion, hypnotic analgesia can easily be viewed as a negative hallucination of an (ordinarily) painful stimulus, which is not consciously perceived, but which is certainly registered well enough to be detected under specially contrived conditions.

Now the point I wish to make is that there is growing reason to believe that high-susceptible subjects are especially responsive to information that is somehow "dissociated," or split off, from conscious awareness. Moreover, this ability is manifested not only in hypnosis but in other states as well. In particular, the evidence suggests that, even when asleep, high-susceptible subjects process external information more effectively than low-susceptible subjects.

Before presenting this evidence, however, it is important to mention that hypnosis and normal sleep are quite distinct, despite the fact that the word "hypnosis" derives from the Greek word *hypnos* (sleep), and despite the hypnotist's frequent invocation of the chant "go to sleep." Such sleep suggestions are by no means essential to the induction process; indeed, subjects can be intimidated into something like hypnosis by suggestions inducing a tense "hyperalert state" rather than a pleasant relaxed one (Ludwig & Lyle, 1964). And a very famous hypnotherapist, Milton Erickson, employs a variety of induction techniques that make no reference at all to sleep (see Haley, 1967). However, the final argument for the distinctiveness of sleep and hypnosis is based on their very different patterns of brain waves. Hypnotized subjects typically display an EEG pattern much more like a waking than a sleeping state (Evans, 1972). The fact that sleep and hypnosis are in fact quite different psychological states implies that the evidence that follows points to a *general* mode of functioning by high-susceptible subjects—one not limited to hypnosis per se.

SLEEP LEARNING AND SUGGESTIBILITY

Let us begin with some accounts of sleep learning that were initially recorded by Russian investigators (Hoskovek, 1966, reviews these studies). In one such investigation, 20 out of 25 subjects were able to perceive and remember spoken material presented during natural sleep (Svyadoshch, 1962; reported in Hoskovec, 1966). In all these cases, "the actual process of perception of the texts by [subjects] was not a conscious one: they slept and did not realize that during this period they were hearing and remembering speech" (Hoskovec, 1966, p. 310).

Cooper and Hoskovec (1972) have tried to replicate these Russian investigations of sleep learning. The subjects were first hypnotized and given a set (that is, "primed") to perceive and remember material that would subsequently be presented in their sleep. Then, when the subjects were in a light stage of sleep (Stage 1 REM), they were administered a list of ten Russian words, each with its paired

English translation. Immediately after the list of paired words was presented, subjects were awakened and tested for their learning. Under these conditions, about 30% of the material was retained. However, in a waking control condition, 90% of the Russian–English word pairs were mastered. Thus, although the evidence for sleep learning is theoretically exciting, learning while asleep is nowhere near as efficient as learning while awake.

In conducting their study, Cooper and Hoskovec employed subjects highly susceptible to hypnosis. They did so for a reason that is of particular importance to my current discussion. According to the Russian reports, sleep learning is most evident in highly hypnotizable, or suggestible, subjects (Cooper/ Hoskovec, 1972, p. 102). What we have here is the strong possibility that effective processing of information while asleep is correlated with hypnotic susceptibility. This conjecture has been confirmed in a series of fascinating investigations recently summarized by Evans (1972).

All in all, the results of the sleep studies establish that: *a person can register and be affected by information he or she does not consciously perceive* (at least by any conventional standard of "conscious perception"). For it is clear that most (high-susceptible) subjects registered fairly complex suggestions while remaining physiologically asleep, maintained this information in operational form over extended periods of time, and acted upon it when confronted with an appropriate cue word that was also administered during sleep. Moreover, all this was accomplished with subjects who, for the most part, had no waking memory of any of the above events.

Perhaps it is becoming clear why the absorptive account of hypnosis and hypnotic susceptibility, although illuminating, is not entirely satisfactory. The capacity for such absorptive involvement does not easily account for the fact that highly susceptible subjects are so much more responsive to sleep-administered suggestions than the low-susceptible ones. It simply presses credibility too far to assume that sleeping subjects, even highly susceptible ones, become imaginatively absorbed in suggestions administered to them while they are asleep. Something else is necessary to account for this phenomenon, and this "something" seems to involve the subject's ability to register and process information that is not fully represented in ordinary waking consciousness.

GENERAL ANESTHESIA AND UNCONSCIOUS HEARING

A particularly dramatic illustration of this ability is demonstrated by surgical patients under general anesthesia. David Cheek (1959, 1966) and others have for many years been alerting a generally skeptical medical community that anesthetized patients undergoing surgery were able to hear

the ongoing conversation of the operating team. To quote Cheek (1959) directly,

The anesthetized patient may lose all motor reflexes, lose all ability to communicate with the outside world, lose all sense of pain, but the anesthetized patient is able to hear and remember important events at a deep level of subconscious thought. This level can be uncovered and the events recalled by hypnotic techniques [p. 101].

A number of clinical accounts establish the authority of this claim (for example, Brunn, 1963; Cheek, 1959) but a report by Levinson (1967) seems to clinch the issue rather dramatically. Levinson's report begins with a description of a chemically anesthetized patient undergoing plastic surgery. During the course of the operation the surgeon put his finger in the patient's mouth, felt a lump there, and said "Good gracious! . . . It may not be a cyst at all; it may be cancer! . . ."

Back in the ward the next day, the patient was totally oblivious to these comments. Nevertheless, she was depressed and weepy. After several abortive attempts to ameliorate her discomfort hypnotically, Levinson finally succeeded in "reaching" her. Under hypnosis, the patient was told that if something was disturbing her, her right hand would lift. It did. Soon, amidst a flood of tears, the patient blurted out the surgeon's "Good gracious!" followed by the rending words "He is saying–this may be malignant." After being reassured, the patient was aroused from hypnosis. Her depression had lifted.

As a result of this dramatic episode, Levinson decided to explore more thoroughly the extent to which anesthetized patients registered complex information. He selected the first ten hypnotizable patients over 21 years of age who were willing to participate in some research on anesthesia and brain waves. Each subject was anesthetized with pentothal and his EEG was continuously monitored throughout the course of the operation. When the patient's EEG indicated he was profoundly anesthetized, a signal was given, and the entire operating theater became suddenly quite. Then the anesthetist, in his most urgent tone of voice, made the following standardized statement: "Just a moment. I don't like the patient's colour! The lips are too blue, very blue! More oxygen please!" (Levinson, 1967, p. 206). After a suitable pause, the anesthetist expressed satisfaction with the patient's condition and the operation proceeded.

Each subject was subsequently seen by the author to assess his recall of the above events. After first hypnotizing the subjects, Levinson age-regressed them back to the time of the operation. Under these circumstances, four out of the ten subjects

were able to repeat practially verbatim the traumatic words used by the anaesthetist. A further 4 patients displayed a severe degree of anxiety while reliving the operation. At a crucial moment they woke from the hypnosis and refused to participate further. The remaining 2 patients, though seemingly capable of reliving the operation under hypnosis, denied hearing anything [Levinson, p. 202].

To be sure, Levinson's study does not tell us some things we would like to know. For example, we don't know whether hypnosis was absolutely essential for the retrieval of the traumatic information acquired under anesthesia. Nor do we know whether anesthetized subjects low in susceptibility could register and/or recall this information as well as the high-susceptible subjects employed in the investigation. Still, it seems unequivocally clear that at least some chemcially anesthetized patients who are hypnotizable do in fact register and retain meaningful and complex information; yet, the information processed in an anesthetized condition is evidently retained in a form that is dissociated from ordinary conscious awareness and is retrievable only with special effort and techniques.

Despite its unavailability to ordinary awareness and memory, information acquired under anesthesia can have a dramatic impact upon a person's functioning (recall, for example, the first patient's weepy depression after "hearing" under anesthesia that she might have cancer). As Check (1966) notes, "unconscious people are terribly vulnerable to pessimistic thoughts . . ." (p. 275). Consequently, he admonishes surgical teams to be very careful about what they say while operating on anesthetized patients. In fact, he goes further and proposes that they make optimistic and hopeful comments during the course of surgery. Once again, there is evidence that supports his advice. Anesthetized subjects exposed to benign suggestions showed a significant reduction in the need for pain-relieving medication during the postoperative period (Hutchings, 1961). In another study (Pearson, 1961), 43 anesthetized subjects receiving tape-recorded suggestions for a quick recovery were released from the hospital an average of 8.63 days after surgery; 38 subjects receiving tape-recorded music and/or silence were released an average of 11.05 days after surgery. The 2.42 days' difference in the length of time spent in the hospital by these two patient groups is statistically significant. These findings are especially persuasive since the investigation was run double-blind: none of the attending surgeons knew which tape recording their patient was hearing (since the patient wore earphones), and the discharging physician was also ignorant in this regard. Consequently, the decision about when to release a patient could not be influenced by a knowledge of which tape recording the patient had received.

Clearly, these studies support the contention that people can register information and be profoundly affected by it even though they have no conscious perception of the information in question. A demonstration of this process with anesthetized patients perhaps makes it easier to accept the possibility that a similar dissociation of input from conscious perception may occur in hypnosis, especially deep hypnosis. We have already seen how severe pain can be registered at one level while remaining unappreciated at other, more conscious levels of experience. And we can now see more clearly how hypnotically deaf subjects can honestly deny hearing a verbal suggestion or a loud noise and yet respond to them; for it now makes very good sense to say that such persons do not consciously *realize* they hear the auditory input. To claim that the subjects' responsiveness to such an input proves they were not deaf is certainly true, but it misses the crucial point. One might as well argue that the anesthetized subject "really heard" the surgeon's remark or "really felt" the pain of the surgeon's knife. To be sure, anesthetized subjects evidently do discern sound (and perhaps pain) *at some level;* but it is equally clear that they do not consciously hear or hurt in the same exquisite way that they would without the anesthesia. From the patient's point of view, the difference is decisively important. Similarly, the fact that deeply hypnotized subjects respond to sound when they are "deaf" and show some evidence of pain when they are analgesic does not mean they experience sound and pain at the same level or in the same fashion as they would in an ordinary waking state. And, again, the difference is decisive.

DISSOCIATION AND ABSORPTION

I have been maintaining that highly hypnotizable subjects can dissociate better than their low-susceptible counterparts. By dissociation I have meant the ability to register (and sometimes respond to) information that is not consciously perceived. This superior capacity for dissociation in highly hypnotizable subjects not only is revealed in hypnosis—where it seems basic to trance logic—analgesia, and other classic hypnotic phenomena but is also manifested in responsiveness to sleep-administered suggestions and to helpful or hurtful comments made while the subject is anesthetized.

This superior capacity for dissociation is doubtless operative in waking life too, as suggested by the experience inventories reviewed in the last chapter. A particularly striking example of such waking dissociation was brought to my attention by an extraordinarily hypnotizable young lady who was also a very talented singer. She acknowledged nearly panicking on several occasions during operatic performances because she had no clear memory of having sung an aria that, according to ongoing music, she must have just completed. It is as if the young lady had been so absorbed in singing that even the sound of her own voice was somehow dissociated; that is, it was not fully integrated into a conscious awareness of herself singing. In effect, there had been very little of "her" left over to notice that "she" was singing.

Perhaps this illustration provides a clue regarding how dissociative and absorptive aspects of hypnosis are related. Specifically, I would like to argue that the capacity for dissociation of a highly susceptible subject facilitates his or her absorptive involvement in reading, drama, hypnosis, and so forth. The rationale for this position is briefly presented in the following paragraphs.

There is clearly adaptive value in processing information without having to do so consciously. If we were forced to attend consciously to every facet of our environment, we could never concentrate on any one thing for very long. We would be, to understate the case, highly distractible. On the other hand, there is considerable advantage in processing peripheral information outside of awareness—in other words, preattentively (Neisser, 1967). For if we were *totally* unresponsive to anything except what occupied consciousness, our cave-dwelling ancestors, for example, would have been easy prey indeed for various stealthy creatures looking for dinner. It is crucial that we be able to register background sounds at a relatively low level of analysis without having to continuously focus conscious attention on them. In this way, when something that may be significant does happen (a twig snapping on the ancient veldt; our name paged at a modern airport), we can quickly attend to the input consciously and take appropriate action.

What I am suggesting is that highly susceptible people are better able than low-susceptible ones to process and appraise information preattentively—that is, without being distracted from their primary involvement. Recall, for example, that high-susceptible subjects were seldom disturbed by suggestions administered to them while they slept, whereas low-susceptible subjects were frequently awakened by the presentation of the suggestions. Thus, low-susceptible persons may need to awaken somewhat in order to determine whether the noise they registered while asleep constitutes a significant input; high-susceptible persons, on the other hand, may be able to make this "decision" at a lower level of analysis that does not disturb

their sleep. Similarly, deeply hypnotized high-susceptible subjects may process and appraise peripheral information preattentively, thereby preserving their effortless absorption in the hypnotist's ongoing suggestions. By contrast, low-susceptible subjects may find themselves constantly "peeking" at various internal and external stimuli in order to appraise them, thus preventing the total and uninterrupted concentration necessary for deep hypnosis (cf. Evans et al., 1969, p. 475). Certainly the study of Van Nuys (1973) reviewed earlier suggests that low-susceptible subjects are more distractible than the high-susceptible ones.

It may be, of course, that low-susceptible subjects can also concentrate uninterruptedly on hypnotic suggestions, but only with extraordinary effort. But this effortful, actively directed attention seems to be precisely what the high-susceptible subjects do *not* engage in. Rather, they typically experience their attention as effortless, almost as if the hypnotist were doing their concentration for them (Weitzenhoffer & Sjoberg, 1961). It is this effortless concentration, which we earlier called *passive attention,* that seems characteristic of deeply hypnotized individuals. Perhaps, then it is the seemingly effortless attention to the task at hand (hypnotic suggestions, reading of a novel, and so on) that is permitted and preserved by the highly susceptible subjects' talent for dissociation; conversely, the relative lack of such talent on the part of the low-susceptible subjects may be the reason why they often experience themselves as working hard to concentrate—the better to overcome various internal and external distractions by "brute force."

Self-Exploration in the Hypnotic State

Milton H. Erickson

This brief study is reported in detail for a number of reasons. It is an account of a classroom experiment proposed and executed by a medical student as an intellectual project for classroom purposes. Actually, it was an unconscious seeking by the student for specific psychotherapy in the guise of an intellectual effort.

The fashion in which the proposed task was to be done, apparently to illuminate the intellectual aspects, served in reality to define the manner in which the student wished unknowingly to achieve his therapy.

One of a group of medical students being trained in hypnosis had shown an almost compulsive obsessional interest in psychiatry and had studied avidly on the subject. He early volunteered to be a hypnotic subject for the group but had placed a restriction on his role as a subject by declaring that no intimate or personal questions be put to him.

He proved to be easily trained and most capable of developing complex hypnotic phenomena.

After some weeks work with the group, at the beginning of a session, this student announced his wish to raise a special question for the evening's work and discussion.

This question he explained as follows: People normally forget many things and, hence, do not know that they have forgotten them. These things may be only of past significance or they may be of actual present but unknown and unrecognized significance. They may be of a minor or a major character and importance. And they may be of a traumatic or a nontraumatic nature.

Therefore, would it be possible for a person to set himself the task of remembering some definite but actually long-forgotten event, and to recall it vividly and comprehensively?

The suggestion was offered that he might spend the next half hour endeavoring to recover a forgotten memory of something that had occurred previous to his tenth year and about which he had not even thought for at least fifteen years.

Half an hour later he reported that the task was hopeless. He had recalled innumerable things but they were memories about which he had had no occasion to think, and they did not constitute recoveries of forgotten things.

He then raised the question of whether or not he could be given the same task in an hypnotic trance. He was answered that he could be given the task but that he would have to discover for himself whether or not he could perform it. He agreed to that stipulation.

He was hypnotized deeply and instructed to review mentally his question and to spend at least ten minutes considering the feasibility of the task.

After ten minutes he stated that the entire problem still looked hopeless to him.

Still maintaining him in the trance state, he was asked if he wanted any help or guidance and he replied that any assistance would vitiate the purpose of the effort, since such assistance would direct and aid in memory recovery and it was his desire to see if such a memory recovery could be effected by a person in either the waking or the trance state and accomplished solely by personal efforts in mental searching.

He was told that he would be given no aid but that certain general remarks could be made to him which would give him more opportunity to do the task.

The time of 7:30 p.m. was announced. He settled himself in a chair, still in a deep trance, bowed his head and closed his eyes.

At 7:50 p.m. he called, "Dr. Erickson, I have a feeling that I am getting something but I don't know what it is. But I am curious." Reply was made, "Thank you for telling me."

About ten minutes later he asked if it were warm or cold. Reply was made, "I find the temperature comfortable."

About five minutes later he announced, "I am getting scared, awful scared but I can't think of anything." No reply was made.

Within a few minutes he presented a distressing picture of indescribable terror that seriously alarmed the medical students. Falteringly he gasped, "I'm scared, awful, awful scared. I'm going to get sick. But I don't know why. Tell me to rest."

He was told, "Stay just where you are in your mind, but rest a few minutes."

Immediately he relaxed and declared, "I am terribly scared but I don't remember anything. It is the awfullest feeling. I think I am going to get sick. Don't let me get sick."

He was told, "I do not know what you are doing. Getting sick might be part of it. I will not tell you how to do your task."

To this was added, "Do you want to wake up and rest or just rest in the trance with your gears in neutral, the engine just idling, neither going ahead nor backing up?"

He answered, "Just as I am."

A few minutes later, he asked the time and, as it was stated, the look of intense terror reappeared and retching but no vomiting developed. His breathing was labored and spasmodic, his hands clasped and unclasped convulsively, and he seem about ready to collapse.

Suddenly he gasped, "Rest."

Immediately he was told, "Hang on but rest."

Again he relaxed and declared, "It's too big, I can't do it. Tell me how." He was told, "I can't tell you how but I can offer a suggestion. You say it's too big. Why not do it a part here, a part there, instead of the whole thing at once, and then put the parts together into the whole big thing?"

He nodded his head, asked the time and again manifested, as the time was stated, intense emotions of varied types. Rage, terror, grief, fear, hatred, hysteria, sickness, despair, bravado, shock, horror, agony were the words written down by the students as they watched him and recorded their interpretations of what they saw manifested by him and the writer was willing to agree with them.

Finally a state of what appeared to be stark terror developed. His face was contorted, his hands were tightly clasped, his jaws were clenched, his breathing was labored, his neck muscles were taut, and his body was rigid.

After about two minutes he shuddered, relaxed, sighed and said, "Rest."

Asked how he wished to rest, he answered, "I've got started. I've got the feelings. I don't know what the memory is. Wake me up and let me rest and then hypnotize me and just tell me to finish the job. I still got the whole thing to do yet. But I got to rest."

He was awakened with instructions to rest and to have a comprehensive anmesia for what had happened in the trance. He awakened, wiped the perspiration from his face, remarked that he must have eaten something that disagreed with him because he felt sick to his stomach, wandered about the room opening windows, remarking about the heat, and added that he hoped to learn something if the writer would start discussing the question he had propounded. Thereupon he returned to his chair, sat down, but jumped up and asked one of his classmates what the assignment was in dermatology. Without waiting for an answer, he started a casual conversation with another student.

After about ten minutes he returned to his chair, sat down, looked expectantly at the writer, and developed a deep somnambulistic trance.

He was told, "You said just before you took your rest, 'I still got the whole thing to do.' The time is now nine o'clock."

He closed his eyes, a look of interest appeared on his face, then one of amusement. Many head movements were made as if he were looking from side. to side. This lasted for a few minutes and then his head movements became jerky and his hands and arms moved slightly in a jerky fashion. Suddenly a look of anger appeared on his face, followed by a short jerk of his body. Then he stiffened in his chair, his face contorted, his hands clenched and his biceps contracted. There followed then a tremendous variety of facial expressions as described above, with much jerking of the head from side to side and twisting of his body.

After about ten minutes of this he slumped exhausted in the chair, gasped "Rest."

Immediately he was told, "Stay where you are in your mind and rest."

He relaxed and declared, "I'm through. I did it. But I don't know what to do now. You got to tell me or I'll forget it all over."

He was answered, "I can give you some suggestions. Listen carefully, I think you have recovered a long-forgotten traumatic memory. (He nodded affirmatively.) You know it now in your unconscious mind. You do not know it in your conscious mind. Keep it fully remembered in your unconscious mind. I will awaken you and let you find out for yourself if you want to know it consciously. Is that all right?"

Since he nodded his head affirmatively, he was told to awaken with only a conscious amnesia and to rest awhile. Then the writer would discuss matters.

He awakened, complained of feeling "horribly washed out," "sick," "tired," and "like I just took an awful beating."

He added, "I'd swear that someone had just been kicking me around and punching me. My gluteals feel like they've been kicked. And my ribs hurt. I feel as if Joe Louis had given me a workover."

He went out to the water fountain, took a drink, returned and asked the same student about the dermatology assignment and again did not wait for an answer.

He wandered about the room, began and interrupted conversations and was exceedingly restless.

Finally he sat down and remarked that it was getting very late, that the writer ought to discuss the question he had propounded at the beginning of the evening.

The writer began by summarizing the question he had raised and then went on to state that such a forgotten memory as he proposed to discover would probably be a rather deeply repressed memory. Hence, there was a good probability that the repression would derive from a traumatic character of the memory.

Therefore, recovery of such repressed memory would entail a lot of distress, pain and actual misery. Furthermore, self-protective tendencies would make such recovery slow and difficult.

With hypnosis there could be a more rapid recovery of the memory and the self-protective tendencies would be greatly minimized. However, such recovery would first be limited to the unconscious mind. Then there would arise the question of whether or not the unconscious knowledge could or would be shared with the conscious mind. If it should be, then the person would have to experience mentally the original trauma with all the personal pain that would accompany the recovery of the repressed material.

In his case there would be a number of questions he would have to consider. Would he be content to recover it and let it remain in his unconscious? Or would he want to know it consciously? Also, while his willingness to work on such a problem in the presence of his classmates implied his willingness to have them see his behavior in so doing, would he want them to see his conscious reactions to a conscious realization?

Then, too, even if he were willing for that, would he want them to know the content of the repressed material?

As for the method of achieving a conscious understanding, there were certain considerations he should have in mind. Would he want the whole thing to irrupt into his conscious mind all at once? Or would he prefer to have it come piecemeal, a part at a time, with the possibility of halting the process and mustering his strength so that he could more easily endure the next development? Would he want to separate the affective from the cognitive elements and experience the one or the other first? Or would he like to have the recovery follow the same course of development, the same chronology, as the original experience?

He interrupted to declare that the latter sounded best and to ask when a beginning could be made.

Reply was made, "The other students are here."

Thoughtfully he answered, "I don't care what they see, but I don't want them to know until I know first. We're all medics, so I figure that they ought to be able to take it. But I want the first look. When can we start?"

He was told, "It is now after 10:00 o'clock. What do you think you have been doing? Why do you feel so tired, so beaten up?"

After a long pause he said, "You mean, I've done that job I talked about when I came, that I know it in my unconscious and that you are waiting for me to figure out if I want to know it consciously? I'm pretty sure that's right—I better think it over. I'm not just beginning the job. I'm on the home-stretch and I'm sick. Give me a few minutes."

Shortly he declared, "I'm going to take it just like it really happened. What time is it?"

He was told 10:30.

He smiled and began, "That's funny. A scene just flashed into my mind. It's just as clear as if I were there looking on. I'm back in Oklahoma. Let's see. I'm almost eight years old. And there is that shirttail cousin of mine. I haven't seen him since I was eight years old. He moved away." Then, in the manner of one who is hallucinating visually a past experience, he continued, "Us kids are playing. We got short pants on and we are having fun." Then in a detached fashion he added, "Nothing traumatic about this. I can see us wrestling and pushing and kicking up in the straw. We are in the cowbarn. We are having a whale of a time. Hey, he pushed me. That hurt. I hit him. He hits back. What a fight. Slugging away. Oh no, no, no, no, don't, don't, don't."

At this point, he stopped verbalizing, closed his eyes, shuddered and there followed a duplication of his previous disturbed behavior, with one new addition. Repeatedly he seemed to be endeavoring to speak but unable to do so.

For about twenty minutes he was absorbed in the throes of this experience and finally he collapsed in his chair in exhaustion and said, "Thank God, he will live."

Slowly he straighted up in his chair and remarked, "Yes, he lived and I forgot the whole thing. I haven't even remembered him. I never dared. I couldn't. I haven't remembered it for years and years—more than fifteen years. I just put it out of my mind completely."

After further similar comments, he suddenly remarked, "I might as well tell the rest of you what it's all about," and he proceeded to relate the story.

In summary, his account was as follows:

One summer day before his eighth birthday, he was playing in the cowbarn with a distantly related boy of his own age, named Johnny. They were wrestling and tussling and unintentionally they hurt each other. This led to an active fight and Johnny, smaller than he, was getting the worst of the battle. To even the contest, Johnny grabbed a pitchfork and attempted to jab him. In turn, he seized a pitchfork used in cleaning the barn and unfortunately stabbed Johnny deeply in the left calf. When Johnny screamed, he horrifiedly jerked the fork tine out and was even more horrified by the pulsing stream of blood.

Johnny ran screaming and limping to the house, while he turned and ran to the pump and began pumping water frantically into the horse trough.

As he learned later, his father applied a tourniquet and summoned a physician. While waiting for the doctor, the father came to the well and, seizing him, went to the horse trough, sat down and proceeded to spank him thoroughly as he lay across his father's knee, staring at the green scum of algae in the horse trough. Then his father roughly dragged him to the house and made him stand and look at Johnny.

The physician arrived, dressed the wound and then wanted to see the fork.

His father cuffed him and sent him to get the fork, which he did in a turmoil of emotion.

After examing the fork, the doctor administered anti-tetanus serum, explaining the reason. Upon learning this the father beat his son again.

Just before the doctor left, Johhny developed anaphylactic shock. His eyes swelled shut, his tongue enlarged and protruded from his mouth and he became a "horrible greenish color."

He saw the doctor give another injection, which he thought was again anti-tetanus (afterwards he learned it was "medicine to help Johnny live"), saw the doctor insert a spoon in Johnny's mouth (to lessen respiratory embarrassment) and then take out a knife (scalpel) to cut Johnny's throat (do a tracheotomy) and he was all the more terrified that Johnny was to be "butchered like a pig."

However, Johnny responded to the adrenalin injection and no tracheotomy was performed, but the doctor did explain the reason for considering a tracheotomy. However, to him, it still sounded like a plan to butcher Johnny.

His father, after the doctor left, trounced him soundly again, and forced him to stand for hours by Johnny's bedside and to watch and give the alarm if Johnny developed "breathing trouble so he would have to have his throat cut."

All that night he dreamed of Johnny's skin turning a "horrible green like the scum in the horse trough."

The next day, he was forced to watch the doctor redress the wound, the surrounding area of which was "all awful color, green and nasty." Furthermore, the doctor in examining the wound, remarked that it was a most "nasty thing."

Later that day, he neglected to pump water for the horses, and was again thoroughly spanked by his father, while in the same position as the previous day.

Shortly thereafter, Johnny's parents moved out of state and all contact was lost.

As far as he could determine, the entire matter then became a closed incident, and a year later his parents moved to a distant city, and farm life became a forgotten thing.

Tired, exhausted, self-absorbed, the student took his departure with the others, who had been instructed not to discuss the matter till later.

A week later the student visited the writer, stating that he had learned some amazing things about himself as a result of his recovered memory.

First of all, he doubted if he was as seriously interested in psychiatry as he had previously thought. Internal medicine was proving more interesting.

Secondly, his attitude toward dermatology had changed completely. Previously, he had been unable to study the textbook, despite repeated efforts. Either he went to sleep or immediately became distracted. Each time he went to the dermatology clinic, he became sick and had to leave. Also, despite frequent faculty warning, he had consistently avoided the lectures given on the subject. Now he was studying dermatology with interest and he enjoyed the clinics. (He eventually secured a good grade in that subject.)

He was seen regularly in class sessions for the rest of the year and also throughout his internship, during which time he discussed his future plans, which included a residency in internal medicine. However, he still retained a good, though secondary, interest in psychiatry.

He has since completed a residency in internal medicine and is now in private practice and he utilizes his knowledge of psychiatry extensively in handling his patients.

SECTION 6

ISOLATION, HEALING, DREAMING, AND DYING

While the schizophrenic's inner changes in brain function and psychological processes, such as attention, are one route to an altered state, external changes in a person's surroundings can also alter his consciousness. Peter Suedfeld surveys the popular and technical lore on the effects of social isolation in situations like Arctic exploration, solitary confinement, and space flight. Although the common expectation is that total solitude drives people mad, this is not necessarily the case. It seems more likely to be true when isolation is involuntary and when the person is anxious about it. But for millenia, people like yogis and shamans have voluntarily sought isolation in order to come into contact with a higher state of being. Alone, a person is confronted with the inner world of thought and fantasy as the distractions of social life are muted. The effect of isolation is often an altered state, but whether the affective tone of that state is upsetting, mellowing, or transcendent depends on the person's motives and inner resources.

People in other cultures are more adept at entering altered states than are we in the West, as the Eastern techniques of meditation attest. Still another traditional route to altering consciousness is through chanting and dancing. The Kung Bushmen of the Kalahari Desert in southern Africa gather as a tribe for all night sessions of chant and dance during which the tribal healers enter an altered state. While in this state, psychologist and ethnographer Richard Katz tells us, the healers experience another realm of existence where the gods and ghosts are real, and a healing energy surges through them. While in this state, the healers treat those who have physical, mental, or spiritual troubles. Everyone present helps the healer enter and work in this state, and by dawn the whole group shares a renewed closeness from their contact with the healer's altered state.

Any normal state of consciousness can be the baseline from which an altered state is defined. While by far the majority of altered states take waking awareness as the baseline, Charles Tart reports an instance where dreaming is the baseline state. He himself has on occasion experienced a "high" dream, which is set apart from normal dreaming by its intense vividness and a sense of dissociation. The dreamer seems to "wake" from an ordinary dream so that he feels as though he is in his waking awareness as the dream world continues to unfold. During a high dream the dreamer finds himself in the dream world, but at the same time there is also a feeling of being in an altered state such as psychedelic drugs induce. The high dream does not change the content of what is dreamed, but rather the state from which the dream is experienced.

Finally, psychiatrist Raymond Moody, Jr. summarizes the reports he has gathered from more than a hundred people who have had a close brush with death, many of whom were pronounced clinically dead but were then resuscitated. Dying is itself an altered state of consciousness, and from these reports it seems much less fearsome than commonly thought. While not everyone reports the identical series of experiences, there is enough commonality that a general map of the most common landmarks of this altered state can be drawn. The dying person often sees his own body as though he were floating above it, sees wondrous lights or meets other "beings" who have come to help him along, and feels intense joy and relief.

Social Isolation: A Case for Interdisciplinary Research

Peter Suedfeld

There is a fantasy story about a supernatural traveller, who wanders about magically granting the wishes of evil people, to their eventual regret. One of these episodes is as follows:

> So too in Wocrahin a swaggering bully came down the street one market day, cuffing aside children with the back of his hand and housewives with the flat of his sword. 'Oh that my way were not cluttered with such riffraff!" he exclaimed, his shoulder butting into the traveller's chest. 'As you wish, so be it,' said the traveller, and when the bully turned the corner the street he walked was empty under a leaden sky—and the buildings either side, and the taverns and the shops. Nor did he again in all eternity have to push aside the raffraff he had cursed; he was alone. (Brunner, 1970, p. 93).

This story seems to evoke a universal feeling of horror. People find the bully's fate so terrible as to be worse than the fate of the traveller's other victims, who usually wind up dead. What is there about social isolation that evokes such revulsion, and what do experimental psychologists have to say about this condition?

It may well be that the awesome implications of isolation do not begin to appear unless the isolation is prolonged, or is combined with other variables which intensify its effect. If the effects themselves are in fact exacerbated by such factors as sensory deprivation, unfamiliarity, or anxiety, then one might expect that in severe environments the effects of isolation will emerge relatively rapidly. This is not the case in most experiments; but it has often been the case in real-life isolation situations. It has been reported, for example, that 90% of shipwreck survivors die within three days, even though they may not be physically injured, and even when it would take much longer to die of exposure, starvation, or thirst (Bombard, 1953). There appears to be considerable evidence from Western sources that isolation for an extended period and/or combined with other adverse factors leads to effects which would normally be considered pathological symptoms: hallucinations, delusions, the development of obsessive rituals, periods of severe anxiety, feelings of unreality, and the like.

While several authors have discussed individual differences in the response to isolation, agreeing that the adaptation tends to be somewhat idiosyncratic, related to personality structure and tends to take the form of an exaggeration of one's normal methods of coping with internal and external problems (Haggard, 1964), there seems to be general agreement that there is a considerable amount of stress generated by solitude. Indeed, not only the experimental literature but also anecdotal reports indicate that isolation is adverse in its effects. Individuals even of such great ego strength as Admiral Byrd report a variety of bizarre symptoms (Byrd, 1938).

On the other hand, Admiral Byrd survived the polar winter in complete isolation with his physical and mental faculties intact (1938). Edith Bone, who spent seven years in a Hungarian prison, most of it in solitary confinement, developed a wide variety of activities, both cognitive and motoric, and managed to adapt successfully (Bone, 1957). Joshua Slocum, Sir Francis Chichester, and other solitary sailors have circumnavigated the world, and overcome the effects of isolation and other threatening factors. It may be pointed out that here is another case in which "history is written by the victors"—that is, those castaways, solitaries, and prisoners who cannot adapt do not survive long enough to write books about their experiences, although Glen Bennet of the University of Bristol is analyzing the diaries of Donald Crowhurst, the solo yacht racer who apparently went insane and committed suicide during a round-the-world race. However, it is clear that even massive doses of isolation, coupled with physical danger, deprivation, and uncertainty, are not necessarily intolerable. We know from the experimental literature that repeated confinement sessions evoke progressively fewer symptoms, indicating that adaptation is taking place, and Saito et al. (1970) have observed a similar progression from high stress, through calm adaptation, to boredom in individuals isolated for long periods of time.

Modern man is at first distressed by aloneness because he does not know how to behave; but as he becomes more familiar with the environment, he develops ways of coping (Haggard, 1964; Suedfeld, 1969 b). Eventually, in fact, these ways may become functionally autonomous. Burney (1961), who spent 526 days in solitary confinement in a Gestapo prison, was extremely stressed for a prolonged initial period. "I soon learned that variety is not the spice, but the very stuff of life. We need the constant ebb and flow of wavelets of sensation, thought, perception, action and emotion, lapping on the shore of our consciousness . . ." (p. 8). Yet, when he was finally able to have contact with fellow prisoners, he "found conversation an embarrassment" (p. 146), and thought of his cell door as a castle wall behind which he had developed habits which to him represented stability and security, and which he was reluctant to abandon. It may be noted here that the optimal adjustment to isolation and to sensory deprivation is apparently made by those subjects who are able to relax and enjoy the flow of fantasy and other primary process material which apparently cannot be efficiently warded off in these situations (Haggard, 1964; Myers, 1969).

It is intriguing that some clinical workers have recently tried removal from social stimuli as an adjunct to therapy. Perhaps the oldest systematic use of isolation in this regard was in ancient Greece, where patients coming to the Oracle of Trophonius were isolated in a small subterranean chamber as a kind of shock treatment which reportedly induced regression and personality change (Kouretas, 1967). The development of Morita therapy in Japan provided another use of isolation in therapy, a therapy which has been quite popular in Japan and has recently been discussed quite intensively by some Western clinical psychologists. The patient in Morita therapy undergoes at least one week, and sometimes more, of isolation and bedrest, during which the patient becomes attuned to both his own psychological processes and to the influence of the absent, but significant, therapist (Reynolds, 1969).

Other therapeutic uses of isolation have included using the technique as a timeout to reduce anti-social behaviour (Tyler & Brown, 1967; Pendergrass, 1972); treatment of anorexia nervosa by secluding the patient after every meal, with the unexpected concomitant of reducing excessive drinking (Lobb & Schaeffer, 1971); improved speech among isolated stutterers, apparently with maintenance of the improvement after isolation (Svab, Gross & Langova, 1972); solitary as opposed to classroom study leading to better learning by retardates (Jenkins et al., 1972), and a general increase in their activity (Altman, 1971); and a large number of studies in which social isolation, usually coupled with some amount of stimulation reduction, was found to be beneficial in the treatment of various neurotic and psychotic symptoms (Suedfeld, in press).

Let us now turn to nonlaboratory situations. High altitude fighter and test pilots have reported reactions, involving confusion, inability to concentrate, absence of awareness, and the like (Bennett, 1961). This led to apprehension that similar phenomena in space flight might endanger the safety of astronauts. While psychologists discussed and made proposals for the solution of such problems (e.g., NASA, 1966), it turned out that flights with only one person aboard would be minimal in number and duration. Thus, simulations using isolated groups, as run by NASA, the Navy, and other agencies, turned out to be much more relevant to the real problems not only of space flight but of nuclear submarines, saturation divers, etc. (Fraser, 1966; Radloff & Helmreich, 1968). At any rate, the effects of this type of special environment can be characterized as in many ways similar to those of sensory deprivation and individual isolation, and adverse effects over projected long-duration flights can probably be averted by appropriate manipulation of the physical and social environment (Suedfeld, 1968).

Social isolation has also been used quite widely in penal systems, usually to "soften up" prisoners for interrogation (Krivitsky, 1939), or as punishment (e.g., Dickens, 1843). It is beyond doubt that the use of social isolation in the prison situation has effects on the personality of the prisoners, and in fact may be a significant factor in the induction of "prisonization" (Scott & Gendreau, 1969); whether it can be used to produce beneficial behavioural change is a moot point (Tabarkova, 1967-8; Suedfeld & Roy, in preparation), but at any rate it is certainly a topic which evokes great furor and controversy (Association for Legal Justice, 1969-73; *Rough Times,* 1973).

One problem with these lines of thought is that they start with the assumption that isolation is necessarily stressful, and thus view it mostly as a problem to be avoided or solved (see e.g. Poulton, 1970). The same feeling underlies much of the related conceptual and empirical work (Appley & Turnbull, 1967; Rasmussen, 1973). This attitude reflects a subtle bias in all of the literature which is discussed above. We have a tendency to take for granted that our data and descriptions point to universal human reactions. But really to understand the effects of social isolation, one must go beyond the easily available psychological references, which tend to be produced by people who, if not denotatively modern Westerners, are culturally so.

When we turn to antiquity, the most famous quote is Aristotle's comment that "to live alone, one must be either a beast or a god" (*Politics,* II). But Aristotle was a product of the same general type of culture which we now share. Kingsley in his book *The Hermits* (undated), stated the point well: "We, here in England, like the old Greeks and Romans, dwellers in the dizzy mart of civilized life, have got to regard mere bustle as so integral an element of human life, that . . . if we meet anyone who loves to be alone, [we] are afraid that he must needs be going mad" p. 127).

Other cultures have not been so generally negative about isolation. For example, the use of a period of aloneness in order to come into contract with higher levels of being, has been for a long time an institutionalized feature of many societies. Moses first encountered God when he was wandering as a solitary shepherd (Exodus, 3); and he spent 40 days and 40 nights alone with God in the mountain after the escape from Egypt. It was, in fact, this long period of absence which led to the revolt of the

Israelites and the breaking of the tablets (Exodus, 24-33). The prophets of the Old Testament, as Berdyaev (1938) suggests, were the products of the desert; and Christ rejected the Devil and reached firmness in his ethical precepts after a long period of fasting and solitude in the wilderness (Matthew, 4).

The desert has continued to exert its fascination on holy men, there being at one time as many as five thousand Christian hermits in the deserts of the Near East during the first five hundred years of Christianity. It has been pointed out (Waddell, 1942) that these hermits did not isolate themselves because of a hatred of humanity, nor did they for the most part recommend what modern standards would consider a neurotic form of asceticism or alienation. They themselves lived ascetically, but they counselled common sense and love of fellow men. Kingsley (undated) discusses their constant attempts to stop the incessant petty warfare and persecution of the communities near their hermitages, their attempts to free the salves, and to foster what we would all call true Christianity (see also Anson, 1964).

As civilization developed the pull of community became stronger, and the hermits banded together to form the first monastic orders. Their spiritual descendants in medieval Europe, hermits and anchorites, represented to a great extent the debasement of the early Christian original. Judging by the evidence which remains, many of them probably were diagnosable as mentally ill, and towards the very end of the 16th century, which saw the disappearance of such practices, some of them apparently were charlatans (Kingsley, undated).

Reports of the experiences of the desert fathers repeatedly emphasize their encounters with demons, devils, and supernatural beasts. The first solitary, St. Antony, who spent 80 years alone (from about 270 to 356 A.D.), encountered so many of these creatures that he began the first attempt at developing a science of demonology. Kingsley hypothesizes that some of these visions were based on paintings which the hermits had seen in Egyptian tombs, and which they therefore connected with devil worship; hallucinations were possibly exacerbated by malnutrition and periodic fevers. Of course, our recent data suggest that isolation per se may be a sufficient, even if not a necessary, cause of such experiences.

Related to these reports are the practices of some Indian tribes in North America. Some of these tribes made it a practice for the individual to go into the plains or forest alone, sometimes fasting or physically torturing himself, in order to seek communion with animistic spirits and thus obtain mystical power. These trips lasted from four days to as much as a month. In some tribes this was a single trial, in others the men repeated their quest periodically. Among the Pawnees, the Gros Ventre, and the Kasha, the power came in hallucinations and dreams (Murie, 1914; Cooper, 1956; Honigmann, 1949). The successful seeker returned from his exile with magical rites and symbols (Honigmann, 1949), magic songs (Sapir & Swadesh, 1955; Cooper, 1956) or a transference of the powers of his father to himself (Fortune, 1932).

The influence of these visions can be seen in one dramatic example. Wavoka, a Paiute Indian, after spending four days in apparent coma alone in a mountain, saw a vision of a Messiah figure who took him to a village peopled by the ghosts of his dead relatives. These ghosts taught him the magic ghost dance, and taught him how to make the so-called "ghost shirt," through which bullets could not pass. The ghost dance religion spread rapidly among the Plains Indians, and culminated in the last of the great Indian wars, involving the death of Sitting Bull and the final defeat of the Indians at Wounded Knee in 1890 (Tebbel, 1967).

Literature on the use of solitude in Far Eastern cultures, particularly in conjunction with various types of mental and physical exercises, in order to induce desired altered states of consciousness, also indicates the cultural nature of isolation effects. It is clear that individuals versed in these techniques are able to control both physiological and mental processes in ways not available to the ordinary person (Tart, 1969; Wallace & Benson, 1972). Meditation is aided by the lack of distraction fostered in isolation, and the highest levels of consciousness are reached through a physical removal from normal stimulation (Conze, 1972).

What can we say about universal effects of social isolation? Briefly, there appears to be trustworthy evidence that isolation disrupts the ordinary everyday coping procedures, and leads to special kinds of psychological events. These frequently include hallucinations and vivid dreams, unusual states of excitement and arousal, and a great openness to experience. These unusual states last for varying, but sometimes quite prolonged, periods. If the individual does not then return to the normal social environment, he begins to adapt and to develop habitual methods of behaving in isolation. These may appear bizarre by "normal" standards, but in fact represent a best fit response to a bizarre environment.

One promising conceptual approach to these phenomena is a view of the human being as an organism which needs a constant flow of information to guide his behaviour. When he encounters a novel situation, particularly one which has potentially dangerous consequences (i.e., natural rather than experimental environments), his first concern is to identify informational anchor points and develop a set of adaptive responses. The more unfamiliar the environment, the more intense the need for such anchors, and the greater the anxiety and general arousal which stem from that need. Furthermore, the less information is available, the more the individual attends to and elaborates residual stimuli, whether internal or external.

It is here that the role of cultural differences is relevant. The ancient Jewish prophet, the early Christian hermit, the Indian yogi, the Tibetan Lama, the Plains Indian warrior, all filled roles which were well established and understood. They expected and chose to undergo the experience; they had available the appropriate kinds of cognitive and emotional reactions. In many cases, they were individuals of rich inner resources, upon which they could draw to provide a sufficiency of stimulation and information so that novel experiences could be interpreted in non-threatening ways.

In contrast, the shipwrecked sailor, the suddenly incarcerated political prisoner, and the polar explorer, are plunged into isolation without much preparation for it, even though they may have had considerable physical preparation and training in dealing with life-threatening stresses. In our other-directed society, perhaps the most salient normal source of behavioural guidelines is the observation of the behaviour of others. When this form of information is gone, an added difficulty is imposed upon the already stressed individual. Novelty, uncertainty, stimulus reduction, and anxiety evoke high arousal and initiate a frantic search for stimulation and information, leading to emotional storms and vivid fantasies. Although these may actually be adaptive reactions, they may be interpreted as symptoms of breakdown and insanity (Janik & Kalvach, 1968), thus increasing the anxiety and distress of the individual.

The cycle is broken only when the situation is terminated, when the environment becomes familiar and at least minimally safe, when the individual learns to "relax and enjoy it"—or when he becomes truly psychotic or dies.

REFERENCES

ALTMAN, R. The influence of brief social deprivation on activity of mentally retarded children. *Training School Bulletin,* 1971, *68,* 165-169.

ANSON, P. F. *The Call of the Desert.* London: SPCK, 1964.

APPLEY, M. H. & TURNBULL, R. *Psychological Stress.* New York: Appleton-Century-Crofts, 1967.

ASSOCIATION FOR LEGAL JUSTICE, Dublin, Eire. Series of newsletters concerning the treatment of detainees by British forces in Northern Ireland, 1969-73.

BENNETT, A. M. H. Sensory deprivation in aviation. In P. Solomon et al. (Eds.), *Sensory Deprivation.* Cambridge, Massachusetts: Harvard University Press, 1961. pp. 161-173.

BERDYAEV, N. *Solitude and Society.* London: Centenary Press, 1938.

BOMBARD, A. *The Voyage of the Heretique.* New York: Simon & Schuster, 1953.

BONE, E. *Seven Years Solitary.* London: Hamish Hamilton, 1957.

BRUNNER, J. Break the doors of hell. In H. S. Santesson (Ed.), *The Mighty Swordsmen.* New York: Lancer, 1970. pp. 86-131.

BURNEY, C. *Solitary Confinement,* 2nd Ed. London: Colin MacMillan, 1961.

BYRD, R. E. *Alone.* New York: Putnams, 1938.

CONZE, E. *Buddhist meditation.* London: Unwin, 1972.

COOPER, J. The Gros Ventre of Mantana: Part 2, *Religion and Ritual,* V. Flannery (Ed.), Washington, D.C.: Catholic University, 1956.

DICKENS, D. *American Notes.* In A. Land (Ed.), *The Works of Charles Dickens,* 28. New York: Scribner's, 1907 (original publication 1843).

DUBOS, R. Environmental determinants of human life. In D. C. Glass (Ed.), *Environmental Influences.* New York: Rockefeller University Press and Russell Sage Foundation, 1968. pp. 138-154.

EISENBERGER, R. Is there a deprivation-satiation function for social approval? *Psychological Bulletin,* 1970, *74,* 255-275.

ENDO, G. T. Social drive or arousal: A test of two theories of social isolation. *Journal of Experimental Child Psychology,* 1968, *6,* 61-74.

EPSTEIN, Y. M. Effects of crowding on cognitive performance and social behavior. New Brunswick, N. J.: Rutgers University, 1972.

ERICSON, M. T. Effects of social deprivation and satiation on verbal conditioning in children. *Journal of Comparative and Physiological Psychology,* 1962, *55,* 953-957.

FORTUNE, R. *Omaha Secret Societies.* New York: Columbia University Press, 1932.

FRASER, T. M. The effects of confinement as a factor in manned space flight. NASA Contractor Report No. 511, 1966.

FULLER, J. L. & CLARK, L. B. Genetic and treatment factors modifying the post-isolation syndrome in dogs. *Journal of Comparative and Physiological Psychology,* 1966, *61,* 251-257.

GEWIRTZ, J. L. & BAER, D. M. The effect of brief social deprivation on behaviors for a social reinforcer. *Journal of Abnormal and Social Psychology,* 1958, *56,* 49-56. (a)

HAGGARD, E. A. Isolation and personality. In P. Worchel & D. Byrne (Eds.), *Personality Change.* New York: Wiley, 1964. Pp. 433-469.

HARLOW, H. The nature of love. *American Psychologist,* 1958, *13,* 673-685.

HAYTHORN, W. W. The miniworld of isolation: Laboratory studies. In J. E. Rasmussen (Ed.), *Man in Isolation and Confinement.* Chicago: Aldine, 1973. Pp. 219-239.

HILL, K. T. & STEVENSON, H. W. Effectiveness of social reinforcement following social and sensory deprivation. *Journal of Abnormal and Social Psychology,* 1964, *68,* 579-584.

HONIGMANN, J. *Culture and Ethos of Kasha Society.* New Haven: Department of Anthropology, Yale University Press, 1949.

JANIK, A. & KALVACH, Z. [Psychopathological aspects of social isolation.] *Psychiatrie, Neurologie und Medizinische Psychiatrie,* 1968, *20,* 361-368.

JANIS, I. L. *Air War and Emotional Stress.* New York: McGraw-Hill, 1951

JENKINS, J.R., GORRAFA, S., & GRIFFITHS, S. Another look at isolation effects. *American Journal of Mental Deficiency,* 1972, *76,* 591-593.

KINGSLEY, S. *The Hermits.* New York: McClellan & Co., undated.

KOURETAS, D. The Oracle of Trophonius: A kind of shock treatment associated with sensory deprivation in ancient Greece. *British Journal of Psychiatry,* 1967, *113,* 1441-1446.

KOZMA, A. The effects of anxiety, stimulation and isolation on social reinforcement effectiveness. *Journal of Experimental Child Psychology,* 1969, *8,* 1-8.

KOZMA, A. Instructional and isolation effects on susceptibility to social reinforcement. *Canadian Journal of Behavioural Science,* 1971, *3,* 388-392.

KRIVITSKY, W. G. *In Stalin's Secret Service*. New York: Harper, 1939.

LEWIS, M. & RICHMAN, S. Social encounters and the effect on subsequent social reinforcement. *Journal of Abnormal and Social Psychology*, 1964, *69*, 253-257.

LOBB, L. G. & SCHAEFER, H. H. Successful treatment of anorexia nervosa through isolation. *Psychological Reports*, 1971, *30*, 245-246.

MARTIN, D. G. & SCHROEDER, D. The effects of social isolation with motor restraint on a figure placement task. *Psychonomic Science*, 1968, *12*, 353-354.

MERTON, T. *Seeds of Contemplation*. Norfolk, Conn.: New Directions, 1949.

MURIE, J. Pawnee Indian society. *Anthropology Papers, New York American Museum of Natural History*, 1914, *11*, 543-644.

MYERS, T. I. Tolerance for sensory and perceptual deprivation. In J. P. Zubek (Ed.), *Sensory Deprivation: Fifteen Years of Research*. New York: Appleton-Century-Crofts, 1969. Pp. 289-331.

NASA (National Aeronautics and Space Administration). The effects of confinement on long duration manned space flights: Proceedings of the NASA Symposium, 1966.

PENDERGRASS, V. E. Timeout from positive reinforcement following persistent, high rate behavior in retardates. *Journal of Applied Behavior Analysis*, 1972, *5*, 85-91.

POULTON, E. C. *Environment and Human Efficiency*. Springfield, Illinois: Charles C. Thomas, 1970.

POWYS, J. C. *A Philosophy of Solitude*. New York: Simon & Schuster, 1933.

RABBIE, J. M. Differential preference for companionship under threat. *Journal of Abnormal and Social Psychology*, 1963, *67*, 643-648.

RADLOFF, W. & HELMREICH, R., *Groups Under Stress: Psychological Research in Sealab II*. New York: Appleton-Century-Crofts, 1968.

RASMUSSEN, J. (Ed.) *Man in Isolation and Confinement*. Chicago: Aldine, 1973.

REYNOLDS, D. K. Directed behavior change: Japanese psychotherapy in a private mental hospital. Ph.D. dissertation, University of California (Los Angeles), 1969. Cited in H. Wagatsuma, Research and observations: Far East. *Transcultural Psychiatric Research*, 1972, *9*, 112-114.

ROUGH TIMES. A number of articles during 1973 appearing in *Rough Times* concerning the use of solitary confinement in American penitentiaries.

SADLER, O. & TESSER, A. Some efforts of salience and time upon interpersonal hostility and attraction during social isolation. *Sociometry*, 1973, *36*, 99-112.

SAITO, D. I., KITAMURA, S., & TADA, H. A study of social isolation. *Tohoku Psychologica Folia*, 1970, *28*, 109-111.

SAPIR, E. & SWADESH, M. *Native Accounts of Nootka Ethnography*. Bloomington, Indiana: Indiana University Research Center of Anthropology, Folklore and Linguistics, 1955.

SCHACHTER, S. *The Psychology of Affiliation*. Stanford, California: Stanford University Press, 1959.

SCOTT, G. D. & GENDREAU, P. A. Psychiatric implications of sensory deprivation in a maximum security prison. *Canadian Psychiatric Association Journal*, 1969, *14*, 337-341.

SCOTT, J. P. Development of social motivation. In D. Levine (Ed.), *Nebraska Symposium on Motivation*, Vol. 15. Lincoln, Nebraska: University of Nebraska Press, 1967. Pp. 11-132.

SUEDFELD, P. Isolation, confinement, and sensory deprivation. *Journal of the British Interplanetary Society*, 1968, *21*, 222-231.

SUEDFELD, P. Changes in intellectual performance and in susceptibility to influence. In J. P. Aubek (Ed.), *Sensory Deprivation: Fifteen Years of Research*. New York: Appleton-Century-Crofts, 1969. Pp. 126-166. (a)

SUEDFELD, P. Theoretical formulations: II. In J. P. Zubek (Ed.), *Sensory Deprivation: Fifteen Years of Research*. New York: Appleton-Century-Crofts, 1969. Pp. 43-448. (b)

SUEDFELD, P. The psychiatric relevance of sensory deprivation: A selective review. *Comments on Contemporary Psychiatry*, in press.

SUEDFELD, P. & ROY, C. Using social isolation to change the behaviour of disruptive inmates. In preparation.

SVAB, L., GROSS, J., & LANGOVA, J. Stuttering and social isolation: Effect of social isolation with different levels of monitoring on stuttering frequency: A pilot study. *Journal of Nervous and Mental Disease*, 1972, *155*, 1-5.

TABARKOVA, H. [Effects of the delinquent's unwilling isolation of the association experiment.] *Psychologia a Patorpsychologia Dietata*, 1967-8, *3*, 547-556.

TART, C. T. (Ed.) *Altered States of Consciousness*. New York: Wiley, 1969.

TEBBEL, J. *The Compact History of the Indian Wars*. New York: Tower, 1967.

TYLER, V. O. Jr. & BROWN, G. D. The use of swift brief isolation as a group control device for institutionalized delinquents. *Behaviour Research and Therapy*, 1967, *5*, 1-9.

WADDELL, H. *The Desert Fathers*. New York: Sheed & Ward, 1942.

WALLACE, R. K. & BENSON, H. The physiology of meditation. *Scientific American*, 1972, *26*, 84-90.

WALTERS, R. H. & HENNING, G. B. Social isolation, effective instructions, and verbal behavior. *Canadian Journal of Psychology*, 1962, *16*, 202-210.

WALTERS, R. H. & PARKE, R. D. Emotional arousal, isolation, and discrimination learning in children. *Journal of Experimental Child Psychology*, 1964, *1*, 163-173.

WALTERS, R. H. & RAY, E. Anxiety, social isolation and reinforcer effectiveness. *Journal of Personality*, 1960, *28*, 358-367.

WEININGER, O. Effects of parental deprivation: An overview of literature and report on some current research. *Psychological Reports*, 1972, *30*, 591-612.

WHO (World Health Organization), *Deprivation of Maternal Care* (Public Health Papers, No. 14). Geneva: WHO, 1962.

ZAJONC, R. B. Social facilitation. *Science*, 1965, *149*, 269-274.

ZIMMERMAN, J. G. *Solitude*. London: Vernor & Hood, etc., 1804.

ZUBEK, J. P. (Ed.) *Sensory Deprivation: Fifteen Years of Research*. New York: Appleton-Century-Crofts, 1969.

ZUBEK, J. P. Behavioral and physiological effects of prolonged sensory and perceptual deprivation: A review. In J. E. Rasmussen (Ed.), *Man in Isolation and Confinement*. Chicago: Aldine, 1973. Pp. 9-83.

ZUCKERMAN, M. Field dependency as a predictor of responses to sensory and social isolation. *Perceptual and Motor Skills*, 1968, *27*, 757-758.

ZUCKERMAN, M., PERSKY, H., LINK, K. E., and BASU, G. K. Experimental and subject factors determining responses to sensory deprivation, social isolation and confinement. *Journal of Abnormal Psychology*, 1968, *73*, 183-194.

ZUCKERMAN, M., PERSKY, H., LINK, K. E., and BASU, G. K. Responses to confinement: An investigation of sensory deprivation, social isolation, restriction of movement and set factors. *Perceptual and Motor Skills*, 1968, *27*, 319-324.

The Painful Ecstasy of Healing

Richard Katz

For ninety-nine percent of human history, our species lived as hunters and gatherers, existing on what the land provided. During this long epoch, human beings forged basic ways of living together and ideas of the forces that mold man's fate.

Few cultures of hunters and gatherers survive today. One of them is the !Kung of the Kalahari Desert in Botswana, Africa (the exclamation point in !Kung represents one of four clicking sounds in their language).

The !Kung call themselves "Zhun/Twasi," which means simply "people." They live in a land that yields food and water only sparingly. They survive by joining in groups to hunt and gather, and sharing what they collect. But the !Kungs' everyday life goes beyond survival in a harsh land; it has a profound spiritual dimension. This spirituality is highlighted by intense and exhilarating all-night healing dances. In these dances they share a spiritual power that heals, protects, and gives well-being to them all.

I lived with the !Kung in 1968 as a member of the Harvard Kalahari Project. During this time, I worked closely with team members, especially Richard Lee, who also served as my translator, and later with Megan Biesele. Since then I have kept in touch with !Kung affairs. As a psychologist, I was most interested in how the !Kung deal with illness, health, and growth. Their approach to healing leads them to include everyone in the dance, whether obviously ill or not, for in healing, the !Kung make no distinction among their physical, emotional, and spiritual needs.

The healing dance is their main method for treating sickness, though the !Kung also use medicinal herbs and salves for minor injuries and infections. Recently the !Kung have had occasional access to antibiotics, which they sometimes use against infection. But they rely on the healing dance for the treatment of virtually every illness. Two illnesses I saw treated in the dance were emphysema and what we in the West would call depression.

But the !Kung bring more than just their medical and psychological problems to the dance; rips in the social fabric, such as arguments between villages or disagreements about the distribution of meat, are often mended in the dance. Once, partisans of each side in a divorce dispute formed their own separate halves of what should have been a single large circle of singers. After a heated exchange between the sides, the protagonists from each side agreed to resolve their differences, got up, and sat together. Then the two sides joined in a single circle, and the healing dance began in earnest.

Spiritual exercise. If someone's illness takes a serious turn, a dance may be convened. More often, however, there will be a smaller healing ceremony in which one or two healers, with several singers, work exclusively on the sick person. The healing dance, since it speaks to so many different needs, is not strictly tied to any specific illness. And since the healing energy originates from the gods, the dance is itself a spiritual exercise.

The !Kung were pleased by my interest in their way of healing. They spoke willingly and eagerly, and received me warmly into their healing dance. Several asked me to tell my people the story of how they heal. I take their charge seriously, for though their way of seeing things is very different from our own, they deal with issues we all face, ranging from the treatment of illness to the relationship of man with the universe. While their unique answers need never be ours, their perspective can be useful.

In the healing dance of the !Kung everyone shares in a spiritual power called "n/um." Some translate n/um as "medicine," but it is more than just medicine. N/um is energy. The !Kung say it is found in the fire, in the healing songs, and most of all in the healers, in whom it concentrates in the pit of their stomachs and the base of their spines. The dance activates the n/um in the healers; their singing and their dance movements, they say "heat up" the n/um. When n/um reaches boiling, it vaporizes and rises up the spine. Tsau, one of the stronger healers, describes the feeling of n/um as a tingling in the base of his spine that works its way up his backbone, until it "makes your thoughts nothing in your head."

As n/um reaches the base of a healer's skull, he enters a state of transcendence called "!kia." Once in this state, the dancer can heal. !Kia, usually translated as "trance," is actually a state of enhanced awareness, in which the healer claims, among other things, to see over great distances, inside other people's bodies, and to be able to contact the gods. Tsau speaks of how boiling n/um produces !kia:

"N/um lifts you up in your belly and lifts you in your back, and then you start to shiver. N/um makes you tremble; it's hot. Your eyes are open but you don't look around; you hold your eyes still and look straight ahead. But when you get into !kia, you're looking around because you see everything, because you see what is troubling everybody."

The !Kung enter !kia in order to heal, and their healing has three main aspects: "seeing properly," pulling out the sickness, and arguing with the gods. Seeing properly allows the healer to locate and diagnose the sickness. As Bo, another strong healer, said, "You have to be absolutely steady to see sickness, steady-eyed, no shivering and shaking; you need direct looking. Your thoughts don't whirl, and the fire doesn't float about you when you are seeing properly." Seeing properly enables the healer to see beyond mere appearances to othe realities. During !kia , the reality of the unseen dominatcs. Toma says, "In !kia you see everybody. You see that the insides of well people are fine. You see the insides of the one the ghosts are trying to kill."

Insulting the gods. Like healers in other parts of the world, the !Kung lay on hands to pull out sickness. They place their fluttering hands on either side of the person's chest, or wherever the sickness is located. They touch the person lightly, or more often vibrate their hands close to the skin's surface. At times the healer wraps his body around the person, rubbing his sweat—believed to carry healing properties—on the sick person. The sickness is drawn into the healer. Then the healer expels the sickness from his own body, shaking it from his hand out into space, his body shuddering with pain.

Ordinarily the !Kung do not speak of the gods. But as the healer works, he not only talks directly to the gods, he may also bargain with them, insult them, or even do battle with them. The healer struggles with the ghosts, the spirits of the dead, whom the gods send to carry away a sick person. If a healer's n/um is strong, the ghosts will retreat and the sick one will live. This struggle is at the center of the healer's skill, art, and power.

The healing dance goes from dusk to dawn, often several times a week. Most of the community come to the open center space of the village, where the dance revolves around a fire. The women sit around the flames, shoulder to shoulder, legs intertwined, and sing the healing songs to the beat of their rhythmic clapping. The dancers circle around them; they are mostly men, who do most of the healing, although singers sometimes heal as well. Toward the edges of the open village, around several smaller fires, others sit, talk, and rest, supporting the dance with their presence, at times singing and dancing.

At the start, the singers and dancers warm up, and the mood is casual and jovial. Many of the dancers are adolescents showing off new dance steps. Laughter and banter fill the air. Then, almost imperceptibly, the mood grows intense; experienced healers begin to dance. The singing and clapping become spirited, the dancing focused.

Profound awe, no piety. But laughter is never far away. Our distinction between the sacred and the profane does not exist in the same way for the !Kung. The dance is their most intensely spiritual event, but during it they exchange some of their spiciest jokes and tease each other with friendly vigor about their dancing. The dance does not have an atmosphere of solemn piety, though the sense of awe is profound. As energy boils and the mood of the dance intensifies, laughter recedes, but only because working with those in !kia requires great concentration and care. Even when the mood is most tense, and all are filled with concern for a dancer overwhelmed with !kia, someone may joke, lightening the atmosphere and giving reassuring support.

Toward the middle of the night, in the darkness of the desert, the fire flickers its captivating, pulsating light on the singers and dancers. Feeling is high; the dancers sweat profusely. Transcendence is at hand. Soon a healer or two begins to stagger, then one falls. He may shudder and shake violently, his whole body convulsing in pain and anguish. Others may walk about stiff-legged, their eyes glazed. The state of !kia has come, and the healing begins.

Healing for the !Kung is much more than curing physical or psychological ailments, although it includes that. Healing nurtures each person's emotional and spiritual growth as well. The dance heals the whole person. The healer who is in !kia goes to each person at the dance whether he shows symptoms of illness or not. All receive the protection of healing. The healer pleads and argues with the gods to save the person from illness. He lays his hands on each one, and pulls out the sickness with eerie, earth-shattering screams and howls that show the pain and difficulty of his healing. The healing goes on for several hours.

As the dance moves into the early morning hours, a calm sets in. Some dancers doze. The talk is quiet, the singing soft. The dance is resting. Before dawn comes it awakes again as sleeping forms rise and move toward the dance circle. Once again, the singing becomes strong, the dancing active. There is usually another period of healing as the sun begins to throw its golden light and warmth on the group huddled around the dance. Before the sun becomes too warm, the healing usually subsides, the singing slowly softens, then stops. The dance is over.

Excruciating pain. To the Western eye it may seem that the men, more often involved in the dramatic role of dancing, are more important than the women to the dance. This is not so. Men and women make different, but equally valued, contributions. The singers and dancers need each other's help to activate the healing energy. Though the actions of the men and women at the dance differ, their experience of transcendence—the heart of the dance—is the same. Men and women are bound together by their shared, enhanced consciousness.

The healer's vocation is open to all, and most of the young men, and many of the women, seek to become healers. About half the men and a third of the women succeed. The training is difficult. Not everyone can stand the excruciating pain of boiling n/um, said to be "hot and painful, just like fire." It makes one cry and writhe in agony.

Part of the pain comes from facing one's own death. To heal, one must die and be reborn. This is no allegorical rite of passage, but a terror-filled experience of death and rebirth. Dem, a powerful healer, says, !kia your heart stops, you're dead, your thoughts are nothing, you breathe with difficulty. You see ghosts killing people, you smell burning, rotten flesh. Then you heal, you pull sickness out. Then you live." Healers insist that this death is as terrible as "the death that kills us all." The terror of !kia remains despite years of healing, and accepting this recurrent death is the core of the healer's training.

The singers, dancers, and everyone at the dance help those seeking !kia. They may, for example, help the seekers regulate the intensity and speed with which n/um boils up inside them so as to keep a balance between the fear of !kia and the intensity of the boiling n/um. If !kia is coming on so rapidly that a dancer's fear is out of control, they may urge him to stop dancing or lie down and drink some water to cool down his boiling n/um. If his fear can be contained or, even better, accepted, he will want the n/um to boil more strongly. The stronger his n/um, the stronger the healing power.

The dancers must continually regulate the intensity and rapidity with which their n/um boils. Others lend emotional and physical support to aid their efforts. In one dance, for example, a young man new to !kia was on the brink of being overwhelmed by this energy. His fear was out of control, and he raced away from the dance. Immediately, two men brought him back to the dance and "danced him," one holding him from the back, the other supporting him from the front. The three danced as one, and the singing reached new levels of intensity. The young dancer now faced what he feared most, in an even more intense form. But with this support he could overcome his fear, experience !kia, and then heal.

No special privileges.   When I asked the !Kung to tell stories about pictures I showed them, I found some psychological differences between those who healed and those who did not. Healers have richer fantasies than nonhealers. Healers are also more inner-directed, more able to cope with unfamiliar situations, and more emotional. All these things prepare a person to accept an enhanced state like !kia; these characteristics are both predispositions that may lead one to become a healer and attributes of the healer that

intensify and are intensified by !kia perhaps 1,000 times. So many profound experiences must affect the quality of the healer's inner life.

Even though the healers have special psychological qualities, they enjoy no special privileges. Healers, like all !Kung, are first hunters and gatherers, and only secondarily healers. Yet for a very few of the most powerful healers things are somewhat different. With these few, a spiritual quality seems to pervade their daily behavior. They, for example, dance frequently, sometimes every day. They can heal themselves and others without needing the support of a full dance. Unlike the ordinary healers, the most powerful healers say they travel to the invisible village of the dogs during !kia in their struggle to keep sickness away. Their healing abilities and general wisdom are widely acknowledged. But they neither accumulate marks of prestige nor do they hoard power.

Healing and spiritual powers are held in great respect, but just as the !Kung freely share their food and water, they share their healing energy. N/um cannot be hoarded; the more it is aroused in one person, the easier it is for someone else to share it. As one healer enters !kia it becomes more likely that another will also. Through the healing dance, members of the group enhance each other's well-being. Through the dance, each person receives more healing than he or she could possibly derive through individual efforts.

Social ecology among the !Kung in unusual. Compared to other cultures, the percentage of !Kung who become healers is large. But since most of them must also hunt and gather to survive, only a few of the most powerful healers, perhaps one out of a hundred, can put hunting and gathering aside for a more intense involvement with healing and the spirit. The !Kung see the need for feeding both the body and the spirit. The work to acquire food—or healing energy—is shared by all, as is its use.

This approach to healing and the !Kung's communal way of life is threatened. Capitalism is bearing down on this egalitarian hunting-gathering society, pushing its members into a more sedentary existence as serfs to another tribe and as exploited laborers to the white Afrikaner farmers. The land, traditionally a storehouse used collaboratively by all, is now passing into the hands oof Bantu cattle raisers, who fence it off as private property. Where everything was once shared, a cash economy is being introduced that encourages people to accumulate personal property and hoard their wealth. Private ownership of goods attacks the principle of sharing—the heart of the healing dance and the hunting-gathering way of life. And missionaires from South Africa, who seek to convert the !Kung to organized religion, further erode support for the dance.

The healing dance has not always taken its present form, and several newer dances have recently emerged. Perhaps the !Kung form of healing may survive by changing to meet the new cultural conditions. But the esoteric principles at the core of the tradition must be kept to preserve its validity.

Shared wisdom.   What might the !Kung healing methods mean for us in the industrialized West? Their healing tradition offers us a valuable perspective on consciousness and human growth. This includes knowledge about the activation, use, and regulation of spiritual energy; the awareness that healing involves the emotional and spiritual sides of a person; the possibility of an intimate connection between everyday life and enhanced states of consciousness; and the sharing of healing power.

While only direct and personal contact with the !Kung healers and community reveals the full experience of !kia healing, its wisdom is more easily shared. Our culture cannot apply the !Kung approach to healing in any literal way. But its basic ingredients—such as treatment of the whole person rather than an isolated part of him—can blend and merge with our own attitudes toward health. The !Kung show us that rigid distinctions between health and illness hide the fact that healing can benefit all, not just those with obvious symptoms. Their collaborative effort, in which the whole community cooperates to release healing energy that is freely shared with all, contrasts sharply with the isolation of the sick and the cost of medical care in our own culture. The !Kung also show us how to contact the spiritual realm as a source of healing energy, and that contact with this realm need not have the stiff solemnity of a Sunday service. These lessons from the !Kung might help us dismantle some of our own cultural barriers to healing and spiritual growth.

The High Dream

Charles T. Tart

People have generally regarded a dream occurring at night as a unitary phenomenon: a dream is a dream is a dream.... Close questioning of people about the formal nature (as opposed to the particular content) of their dreams will reveal many differences between one person's dreams and another's. For example, we have always known some people dream in color while others never report color. This fact of individual differences suggests that there might be not only *quantitative* differences among various dreams of the same individual (such as in intensity of imagery, affect, feeling of control, et.) but perhaps *qualitative* differences,, i.e., that there may in fact be several psychologically and experientially distinct phenomena that have been indiscriminately lumped together under the term "dream."

Modern laboratory studies of sleep and dreaming have now indicated there are at least two distinct types of mental activity occurring during sleep, one associated with a stage 1 EEG pattern and the other associated with a stage 2, 3, or 4 EEG. The stage 1 mental activity has the characteristics we usually associate with dreaming: vivid visual imagery, being located at some distant place, interacting with other characters, intense emotions, lack of recognition that one is actually lying in bed asleep, etc. The mental activity in the other stages of sleep is thought-like, and has little or no visual imagery. Typical reports are on the order of "I was wondering what to buy at the store tomorrow." Further, non-stage 1 mental activity seems such less likely to be recalled by most subjects.

An even more interesting type of dream has been occasionally reported by introspective writers, which van Eeden called the "lucid" dream. This has the unusual characteristic that the dreamer "wakes" from an ordinary dream in that he feels he is suddenly in possession of his normal waking consciousness and knows that he is actually lying in bed asleep: *but,* the dream world he is in remains perfectly real. What stage of sleep this lucid dream might be associated with is unknown. There are occasional references to learning how to produce this sort of dream as a dream yoga, leading to liberation, but other than that almost nothing is known about it. I have had a lucid dream about three times in my life, during the past ten years, and so can testify to its experiential reality. Each time it occurred

from a normal dream: for a few seconds my state of consciousness would shift to a "full waking" state in which I seemed possessed of all my normal mental faculties, yet the dream world stayed perfectly real and I was experientially located "in" it. At the same time, I had to maintain a curious sort of mental "balance of activation" which I cannot describe adequately. If I pushed the activation too high I would actually wake up; if I didn't keep it high enough I would slip back into ordinary dream consciousness. I could not maintain the right balance for more than about half a minute on each occasion.

It appears then that there are at least three distinct types of mental activity that occur during sleep: "dreaming," associated with a stage 1 EEG pattern, "sleep thinking," associated with a stage 2, 3, or 4 pattern, and the "lucid dream."

I would now like to describe what may be a fourth type of dreaming activity, which I shall term the "high dream." I have had this type of dream about a dozen times in the past few years, subsequent to personal experience with psychedelic chemicals, although usually not in close temporal proximity to a psychedelic experience. This experience is a distinct shift to a new type of consciousness within the dream state, like being "high" on a psychedelic chemical, although not exactly the same. I have talked to many people who have had chemical psychedelic experiences but found only a few of them also noting high dreams. I will present a few dreams (mine and others) below to illustrate the phenomena before attempting a formal definition. All of these dreams are from people who have had many years interest in their dreams and so were good observers of dream processes, as well as having had chemically induced psychedelic experiences.

My first dream of this sort occurred several hours after the end of an LSD-25 session (dosage of 175 mg), so there was probably still some chemical activity occurring, although I had felt almost completely normal on going to bed. Several hours after falling asleep I found myself in a condition that was not sleep, dreaming, or waking. In it I was holding on to a gestalt concept of my waking personality, and with this nebulously articulated concept as a constant background I was examining statements about personality characteristics: slow to anger, high interest in outdoors, etc. Each concept would be examined and, if acceptable, "programmed" into the waking personality that would emerge on the morrow. If unacceptable the statement was thrown away rather than being programmed. Exactly what this programming operation was was clear in this high dream, but could not be recalled clearly on waking. Like many psychedelic experiences, the memory cannot be re-experienced in ordinary consciousness.

Another dream from a young woman illustrates the great shift in sensory qualities of the high dream:

> I was sitting on a large square pillow, an intense blue (pillow), or lying across it at an angle, and it was large enough so that I could do this easily. The pillow was spinning slowly and all sorts of intense colors were happening at the corners and edges. Mostly it was the feeling rather than any visual cue, a feeling of being very much with it and whole. I woke up happy to have had a little glimpse of the peace I had gone to bed seeing.

Note that the dreamer emphasized that it is not simply the sensory quality alone which distinguishes the high dream from ordinary dreams. Asked to comment futher on the differences between such dreams and her ordinary dreams she wrote:

> Ordinary dreams usually center around action of some sort with other characters and usually take place in an everyday world. None of this is true of high dreams. The real distinction is the state of mind which in a high dream is one which would be found with marijuana or LSD, time and perceptual distortions which, however, are only pointers for the change, which is an altered and more exclusive point of view. . . .

At this point I shall attempt a formal definition of the high dream: it is an experience occurring during sleep in which you find yourself in another world, the dream world, *and* in which you recognize *during* the dream that you are in an altered state of consciousness which is similar to (but not necessarily identical with) the high induced by a chemical psychedelic. It is important to emphasize that it is not the *content* of the dream, but *what* is dreamed about that distinguishes the high dream from the ordinary dream: one could dream of taking LSD, e.g., without the change in the mental processes that constitute the high dream, just as one can dream of waking up without it being a lucid dream. This is a rough definition, but a more precise definition will not be possible until much more is known about the high dream. It is quite possible that there may be several distinct types of high dreams also, just as there seem to be some differences in chemically produced highs which are a function of the particular chemical substance used (as well as set and setting).

A fascinating possibility, that some sort of high state of conciousness can be carried over from dream to waking, is illustrated by the following dream from a male:

> I dreamed I got high on some sort of gaseous substance, like LSD in gas form. Space took on an expended, high quality, my body (dream body) was filled with a delicious sensation of warmth, my mind "high" in an obvious but indescribable way. It only lasted a minute and then I was awakened by one of the kids calling out and my wife getting up to see what was the matter. Then the most amazing thing happened: I stayed high even though awake! It had a sleepy quality to it but the expanded and warm quality of time and space carried over into my perception of the (dimly lit) room. It stayed this way for a couple of minutes, amazing me at the time because I was clearly high, as well as recalling my high dream. Then I drifted back into sleep as my wife returned to bed. I think I slipped into a high dream state for a minute or two but can't recall clearly, as I fell asleep. . . . It was definitely a high condition, although not quite the same as an LSD high: I can't explain the difference. This high state was clearly different from ordinary dream consciousness, ordinary waking consciousness, and "ordinary" highs, and the high state itself was unchanged by the transition from dream to waking.

Thus we may not only have a pronounced shift in mental functioning during the dream state, but such a shift can carry over to a subsequent waking state.

Little more can be said about the high dream at this point: the examples presented above comprise almost my entire collection of them, and are from only a few individuals. How frequently does the high dream occur? Can all the characteristics of chemically induced highs be reproduced in it? Are there phenomena that do not occur in chemically induced highs? The high dream exists as a distinct entity from ordinary dreams in at least a few individualists, but other questions about it cannot be answered until (a) many spontaneous high dreams are collected for analysis, or (b) we learn to produce high dreams at will for study.

The Experience of Dying

Raymond Moody, Jr.

WHAT IS IT LIKE TO DIE?

During the past few years I have encountered a large number of persons who were involved in what I shall call "near-death experiences." I have met these persons in many ways. At first it was by coincidence. In 1965, when I was an undergraduate student studying philosophy at the University of Virginia, I met a man who was a clinical professor of psychiatry in the School of Medicine. I was struck from the beginning with his warmth, kindliness and humor. It came as a great surprise when I later learned a very interesting fact about him, namely, that he had been dead—not just once but on two occasions, about ten minutes apart—and that he had given a most fantastic account of what happened to him while he was "dead." I later heard him relate his story to a small group of interested students. At the time, I was most impressed, but since I had little background from which to judge such experiences, I "filed it away," both in my mind and in the form of a tape recording of his talk.

Some years later, after I had received my Ph.D. in philosophy, I was teaching in a university in eastern North Carolina. In one course I had my students read Plato's *Phaedo,* a work in which immortality is among the subjects discussed. In my lectures I had been emphasizing the other doctrines which Plato presents there and had not focused upon the discussion of life after death. After class one day a student stopped by to see me. He asked whether we might discuss the subject of immortality. He had an interest in the subject because his grandmother had "died" during an operation and had recounted a very amazing experience. I asked him to tell me about it, and much to my surprise, he related almost the same series of events which I had heard the psychiatry professor describe some years before.

At this time my search for cases became a bit more active, and I began to include readings on the subject of human survival of biological death in my philosophy courses. However, I was careful not to mention the two death experiences in my courses. I adopted, in effect, a wait-and-see attitude. If such reports were fairly common, I thought, I would probably hear of more if I just brought up the general topic of survival in philosophical discussions, expressed a sympathetic attitude toward the question, and

waited. To my amazement, I found that in almost every class of thirty or so students, at least one student would come to me afterwards and relate a personal near-death experience.

What has amazed me since the beginning of my interest are the great similarities in the reports, despite the fact that they come from people of highly varied religious, social, and educational backgrounds. By the time I entered medical school in 1972, I had collected a sizable number of these experiences and I began mentioning the informal study I had been doing to some of my medical acquaintances. Eventually, a friend of mine talked me into giving a report to a medical society, and other public talks followed. Again, I found that after every talk someone would come up to tell me of an experience of his own.

As I became more widely known for this interest, doctors began to refer to me persons whom they had resuscitated and who reported unusual experiences. Still others have written to me with reports after newspaper articles about my studies appeared.

At the present time, I know of approximately 150 cases of this phenomenon. The experiences which I have studied fall into three distinct categories:

(1) The experiences of persons who were resuscitated after having been thought, adjudged, or pronounced clinically dead by their doctors.

(2) The experiences of persons who, in the course of accidents or severe injury or illness, came very close to physical death.

(3) The experiences of persons who, as they died, told them to other people who were present. Later, these other people reported the content of the death experience to me.

From the vast amount of material that could be derived from 150 cases, selection obviously has occurred. Some of it has been purposeful. For example, although I have found reports of the third type to complement and to agree very well with experiencces of the first two types, I have for the most part dropped them from consideration for two reasons. First, it helps to reduce the number of cases studied to a more manageable level, and second, it enables me to stick as close as possible to first hand reports. Thus, I have interviewed in great detail some fifty persons upon whose experiences I am able to report. Of these, the cases of the first type (those in which an apparent clinical death actually occurs) are certainly more *dramatic* than those of the second type (in which only a close brush with death occurs). Indeed, whenever I have given public talks on this phenomenon, the "death" episodes have invariably drawn most of the interest. Accounts in the press have sometimes been written so as to suggest they are the *only* type of case with which I have dealt.

However, in selecting the cases to be presented, I have avoided the temptation to dwell only on those cases in which a "death" event took place. For, as will become obvious, cases of the second type are not different from, but rather form a continuum with, cases of the first type. Also, though the near-death experiences themselves are remarkably similar, both the circumstances surrounding them and the persons describing them vary widely. Accordingly, I have tried to give a sample of experiences which adequately reflects this variation. With these qualifications in mind, let us now turn to a consideration of what may happen, as far as I have been able to discover, during the experience of dying.

Despite the wide variation in the circumstances surrounding close calls with death and in the types of persons undergoing them, it remains true that there is a striking similarity among the accounts of the experiences themselves. In fact, the similarities among various reports are so great that one can easily pick out about fifteen separate elements which recur again and again in the mass of narratives that I have collected. On the basis of these points of likeness, let me now construct a brief, theoretically "ideal" or "complete" experience which embodies all of the common elements, in the order in which it is typical for them to occur.

A man is dying and, as he reaches the point of greatest physical distress, he hears himself pronounced dead by his doctor. He begins to hear an uncomfortable noise, a loud ringing or buzzing, and at the same time feels himself moving very rapidly through a long dark tunnel. After this, he suddenly finds himself outside of his own physical body, but still in the immediate physical environment, and he sees his own body from a distance, as though he is a spectator. He watches the resuscitation attempt from this unusual vantage point and is in a state of emotional upheaval.

After a while, he collects himself and becomes more accustomed to his odd condition. He notices that he still has a "body," but one of a very different nature and with very different powers from the physical body he has left behind. Soon other things begin to happen. Others come to meet and to help him. He glimpses the spirits of relatives and friends who have already died, and a loving, warm spirit of a kind he has never encountered before—a being of light—appears before him. This being asks him a question, nonverbally, to make him evaluate his life and helps him along by showing him a panoramic, instantaneous playback of the major events of his life. At some point he finds himself approaching some sort of barrier or border, apparently representing the limit between earthly life and the next life. Yet, he finds that he must go back to the earth, that the time for his death has not yet come. At this point he resists, for by now he is taken up with his experiences in the afterlife and does not want to return. He is overwhelmed by intense feelings of joy, love, and peace. Despite his attitude, though, he somehow reunites with his physical body and lives.

Later he tries to tell others, but he has trouble doing so. In the first place, he can find no human words adequate to describe these unearthly episodes. He also find that others scoff, so he stops telling other people. Still, the experience affects his life profoundly, especially his views about death and its relationship to life.

It is important to bear in mind that the above narrative is not meant to be a representation of any one person's experience. Rather, it is a "model," a composite of the common elements found in very many stories. I introduce it here only to give a preliminary, general idea of what a person who is dying may experience. Since it is an abstraction rather than an actual account, I will discuss in detail each common element, giving many examples.

Before doing that, however, a few facts need to be set out in order to put the remainder of my exposition of the experience of dying into the proper framework.

(1) Despite the striking similarities among various accounts no two of them are precisely identical (though a few come remarkably close to it).

(2) I have found no one person who reports every single component of the composite experience. Very many have reported most of them (that is, eight or more of the fifteen or so) and a few have reported up to twelve.

(3) There is no one element of the composite experience which every single person has reported to me, which crops up in every narrative. Nonetheless, a few of these elements come fairly close to being universal.

(4) There is not one component of my abstract model which has appeared in only one account. Each element has shown up in many separate stories.

(5) The order in which a dying person goes through the various stages briefly delineated above may vary from that given in my "theoretical model." To give one example, various persons have reported seeing the "being of light" before, or at the same time, they left their physical bodies, and not as in the "model," some time afterward. However, the order in which the stages occur in the model is a very typical order, and wide variations are unusual.

(6) How far into the hypothetical complete experience a dying person gets seems to depend on whether or not the person actually underwent an apparent clinical death, and if so, on how long he was in this state. In general, persons who were "dead" seem to report more florid, complete experiences than those who only came close to death, and those who were "dead" for a longer period go deeper than those who were "dead" for a shorter time.

THE POLITICS OF CONSCIOUSNESS

There is a politics of consciousness played out in the value (or lack of value) that people, groups, or cultures place on a particular state. Some critics complain that in the West we put an undue value on the rational waking state to the detriment of states more conducive to intuitive and creative insights. This has been a longstanding debate in the West; during the 1950s it focused on C. P. Snow's concept of the "two cultures"—the arts and the sciences. In this decade its symbol has been the two halves of the brain, with the left hemisphere embodying the rational mode of consciousness, the right the creative and intuitive. This is but one of many battlelines in the politics of consciousness.

MYSTICISM AND MADNESS

A longstanding dispute in the politics of consciousness has revolved around the nature of the mystical experience. In a revealing survey, pollsters Andrew Greeley and William McCready discovered that two out of five Americans in a random sample had experienced at least once in their lives a mystic moment where they felt they had become completely "one" with the universe. Despite the commonness of this experience, virtually no one in their sample had ever told anyone about it before. Why? In our culture, they feared, this mystical experience would be seen as a symptom of mental illness rather than a spiritual breakthrough.

A much less cautious view of the transcendental experience is taken by British psychiatrist R. D. Laing, who acknowledges that the distinction is often hazy between a state that is mad and one that is mystical. Much of how the judgment goes depends more on the dominant views of society than the specifics of the state itself. In both mystical and mad states of consciousness, the person loses touch with commonly shared views of reality. For the mystic, a voyage into an altered state is an essential part of the inner pilgrimage, but that voyage invariably ends in a return to the normal, shared state of consciousness which is then enhanced by a higher perspective gained in the altered state. The schizophrenic, Laing suggests, may sometimes follow the same inner voyage the mystic takes. The psychotic state may allow some schizophrenics to face and finally subdue "demons" and dilemmas that plague us all. When they emerge from the psychosis, like the mystic, they may be more "sane"—more fully adjusted to life—than those of us who never make such a voyage.

Concerned by the upsurge of interest in altered states and the mystical experience, the American Psychiatric Association commissioned a task force to look into the nature of mysticism from a psychiatric viewpoint. After a thorough survey of the classical literature on mysticism, the committee was unable to make a firm distinction between a mystical state and psychopathology. Their difficulty, the report acknowledged, was in large part due to their psychoanalytic orientation; this perspective has no place in it for spiritual development *per se*, but rather reduces such experiences to one sort or another of adaptive or defensive process.

Psychologist Arthur J. Deikman, in a critique of the Committee's report, contends that it reveals more about the limits of his own profession than about the mystical experience. The report, says Deikman, displays a misunderstanding of the nature of the goal of spiritual methods, and reduces them to terms more comfortable to the psychoanalytic viewpoint.

There is an experience common to all ventures into altered states of consciousness, writes mythographer Joseph Campbell—a core found also as a universal motif of myths. Whether the altered state be that of the schizophrenic, the taker of LSD, the shaman, the yogi, or the mystic, a common thread runs through them all. The pattern begins with a break away from the prevailing social order and its reality, progresses through a retreat into the inner psyche and a series of darkly terrifying encounters or, with luck, fulfilling and harmonizing encounters, and finally returns to a normal state with new courage and insight. The function of myths is to guide people through such journeys of inner descent and return. From this view, the schizophrenic's acute psychosis is part of an innate program for self-exploration which, if allowed to unfold on its own, will bring the person through to a new level of being. The schizophrenic, Campbell suggests, is plunged into the same sort of inward journey that the shaman and mystic seek voluntarily, in the hopes of a richer and more joyous life upon return. This journey in consciousness is a basic motif of myths throughout the world; it is the enternal voyage of the hero.

From the perspective of what we know about the brain, the psychotic state and the altered states that the yogi enters by dint of his own efforts are most likely very different. But in terms of the loosening of one's self-concepts and view of reality, they may in the end function similarly: to give the person who follows either route to a fortunate end an enlarged vision of the self and the world. But it is well to remember the caution that C. G. Jung offered to the novelist James Joyce, famous for his loose, seemingly mad, free associative prose. Joyce's daughter was hospitalized as psychotic, and the novelist asked Jung what was the difference between his own creative state and his daughter's madness. Replied Jung, "You dive, she falls."

Are We a Nation of Mystics?

Andrew Greeley
William McCready

Until the day he died, Blaise Pascal, the French philosopher, carried on his person the words he wrote after his conversion experience:

> From about half past ten in the evening to
> about half an hour after midnight.
> Fire.
> God of Abraham, God of Isaac, God of Jacob,
> Not the God of philosphers and scholars.
> Absolute Certainty: Beyond reason.
> Joy. Peace.
> Forgetfulness of the world and everything
> but God.
> The world has not known thee,
> but I have known thee.
> Joy! joy! joy! tears of joy!

Such extraordinary experiences—intense, overwhelming, indescribable—are recorded at every time in history and in every place on the globe and, as we shall argue later, are widespread, almost commonplace, in American society today. In times past, Joan of Arc had such an experience before leading her army into battle; St. Paul was knocked off his horse by a flash of light; Jesus apparently had at least two such experiences—at the time of his temptation and on Mount Thasor; the Buddha and Mohammed began their religious preaching after such interludes; the shamans of the Indian tribes of the Central Plains and the dancers of Bali go into mystic trances; Thomas Aquinas, just 700 years ago, described his life work as "straw" (*mihi videtur ut pavia*) after an intense ecstatic experience, and died, almost gladly, a few months thereafter; Abraham Lincoln may have had an intense mystical experience between the death of his son and the signing of the Emancipation Proclamation; Juan de la Cruz wrote his haunting lines, "Upon a gloomy night,/With all my cares in loving ardours flushed,/ (O venture of delight!)/With nobody in sight/I went abroad when all my house was hushed," in prison; G. K. Chesterton describes an ecstatic trance in front of a toy-shop window; Paul Claudel saw the whole of reality converge by a pillar in Notre Dame de Paris at the first vespers of Christmas.

But wherever the place and whatever the trigger and whoever the person, there run through the accounts of such interludes certain common themes—joy, light, peace, fire, warmth, unity, certainly, confidence, rebirth. Easterner and Westerner, saint and sinner, man and woman, young person and old, all seem to report a virtually identical experience—intense, overpowering joy which seemed literally to lift them out of themselves (in some instances the ecstatics thought they could actually see themselves from the outside).

No one with any familiarity with history or anthropology or psychology can deny that such events occur. They are a form of "altered state of consciousness"—to use the current approved phrase—something like intoxication or delirium or a hypnotic trance but different in their intensity, their joyfulness and their "lifting out" dimension. In some cases, such experiences were triggered by drugs, in others by ritual dances, in still others by disciplined meditation; but most such "ecstatic interludes" about which we have accounts seem to be purely spontaneous—a man casually walking by a tennis court suddenly is caught up in a wave of peace and joy "as time stands still."

Such profoundly skeptical writers as Karl Mannheim, Sigmund Freud and Bertrand Russell have commented on the existence of these "oceanic" feelings. Freud, who never had such an experience himself, was interested in them and included a description of the experience of his friend Romain Rolland in his book "Civilization and Its Discontents": "A peculiar feeling, which never leaves him personally, a feeling which he would like to call a sensation of 'eternity,' a feeling as of something limitless, unbounded, something 'oceanic.' It is purely subjective experience, not an article of belief . . . ."

The best known study of ecstasy is still "The Varieties of Religious Experience" by William James. He characterizes such experiences as "ineffable" (defying expression), "noetic" (providing an overwhelming experience of understanding), "transient" (lasting but a short time, although the "afterflow" may persist a lifetime) and "passive" (the person feels "grasped" by some sort of superior power).

James himself did not know what to make of these experiences. He was too careful a scholar to write ecstatics off as madmen, but too skeptical an agnostic to accept their testimony that the world was as benign and as joyous as they perceived it. Toward the end of his book, he offered a cautious concluding judgment: "Nonmystics are under no obligation to acknowledge in mystical states a superior authority conferred on them by their intrinsic nature. Yet . . . the existence of mystical states absolutely overthrows the pretension of nonmystical states to be the sole and ultimate dictator of what we may believe."

The mainstream of psychoanalytic writing on ecstatic episodes is much less gentle. Its contention is that the mystical experience is a form of regression. It is "like schizophrenia," an "escape from reality." But, unlike the schizophrenic, the mystic does not retreat all the way into an inner reality. Stimulated by a severe "life crisis," an unacceptable external reality, one retreats to the world of infancy where one can deal with (or bypass) frustration and disappointment through an intense sensate experience. The mystic is a neurotic, a misfit, an incipient psychotic; he cannot cope with the real world, so he flees to one of make-believe.

The verdict is not unanimous. The psychologist Abraham Maslow thought that "peak experiences" or "core experiences" were benign and healthy. Some psychologists who have identified with the counterculture suggest that ecstasy induced by drugs or fasting or contemplation or self-hypnotism may be a means of personal growth. But it is still fair to say, on the basis of the published literature, that most psychologists tend to think that ecstatic episodes are either bizarre evidence of a disturbed personality or a potentially dangerous search for novelty among unbalanced young people in the counterculture. Most Americans would doubtless go along with such judgments.

Though we, the writers of this article, are thoroughly unmystical ourselves, we discovered that a few people we knew had experienced such episodes. On the whole, they did not seem to us to be schizophrenic personalities or even any more neurotic than the general run. So, motivated by no more elaborate theoretical concern than curiosity, we managed to find room in a representative national survey of ultimate values among some 1,500 American adults for a handful of questions on mystical experiences. We wondered how many people in American society have had "mystical" or "oceanic" experiences, what kinds of people are likely to have them, and what impact these episodes have on their lives.

At first blush it may seem just a trifle mad to use the techniques of a national sample survey to fathom the unfathomable, explain the inexplicable, eff the ineffable; but we would argue that the national sample may be the only way to begin the study of mystical experiences in modern society. There is no other technique to determine how often and to whom such experiences happen. Those mystics who are discovered by a national survey are likely to be very different from the college freshman who volunteers for psychological experimentation or the wandering mystic who drops into a researcher's laboratory.

Furthermore, artificially induced ecstatic experiences produced by drugs or contemplative exercises or the various kinds of hypnotism or "mysticism machines" now being used in some laboratories are not necessarily the same things as the spontaneous experiences our respondents report. The basic difference between a spontaneous ecstatic interlude and one induced by a hallucinogenic drug, for example, is that one is induced by a drug and the other is not. However similar they may seem to be, they differ in that one critical respect at least. It may turn out that laboratory experiences and "natural" ones are indeed similar, but the only way that can be established is to study those who have had natural experiences.

We limited our investigation to those who reported having solitary mystical experiences. Group mystical experiences may occur in some segments of the population, such as young people living in community, but these communities are hard to ferret out with existing sampling techniques and are not typical of the national population, which was our basic interest.

The toughest problem was to figure out how to ask the question. Do you just walk into people's homes and ask them if they have ever had a "religio-mystical experience"? We did in one of our pretests and 50 percent of the respondents said they had. Our instincts—on which all question-worders rely heavily in the survey game—suggested that this might be too high a proportion. Another try was to ask whether they had ever felt as though they had become completely one with God or the universe. About 45 percent insisted they had. Finally, we settled on a question which seemed to reflect what the mysticism literature described as the core of the experience: Have you ever had the feeling of being very close to a powerful spiritual force that seemed to lift you out of yourself?

About 600 persons—two-fifths of the 1,500 persons asked the question—reported having had at least one such experience. About 300 said they had had it several times, and 75 said they had had it often.

Does such a question really get at whether a person has had a "mystical experience" in the classic meaning of the word? Until further research is done, we cannot say for sure. Obviously, one has to know far more about the experience that an individual respondent has had than can be gleaned in a first-round exploration. No survey question is ever perfect and doubtless this one is in many respects inadequate. If there is more research on mysticism, whoever does it will probably find better ways to ask the question. On the other hand, someone has to ask the question for the first time or there will be nothing on which to improve.

But we are moderately hopeful that the wording of the question is accurate enough for our present exploratory purposes. Those who say "yes" to it report that they have had an experience of a powerful spiritual force which seemed to lift them out of themselves. This "lifting out" *(exsto*—I stand out—whence the word "ecstasy") seems to be characteristic of all the mystical experiences about which we have read in the literature. Furthermore, more than two-thirds of those who have had such experiences placed the experience at the top end of a seven-point intensity scale. We are then dealing with people who report an intense experience of being lifted out of themselves by a powerful spiritual force. More than this we cannot say. Even if some (many, most) of these experiences are not "mystical" in the classic sense of the word, it is nonetheless a striking phenomenon that a large segment of the population is prepared to report such an intense experience. Whatever the nature of that experience, and however much it might fit the definition of traditional mysticism, it is in itself worth investigating.

Since there was not the time or the money to ask for a detailed description of each experience, we presented the respondents with two lists from which to check off answers. One list offered choices of what triggered the experience, and the other what the experience was like. Sure enough, the pattern we anticipated did indeed emerge. "A feeling that I couldn't possibly describe was happening to me," "the sensation that my personality had been taken over by something much more powerful than I am," "a sense of a new life or living in a new world," and "a sense that I was being bathed in light" clustered together in a pattern. Not only did such a cluster emerge (we called it the "twice-born" factor), but the principal relationships we are going to discuss in the rest of this article were precisely with those "mystics" who scored high on the scale created from the cluster.

We have, then, a substantial segment of the American population who have had intense spiritual experiences. We cannot now prove with certainty that they are all mystics, but we can ask what kind of people have such intense spiritual experiences. To suspend judgment on whether these are "real" mystical experiences, we will put quotes around the word "mystical" for the rest of this article.

Who are the ones who have "mystical" experiences? People in their 40's and 50's are somewhat more likely to report "mystical" interludes than those in their 70's or their teens. Protestants are more likely to experience them than Jews, and Jews more likely than Catholics. Within the Protestant denominations, it is not the fundamentalists who are the most frequent "mystics" but the Episcopalians (more than half of them). And within the two major denominational groups, the Irish are more likely than their co-religionists (be they Protestant or Catholic) to be "mystics."

Who are those who have these episode often? They are disproportionately male, disproportionately black, disproportionately college-educated, disproportionately above the $10,000-a-year income level and disporportionately Protestant.

They are not, then, the socially or economically disadvantaged in our society. If our ecstatics are running

from anything, it is not from their social condition; and while "mystics" are disproportionately black, it is not the poor blacks but the college-educated ones who are most likely to have had such experiences. Furthermore, the "mystics" have positive and happy recollections of their childhood; they report close relations between their mothers and fathers and between themselves and each of their parents. They also report a religious approach by their fathers and mothers that was characterized by "joyousness." (Apparently it is the father's religious joyousness in particular which predicts ecstatic experiences in the child.) Finally, the whites who had such experiences are less likely to be racially prejudiced.

Most of our "mystics"—though not all—are religious in the sense that they are affiliated with one of the major denominations and they attend church, but there is a tendency for them not to be "churchy." They also seem to have an extremely strong sense of confidence in life after death.

There is nothing on the surface, then, which would indicate that, either socially or psychologically, the ecstatics are deprived or disturbed. One would have liked, of course, to administer complex personality tests or to attempt indepth clinical interviews, but these are prohibitively expensive techniques. We did administer the brief Psychological Well-Being Scale developed by Prof. Norman Bradburn. The relationship between frequent ecstatic experiences and psychological well-being was .40, the highest correlation, according to Bradburn, he has ever observed with his scale. We tried to explain away or at least to diminish the strength of this correlation by taking into account a number of variables (education, sex, age, race) that might be responsible for it. The result was that the correlation remained virtually unchanged, declining only from .40 to .39.

Friends and professional colleagues began to drift into our offices, write letters, and telephone with, "Say, I wonder if you'd be interested in some experiences I've had . . ." Colleagues could remain absolutely silent at a seminar while others expressed polite and occasionally not so polite skepticism about our data, and then afterward come up to us in the corridor and detail really spectacular ecstatic episodes. We fear the secret must be let out: Even at one of the world's most empirical places, the National Opinion Research Center, there are "mystics" on the loose, and they are not completely absent from the senior positions. Heaven only knows, but there are probably some around William James Hall at Harvard University.

We also discovered that at any social gathering we need only raise the subject of our research to find at least one person in the group who has had ecstatic experiences. At first, we simply enjoyed this phenomenon because it promptly shut up the skeptics; now we are also pleased with the information provided by these very unsystematic interviews since it puts flesh on the bones of our statistical findings. From a few more than 20 such random interviews we have made a number of conclusions which could serve as the basis for further research:

(1) Like the mystics of the classic tradition, the interviewees perceived the phenomenon as fundamentally cognitive. They *saw*—not a person or a vision necessarily—the "way things really are." The core of the event is *knowing* something or Something. The joy, peace, heat, light and other such aspects of the experience are perceived as the result of the "knowledge." The truth of what they "know" is unshakable conviction, even if they are not able to put such truth into precise language that would have any meaning for those who have never experienced like episodes. "It was like a rose blooming in the snow and my life has never been the same since."

(2) Virtually all of the respondents have never spoken about their experiences to anyone—spouse, friends, family, clergyman. When a discussion of statistical research on the subject "legitimizes" talk about it, the revelation comes as something utterly astonishing even to those who know the person well. "Why didn't you tell me about it before?" is the standard question, to which the standard reply is, "It just didn't seem to be the kind of thing people talk about." Least of all does one talk about it to a clergyman. One woman remarked that she could not even mention it to her brother, who was one, because, as she said, the clergy simply don't believe in those things any more, and he would want her to see a psychiatrist.

(3) Some of the episodes are spontaneous, with no apparent "trigger." Others are occasioned by clearly defined triggers, some of them crisis situations of the sort that psychoanalytic writers postulate, but others not. "I was sitting in the window studying for an exam, and the whole world poured in on me."

(4) Some experiences are overwhelming in intensity. Joy, confidence, heat, light, fire, laughter, enthusiasm are so powerful as almost to sweep the one caught by such an experience off his feet. To cope with such intensity requires a fair amount of ego strength and support from those around one. We suspect that many who end up on a psychiatrist's couch may be those who cannot cope with such intense experiences. Hence the analysts form their conclusions of the phenomenon from a very biased sample. Other experiences, however, may be much more gentle—powerful, indeed, but subtle rather than overwhelming. "I stood on the pier, looking at the stars and everything was so peaceful it seemed like I was in eternity and it would never end."

Some of the respondents can't remember *not* having "mystical" experiences, while others seem to have had them only once or twice. But both groups insist that the experience was either the most important thing that ever happened in their lives or one of the most important things, that they have shaped their behavior and many of their decisions on the basis of the experience. Interestingly

enough, no one to whom we have spoken wants such experiences again; they are astonished that some people might deliberately seek them. Ecstatic interludes are glorious when they happen, and they are critically important to the people who have them, but they are disconcerting, disruptive, disturbing. It is as though people are saying, "Thanks, but no thanks." One person told us, "It was so joyful that it hurt; I don't ever want it to happen again. I couldn't stand such pain, and I couldn't stand the worse pain of it stopping."

(5) We encountered a number of people for whom sexual intercourse was the "trigger" of their ecstatic interlude (about 20 percent of the sample). These respondents agreed that, while their experience was occasioned by orgasm, it was categorically different from orgasmic pleasure and much more powerful. As far as we know, explicit sexual trigger has been noted only once before—by Marghanita Laski in her book "Ecstasy." "I had just settled into the 'afterglow,' " said one interviewee, "when something else happened which made the pleasure of that almost perfect lovemaking seem almost not to matter. I was possessed by something or someone whose demands made my very sexy partner seem dull and uninteresting. I was scared silly and thought I would lose my mind with pleasure." Perhaps the reason such scant attention is paid to such a trigger is that, in the Western tradition, most of the "mystics" who wrote about their experiences for us were celibate (though they certainly used passionate sexual imagery to describe the event).

(6) The people we interviewed were, with one exception, all "religious" in the broad sense of the word, though many of them were not "churchy." We asked one person who had no formal religious affiliation and was an infrequent church attender what he thought about the question of human survival after death. He resonded, "I don't have any explicit or verbal answer to that question. All I know is that, once you have experiences like I've had [he had had two of them], the question doesn't seem very important. You know things will be all right, and you don't bother yourself worrying about details."

(7) There is a curious loss of time perspective associated with the ecstatic interlude. "Time stands still" is a phrase we heard frequently. Hours seem like seconds, or a few moments like hours. It is during that period of time confusion, apparently, that the unity and convergence of all things are perceived. One respondent told us how he frequently walks down to a pier jutting into a small lake on an evening and the next thing he knows it's sunrise. Another described her sister finding her in church several hours after she had gone in, though it seemed to her only a few moments had passed. John Brodie, the articulate, sophisticated former quarterback for the San Francisco 49ers, has described a phenomenon of time lag when dropping back to throw a pass.

(8) For all but one of the respondents. the experi-

ence was benign. In the one exception, the structure of the experience was the same: Time stood still, the universe was perceived as converging, one's place in it was clearly specified. But the universe in this instance was hostile, vindictive; and instead of joy and peace, the person experienced what he called "cosmic buzz." We were able to tease out of our national survey some evidence of similar phenomena, which we called "dark night" mysticism. (It is more like the dark night of the senses of classical mysticism than the dark night of the soul with its more specifically religious connotation.) Those who have such experiences seem most likely to be from unreligious backgrounds and from fairly aloof, and reserved family relationships. "If God is responsible for those things," said our agnostic respondent, "I don't want any part of him. He is Ingmar Bergman's spider."

(9)   All of the respondents were creative, happy, dynamic individuals, though we would hesitate to say whether their creative proclivities were a cause or effect of their ecstatic episodes (or neither). One might say of most of them that they were intense individuals, but on the basis of their career performances and achievements, as well as the quality of their relationships with family and friends, the intensity seemed constructive rather than neurotic. "What the hell," said one young woman, "you gotta do something till it or he or she or whoever or whatever it is gets around to coming back again."

(10)   There seems to be some relationship, which we have not yet been able to understand, between "mystical" experience and consciousness of death. We use the word "consciousness" advisedly, because we are not disposed to say our interviewees are more afraid of death. They are more aware of death, but this awareness does not seem to be morbid. As one very active young woman put it, "I am not afraid of death, but it's very much on my mind. Sometimes to think about it makes me relaxed and peaceful."

(11)   A "sudden death" experience has triggered "mystical" interludes for some of our interviewees. Their descriptions parallel the pattern recorded by sudden death researchers—the rapid turnover of anger, life passing in review, resignation, peace, serenity, and then ecstatic joy (and the next thing you know, you're in a snowbank and have to study for the final examinations after all). In "The Accident," G. K. Chesterton describes with characteristic flair one such event in his life on the occasion of a runaway hansom:

But in those few moments, while my cab was tearing toward the traffic of the Strand . . . I really did have, in that short and shrieking period, a rapid succession of a number of fundamental points of view. I had, so to speak, about five religions in almost as many seconds. My first religion was pure Paganism, which among sincere men is more shortly described as extreme fear. Then there succeeded a state of mind which is quite real, but for which no proper name has ever been found. The ancients called it Stoicism . . . It was an empty and open acceptance of the thing that

happens—as if one had got beyond the value of it. And then, curiously enough, came a very strong contrary feeling—that things mattered very much indeed, and yet that they were something more than tragic. It was a feeling, not that life was unimportant, but that life was much too important ever to be anything but life. I hope that this was Christianity. At any rate, it occurred at the moment when we went crash into the omnibus.

Again, we don't know what to make of this phenomenon. It may be merely an evolutionary adaptation by which certain human beings who are better able to cope with death are more likely to survive and reproduce than those who are terrorized into powerlessness at the threat of death.

If we are forced to depart from our sociological agnosticism—as well as our own woeful inexperience—and to try to guess what really happens in "mystical" interludes, we would say that we think they are episodes of intense and immediate cognition in which the total personality of a person is absorbed in an intimate though transient relationship with the basic forces, cycles and mechanisms at work in the universe and in his own psychosomatic composite—gravity, cosmic rays, light, heat, electromagnetism, cycles of breathing, circulation, digestion, day, year, life, death.

We are all inextricably caught up in these various ongoing processes but hardly ever notice them, much less "break through" to their harmonious interaction. The "mystic," we think, intuits all of these things at work in a single all-encompassing insight. The capacity for such comprehensive, intense and transient knowledge is probably latent in all of us, but for reasons of nature or nurture, it is likely to be stronger in some than in others. We have no explanation why the experience is almost always joyous—save that the universe or the universal forces (or "being," if one wishes to be philosophical) seem to be intuited in these interludes as gracious and benign.

Both our representative national sample and our random personal interviews seem to suggest that ecstatic episodes are relatively frequent in American society; and for most people they are positive, constructive and healthy, though sometimes they are so intense that those who have them are not eager to go through such an experience again. What conclusions would we draw from such findings?

First, we submit what all researchers submit, that there ought to be more research. It is indeed interesting that a phenomenon as widespread as "mystical" experiences apparently are has been almost totally ignored and unstudied by social scientists. We think the churches have been even more remiss than social science in paying attention to intense religious experience. None of our respondents had discussed his or her ecstatic interludes with the clergy. One put it, "I knew it had to do with God and religion; but I didn't think it had anything to do with the church." It may be that in their passion to be "with it," church leaders have missed those kinds of people who are "with" something that is at the core of all religion.

We also conclude that mental-health workers ought to be much more cautious than they are in equating such experiences with schizophrenia. Doubtless some "visionaries" are schizophrenics. But our data strongly suggest that others are not. Some personalities, however, seem ill-equipped to cope with such intense joy. They need support from mental-health workers, and the implicit hint that they are nothing but schizophrenics could easily turn them into schizophrenics. We asked one man whose wife went into an extraordinarily powerful ecstatic episode after an afternoon's lovemaking what he thought was happening. "Well," said this Jesuit-trained Chicago Slav, "I figured she was having a mystical experience. I thought it was nice, but I didn't know who was going to put the kids to bed or make my lunch the next morning." And how did he react? By helping—doing those chores himself. His wife quickly added that if it hadn't been for this combination of support and down-to-earth realism, she might have ended up in the hospital. Not all those who find themselves "surprised by joy"—to use C. S. Lewis's words—are so lucky.

Finally, is the world as joyous and as benign, as loving and dazzling a place as the "mystics"—those in the classic literature as well as in our samples—claim it is?

Well, as sociologists, we can't say for sure.

But it would be nice if it were.

THE MYSTICAL EXPERIENCE

What is a mystical experience like? What feelings does one have during it? Although it is often difficult to put into words, Andrew M. Greeley and William C. McCready compiled a list of possible descriptions drawn from the writings of Marghanita Laski and others. In a national survey they conducted, they asked some 600 persons who said they had had one or more mystical experiences to check off suitable descriptions. Many of those questioned checked off more than one description. The descriptions, and the percentages that each received, follow:

DESCRIPTION	PER CENT
A feeling of deep and profound peace	55
A certainty that all things would work out for the good	48
A sense of my own need to contribute to others	43
A conviction that love is at the center of everything	43
A sense of joy and laughter	43
An experience of great emotional intensity	38
A great increase in my understanding and knowledge	32
A sense of the unity of everything and my own part in it	29
A sense of a new life or living in a new world	27
A confidence in my own personal survival	27
A feeling that I couldn't possibly describe what was happening to me	26
A sense that all the universe is alive	25
A sensation that my personality has been taken over by something much more powerful than I am	24
A sense of tremendous personal expansion, either psychological or physical	22
A sensation of warmth or fire	22
A sense of being alone	19
A loss of concern about worldly problems	19
A sense that I was being bathed in light	14
A feeling of desolation	8
Something else	4

Transcendental Experience

R. D. Laing

We are living in an age in which the ground is shifting and the foundations are shaking. I cannot answer for other times and places. Perhaps it has always been so. We know it is true today.

In these circumstances, we have every reason to be insecure. When the ultimate basis of our world is in question, we run to different holes in the ground, we scurry into roles, statuses, identities, interpersonal relations. We attempt to live in castles that can only be in the air because there is no firm ground in the social cosmos on which to build. We are all witnesses to this state of affairs. Each sometimes sees the same fragment of the whole situation differently; often our concern is with different presentations of the original catastrophe.

. . . I wish to relate the transcendental experiences that *sometimes* break through in psychosis, to those experiences of the divine that are the living fount of all religion. . . .

If we can begin to understand sanity and madness in existential social terms, we shall be more able to see clearly the extent to which we all confront common problems and share common dilemmas.

Experience may be judged as invalidly mad or as validly mystical. The distinction is not easy. In either case, from a social point of view, such judgements characterize different forms of behavior, regarded in our society as deviant. People behave in such ways because their experience of themselves is different. It is on the existential meaning of such unusual experience that I wish to focus.

Psychotic experience goes beyond the horizons of our common, that is, our communal, sense.

What regions of experience does this lead to? It entails a loss of the usual foundations of the "sense" of the world that we share with one another. Old purposes no longer seem viable; old meanings are senseless; the distinctions between imagnination, dream, external perceptions often seem no longer to apply in the old way. External events may seem magically conjured up. Dreams may seem to be direct communications from others; imagination may seem to be objective reality.

But most radical of all, the very ontological foundations are shaken. The being of phenomena shifts and the phenomenon of being may no longer present itself to us as

before. There are no supports, nothing to cling to, except perhaps some fragments from the wreck, a few memories, names, sounds, one or two objects, that retain a link with a world long lost. This void may not be empty. It may be peopled by visions and voices, ghosts, strange shapes and apparitions. No one who has not experienced how insubstantial the pageant of external reality can be, how it may fade, can fully realize the sublime and grotesque presences that can replace it, or that can exist alongside it.

When a person goes mad, a profound transposition of his place in relation to all domains of being occurs. His center of experience moves from ego to self. Mundane time becomes merely anecdotal, only the eternal matters. The madman is, however, confused. He muddles ego with self, inner with outer, natural and supernatural. Nevertheless, he can often be to us, even through his profound wretchedness and disintegration, the heirophant of the sacred. An exile from the scene of being as we know it, he is an alien, a stranger signaling to us from the void in which he is foundering, a void which may be peopled by presences that we do not even dream of. They used to be called demons and spirits, and they used to be known and named. He has lost his sense of self, his feelings, his place in the world as we know it. He tells us he is dead. But we are distracted from our cosy security by this mad ghost who haunts us with his visions and voices which seem so senseless and of which we feel impelled to rid him, cleanse him, cure him.

Madness need not be all breakdown. It may also be breakthrough. It is potentially liberation and renewal as well as enslavement and existential death.

There are now a growing number of accounts by people who have been through the experience of madness. . . .

Certain *transcendental experiences* seem to me to be the original wellspring of all religions. Some psychotic people have transcendental experiences. Often (to the best of their recollection), they have never had such experiences before, and frequently they will never have them again. I am not saying, however, that psychotic experience necessarily contains this element more manifestly then sane experience.

We experience in different modes. We perceive external realities, we dream, imagine, have semi-conscious reveries. Some people have visions, hallucinations, experience faces transfigured, see auras and so on. Most people most of the time experience themselves and others in one or another way that I shall call *egoic*. That is, centrally or peripherally, they experience the world and themselves in terms of a consistent identity, a me-here over against a you-there, within a framework of certain ground structures of space and time shared with other members of their society.

This identity-anchored, space-and-time-bound experience has been studied philosophically by Kant, and later by the phenomenologists, e.g. Husserl, Merleau-Ponty. Its historical and ontological relativity should be fully realized by any contemporary student of the human scene. Its cultural, socioeconomic relativity has become a commonplace among anthropologists and a platitude to the Marxists and neo-Marxists. And yet, with the consensual and interpersonal confirmation it offers, it gives us a sense of ontological security, whose validity we *experience* as self-validating, although metaphycially-historically-ontologically-socioeconomically-culturally we know its apparent absolute validity as an illusion.

In fact all religious and all existential philosophies have agreed that such *egoic experience* is a preliminary illusion, a veil, a film of *maya*—a dream to Heraclitus, and to Lao Tzu, the fundamental illusion of all Buddhism, a state of sleep, of death, of socially accepted madness, a womb state to which one has to die, from which one has to be born.

The person going through ego-loss or transcendental experiences may or may not become in different ways confused. Then he might legitimately be regarded as mad. But to be mad is not necessarily to be ill, notwithstanding that in our culture the two categories have become confused. It is assumed that if a person is mad (whatever that means) then *ipso facto* he is ill (whatever that means). The experience that a person may be absorbed in, while to others he appears simply ill-mad, may be for him veritable manna from heaven. The person's whole life may be changed, but it is difficult not to doubt the validity of such vision. Also, not everyone comes back to us again.

Are these experiences simply the effulgence of a pathological process or of a particular alienation? I do not think they are.

In certain cases, a man blind from birth may have an operation performed which gives him his sight. The result—frequently misery, confusion, disorientation. The light that illumines the madman is an unearthly light. It is not always a distorted refraction of his mundane life situation. He may be irradiated by light from other world. It may burn him out.

This "other" world is not essentially a battlefield wherein psychological forces, derived or diverted, displace or sublimated from their original object-cathexes, are engaged in an illusionary fight—although such forces may obscure these realities, just as they may obscure so-called external realities. When Ivan in *The Brothers Karamazov* says, "If God does not exist, everything is permissible," he is *not* saying, "If my super-ego, in projected form, can be abolished, I can do anything with a good conscience." He *is* saying, "If there is *only* my conscience, then there is no ultimate validity for my will."

Among physicians and priests there should be some who are guides, who can educt the person from this world and induct him to the other. To guide him in it and to lead him back again.

One enters the other world by breaking a shell: or through a door: through a partition: the curtains part or rise: a veil is lifted. Seven veils: seven seals, seven heavens.

The "ego" is the instrument for living in *this* world. If the "ego" is broken up or destroyed (by the insurmountable contradictions of certain life situations, by toxins, chemical changes, etc.), then the person may be exposed to other worlds, "real" in different ways from the more familiar territory of dreams, imagination, perception or fantasy.

The world that one enters, one's capacity to experience it, seem to be partly conditional on the state of one's "ego."

Our time has been distinguished, more than by anything else, by a drive to control the external world, and by an almost total forgetfulness of the external world, and by an almost total forgetfulness of the internal world. If one estimates human evolution from the point of view of knowledge of the external world, then we are in many respects progressing.

If our estimate is from the point of view of the internal world and of oneness of internal and external, then the judgement must be very different.

Phenomenologically the terms "internal" and "external" have little validity. But in this whole realm one is reduced to mere verbal expedients—words are simply the finger pointing at the moon. One of the difficulties of talking in the present day of these matters is that the very existence of inner realities is now called in question.

By "inner" I mean our way of seeing the external world and all those realities that have no "external," "objective" presence—imagination, dreams, fantasies, trances, the realities of contemplative and meditative states, realities of which modern man, for the most part, has not the slightest direct awareness.

For example, nowhere in the Bible is there any argument about the *existence* of gods, demons, angels. People did not first "believe in" God: they experienced His presence, as was true of other spiritual agencies. The question was not whether God existed, but whether this particular God was the greatest god of all, or the only God; and what was the relation of the various spiritual agencies to each other. Today, there is a public debate, not as to the trustworthiness of God, the particular place in the spiritual hierarchy of different spirits, etc., but whether God or such spirits *even exist* or ever have existed.

Sanity today appears to rest very largely on a capacity to adapt to the external world—the interpersonal world, and the realm of human collectivities.

As this external human world is almost completely and totally estranged from the inner, any personal direct awareness of the inner world already has grave risks.

But since society, without knowing it, is *starving* for the inner, the demands on people to evoke its presence in a "safe" way, in a way that need not be taken seriously, etc., is tremendous—while the ambivalence is equally intense. Small wonder that the list of artists, in say the last 150 years, who have become shipwrecked on these reefs is so long—Holderlin, John Clare, Rimbaud, Van Gogh, Nietzsche, Antonin Artaud. . . .

Those who survived have had exceptional qualities—a capacity for secrecy, slyness, cunning—a thoroughly realistic appraisal of the risks they run, not only from the spiritual realms they frequent, but from the hatred of their fellows for anyone engaged in this pursuit.

Let us *cure* them. The poet who mistakes a real woman for his Muse and acts accordingly. . . . The young man who sets off in a yacht in search of God. . . .

The outer divorced from any illumination from the inner is in a state of darkness. We are in an age of darkness. The state of outer darkness is a state of sin—i.e., alienation or estrangement from the *inner light.* * Certain actions lead to greater estrangement; certain others help one not to be so far removed. The former used to be called sinful.

The ways of losing one's way are legion. Madness is certainly not the least unambiguous. The countermadness of Kraepelinian psychiatry is the exact counterpart of "official" psychosis. Literally, and absolutely seriously, it is as *mad,* if by madness we mean any radical estrangement from the totality of what is the case. Remember Kierkegaard's objective madness.

As we experience the world, so we act. We conduct ourselves in the light of our view of what is the case and what is not the case. That is, each person is a more or less naive ontologist. Each person has views of what is and what is not.

There is no doubt, it seems to me, that there have been profound changes in the experience of man in the last thousand years. In some ways this is more evident than changes in the patterns of his behavior. There is everything to suggest that man experienced God. Faith was never a matter of believing. He existed, but of trusting, in the presence that was experienced and known to exist as a self-validating datum. It seems likely that far more people in our time experience neither the presence of God, nor the presence of his absence, but the absence of his presence.

We require a history of phenomena, not simply more phenomena of history.

As it is, the secular psychotherapist is often in the role of the blind leading the half-blind.

The fountain has not played itself out, the frame still shines, the river still flows, the spring still bubbles forth, the light has not faded. But between *us* and It, there is a veil which is more like fifty feet of solid concrete. *Deus absconditus.* Or we have absconded.

Already everything in our time is directed to categorizing and segregating this reality from objective facts. This is precisely the concrete wall. Intellectually, emotionally, interpersonally, organizationally, intuitively, theoretically, we have to blast our way through the solid wall, even if at the risk of chaos, madness and death. For from *this* side of the wall, this is the risk. There are no assurances, no guarantees.

Many people are prepared to have faith in the sense of scientifically indefensible belief in an untested hypothesis. Few have trust enough to test it. Many people make-believe what they experience. Few are made to believe by their experience. Paul of Tarsus was picked up by the scruff of the neck, thrown to the ground and blinded for three days. This direct experience was self-validating.

We live in a secular world. To adapt to this world the child abdicates its ecstasy. *("L'enfant abdique son extase":* Malarmé.) Having lost our experience of the spirit, we are expected to have faith. But this faith comes to be a belief in a reality which is not evident. There is a prophecy in Amos that a time will come when there will be a famine in the land, "not a famine for bread, nor a thirst for water, but of *hearing* the words of the Lord." That time has now come to pass. It is the present age.

From the alienated starting point of our pseudo-sanity, everything is equivocal. Our sanity is not "true" sanity. Their madness is not "true" madness. The madness of our patients is an artifact of the destruction wreaked on them by us and by them on themselves. Let no one suppose that we meet "true" madness any more than that we are truly sane. The madness that we encounter in "patients" is a gross travesty, a mockery, a grotesque caricature of what the natural healing of that estranged integration we call sanity might be. True sanity entails in one way or another the dissolution of the normal ego, that false self competently adjusted to our alienated social reality; the emergence of the "inner" archetypal mediators of divine power, and through this death a rebirth, and the eventual re-establishment of a new kind of ego-functioning, the ego now being the servant of the divine, no longer its betrayer.

---

*M. Eliade, *The Two and the One* (London: Harvill Press, 1965), especially Chapter I.

What Mysticism Is

Group for the Advancement of Psychiatry

The word *mystical* is used to describe experiences that have for their goal a union with a supernatural power, in contrast to other experiences which are more appropriately called "magical," "esoteric," "visionary," "occult" or "metaphysical." Differing from the usual practices of institutional religions, mysticism involves a relationship with the supernatural which is not mediated by another person; the goal of mystical union is reached during the course of this relationship. The union itself is considered ultimate reality, compared with which the events of everyday life are dim and uncertain.

The mystic asserts that the experience of union is not achieved by rational intellectual functions or through the ordinary senses, but from the depths of the soul. He is driven toward his goal by an outgoing love for the supernatural object. Although his description may employ sexual metaphors to describe this love, he asserts that it is not the sexually contaminated love of a man for a woman. Neither is it the self-seeking love of a child.

There is probably a mystical element in all institutional religions—at least for some adherents. The tendency of the mystical approach to isolate individuals, or to alienate them from established authority, is one of the reasons that churches tend to discourage it, inasmuch as they are dependent on social organization. On the other hand, a mystical leader may dominate a religious group. In cases of "secular" mysticism, it may be denied that the practice is religious in nature, although here we become involved with questions of definition.

Mystical experiences vary widely in content, but they share certain characteristics. The basic technique for achieving the mystical goal, used by mystics of all times and places, is commonly called contemplation. Successful contemplation requires arduous practice. Through it the mind gradually finds ways of eliminating thoughts of the self and the ordinary world as well as abandoning all imaginative or reasoning thought processes. The ultimate direct encounter with the supernatural—the unitive state—occurs during a period of mental emptiness. It appears, as it were, on a blank screen. Although the mystic has worked hard to find his way there, he feels that he is a passive recipient of the event.

The training process often begins with meditation—an exercise in which thought is consciously restricted to an isolated aspect of the potential mystic's belief system: a single sacred word, one aspect of God, or a short passage from the Bible, for example. All other ideas are rejected. This type of thinking is gradually succeeded by a state of emptiness in which rational thinking processes are eliminated, comparable to the alteration of consciousness that follows sensory deprivation in experimental studies. During this "quiet" period, the mystic becomes aware of the supernatural while remaining distinct from it; an awareness of the self as an independent agency continues to exist. The state of true contemplation, or union, follows.

There are two aspects of the contemplative state, the transcendental and the immanent; they differ in relative strength from one mystic to another. Perceived from the transcendental aspect, the supernatural object is "the wholly other" or "the Cloud of Unknowing"—the numinous; feelings of strangeness and awe in relation to it predominate, with corresponding feelings of humility concerning the self. On the other hand, a belief in the immanent nature of the supernatural, conceived as a part of the self, contributes to a more intimate and more joyful relationship with it.

The ultimate in the contemplative state, although not essential to it, is the occurrence of an ecstatic trance. The mystic is physically transfixed, unable to move or speak, and he experiences a tremendous lucidity. A state of rapture is differentiated from the state of ecstasy on the basis of its sudden, violent onset and the occurrence of gross mental disorganization.

Great mystics, like great artists, take advantage of the ideas of their historical forebears, even though their search is private and creative. They usually have been adherents of traditional religious groups and make use of the religious forms to which they have been exposed. While doing so, however, their private and creative nature often puts them on a course that defies traditional practices, and they may find themselves at war with established authority.

Mystics agree that the mystical experience is ineffable, yet often they have felt the need to explain it. In reading the literature of the mystics, it is well to bear in mind that when attempting to describe the indescribable they have been forced to use symbolic terms. Images likening the mystic to the pilgrim, the lover, or the alchemist are among those which have been commonly used. Mystical writers stress the inadequacy of such symbolic language and warn the reader of its dangers and limitations. They excuse their recourse to it on the ground that no other language is available to them.

The natural history of the contemplative process tends to follow a more or less typical course that has been called "the Mystic Way."[1] It is marked by alternating periods of joy and suffering. Indeed, suffering is considered essential to the attainment of the unitive state. Typically, the Mystic Way is inaugurated by the sudden onset of an exalted experience known as conversion. Mystical conversion, which should be distinguished from the usual conversion to a religious belief, is characterized by the sudden expansion of the mystic's frame of reference from a narrow, self-centered state to a broader view of himself in the world and a beginning awareness of the transcendent. This stage, as well as others of the Mystic Way, may be accompanied by visions or voices, a radiant light, and an increased lucidity involving one or all of the senses.

Clearly aware of his imperfections in relation to the supernatural, the mystic may now enter the state of purgation, a state that is filled with pain and suffering. In it he attempts to purify himself by ascetic self-mortification: He simplifies his existence, leads a life of poverty and chastity, and detaches himself from worldly pursuits and desires.

Once the mystic has succeeded in this initial divestment of his impurities and sensual claims, he emerges—both symbolically and literally—from the darkness into a bright light; this is the state of illumination. Suffering is again replaced with joy. There is a heightening of the sense perceptions and an apprehension of the supernatural. This is not as complete as in the later stage of union, since the self is still perceived as a distinct entity. Auditory and visual hallucinations, and phenomena such as automatic writing, commonly appear during this phase.

Typically, illumination is followed by the most painful and horrifying experience of the Mystic Way. The bright light, the lucidity, and the perception of the supernatural object are replaced by a great darkenss, a feeling of having been abandoned by the object, and a conscious rejection of personal satisfactions. Similar to the earlier stage of purgation, it is deeper and more terrifying. The mystic, deprived and abandoned, feels so empty that contemplative activity is no longer possible and the visions and voices of the illuminative phase usually disappear. The emotions that accompany this period have caused it to be called the "mystic death" or "the dark night of the soul." It carries on the purification of the stage of purgation to its ultimate end, the total abandonment of any desire for self-satisfaction.

Thus prepared, the chosen few finally reach the mystical goal of union, a state of joy and absolute certainty. The actual experience is said to be timeless, yet often lasts for only a moment—"the space of an Ave Maria," according to St. Augustine. It remains forever implanted in the mystic's being. It is spontaneous, but at the same time the product of a long and difficult process. Although the mystic says that he seeks no reward for his labors, he feels that his outgoing love has been returned in kind and that he achieves an "ineffable peace" and a sense of moral perfection.

The mystic who conceives of the supernatural object as an awesome, distant figure is apt to describe this union in terms of a godlike transformation (called deification). When the supernatural is seen as a personal, intimate companion, the mystic may speak of a "spiritual marriage between God and the soul." Once having attained this peak experience, brief as it may be, the mystic is enabled to live his life henceforward on transcendental levels of reality. Endowed with great vitality and great certitude about the nature of his experience, the former recluse may now emerge as an active leader who regards the salvation of the world as his duty—not surprising, in view of his identification with a godlike figure. It should be emphasized that all mystics do not reach this state of union. Jewish mystics, for example, describe only a clinging to God, rather than a merging with Him.

The mysticism of the East insists on still another step along the mystical path: total annihilation of the self and its absorption into the Infinite, as expressed in the Sufis' Eighth Stage of Progress and Buddhists' Nirvana.

* * *

The inability of this Committee to make a firm distinction between a mystical state and a psychopathological state may be due, in part at least, to more fundamental theoretical problems in psychiatry. The many ways in which human behavior and thought can be perceived make numerous points of view inevitable. For example, there are those who draw fine lines between various psychiatric diagnoses as irrelevant and who perceive in schizophrenia a manifestation to be prized as a way toward better adaptation. Pathology may be uncovered in the nature of—and the method of resolution of—the conflicts in someone who seems to be brimming over with mental health, while the thought and behavior of the most disturbed patient may be viewed as a contribution to his well-being. Therefore we should not expect to be able to reach a consensus on the line distinguishing mysticism from mental disorder. From one point of view all mystical experiences may be regarded as symptoms of mental disturbance, and from another, they may be regarded as attempts at adaptation.

By and large, the psychoanalytic orientation of the majority of the Committee on Psychiatry and Religion has determined the approach to this report. Given that psychoanalysis is an open-ended theoretical system, we might have gone further with our psychoanalytic interpretation had caution or disagreement not stopped us. For one thing, we might have expanded our discussion on the nature of the childhood events that contribute to adult proclivities toward mysticism. To cite one example, we could have theorized about a possible connection between the development of awe in childhood and mystical states in adulthood. Saint Catherine of Siena was a mystic who reported having highly developed feelings of awe at the age of five, when she saw the Lord "in the most sacred and awe-inspiring garb imaginable" above the Sienese church of San Domenico. Greenacre has suggested that childhood feelings of awe which may later be associated with inspiration, creativity and religious feeling are often derived from awe (as distinguished from envy) of the phallus.[1,2] In the girl, awe is more liable to be aroused, according to Greenacre, if the child sees an adult phallus rather than a boy's.

Deikman makes use of the concepts of automatization of Hartmann and of deautomatization of Gill and Brenman in explaining the dynamics of mystical states. Automatization permits us to carry on our usual activities without having to figure out each complicated step. Deautomatization signifies a breakdown in this process. Deikman has suggested that deautomatization takes place in the mystic; and because stimulus-processing is less efficient in deautomatization, the mystic is enabled to discover new or long-forgotten experiences, as well as cognitive or sensory states that had been excluded by the rigidities of automatization. This same process may apply equally to creativity.[6,7]

In writing about creative thinking in *The Hidden Order of Art,* Anton Ehrenzweig has proposed a different concept, using "dedifferentiation" as his key term. Differentiation refers to the gradually increasing ability to make distinctions, beginning with the distinction between self and object; dedifferentiation signifies the loss or suspension of this ability. Acknowledging the similarity between mysticism and creativity, Ehrenzweig writes, "Any—not only religious—creative experience can produce an oceanic state. In my view this state need not to be due to a 'regression' to an infantile state, but could be the product of extreme dedifferentiation in lower levels of the ego which occurs during creative work. Dedifferentiation suspends many kinds of boundaries and distinctions, . . . [inducing] a mystic oceanic feeling that is distinctively manic in character [using *manic* in the Kleinian sense] . . . . Dedifferentiation transforms reality according to the structural principles valid on those deeper levels." In the process, Ehrenzweig notes, "perfect integration is possible because of unlimited mutual interpenetration of oceanic imagery."[8]

The stress on absence of automatization, on loss of efficiency in stimulus-processing, and on the absence of differentiation seems to obscure the extraordinary complexity of the events that take place in the psyche, and the speed at which they occur, so bewildering that the sluggish conscious mind cannot keep up with them any more than a mathematician can keep up with a computer. Highly creative people and high-level mystics are able to function in hyperautomatized ways, capable of finer differentiations than others, even though they may have gone through a chaotic, seemingly undifferentiated experience before they got there. It is the final differentiation, bringing supreme order out of chaos, that is significant, not the fact of chaos—a state that most of us, at least those who are not terribly rigid, have no difficulty at all in experiencing.

Looking at mysticism from the point of view of identity formation, it can be seen as a different though parallel process.[9] Identity is a unique integration of psychological, social, historical and educational attributes which, when successful, results in a harmonious human being. In this view, mystical experiences, like creative experiences, are attempts at integration or reintegration by people who have not achieved satisfying results in identity formation or, to put it another way, have too many conflicts that cannot be resolved harmoniously. Identity formation is associated with internal resolution and is more or less permanent. In creativity, the resolution is projecting outside of the mind (as in a painting or a scientific discovery) and in itself does not involve a permanent change in the creator. Hence, it needs to be repeated again and again. Perhaps from this point of view mystical processes lie between identity formation and creativity, because the integrative process, involving the projection of images of the self and of others into theological or natural forces, may, if successful, initiate permanent changes in the personality or identity.

In the analytic psychology of Jung, himself a mystic, mysticism is held to be a fundamental category of human experience. Eric Neumann, in particular, has discussed mysticism from a Jungian point of view. Man, he writes, is a *Homo mysticus.* Mystical phenomena contribute to personality development and are essential to all creative processes. Mystical experiences are not only theistic, extroverted and introverted. They give rise to love, artistic creation, great ideas and delusions. While Neumann agrees with Freudian psychoanalysts that projection plays a role in mysticism, he believes that the failure of many analysts to recognize the vital significance of archetypes and the collective unconscious gives rise to psychoanalytic interpretations that are reductionistic and personalistic. For mysticism is grounded in the encounter between the ego and the numinous (the supernatural presence, as perceived) that takes place deep in the collective unconscious. Because of this, mysticism is inherent in man, and every mystical experience (or, in Jungian terms, every encounter between the ego and the numinous) transforms his personality, and what is more, "the development of [man's] natural phases with their archetypal encounters gives a mystical stamp to the development of every man, even though he may be unaware of it."[10]

Of especial interest to students of mysticism is Neumann's statement that mysticism originates in childhood and continues to metamorphose throughout life. Man is "in constant mystical motion." The many varieties of mysticism appear in relation to developmental phases in the individual. Among them, several stand out as contrasting forms.

Source mysticism, or "uroborus mysticism," is seen in children, in primitive people, and in pathological and unstable personalities. It appears when man cannot face conflict but yearns to return to the paradise of the maternal womb or the Great Mother archetype, a state known as "uroborus incest." Nihilistic, its aim is world-destructive, and it is noncreative.

Hero mysticism, or "the Fight with the Dragon," is characteristic of puberty and early adulthood. In it, conflict and life in this world are accepted; its mission is world-transforming. Instead of a return to the Great Mother-Womb, there is union with the Godhead or one of the great archetypal leaders. The story of David and Goliath exemplifies hero mysticism. Stimulated by conflict, it is creative.

Finally, there is the highest form of mysticism known as *last stage mysticism,* or "imminent world-transforming mysticism," which appears in the latter part of the life cycle. Here, a unity with the world is attained; conflict and the hostile world are eliminated in favor of peace; man becomes a fully integrated being, creatively renewed. He exists in time and in this world—not outside, as in more primitive forms of mysticism. He is in a constant mystical state in which the world and its objects, including his innermost self, are transparent. Now there is no conflict between the Jungian ego and the self, or the conscious and the unconscious. What may appear as hostility to the world is, rather, an intent to recreate and renew it.

* * *

The attempt in this epilogue to brief the reader on other ways of looking at our subject may threaten to turn confusion into bedlam. The mystic, however, learns to live with paradox, to accommodate himself to opposing views, and finally to unite them. The fullest understanding of mysticism undoubtedly requires a similar effort.

REFERENCES

1. Evelyn Underhill. *Mysticism* (New York: E. P. Dutton, 1961).
2. Quoted in *ibid.,* 12th ed., pp 292-293. [Original from *The Life of St. Teresa of Jesus,* written by herself.]

1. Phyllis Greenacre. "Penis Awe and Its Relation to Penis Envy" In *Drives, Affects, Behavior,* R. M. Loewenstein, Ed. (New York: International Universities Press, 1953) pp 176-190.
2. ——. Experiences of Awe in Childhood. *The Psychoanalytic Study of the Child* 11 (1956): 9-30.
3. Paul C. Horton. The Mystical Experience: Substance of an Illusion. *Journal of the American Psychoanalytic Association* 22 (1974): 364-380.
4. D. W. Winnicott. Transitional Objects and Transitional Phenomena. *International Journal of Psychoanalysis* 34 (1953): 89-97.
5. Albert J. Lubin. "From Augustine to Einstein: Some Thoughts on Mysticism, Creativity, and Identity." Paper presented at the San Francisco Psychoanalytic Institute, January 6, 1975.
6. Arthur J. Deikman. Implications of Experimentally Induced Contemplative Meditation. *Journal of Nervous & Mental Disease* 142 (1966): 101-115.
7. ——. Bimodal Consciousness. *Archives of General Psychiatry* 25 (1971): 481-489.
8. Anton Ehrenzweig. *The Hidden Order of Art* (London: Weidenfelt & Nicholson, 1967).
9. See reference 5 above.
10. Erich Neumann. "Mystical Man." In *The Mystic Vision: Papers from the Eranos Yearbooks,* Joseph Campbell, Ed. (Princeton: Princeton University Press, 1968) Bolligen Series Vol. XXX, No. 6, pp 375-415.

Comments on the GAP Report on Mysticism

Arthur J. Deikman

The report by the Group for the Advancement of Psychiatry entitled *Mysticism: Spiritual Quest or Psychic Disorder?* is intended to supply the psychiatric profession with needed information on the phenomena of mysticism, of which most psychiatristss have only a sketchy knowledge. Certain of the sections, especially those on Christian and Hindu mysticism, show an objectivity and scholarship that are quite commendable. As a whole, however, the report displays extreme parochialism, a lack of discrimination, and naive arrogance in its approach to the subject.

From the point of view of scholarship, the basic error lies in the committee's ignoring the importance of the distinction made by both Western and Eastern mystics between lower level sensory-emotional experiences and those experiences that go beyond concepts, feelings, and sensations. Repeatedly, the mystical literature stresses that sensate experiences are not the goal of mysticism; rather, it is only when these are transcended that one attains the aim of a *direct* (intuitive) knowledge of fundamental reality. For example, Walter Hilton, an English mystic from the 14th century, is quite explicit about this distinction:

> . . . visions of revelations by spirits, . . . do not constitute true contemplation. This applies equally to any other sensible experiences of seemingly spiritual origin, whether of sound, taste, smell or of warmth felt like a glowing fire in the breast . . . anything, indeed, that can be experienced by the physical senses.

St. John of the Cross, 16th century, states:

> That inward wisdom is so simple, so general and so spiritual that it has not entered into the understanding enwrapped or clad in any form or image subject to sense, it follows that sense and imagination (as it has not entered through them nor has taken their form and color) cannot account for it or imagine, so as to say anything concerning it, although the soul be clearly aware that it is experiencing and partaking of that rare and delectable wisdom.

A similar distinction between lower (sensate) and higher (transcendent) contemplative states may be found in Yoga texts:

> When all lesser things and ideas are transcended and forgotten, and there remains only a perfect state of imagelessness where Tathagata and Tathata are merged into perfect Oneness. . . .

Western mysticism, from which the authors derived most of their examples, constitutes only a minor segment of the literature in the field of mysticism, and its basic contemplative tradition actually derives from Eastern sources, as acknowledged in the report. Yet the goal of Eastern (Buddhist, Hindu, Taoist, Sufic) mysticism—"enlightenment"—is not visions of angels or Buddhas but the awakening of an inherent capacity to perceive the true nature of the self and the world. Over and over again, these texts warn that the type of mystical experience on which the GAP report focuses is not the goal of the mystical path. Such visionary experiences are regarded as illusions and, at worst, snares for the poorly prepared or the ill guided. An example from the Zen literature follows:

> Other religions and sects place great store by the experiences which involve visions of God or hearing heavenly voices, performing miracles, receiving divine messages, or becoming purified through various rites . . . yet from the Zen point of view all are morbid states devoid of true religious significance and hence only makyo (disturbing illusions).

In the Sufi literature, we find many explicit statements that Sufism is a science of knowing and is not a religion in the way that term is ordinarily understood.

> The Sufis often start from a nonreligious viewpoint. The answer, they say, is within the mind of mankind. It has to be liberated, so that by self-knowledge the intuition becomes the guide to human fulfillment.

The Sufis regard most mystical experience as being essentially emotional with little practical importance—except for the harmful effect of causing people to believe they are being "spiritual" when they are not:

> Sahl Abdullah once went into a state of violent agitation with physical manifestations, during a religious meeting.
> Ibn Salim said, "What is this state?"
> Sahl said: "This was not, as you imagine, power entering me. It was, on the contrary, due to my own weakness."
> Others present remarked: "If that was weakness, what is power?"
> "Power" said Sahl, "is when something like this enters and the mind and body minifests nothing at all."

Despite these clear warnings in the mystical literature, the GAP publication emphasizes lurid, visionary phenomena which lend themselves readily to standard psychiatric interpretations. Because of this, the authors have failed to come to grips with the fundamental claim of mystics: that they acquire direct knowledge of reality. Furthermore, the authors follow Freud's lead in defining the mystic perception of unity as a regression, an escape, a projection upon the world of a primitive, infantile state. The fact is, we know practically nothing about the actual experience of the infant, except that whatever it is, it is not that of a small adult. No one who has read carefully the accounts of "enlightenment" can accept this glib equation of mystical = infantile. An infant mind could hardly have had the experience that conveyed the following:

> The least act, such as eating or scratching an arm, is not at all simple. It is merely a visible moment in a network of causes and effects reaching forward into Unknowingness and back into an infinity of Silence, where individual consciousness cannot even enter. There is truly nothing to know, nothing that can be known.
> The physical world is an infinity of movement, of Time-Existence. But simultaneously it is an infinity of Silence and Voidness. Each object is thus transparent. Everything has its own special inner character, its own karma or 'life in time,' but at the same time there is no place where there is emptiness, where one object does not flow into another.

To confuse lower level sensory-emotional experiences with the transcendent "Knowledge" that is the goal of mysticism seriously limits the usefulness of the report and tends to perpetuate in the reader the ignorant parochial position that was standard in most psychiatric writings before the GAP publication and now, unfortunately, is likely to be reinforced.

This naive reductionism is all the more striking in the context of the numerous reports from physicists indicating that the world is actually more like the one that the mystics describe than the one on which psychology and psycho-analysis are based. Contemporary scientists have ample evidence that the world of discrete objects is an illusion, a function of the particular scale of our perception and time sense. For them, it is commonplace that the phenomena of biology and physics point to a continuous world of gradients, not a collection of objects. Percy Bridgman, Nobel Laureate in physics, comments:

> It has always been a bewilderment to me to understand how anyone can experience such a commonplace event as an automobile going up the street and seriously maintain that there is identity of structure of this continually flowing, dissolving and reforming thing and the language that attempts to reproduce it with discrete units, tied together by remembered conventions.

What is missing from the GAP report is any acknowledgment that the mystic who has completed his or her development may have access to an intuitive, immediate knowledge of reality. The authors assume that the known sensate pathways are the only means to acquire knowledge of what is real. In fact, studies of how scientific discoveries were actually made show in almost every instance that this is not the case at all. Another Nobel prize-winning physicist, Eugene Wigner, has remarked:

> The discovery of the laws of nature requires first and foremost intuition, conceiving of pictures and a great many subconscious processes. The use and also the confirmation of these laws is another matter . . . logic comes after intuition.

"Intuition" can be considered a lower order example of the latent capacity to which mystics refer.

The eclectic ignorance of the authors has led them at one point to lump together Einstein, Jesus, Abraham Lincoln, biofeedback, Vincent Van Gogh, and St. John of the Cross. Interestingly enough, if the authors had pursued the case of Einstein alone, they might have come to the epistemological issue that is the core of mysticism—and paid proper attention to it; for Einstein's modern discoveries, as well as the discoveries of natural philosophers thousands of years earlier, were based on an intuitive perception of the way things are. Such perceptions are the source of our greatest advances in science. Michael Polanyi, at one time Professor of Physical Chemistry at the University of Manchester, made an extensive and thorough study of the actual process of scientific discovery and found that the revolutionary ideas of geniuses such as Einstein had "come to them" by some form of direct intuition, often presented as imagery.[10] Polanyi was led by his data to propose a theory of knowledge and human consciousness that is clearly "mystical." Furthermore, at least two books have been published recently documenting the strikingly close correspondence between the scientific conceptions of physicists and the insights of mystics.[2, 9]

Thus, it is truly remarkable to have a group of psychiatrists issue a report in 1976, in which the only comment they make on the mystic perception of unity is that it represents a "reunion with parents." Nowhere in the report do we find a discussion of the possibility that the perception of unity occurring in the higher forms of mysticism may be correct and that the ordinary perception of separateness and meaninglessness may be an illusion, as mystics claim. Clearly, mystic perception could be true whether or not a particular mystic might wish, in fantasy, to be reunited with his or her mother.

The GAP report states:

> The psychiatrist will find mystical phenomena of interest because they can demonstrate forms of behaviour intermediate between normality and frank psychosis; a form of ego regression in the service of defense against internal or external stress; and a paradox of the return of repressed regression in unconventional expressions of love.

How totally provincial our profession has become if this is a summary statement from a group that claims to be devoted to "advancing" psychiatry!

It is interesting that the only place in which the authors are able to allow themselves to think in positive terms of mysticism is when they discuss the concept of "creativity." Apparently, creativity is OK. In this section of the report, the authors venture to speculate:

> At the same time, intense or external perceptions may be heightened, and this sensitivity may open a path to hidden aspects of reality.

Unfortunately, that one sentence, like a lonely ray of

sunshine, is soon swallowed up by a return of the monotonous clouds of reductionism. The very next chapter, entitled "Case Report," concerns a woman in psychotherapy who reported having had the sort of low level, sensate mystical experience on which the authors focus. The report provides the following conclusion:

> Her interests were reinvested in the fantasy universe, representing God, in which such problems do not exist, and she felt herself united with this God-Universe, a substitute for an unavailable or rejecting parent. The mystical union made up for the rejection she feared from her father, now represented by the therapist in another man . . . so, while a psychiatric diagnosis cannot be dismissed, *her experience was certainly akin to those described by great religious mystics*(!) (emphasis mine) who have found a new life through them.

In the last paragraph it becomes even more presumptuous and confused:

> The mystical state itself provided the illusion of knowledge. But unlike many mystical states in which the search ends with illusion, it stimulated her to seek further knowledge and led directly to the disappearance of her inhibition to serious reading(!) This continued search is characteristic of those in whom mystical states contribute towards creative activity.

The authors of this report are intelligent, educated, sincere men. It is hard to believe that they would display such provincialism, carelessness, and bias if they were discussing schizophrenia. Judging by this and other, similar psychiatric discussions, our profession, when it comes to mysticism, does not feel the need to ask serious questions about its own assumptions, nor to take the devil's advocate's position toward its too-easy conclusions. Ironically, the authors are capable of pointing out the problem in others. In discussing "the naive Western observers of the Indian scene" they say:

> Confronted by such common symbols as that of the representation of the divine activity in sexual form, and bewildered by the profusion of deities in the Hindu pantheon, they could impute to Hinduism a 'decadence' following from its essence, and they fail to apply to that religion the discrimination between enlightened and superstitious observance which they would be sure to demand for their own.

Exactly.

In trying to understand the phenomenon of the GAP report itself, I am led to two principal considerations. First, in order to understand and have some appreciation of "mysticism," it is necessary that psychiatrists participate to some extent in the experience. When it comes to its own discipline, the psychiatric profession is unwavering in its requirement that one must "know" through experience, not just description. Who can really understand "transference" without experiencing it? Actual experience is necessary because the position of the outside observer has its limits, particularly in areas not well adapted to language. I can give an example of the necessity for participation from my own research on meditation and mysticism. In surveying the literature, I had noticed that contemplation

and renunciation were the two basic processes specified for mystical development by almost all mystical authors, East and West. I proceeded to study the effects of meditation in the laboratory and, naively, assumed that renunciation meant giving up the things of the world—in a literal sense. It was only later, when I both studied and participated in Soto Zen training, that I came to understand that renunciation refers to an attitude, not to asceticism, per se. That understanding enabled me to formulate the hypothesis of "bimodal consciousness," based on motivational considerations.[4] The hypothesis, in turn, enabled me to understand a wide variety of unusual states of consciousness.

Perhaps by stating that I have, myself, practiced meditation, I will automatically disqualify myself in the eyes of some readers as having any credibility in these matters. I refer those readers to the paper by Charles Tart, wherein he presents a compelling case for the development of "state-specific sciences"—sciences whose mode of investigation is specifically adapted to the area it is investigating.[13] Indeed, participation by scientists in these areas of mysticism would result in an understanding that is less exotic and less religious—and would help rid ourselves of the clap-trap associated with mysticism that constitutes a burden to scientist and mystic alike.

Unfortunately, such participation is not likely to occur because of the other basic problem confronting psychiatrists when they approach this field: arrogance—reflecting the arrogance of Western civilization. In this connection, it is interesting that the fundamental requirement for participating in any of the mystical traditions has been, and still is, humility. This is so, not because humility is a virtue, something that earns one credit in a heavenly bank account, but because humility is instrumental—it is the attitude required for learning. Humility is the acceptance of the possibility that someone else or something else has something to teach you which you do not already know. In crucial sections of the GAP report, there is no sign of humility. It seems to me that in our profession we display the arrogance of the legendary British Colonial who lived for 30 years in India without bothering to learn the language of the inhabitants, because he considered them to be inferior. Perhaps medicine's long battle to free itself from religious control, from demonology and "divine authority," has left us with an automatic and costly reaction against anything that bears the outward signs of religion. In point of fact, mystics outside the Western tradition tend to share our suspicion and describe their disciplines as a science of development—not a religion, as ordinarily understood.

The authors of the GAP report have selectively ignored the central issues of mysticism and have made traditional interpretations of the secondary phenomena. If our profession is to advance, we must recognize our defenses against ideas that would change our assumptions. Mysticism, studied seriously, challenges basic tenets of

Western cultures: a) the primacy of reason and intellect; b) the separate, individual nature of man; c) the linear organization of time. Great mystics, like our own great scientists, envision the world as being larger than those tenets, as transcending our traditional views. By not recognizing our defensiveness and by permitting our vision to be narrowed so as to exclude the unfamiliar, we betray our integrity as psychiatrists, showing no more capacity for freedom from prejudice than persons totally ignorant of psychodynamics—perhaps less.

Psychiatry's aversion to things ecclesiastical should not blind the profession to the possibility that "real gold exists, even though false coin abounds." It is unfortunate that the GAP report carries us little further toward gaining for ourselves that wider base for human fulfillment that we need. The attitude reflected in the report is myopic and unnecessarily fearful of an avenue of human endeavor, aspiration, and discovery thousands of years old—one productive of outstanding achievements in science and literature that we are only now beginning to recognize. Yet, if we learn nothing more from mystics than the need for humility, they will have contributed greatly to Western culture in general and to the profession of psychiatry in particular.

REFERENCES

1. Bridgman, P. W. *The Nature of Physical Theory.* John Wiley & Sons, New York, 1964.
2. Capra, F. *The Tao of Physics.* Shambala, Berkeley, 1975.
3. *The Complete Works of St. John of the Cross,* Vol. 1. Newman Press, Westminister, 1953.
4. Deikman, A. Bimodal consciousness. Arch. Gen. Psychiatry, *25:* 481-489, 1971.
5. Goddard, D., Ed. *A Buddhist Bible.* Dwight Goddard, Thetford, Vermont, 1938.
6. Greene, M., Ed. *Toward a Unity of Knowledge.* (Psychol. Issues, *22:* 45, 1969.) International Universities Press, New York, 1969.
7. Hilton, W. *The Scale of Perfection.* Burns & Oates, London, 1953.
8. Kapleau, P. *The Three Pillars of Zen.* Beacon Press, Boston, 1967.
9. LeShan, L. *The Medium, the Mystic and the Physicist.* Viking Press, New York, 1974.
10. Polanyi, M. *Personal Knowledge.* University of Chicago Press, Chicago, 1958.
11. Shah, I. *The Sufis.* Anchor Books (Doubleday & Co., Inc.), Garden City, N. Y., 1971.
12. Shah, I. *The Way of the Sufi.* E. P. Dutton & Co., New York, 1970.
13. Tart, C. States of consciousness and state-specific sciences. Science, *176:* 1203-1218, 1972.

Schizophrenia – The Inward Journey

Joseph Campbell

In the spring of 1968 I was invited to deliver a series of talks on schizophrenia at the Esalen Institute at Big Sur, California.

A few weeks later there came in the mail an envelope from John Weir Perry, M.D., of San Francisco, containing the reprint of a paper on schizophrenia that he had published in 1962 in the *Annals of the New York Academy of Sciences;* and to my considerable amazement I learned, on reading it, that the imagery of schizophrenic fantasy perfectly matches that of the mythological hero journey, which I had outlined and elucidated, back in 1949, in *The Hero with a Thousand Faces.*

My own had been a work based on a comparative study of the mythologies of mankind, with only here and there passing references to the phenomenology of dream, hysteria, mystic visions, and the like. Mainly, it was an organization of themes and motifs common to all mythologies; and I had had no idea, in bringing these together, of the extent to which they would correspond to the fantasies of madness. According to my thinking, they were the universal, archetypal, psychologically based symbolic themes and motifs of all traditional mythologies; and now from this paper of Dr. Perry I was learning that the same symbolic figures arise spontaneously from the broken-off, tortured state of mind of modern individuals suffering from a complete schizophenic breakdown: the condition of one who has lost touch with the life and thought of his community and is compulsively fantasizing out of his own completely cut-off base.

Very briefly: The usual pattern is, first, of a break away or departure from the local social order and context; next, a long, deep retreat inward and backward, as it were, in time, and inward, deep into the psyche; a chaotic series of encounters there, darkly terrifying experiences, and presently (if the victim is fortunate) encounters of a centering kind, fulfilling, harmonizing, giving new courage; and then finally, in such fortunate cases, a return journey of rebirth to life. And that is the universal formula also of the mythological hero journey, which I, in my own published work, had described as: 1) separation, 2) initiation, and 3) return:

A hero ventures forth from the world of common day into a region of supernatural wonder: fabulous forces are there encountered and a decisive victory is won: the hero comes back from this mysterious adventure with the power to bestow boons on his fellow men.

That is the pattern of the myth, and that is the pattern of these fantasies of the psyche.

Now it was Dr. Perry's thesis in his paper that in certain cases the best thing is to let the schizophrenic process run its course, not to abort the psychosis by administering shock treatments and the like, but, on the contrary, to help the process of disintegration and reintegration along. However, if a doctor is to be helpful in this way, he has to understand the image language of mythology. He has himself to understand what the fragmentary signs and signals signify that his patient, totally out of touch with rationally oriented manners of thought and communication, is trying to bring forth in order to establish some kind of contact. Interpreted from this point of view, a schizophrenic breakdown is an inward and backward journey to recover something missed or lost, and to restore, thereby, a vital balance. So let the voyager go. He has tipped over and is sinking, perhaps drowning; yet, as in the old legend of Gilgamesh and his long, deep dive to the bottom of the cosmic sea to pluck the watercress of immortality, there is the one green value of his life down there. Don't cut him off from it: help him through.

Dr. Perry introduced me to a paper on "Shamans and Acute Schizophrenia," by Dr. Julian Silverman of the National Institute of Mental Health, which had appeared in 1967 in the *American Anthropologist,* and there again I found something of the greatest interest and of immediate relevance to my studies and thinking. In my own writings I had already pointed out that among primitive hunting peoples it is largely from the psychological experiences of shamans that the mythic imagery and rituals of their ceremonial life derive. The shaman is a person (either male or female) who in early adolescence underwent a severe psychological crisis, such as today would be called a psychosis. Normally the child's apprehensive family sends for an elder shaman to bring the youngster out of it, and by appropriate measures, songs, and exercises, this experienced practitioner succeeds. As Dr. Silverman remarks and demonstrates in his paper, "In primitive cultures in which such a unique life crisis resolution is tolerated, the abnormal experience (shamanism) is typically beneficial to the individual, cognitively and affectively; he is regarded as one with expanded consciousness." Whereas, on the contrary, in such a rationally ordered culture as our own—or, to phrase the proposition again in Dr. Silverman's words, "in a culture that does not provide referential guides for comprehending this kind of crisis experience, the individual (schizophrenic) typically undergoes an intensification of his suffering over and above his original anxieties."

Now let me describe to you the case of an Eskimo shaman who was interviewed in the early 1920s by the great Danish scholar and explorer Knud Rasmussen. Rasmussen was a man of the broadest human sympathy and understanding, who was able to talk in a marvelous way, man to man, with the characters he encountered all the way across the Arctic lands of North America in the course of the Fifth Danish Thule Expedition, which from 1921 to 1924 trekked the whole long stretch from Greenland to Alaska.

Igjugarjuk was a Caribou Eskimo shaman of a tribe inhabiting the North Canadian tundras. When young, he had been visited constantly by dreams that he could not interpret. Strange unknown beings came and spoke to him; and when he woke he remembered all so vividly that he could describe to his friends and family exactly what he had seen. The family, disturbed, but knowing what was happening, sent for an old shaman named Peqanaoq, who, on diagnosing the case, placed the youngster on a sledge just large enough for him to sit on, and in the depth of winter—the absolutely dark and freezing Arctic winter night—dragged him far out onto a lonely Arctic waste and built for him there a tiny snow hut with barely room for him to sit cross-legged. He was not allowed to set foot on the snow, but was lifted from the sledge into the hut and there set down on a piece of skin just large enough to contain him. No food or drink was left with him. He was instructed to think only of the Great Spirit, who would presently appear, and was left there alone for thirty days. After five days the elder returned with a drink of lukewarm water, and after another fifteen, with a second drink and with a bit of meat. But that was all. The cold and the fasting were so severe that, as Igjugarjuk told Rasmussen, "sometimes I died a little." And during all that time he was thinking, thinking, thinking of the Great Spirit, until, toward the end of the ordeal, a helping spirit did in fact arrive in the form of a woman who seemed to hover in the air above him. He never saw her again, but she became his helping spirit. The elder shaman than brought him home, where he was required to diet and fast for another five months; and, as he told his Danish guest, such fasts, often repeated, are the best means of attaining to a knowledge of hidden things. "The only true wisdom," Igjugarjuk said, "lives far from mankind, out in the great loneliness, and can be reached only through suffering. Privation and suffering alone open the mind of a man to all that is hidden to others."

Another powerful shaman, whom Dr. Rasmussen met in Nome, Alaska, told him of a similar venture into the silence. But this old fellow, Najagneq by name, had fallen upon bad times in relation to the people of his village. For shamans, you must know, live in a rather perilous position. When things anywhere go wrong, people tend to blame the local shaman. They imagine he is working magic. And this old man, to protect himself, had invented a number of trick devices and mythological spooks to frighten his neighbors off and keep them safely at bay.

Dr. Rasmussen, recognizing that most of Najagneq's spirits were outright frauds of this kind, one day asked him if there were any in whom he himself believed; to which he replied, "Yes, a power that we call Sila, one that cannot be explained in so many words: a very strong spirit, the upholder of the universe, of the weather, in fact of all life on earth—so mighty that his speech to man comes not through ordinary words, but through storms, snowfalls, rain showers, the tempests of the sea, all the forces that man fears, or through sunshine, calm seas, or small, innocent, playing children who understand nothing. When times are good, Sila has nothing to say to mankind. He has disappeared into his infinite nothingness and remains away as long as people do not abuse life but have respect for their daily food. No one has ever seen Sila. His place of sojourn is so mysterious that he is with us and infinitely far away at the same time."

And what does Sila say?

"The inhabitant or soul of the universe," Najagneq said, "is never seen; its voice alone is heard. All we know is that it has a gentle voice, like a woman, a voice so fine and gentle that even children cannot become afraid. And what it says is: *Sila ersinarsinivdluge,* 'Be not afraid of the universe.' "

Now there were very simple men—at least in our terms of culture, learning, and civilization. Yet their wisdom, drawn from their own most inward depths, corresponds in essence to what we have heard and learned from the most respected mystics. There is a deep and general human wisdom here, of which we do not often come to know in our usual ways of active rational thinking.

In his article on shamanism Dr. Silverman had distinguished two very different types of schizophrenia. One he calls "essential schizophrenia;" the other "paranoid schizophrenia;" and it is in essential schizophrenia alone that analogies appear with what I have termed "the shaman crisis." In essential schizophrenia the characteristic pattern is of withdrawal from the impacts of experience in the outside world. There is a narrowing of concern and focus. The object world falls back and away, and invasions from the unconscious overtake and overwhelm one. In "paranoid schizophrenia," on the other hand, the person remains alert and extremely sensitive to the world and its events, interpreting all, however, in terms of his own projected fantasies, fears, and terrors, and with a sense of being in danger from assaults. The assaults, actually, are from within but he projects them outward, imagining that the world is everywhere on watch against him. This, states Dr. Silverman, is not the type of schizophrenia that leads to the sorts of inward experience that are analogous to those of shamanism. "It is as if the paranoid schizophrenic," he explains, "unable to comprehend or tolerate the stark terrors of his inner world, prematurely directs his attention to the outside world. In this type of abortive crisis solution, the inner chaos is not, so to speak, worked through, *or is not capable of being worked through.*" The lunatic victim is at large, so to say, in the field of his own projected unconscious.

The opposite type of psychotic patient, on the other hand, a pitiful thing to behold, has dropped into a snake-pit deep within. His whole attention, his whole being, is down there, engaged in a life-and-death battle with the terrible apparitions of unmastered psychological energies—which, it would appear, is exactly what the potential shaman also is doing in the period of his visionary journey. And so, we have next to ask what the difference is between the predicament of the "essential schizophrenic" and that of the trance-prone shaman: to which the answer is simply that the primitive shaman does not reject the local social order and its forms; that, in fact, it is actually by virtue of those forms that he is brought back to rational consciousness. And when he has returned, furthermore, it is generally found that his inward personal experiences reconfirm, refresh, and reinforce the inherited local forms; for his personal dream symbology is at one with the symbology of his culture. Whereas, in contrast, in the case of a modern psychotic patient, there is a radical breakoff and no effective association at all with the symbol system of his culture. The established symbol system here provides no help at all to the poor lost schizophrenic, terrified by the figments of his own imagination, to which he is a total stranger; whereas, in the case of the primitive shaman, there is between his outward life and his inward a fundamental accord.

The LSD phenomenon is an intentionally achieved schizophrenia, with the expectation of a spontaneous remission—which, however, does not always follow. Yoga, too, is an intentional schizophrenia: one breaks away from the world, plunging inward, and the ranges of vision experienced are in fact the same as those of a psychosis. But what then, is the difference? What is the difference between a psychotic or LSD experience and a yogic, or a mystical? The plunges are all into the same deep inward sea; of that there can be no doubt. The symbolic figures encountered are in many instances identical (and I shall have something more to say about those in a moment). But there *is* an important difference. The difference—to put it sharply—is equivalent simply to that between a diver who can swim and one who cannot. The mystic, endowed with native talents for this sort of thing and following, stage by stage, the instruction of a master, enters the waters and

finds he can swim; whereas the schizophrenic, unprepared, unguided, and ungifted, has fallen or has intentionally plunged, and is drowning. Can he be saved? If a line is thrown to him, will he grab it?

Let us first ask about the waters into which he has descended. They are the same, we have said, as those of the mystical experience. What, then, is their character? What are their properties? And what does it take to swim?

They are the waters of the universal archetypes of mythology. All my life, as a student of mythologies, I have been working with these archetypes, and I can tell you, they *do* exist and are the same all over the world. In the various traditions they are variously represented; as, for instance, in a Buddhist temple, medieval cathedral, Summerian ziggurat, or Mayan pyramid. The images of divinities will vary in various parts of the world according to the local flora, fauna, geography, racial features, etc. The myths and rites will be given different interpretations, different rational applications, different social customs to validate and enforce. And yet the archetypal, essential forms and ideas are the same—often stunningly so. And so what, then, *are* they? What do they represent?

The psychologist who has best dealt with these, best described and best interpreted them, is Carl G. Jung, who terms them "archetypes of the collective unconscious," as pertaining to those structures of the psyche that are not the products of merely individual experience but are common to all mankind. In his view, the basal depth or layer of the psyche is an expression of the instinct system of our species, grounded in the human body, its nervous system and wonderful brain. All animals act instinctively. They act also, of course, in ways that have to be learned, and in relation to circumstance; yet every species differently, according to its "nature." Watch a cat enter a living room, and then for example, a dog. Each is moved by impulses peculiar to its species, and these, finally, are the ultimate shapers of its life. And so man too is governed and determined. He has both an inherited biology and a personal biography, the "archetypes of the unconscious" being expressions of the first. The repressed personal memories, on the other hand, of the shocks, frustrations, fears, etc., of infancy, to which the Freudian school gives such attention, Jung distinguishes from that other and calls the "personal unconscious." As the first is biological and common to the species, so this second is biographical, socially determined, and specific to each separate life. Most of our dreams and daily difficulties will derive, of course, from the latter; but in a schizophrenic plunge one descends to the "collective," and the imagery there experienced is largely of the order of the archetypes of myth.

Now in every human being there is a built-in human instinct system, without which we should not even come to birth. But each of us has also been educated to a specific local culture system. The peculiar thing about man, which distinguishes us from all other beasts of the kingdom, is that we are born twelve years too soon. No mother would wish it to be otherwise; but so it is, and that is our problem. The newly born has the wit neither of a newly hatched turtle, size of a nickel, nor of a chick with a piece of eggshell still adhering to its tail. Absolutely unable to fend for itself, the infant Homo sapiens is committed for twelve years to a season of dependency on parents or parent substitutes; and it is during these twelve dependent years that we are turned into human beings. We learn to walk as people walk, as well as to speak, think and cogitate in terms of the local vocabulary. We are taught to respond to certain signals positively, to others negatively or with fear; and most of these signals taught are not of the natural, but of some local social order. They are socially specific. Yet the impulses that they activate and control are of nature, biology, and instinct. Every mythology is an organization, consequently, of culturally conditioned releasing signs, the natural and the cultural strains in them being so intimately fused that to distinguish one from the other is in many cases all but impossible. And such culturally determined signals motivate the culturally imprinted human nervous system, as the sign stimuli of nature do the natural reflexes of a beast.

A functioning mythological symbol I have defined as "an energy-evoking and -directing sign." Dr. Perry has termed such signals "affect images." Their messages are addressed not to the brain, to be interpreted there and passed on; but directly to the nerves, the glands, the blood, and the sympathetic nervous system. Yet they pass *through* the brain, and the educated brain may interfere, misinterpret, and so short-circuit the messages. When that occurs the signs no longer function as they should. The inherited mythology is garbled, and its guiding value lost or misconstrued. Or, what is worse, one may have been brought up to respond to a set of signals not present in the general environment; as is frequently the case, for example, with children raised in the circles of certain special sects, not participating in—and even despising or resenting—the culture forms of the rest of the civilization. Such a person will never quite feel at home in the larger social field, but always uneasy and even slightly paranoid. Nothing touches him as it should, means to him what it should, or moves him as it moves others. He is compelled to retreat for his satisfactions back to the restricted and accordingly restricting context of the sect, family, commune, or reservation to which he was attuned. He is disoriented, and even dangerous, in the larger field.

And so, it seems to me, there is a critical problem indicated here, which parents and families have to face squarely: that, namely, of insuring that the signals which they are imprinting on their young are such as will attune them to, and not alienate them from, the world in which they are going to have to live; unless, of course, one is dead set on bequeathing to one's heirs one's own paranoia. More normally, rational parents will wish to have produced socially as well as physically healthy offspring, well enough attuned to the system of sentiments of the culture into which they are growing to be able to appraise its values rationally and align themselves constructively with its progressive, decent, life-fostering, and fructifying elements.

Let me now, therefore, before proceeding to an account of the general course or history of such a break-off—the inward journey (let us call it) of descent and return—just say one more word about the functions normally served by a properly operating mythology. They are, in my judgment, four.

The first is what I have called the mystical function: to waken and maintain in the individual a sense of awe and gratitude in relation to the mystery dimension of the universe, not so that he lives in fear of it, but so that he recognizes that he participates in it, since the mystery of being is the mystery of his own deep being as well. That is what the old Alaskan medicine man heard when Sila, the soul of the universe, said to him, "Be not afraid." For, as beheld by our temporal eyes, nature, as we have seen, is tough. It is terrible, terrific, monstrous. It is the kind of thing that makes reasonable, existentialist Frenchmen call it "absurd!"

The second function of a living mythology is to offer an image of the universe that will be in accord with the knowledge of the time, the sciences and the fields of action of the folk to whom the mythology is addressed. In our own day, of course, the world pictures of *all* the major religions are at least two thousand years out of date, and in that fact alone there is ground enough for a very serious break-off. If, in a period like our own, of the greatest religious fervor and quest, you would wonder why the churches are losing their congregations, one large part of the answer surely is right here. The are inviting their flocks to enter and to find peace in a browsing-ground that never was, never will be, and in any case is surely not that of any corner of the world today. Such a mythological offering is a sure pill for at least a mild schizophrenia.

The third function of a living mythology is to validate, support, and imprint the norms of a given, specific moral order, that, namely, of the society in which the individual is to live. And the fourth is to guide him, stage by stage, in health, strength, and harmony of spirit, through the whole foreseeable course of a useful life.

Let us review, briefly, the sequence of these stages.

The first is, of course, that of the child, dependent for those twelve years, both physically and psychologically, on the guidance and protection of its family. The most obvious biological analogy is to be found among the marsupials: kangaroos, opposums, wallabies, etc. Since these are not placental animals, the fetus cannot remain in the womb after the food provision (the yolk) of the egg has been absorbed, and the little things have to be born, therefore, long before they are ready for life. The infant kangaroo is born after only three weeks of gestation, but already has strong front legs, and these know exactly what to do. The tiny creature—by instinct, again please observe!—crawls up its mother's belly to her pouch, climbs in there, attaches itself to a nipple that swells (instinctively) in its mouth, so that it cannot get loose, and there, until ready to hop forth, remains in a second womb: a "womb with a view."

An exactly comparable biological function is served in our own species by a mythology, which is a no less indispensable biological organ, no less a nature product, though apparently something else. Like the nest of a bird, a mythology is fashioned of materials drawn from the local environment, apparently altogether consciously, but according to an architecture unconsciously dictated from within. And it simply does not matter whether its comforting, fostering, guiding images would be appropriate for an adult. It is not intended for adults. Its first function is to foster an unready psyche to maturity, preparing it to face its world. The proper question to ask, therefore, is whether it is training up a character fit to live in this world as it is, or only in some Heaven or imagined social field. The next function, accordingly, must be to help the ready youth step out and away, to leave the myth, this second womb, and to become, as they say in the Orient, "twice born," a competent adult functioning rationally in his present world, who has left his childhood season behind.

Then next, no sooner have you learned your adult job and gained a place for yourself in this society of ours, than you begin to feel the creak of age, retirement is in prospect, and remarkably soon it arrives with its Medicare, old-age pensions, and all. You have now a disengaged psyche on your hands, your own; a load of what Jung termed "disposable libido." What to do with it? The classical period has arrived of the late-middle-age nervous breakdown, divorce, alcoholic debacle, and so forth: when the light of your life has descended, unprepared, into an unprepared unconscious, and you there drown. It would have been a very much better situation if, during your childhood years, you had been given a sound imprinting of childhood myths, so that when the time came for this backward, downward plunge the scenery down there would have been a bit more familiar. At least for some of the monsters encountered you would have been given names and perhaps even weapons: for it is simply a fact, and a very important one, that the images of mythology that in childhood are interpreted as references to external supernaturals, actually are symbols of the structuring powers (or, as Jung called them, archetypes) of the unconscious. And it will be to these and the natural forces they represent—the forces and voices within you of the soul (Sila) of the Universe—that you will return when you take that plunge, which is to befall you one day, sure as death.

And so, with that challenge before us, let us try to become acquainted with some of the tides and undertows of our inward sea. Let me tell you something of what I have recently heard about the wonders of the inward schizophrenic plunge.

The first experience is of a sense of splitting. The person sees the world going in two: one part of it moving away; himself in the other part. This is the beginning of the regressus, the crack-off and backward flow. He may see himself, for a time, in two roles. One is the role of the clown, the ghost, the witch, the queer one, the outsider. That is the outer role that he plays, making little of himself as the fool, a joke, the one kicked around, the patsy. Inside, however, he is the savior, and he knows it. He is the hero chosen for a destiny. Recently one such savior did me the honor of paying me three visits: a tall, beautiful young man with the beard and gentle eyes and manner of a Christ; LSD was his sacrament—LSD and sex. "I have seen my Father," he told me on the second occasion. "He is old now and has told me just to wait. I shall know when the time comes for me to take over."

The second stage has been described in many clinical accounts. It is of a terrific drop-off and regression, backward in time and biologically as well. Falling back into his own past, the psychotic becomes an infant, a fetus in the womb. One has the frightening experience of slipping back to animal consciousness, into animal forms, sub-animal forms, even plantlike. I think of the legend here of Daphne, the nymph who was turned into a laurel tree. Such an image, read in psychological terms, would be the image of a psychosis. Approached in love by the god Apollo, the virgin was terrified, cried for help to her father, the river-god Peneus, and he turned her into a tree.

"Show me the face you had before your father and mother were born!" We have had occasion before to refer to this meditation theme of the Japanese Zen masters. In the course of a schizophrenic retreat, the psychotic too may come to know the exaltation of a union with the universe, transcending personal bounds: the "oceanic feeling," Freud called it. Feelings arise then, too, of a new knowledge. Things that before had been mysterious are now fully understood. Ineffable realizations are experienced; and in fact, as we read about them, we can only be amazed. I have now read dozens of accounts; and they correspond, often amazingly, to the insights of the mystics and to the images of Hindu, Buddhist, Egyptian, and classical myth.

For example, a person who has never believed in, or even heard of, reincarnation will begin to feel that he has lived forever; that he has lived through many lifetimes, yet was never born and will never die. It is as though he had come to know himself as that Self (*atman*) of which we read in the *Bhagavad Gita:* "Never is it born, never does it die.... Unborn, eternal, permanent, and primeval, it is not slain when the body is slain." The patient (let us now call him that) has united what remains of his consciousness with the consciousness of all things, the rocks, the trees, the whole world of nature, out of which we all have come. He is in accord with that which has indeed existed forever: as we all are, actually, at root, and therein at peace—once again, as stated in the *Gita:* "When one completely withdraws the senses from their objects, like a tortoise drawing in its limbs, then is one's wisdom firmly fixed. In that serenity is surcease of all sorrow."

In short, my friends, what I find that I am saying is that our schizophrenic patient is actually experiencing inadvertently that same beatific ocean deep which the yogi and saint are ever striving to enjoy: except that, whereas they are swimming in it, he is drowning.

There may come next, according to a number of accounts, the sense of a terrific task ahead with dangers to be met and mastered; but also a presentiment of invisible helpful presences that may guide and help one through. These are the gods, the guardian demons or angels: innate powers of the psyche, fit to meet and to master the torturing, swallowing, or shattering negative forces. And if one has the courage to press on, there will be experienced, finally, in a terrible rapture, a culminating overwhelming crisis—or even a series of such culminations, more than can be borne.

These crises are mainly of four typical sorts, according to the kinds of difficulty that will have conduced to the regressus in the first place. For instance, a person who in childhood has been deprived of essential love, brought up in a home of little or no care, but only authority, rigor, and commands, or in a house of tumult and wrath, a drunken father raging about, or the like, will have been seeking in his backward voyage a reorientation and centering of his life in love. Accordingly, the culmination (when he will have broken back to the start of his biography and even beyond, to a sense of the erotic first impulse to life) will be a discovery of a center in his own heart of tenderness and of love in which he can rest. That will have been the aim and meaning of his entire backward quest. And its realization will be represented through an experience, one way or another, of some sort of visionary fulfillment of a "sacred union" with a wifely mothering (or simply a mothering) presence.

Or if it had been a household in which the father had been nobody, a nothing, of no force in the home at all; where there had been no sense of paternal authority, no one of masculine presence who could be honored and respected, but only a clutter of domestic details and disordered feminine concerns, the quest will have been for a decent father image, and that is what will have to be found: some sort of symbolic realization of supernatural daughterhood or sonship to a father.

A third domestic situation of significant emotional deprivation is that of the child who feels itself to have been excluded from its family circle, treated as though not wanted; or with no family at all. In cases, for example, of a second marriage, where a second family has come along, a child of the first may feel and actually find itself excluded,

thrown away, or left behind. The old fairy-tale theme of the wicked stepmother and stepsisters is relevant here. What such an excluded one will be striving for in his inward lonely journey will be the finding or the fashioning of a center—not a *family* center, but a *world* center—of which *he* will be the pivotal being. Dr. Perry told me of the case of a schizophrenic patient who was so completely and profoundly cut off that no one could establish any communication with him at all. One day, this poor mute person, in the doctor's presence, drew a crude circle, and then just placed the point of his pencil in the middle of it. Dr. Perry stopped and said to him, "You *are* in the center, aren't you! Aren't you!" And *that* message got through, initiating the course of a return.

There is a perfectly fascinating inside report of a schizophrenic breakdown in the next-to-last chapter of Dr. R. D. Laing's book *The Politics of Experience.* This is an account given by a former Royal Navy commodore, now a sculptor, of a schizophrenic adventure of his own, at the culmination of which he experienced a fourth type of realization: a sense of sheer light, the sense of a terribly dangerous, overpowering light to be encountered and endured. His account suggests very strongly the Buddha-light described in the *Tibetan Book of the Dead,* which is supposed to be experienced immediately upon death, and which, if endured, yields release from rebirth but is for most too great to bear. The former Royal Navy man, a certain Mr. Jesse Watkins, thirty-eight years of age, had had no previous knowledge of Oriental philosophies or mythologies; yet, as the climax of his ten-day voyage approached, its imagery became all but indistinguishable from that of the Hindu and Buddhist faiths.

It all had begun with an alarming sense of time itself running backward. The gentleman, at home in the living room, had been listening inattentively to a popular tune on the radio when he began to have this uncanny experience. He got up and looked into a mirror to see what might be happening, and though the face that he saw there was familiar, it seemed to be of a stranger, not himself. Taken to an observation ward, he was put to bed and that night had the feeling that he had died, and that those in the ward around him had died too. He continued falling backward in time into a sort of animal landscape, where he wandered as a beast: a rhinoceros making rhinoceros sounds, afraid, yet aggressive and on guard. He felt, too, that he was a baby and could hear himself cry like a child. He was at once the observer and what he observed.

Given newspapers to read, he could make no headway because everything, every headline, opened out to widening associations. A letter from his wife gave the feeling that she was in a different world, which he would never again inhabit. And he felt that, where he was, he had tapped powers, powers inherent in us all. For example, a nasty cut on his finger, which he would not let the attendants treat, he actually healed in a single day by putting, as he declared, "a sort of intense attention on it." He found that by sitting up in bed and staring hard at noisy patients elsewhere in the ward, he could cause them to lie down and be still. He felt that he was more than he had ever imagined himself to be, that he had existed forever, in all forms of life, and was experiencing it all again; but also that he had now before him a great and terrible journey to accomplish, and this gave him a feeling of deep fear.

Now these great new powers that he was experiencing, both of control over his own body and of influence over others, are in India called the *siddhi*. They are recognized there (as they were experienced here, by this Western man) as powers latent in us all, inherent in all life, which the yogi releases in himself. We hear of them in Christian Science; also, in other types of "faith healing," praying people to health, and so forth. The miracles of shamans, saints, and saviors are, again, well-known examples. And as for the sense of an experience of identity with all being, all life, and of transformations into animal forms: consider the following chant of the legendary chief poet, Amairgen, of the first arriving Goidelic Celts, when their leading ship came to beach on the shores of Ireland:

I am the wind that blows o'er the sea;
I am the wave of the deep;
I am the bull of seven battles;
I am the eagle on the rock;
I am a tear of the sun;
I am the fairest of plants;
I am a boar for courage;
I am a salmon in the water;
I am a lake in the plain;
I am the word of knowledge;
I am the head of the battle-dealing spear;
I am the god who fashions fire [= thought] in the head.

We are thus on well-known mythic ground—strange and fluid though it may seem—as we follow in imagination the course of this ten-day inward journey. And its culminating passages too, though strange, will be curiously (in some secret way) familiar.

The voyager, as he tells, had a "particularly acute feeling" that the world he now was experiencing was established on three planes, with himself in the middle sphere, a plane of higher realizations above, and a sort of waiting-room plane beneath. Compare the cosmic image in the Bible, of God's heaven above, the earth beneath, and the waters beneath the earth. Or consider Dante's *Divine Comedy,* the temple towers of India and the Middle American Mayas, the ziggurats of old Sumer. Below are the Hells of suffering; aloft, the Heaven of light; and between, the mountain of ascending souls in stages of spiritual progress. According to Jesse Watkins, most of us are on the lowest level, waiting (*en attendant Godot,* one might say), as in a general waiting room; not yet in the middle room of struggle and quest at which he himself had arrived. He had

feelings of invisible gods above, about, and all around, who were in charge and running things; and in the highest place, the highest job, was the highest god of all.

Moreover, what made it all so terrible was the knowledge that ultimately everybody would have to assume that job at the top. All those around him in the madhouse, who, like himself, had died and were in the middle, purgatorial stage, were—as he phrased it—"sort of awakening." (The meaning of the word *buddha,* let us recall, is "the awakened one.") Those all around him in the madhouse were on their ways—awakening—to assume in their own time that top position, and the one now up there was God. *God was a madman.* He was the one that was bearing it all: "this enormous load," as Watkins phrased it, "of having to be aware and governing and running things." "The journey is there and every single one of us," he reported, "has got to go through it, and you can't dodge it, and the purpose of everything and the whole of existence is to equip you to take another step, and another step, and another step, and so on. . . ."

One is reminded of the figure of the maimed king of the medieval Christian legend of the Grail, and of the question there to be asked by the arriving innocent Grail Knight, who, upon asking it, will have healed the king and himself achieved the kingly role. One thinks also of the head crowned with thorns of the crucified Christ; and of a number of other figures: Prometheus, pinned to a crag of Caucasus, with an eagle tearing at his liver; Loki likewise fixed to a crag, and with the fiery venom of a cosmic serpent dripping forever on his head; or indeed Satan, as Dante saw him, at the center of the earth, as its pivot, corresponding in this position to his prototype, the Greek Hades (Roman Pluto), lord of both the underworld and of wealth—who is exactly (in that marvelous way that we so often find when comparing mythic forms) the Occidental counterpart of India's earth-god Kubera, the very lord of wealth and of the painful turning wheel referred to in this fable.

In the case of our schizophrenic visionary, however, the role of the mad, terribly suffering god at the summit of the universe was felt to be too much for him to assume. For who, indeed, would be able both to face and to accept to himself willingly the whole impact of an experience of what life truly is—what the universe truly is—in the whole of its terrible joy? That perhaps would be the ultimate test of the perfection of one's compassion: to be able to affirm this world, just as it is, without reservation, while bearing all its terrible joy with rapture in oneself, and thereby madly willing it to all beings! In any case, Jesse Watkins, in his madness, knew that he had had enough.

"At times it was so devastating," he said, in speaking of his whole adventure, "that I'd be afraid of entering it again. . . . I was suddenly confronted with something so much greater than oneself, with so many more experiences, with so much awareness, so much that you couldn't take it. . . . I experienced it for a moment or two, but it was like a sudden blast of light, wind or whatever you like to put it as, against you; so that you feel that you're too naked and alone to be able to withstand it."

One morning he decided to let them give him no more sedatives and to come back, somehow, to his senses. He sat up on the edge of his bed, tightly clenched together his hands, and began repeating his own name. He kept on repeating it, over and over, and all of a sudden—just like that—he realized that it was all over, and so it was. The experiences were finished, and he was sane.

And here, I think we can say, is our clue to the method of the adventure, if one is ever to return home. It is this: *not* to identify one's *self* with *any* of the figures or powers experienced. The Indian yogi, striving for release, identifies himself with the Light and never returns. But no one with a will to the service of others and of life would permit himself such an escape. The ultimate aim of the quest, if one is to return, must be neither release nor ecstasy for oneself, but the wisdom and power to serve others. And there is a really great, as well as greatly celebrated, Occidental tale of such a round trip to the Region of Light in the *ten-year voyage* of Homer's Odysseus—who, like the Royal Navy Commodore Watkins, was a warrior returning from long battle years to domestic life, and required, therefore, to shift radically his psychological posture and center.

We all know the great story: Of how, having sailed with his twelve ships away from conquered Troy, Odysseus put into a Thracian port, Ismarus, sacked the city, slew its people, and—as he later reported—"took their wives and much substance," distributing these to his own men. Clearly, such a brute was not ready for domestic life; a complete change of character was required. And the gods, who are always alert to such things, saw to it that he should fall into competent hands.

First Zeus sent upon him a tempest that tore the sails of his ships to shreds and blew them for nine days, out of control, to the land of the Lotus Eaters—land of the hallucinogenic drug "forgetfulness," where, like Watkins in his madhouse, Odysseus and his freaked-out men were set floating on a sea of dream. Then follows the sequence of their mythological adventures, altogether different in kind from anything they had ever known.

There was, first, their encounter with the Cyclops and, after a costly release from his terrible cave, a period of elation, as they sailed on the winds of the god Aeolus; next, however, a dead calm and the toilsome ordeal of the twelve great ships reduced to rowing. They made it to land at the island of the cannibal Laestrygons, who sent eleven ships to the bottom, and the mighty Odysseus, up against forces now greater far than he could master, made away with a terrified crew in the one last hull remaining. Rowing wearily, still on a dead-calm sea, they advanced to what was to prove to be the crux of the entire nightsea adventure, the island of Circe of the Braided Locks, the nymph who turns men into swine.

This would be such a female as our already seriously humbled hero could not manhandle as mere booty. Her power surpassed his own. Fortunately for his fame, however, the protector and guide of souls beyond death to rebirth, the mystery-god Hermes, arrived just in time to protect him with both advice and a charm; so that instead of being metamorphosed, the great mariner, so protected, was taken to Circe's bed, after which she directed him to the underworld and the shades down there of his ancestors. There he also met Tiresias, the blind prophetic sage in whom male and female knowledges are united. And when he had learned there all he could, he returned, much improved, to the formerly very dangerous nymph, who was now his teacher and guide.

Circe next directed him to the Island of the Sun, her own father, where, however—in the source-region of all light—his only remaining ship with its crew was shattered, and Odysseus, tossed alone into the sea, was carried by its irresistible tides right back to his daytime earthly wife (and life), Penelope . . . after an eight-year stop-off on the way with the middle-aged wifely nymph Calypso, and a brief pause, also, on the isle of pretty Nausicaa and her father, in whose nightsea craft he was finally carried in deep sleep home to his own sweet shore—now fully prepared for his life-to-come as a considerate spouse and father.

A significant feature of this great epic of the inward night-sea adventure is its representation of the voyager as never wishing to remain at any of its stations. In the land of the Lotus Eaters, those of his men who ate the flowery food had no desire ever to return home; but Odysseus dragged them weeping to his ships, bound them in the hulls, and rowed away. And evern during his idyllic stay of eight years on the isle of Calypso, he would often be found on the beach alone, gazing homeward, out to sea.

Jesse Watkins too was able ultimately to distinguish himself in his worldly role from the madman in the asylum; and, like the turning point at the fartheest reach of his classical protoptype's course, where the last ship went to pieces at the Island of the Sun, so in this modern mariner's voyage, the turning point was reached at the brink of an experience of blasting light. Jesse Watkins, at that juncture, recognizing that he was not only a terrified madman about to experience annihilation, but also the sane man he once had been at home, from whose sphere of life he had become psychologically dissociated, sat (as we have heard) on his bed, clenched together his two hands, pronounced his daylight body's name, and returned to it, like a diver to the surface of the sea.

The usual and most appropriate mythological figure to symbolize such a return to life is "rebirth," rebirth to a new world; and that, exactly, was the figure that occurred to the mind of this self-rescued patient on experiencing spontaneous remission. "When I came out," he is reported to have told, "I suddenly felt that everything was so much more real than it had been before. The grass was greener, the sun was shining brighter, and people were more alive, I could see them clearer. I could see the bad things and the good thing and all that. I was much more aware."

"Can we not see," remarks Dr. Laing in his commentary on the whole experience, "that his voyage is not what we need to be cured of, but that it is itself a natural way of healing our own appalling state of alienation called normality?"

Something much of the same was the view, also, of both Dr. Perry and Dr. Silverman in the papers earlier mentioned; and, as I have most lately learned, the earliest documented proposal of this view was in a study published by C. G. Jung already in 1902, "On the Psychology and Pathology of So-called Occult Phenomena."

In sum, then: The inward journeys of the mythological hero, the shaman, the mystic, and the schizophrenic are in principle the same; and when the return or remission occurs, it is experienced as a rebirth: the birth, that is to say, of a "twice-born" ego, no longer bound in by its daylight-world horizon. It is now known to be but the reflex of a larger self, its proper function being to carry the energies of an archetypal instinct system into fruitful play in a contemporary space-time daylight situation. One is now no longer afraid of nature; nor of nature's child, society—which is monstrous too, and in fact cannot be otherwise; it would otherwise not survive. The new ego is in accord with all this, in harmony, at peace; and, as those who have returned from the journey tell, life is then richer, stronger, and more joyous.

OTHER VISIONS, OTHER REALITIES

Asian psychologies offer us a fresh viewpoint on consciousness. Each discrete state of consciousness is, in a sense, "a realm of existence." Chögyam Trungpa, a Tibetan lama, translates Tibetan Buddhism into a Western psychological framework, showing that the normal fluctuations of the waking state can encompass all the major realms, from the worst "hell world" of anxiety to the "realm of the gods," where one is rapt in ultimate pleasure. In Buddhist psychology there are six major states: blissful self-absorption, paranoia, passion, stupidity, craving, and anger. Each of these shows up in subtle but distinct differences in how people handle themselves in daily life—walking, talking, eating, and the like. People tend to experience one such state more often than the rest, making it characteristic of their personality. When exaggerated to the point of obsession, they each bloom into a form of neurosis or psychosis. The ability to have insight and detachment from one's basic state is the beginning of the path to personal liberation.

Psychiatry itself, suggests philosopher Jacob Needleman, has by and large reached a cul-de-sac of hopelessness in the face of the suffering and frustrations of everyday human life. "The once magical promise of transformation of the mind through psychiatry," he claims, "has disappeared." For this reason many therapists themselves join in the widespread attraction to the spiritual methods of ancient Asian traditions. One basic difference between psychotherapy and spiritual techniques is that the former changes the *contents* of consciousness, while the latter transforms consciousness *itself*. This change in one's state of consciousness, says Needleman, can bring about a transformation of the person more far-reaching than any therapy might produce.

Ram Dass, a Western psychotherapist-turned-yogi, describes in detail the kind of training Eastern traditions require of those who follow this path to transform their consciousness. Eastern and Western systems of thought, he notes, diverge in their basic view of man. In the West, psychology sees people in terms of their individual ego identity; in the East, consciousness itself, rather than any aspect of the ego, is what a person "really" is. In transforming one's consciousness in Eastern systems, the person has to become detached from models of himself. As he frees himself, he will be more able to experience a greater range of states of consciousness. This range includes the normal state, from which vantage point his old identity is real, but also extends into altered states of consciousness from which that reality is as relative as any other.

The scientific world view deals with but a part of the universe, although it has thoroughly captured the Western intellect. That science should be so ardently embraced by our thinkers is understandable psychologically, says philosopher Huston Smith, but is, paradoxically, illogical. Admittedly science is a powerful probe of the universe, but it is blind to its own limitations; "reality exceeds what science measures." Issues fundamental to man's life lie outside science's domain: questions of values, of purpose, of life's meaning and quality cannot be answered by the scientific method. As people recognize the limitations of science's lens on the world, they turn to other means. For many in the West, this means returning to the wisdom of techniques of traditional cultures, and to experiments with altered states of consciousness, to retrieve an understanding that science cannot offer. In Smith's words, this search is for "the vision philosophers have dreamed, mystics have seen, and prophets have transmitted."

The Six Realms of Existence

Chögyam Trungpa

The six realms, the different styles of samsaric occupation, are referred to as "realms," in the sense that we dwell within a particular version of reality.

The six realms are: the realm of the gods, the realm of the jealous gods, the human realm, the animal realm, the realm of the hungry ghosts, and the hell realm. The realms are predominantly emotional attitudes toward ourselves and our surroundings, emotional attitudes colored and reinforced by conceptual explanations and rationalizations. As human beings we may, during the course of a day, experience the emotions of all of the realms, from the pride of the god realm to the hatred and paranoia of the hell realm. Nonetheless, a person's psychology is usually firmly rooted in one realm. This realm provides us with a style of confusion, a way of entertaining and occupying ourselves so as not to have to face our fundamental uncertainty, our ultimate fear that we may not exist.

SELF-ABSORPTION

The fundamental occupation of the god realm is mental fixation, a meditative absorption of sorts, which is based upon ego, upon the spiritually materialistic approach. In such meditation practice the meditator maintains himself by dwelling upon something.

You do get very dramatic results from such practice, if you are successful at it. One might experience inspiring visions or sounds, seemingly profound mental states, physical bliss and mental bliss. All sorts of "altered states of consciousness" could be experienced or manufactured through the efforts of self-conscious mind. But these experiences are imitations, plastic flowers, manmade, manufactured, prefabricated.

The realm of the gods is realized through tremendous struggle, is manufactured out of hope and fear. The fear of failure and the hope of gain build up and up and up to a crescendo. One moment you think you are going to make it and the next moment you think you are going to fail. Alternation between these extremes produces enormous tension. Success and failure mean so much to us—"This is the end of me," or "This is my achievement of ultimate pleasure."

Finally we become so excited that we begin to lose the reference points of our hope and fear. We lose track of where we are and what we were doing. And then there is a sudden flash in which pain and pleasure become completely one and the meditative state of dwelling on the ego dawns upon us. Such a breakthrough, such a tremendous achievement. And then pleasure begins to saturate our system, psychologically and physically. We no longer have to care about hope or fear. And quite possibly we might believe this to be the permanent achievement of enlightenment or union with God. At that moment everything we see appears to be beautiful, loving, even the most grotesque situations of life seem heavenly. Anything that is unpleasant or aggressive seems beautiful because we have achieved oneness with ego. In other words, ego lost track of its intelligence. This is the absolute, ultimate achievement of bewilderment, the depths of ignorance—extremely powerful. It is a kind of spiritual atomic bomb, self-destructive in terms of compassion, in terms of communication, in terms of stepping out of the bondage of ego. The whole approach in the realm of the gods is stepping in and in and in, churning out more and more chains with which to bind oneself. The more we develop our practice, the more bondage we create. The scriptures cite the analogy of the silkworm which finds itself with its own silk thread until it finally suffocates itself.

Actually we have only been discussing one of two aspects of the realm of the gods, the self-destructive perversion of spirituality into materialism. However, the god realm's version of materialism can also be applied to so-called worldly concerns in the search for extreme mental and physical pleasure, the attempt to dwell on seductive goals of all kinds: health, wealth, beauty, fame, virtue, whatever. The approach is always pleasure-oriented, in the sense of maintenance of ego. What characterizes the realm of the gods is the losing track of hope and fear. And this might be achieved in terms of sensual concerns as well as in terms of spirituality. In both cases, in order to achieve such extraordinary happiness, we must lose track of who is searching and what is the goal.

So the realm of the gods is not particularly painful, in itself. The pain comes from the eventual disillusionment. You think you have achieved a continually blissful state, spiritual or worldly; you are dwelling on that. But suddenly something shakes you and you realize that what you have achieved is not going to last forever. Your bliss becomes shaky and more irregular, and the thought of maintenance begins to reappear in your mind as you try to push yourself back into your blissful state. But the karmic situation brings you all kinds of irritations and at some stage you begin to lose faith in the continuity of the blissful state. A sudden violence arises, the feeling that you have been cheated, that you cannot stay in this realm of the gods forever. So when the karmic situation shakes you and provides extraordinary situations for you to relate with, the whole process becomes profoundly disappointing. You condemn yourself or the person who put you into the god realm or what brought you out of it. You develop anger and disappointment because you think you have been cheated. You switch into another style of relating to the world, another realm. This is what is called *samsara,* which literally means "continual circle," "whirlpool," the ocean of confusion which spins around again and again and again, without end.

PARANOIA

The dominant characteristic of the next realm, the jealous god or *asura* realm, is paranoia. If you are trying to help someone who has an asura mentality, they interpret your action as an attempt to oppress them or infiltrate their territory. But if you decide not to help them, they interpret that as a selfish act: you are seeking comfort for yourself. If you present both alternatives to them, then they think you are playing games with them. The asura mentality is quite intelligent: it sees all the hidden corners. You think that you are communicating with an asura face to face, but in actual fact he is looking at you from behind your back. This intense paranoia is combined with an extreme efficiency and accuracy which inspires a defensive form of pride. The asura mentality is associated with wind, speeding about, trying to achieve everything on the spot, avoiding all possibilities of being attacked. It is trying constantly to attain something higher and greater. To do so one must watch out for every possible pitfall. There is no time to prepare, to get ready to put your action into practice. You just act without preparation. A false kind of spontaneity, a sense of freedom to act develops.

The asura mentality is preoccupied with comparison. In the constant struggle to maintain security and achieve greater things, you need points of reference, landmarks to plot your movement, to fix your opponent, to measure your progress. You regard life situations as games, in the sense of there being an opponent and yourself. You are constantly dealing with them and me, me and my friends, me and myself. All corners are regarded as being suspicious or threatening, therefore one must look into them and be

careful of them. But one is not careful in the sense of hiding or camouflaging oneself. You are very direct and willing to come out in the open and fight if there is a problem or if there is a plot or a seeming plot against you. You just come out and fight face to face, trying to expose the plot. At the same time that one is going out in the open and facing the situation, one is distrustful of the messages that you receive from the situation, so you ignore them. You refuse to accept anything, refuse to learn anything that is presented by outsiders, because everyone is regarded as the enemy.

PASSION

Passion is the major occupation in the human realm. Passion in this sense is an intelligent kind of grasping in which the logical reasoning mind is always geared toward the creation of happiness. There is an acute sense of the separateness of pleasurable objects from the experiencer resulting in a sense of loss, poverty, often accompanied by nostalgia. You feel that only pleasurable objects can bring you comfort and happiness, but you feel inadequate, not strong or magnetic enough for the objects of pleasure to be drawn naturally into your territory. Nevertheless, you try actively to draw them in. This often leads to a critical attitude toward other people. You want to magnetize the best qualities, the most pleasurable, most sophisticated, most civilized situations.

This kind of magnetizing is different from that of the asura realm which is not as selective and intelligent. The human realm by comparison involves a high degree of selectivity and fussiness. There is an acute sense of having your own ideology and your own style, of rejecting things not your style. You must have the right balance in everything. You criticize and condemn people who do not meet your standards. Or else you might be impressed by someone who embodies your style or is superior to you at achieving it, someone who is very intelligent and has very refined taste, who leads a pleasurable life and has the things you would like to have. It might be an historical figure or a mythological figure or one of your contemporaries who has greatly impressed you. He is very accomplished and you would like to possess his qualities. It is not simply a matter of being jealous of another person; you want to draw that person into your territory. It is an ambitious kind of jealousy in that you want to equal the other person.

The essence of the human realm is the endeavor to achieve some high ideal.

There is an heroic attitude, the attempt to create monuments, the biggest, greatest, historical monument. This heroic approach is based on fascination with what you lack. When you hear of someone who possesses remarkable qualities, you regard them as significant beings and yourself as insignificant. This continual comparing and selecting generates a never-ending procession of desires.

The human mentality places a strong emphasis on knowledge, learning and education, on collecting all kinds of information and wisdom. The intellect is most active in the human realm. There is so much going on in your mind as a result of having collected so many things and having planned so many projects. The epitome of the human realm is to be stuck in a huge traffic jam of discursive thought. You are so busy thinking that you cannot learn anything at all.

So it is a very intellectual realm, very busy and very disturbing. The human mentality has less pride than the mentalities of the other realms. In the other realms you find some occupation to hang onto and derive satisfaction from, whereas in the human realm there is no such satisfaction. There is a constant searching, constant looking for new situations or attempts to improve given situations. It is the least enjoyable state of mind because suffering is not regarded as an occupation nor as a way of challenging oneself; rather it is a constant reminder of ambitions created out of suffering.

STUPIDITY

The descriptions of the different realms are related to subtle but distinct differences in the ways individuals handle themselves in daily life—how they walk, talk, write letters, the way they read, eat, sleep and so on. Everyone tends to develop a style which is peculiar to them. If we hear a tape recording of our voice or see a videotape or movie of ourselves, we are often shocked to see our style as someone else sees it. It feels extremely alien. Usually we find other people's point of view irritating or embarrassing.

Blindness to our style, to how others see us, is most acute in the animal realm. I am not speaking of literally being reborn as an animal but of the animal quality of mind, a mentality which stubbornly pushes forward toward predetermined goals. The animal mentality is very serious. It even makes humor into a serious occupation. Self-consciously trying to create a friendly environment, a person will crack jokes to try to be funny, intimate or clever. However, animals do not really smile or laugh; they just behave. They may play, but it is unusual for animals to actually laugh. They might make friendly noises or gestures, but the subtleties of a sense of humor are absent. The animal mentality looks directly ahead, as if wearing blinders. It never looks to the right or left but very sincerely goes straight ahead, trying to reach the next available situation, continually trying to adjust situations to make them conform to its expectations.

The animal realm is associated with stupidity: that is, preferring to play deaf and dumb, preferring to follow the rules of available games rather than redefine them. Of course, you might try to manipulate your perception of any

given game, but you are really just following along, just following your instinct. You have some hidden or secret wish that you would like to put into effect, so when you come to obstacles, to irritations, you just push forward, regardless of whether or not you may hurt someone or destroy something of value. You just go out and pursue whatever is available and if something else comes up, you take advantage of that as well and pursue it.

If somebody attacks you or challenges your clumsiness, your unskilled way of handling a situation, you find a way of justifying yourself, find a rationale to keep your self-respect. You are not concerned with being truthful as long as your deception can be maintained in front of others. You are proud that you are clever enough to lie successfully. If you are attacked, challenged, criticized, you automatically find an answer. Such stupidity can be very clever. It is ignorance or stupidity in the sense that you do not see the environment around you, but you see only your goal and only the means to achieve that goal, and you invent all kinds of excuses to prove that you are doing the right thing.

The extreme animal mentality is trapped in a continual, self-contained, self-justifying round of activity. You are not able to relate with the messages given to you by your environment. You do not see yourself mirrored by others. You may be dealing with very intellectual matters, but the style is animal since there is no sense of humor, no way of surrendering or opening. There is a constant demand to move on from one thing to the next, regardless of failures or obstacles.

POVERTY

In the *preta* or hungry ghost realm one is preoccupied with the process of expanding, becoming rich, consuming. Fundamentally, you feel poor. You are unable to keep up the pretense of being what you would like to be. Whatever you have is used as proof of the validity of your pride, but it is never enough, there is always some sense of inadequacy.

The poverty mentality is traditionally symbolized by a hungry ghost who has a tiny mouth, the size of the eye of a needle, a thin neck and throat, skinny arms and legs and a gigantic belly. His mouth and neck are too small to let enough food pass through them to fill his immense belly, so he is always hungry. And the struggle to satisfy his hunger is very painful since it is so hard to swallow that he eats. Food, of course, symbolizes anything you may want—friendship, wealth, clothes, sex, power, whatever.

Anything that appears in your life you regard as something to consume. If you see a beautiful autumn leaf falling, you regard it as your prey. You take it home or photograph it or paint a picture of it or write in your memoirs how beautiful it was. But after a while you become restless again and look for something else to consume.

You are constantly hungering for new entertainment—spiritual, intellectual, sensual, and so on. Intellectually you may feel inadequate and decide to pull up your socks by studying and listening to juicy, thoughtful answers, profound, mystical words. You consume one idea after another, trying to record them, trying to make them solid and real. Whenever you feel hunger, you open your notebook or scrapbook or a book of satisfying ideas. When you experience boredom or insomnia or depression, you open your books, read your notes and clippings and ponder over them, draw comfort from them. But this becomes repetitive at some point.

It is painful to be suspended in unfulfilled desire, continually searching for satisfaction. But even if you achieve your goal then there is the frustration of becoming stuffed, so full that one is insensitive to further stimuli. You try to hold on to your possession, to dwell on it, but after a while you become heavy and dumb, unable to appreciate anything. You wish you could be hungry again so you could fill yourself up agin. Whether you satisfy a desire or suspend yourself in desire and continue to struggle, in either case you are inviting frustration.

ANGER

The hell realm is pervaded by aggression. This aggression is based on such a perpetual condition of hatred that one begins to lose track of whom you are building your aggression toward as well as who is being agressive toward you. There is a continual uncertainty and confusion. You have built up a whole environment of aggression to such a point that finally, even if you were to feel slightly cooler about your own anger and aggression, the environment around you would throw more aggression at you. It is like walking in hot weather: you might feel physically cooler for a while, but hot air is coming at you constantly so you cannot keep yourself cool for long.

In the hell realm we throw out flames and radiations which are continually coming back to us. There is no room at all in which to experience any spaciousness or openness. Rather there is a constant effort, which can be very cunning, to close up all the space. The hell realm can only be created through your relationships with the outside world, whereas in the jealous god realm your own psychological hang-ups could be the material for creating the asura mentality. In the hell realm there is a constant situation or relationship; you are trying to play games with something and the attempt bounces back on your, constantly recreating extremely claustrophobic situations; so that finally there is no room in which to communicate at all.

At that point the only way to communicate is by trying to recreate your anger. You thought you had managed to win a war of one-upsmanship, but finally you did not get a response from the other person; you one-upped him right out of existence. So you are faced only with your own aggression coming back at you and it manages to fill up all the space. One is left lonely once more, without excitement, so you seek another way of playing the game, again and again and again. You do not play for enjoyment, but because you do not feel protected nor secure enough. If you have no way to secure yourself, you feel bleak and cold, so you must rekindle the fire. In order to rekindle the fire you have to fight constantly to maintain yourself. One cannot help playing the game; one just finds oneself playing it, all the time.

Psychiatry and the Sacred

Jacob Needleman

Modern psychiatry arose out of the vision that man must change himself and not depend for help upon an imaginary God. Over half a century ago, mainly through the insights of Freud and through the energies of those he influenced, the human psyche was wrested from the faltering hands of organized religion and was situated in the world of nature as a subject for scientific study. The cultural shock waves were enormous and long-lasting. But equal to them was the sense of hope that gradually took root throughout the Western world. To everyone, including those who offered countertheories to psychoanalysis, the main vision seemed indomitable: science, which had brought undreamt-of power over external nature, could now turn to explaining and controlling the inner world of man.

The era of pscyhology was born. By the end of the Second World War many of the best minds of the new generation were magnetized by a belief in this new science of the psyche. Under the conviction that a way was now open to assuage the confusion and suffering of mankind, the study of the mind became a standard course of work in American universities. The ranks of psychiatry swelled, and its message was carried to the public through the changing forms of literature, art, and educational theory. Against this juggernaut of new hope, organized religion was helpless. The concepts of human nature which had guided the Judeo-Christian tradition for two thousand years had now to be altered and corrected just as three hundred years earlier the Christian scheme of the cosmos retreated against the onslaught of the scientific revolution.

But although psychiatry in its many forms pervades our present culture, the hope it once contained has slowly ebbed away. The once charismatic psychoanalyst has become encapsulated within the workaday medical establishment, itself the object of growing public cynicism. The behaviorist who once stunned the world by defining man as a bundle of manageable reactions finds himself reduced to mere philosophizing and to the practice of piecemeal psychological cosmetics. In the burgeoning field of psychophysiology the cries of "breakthrough" echo without real conviction before the awesome and mysterious structure of the human brain. And as for experimental psychology, it has become mute; masses of data accumulated over decades of research with animals remain unrelated and seemingly unrelatable to the suffering, fear, and frustration of everyday human life.

The growing feeling of helplessness among psychiatrists and the cries for help from the masses of modern people operate in perverse contrast to the constant psychologizing of the media. Amid the "answers" provided by publications ranging in sophistication from *Reader's Digest* to *Psychology Today,* millions seem quite simply to have accepted that their lives have no great direction and ask only for help to get them through the night. The once magical promise of a transformation of the mind through psychiatry has quietly disappeared.

Of course, questions about the meaning of life and death and one's relationship to the universe may still tear at a person's insides. But now neither psychiatry nor the Church is able to respond even from the same gut level at which such questions can arise—far less from a level of universal knowledge and intuitive relationship which perceives certain cries for help as the seed of the desire for self-transformation.

No one suffers from this lack more than the psychiatrists themselves, more and more of whom despair over their inability to help other human beings in the fundamental way they once dreamed possible. Faced with the accelerating pressure of technology upon the normal patterns of human life, faced with the widespread effects of modern man's twisted relationship to nature, and yearning for a coherent purpose in living, they have come to see themselves as being in the same situation as their patients and the rest of us.

Such, in brief, is the background of a new question that is now arising concerning the hidden structure and distortions of man's inner life. Over the past decade there has taken place in our culture a widespread attraction to ideas and spiritual methods rooted in the ancient traditions of Asia and the Middle East. A large and growing number of psychotherapists are now convinced that the Eastern religions offer an understanding of the mind far more complete than anything yet envisaged by Western science. At the same time, the leaders of the new religions themselves—the numerous gurus and spiritual teachers now in the West—are reformulating and adapting the traditional systems according to the language and atmosphere of modern psychology.

With all these disparate movements, it is no wonder that thousands of troubled men and women throughout America no longer know whether they need psychological or spiritual help. The line is blurred that divides the therapist from the spiritual guide. As one observer, speaking only half facetiously, put it: "The shrinks are beginning to sound like gurus, and the gurus are beginning to sound like shrinks."

But is it so easy to distinguish between the search for happiness and the search for transformation? Are psychotherapy and spiritual tradition simply two different approaches to the same goal, two different conceptions of what is necessary for well-being, peace of mind, and personal fulfillment? Or are they two quite separate directions that human life can take? What is the real difference between sacred tradition and psychotherapy?

Our question concerns psychiatry considered as a means to an end, as the removal of obstacles that stand in the way of happiness. (I choose the word *happiness* only for the sake of brevity; we could equally well speak of the goal of psychiatry as useful living, the ability to stand on one's own feet, or adjustment to society.) These obstacles to happiness—our fears, unfulfilled desires, violent emotions, frustrations, maladaptive behavior—are the "sins" of our modern psychiatric "religion." But now we are asked to understand that there exist teachings about the universe and about man under whose guidance the psychological obstacles, these "sins against happiness," may be accepted and studied as material for the development of the force of consciousness.

Perhaps at this point it would be helpful to pause briefly and reflect upon the general idea of the transmutation of consciousness. The word *consciousness* is used nowadays in so many different senses that it is tempting to single out one or another aspect of consciousness as its primary characteristic. The difficulty is compounded by the fact that our attitude toward knowledge about ourselves is like our attitude toward new discoveries about the external world. We so easily lose our balance when something extraordinary is discovered in science or when we come upon an exciting new explanatory concept: immediately the whole machinery of systematic thought comes into play. Enthusiasm sets in, accompanied by a proliferation of utilitarian explanation, which then stand in the way of direct encounters with the real, moving world.

In a like manner, a new experience of the self tempts us to believe we have discovered the sole direction for the development of consciousness, aliveness, or—as it is sometimes called—presence. The same machinery of explanatory thought comes into play, accompanied by pragmatic programs for "action." It is not only followers of the new religions who may fall victim to this tendency, taking fragments of traditional teachings which have brought them a new experience of themselves and building a religion around them. This tendency in ourselves also accounts for much of the fragmentation of modern psychology, just as it accounts for fragmentation in the natural sciences.

In order to call attention to this tendency in ourselves, the traditional teachings—as in the Bhagavad Gita, for example—make a fundamental distinction between *consciousness* and the *contents of consciousness.* In the light of this distinction, everything we ordinarily take to be consciousness (or our real self) is actually identified as the *contents of consciousness:* our perceptions of things, our sense of personal identity, our emotions, and our thoughts in all their colors and gradations.

This ancient distinction has two crucial messages for us. On the one hand, it tells us that what we feel to be the best of ourselves as human beings is only part of a total structure containing layers of mind, feeling, and sensation far more active, subtle, and unifying than what we have settled for as our best. These layers are incredibly numerous and need to be peeled back, as it were, one by one along the path of inner growth (the "upward path" of our tale) until one touches in oneself the fundamental intelligent force in the cosmos.

At the same time, this distinction also communicates that the awakening of consciousness requires a constant effort. It is telling us that anything in ourselves, no matter how subtle, fine, or intelligent, no matter how close to reality or virtuous, no matter how still or violent—any action, any thought, any intuition or experience—immediately devours our attention and becomes automatically transformed into *contents,* around which gather all the opinions, feelings, and distorted sensations that are the supports of our secondhand sense of identity. In short, we are told that the evolution of man is always (eternally) "vertical" to the downward-flowing stream of mental, emotional, and physical associations within the human psyche. The downward "pull of gravity" is within ourselves. And seen in this light, there are no concentric layers of human awareness that need to be peeled back like the skins of an onion, but only one skin, one veil, that is constantly forming regardless of the quality of the psychic field at any given moment.

From this latter perspective, the main requirement for understanding the nature of consciousness is the repeated *effort* to be aware of whatever is taking place in the whole of ourselves at any given moment. All definitions or systematic explanations, no matter how profound, are secondary. Thus teachings about consciousness, both of the ancient masters and of modern psychologists, can be a distraction if they are presented to us in a way that does not support the effort to be aware of the totality of ourselves in the present moment.

In traditional cultures special terms surround this quality of self knowledge, connecting it to the direct human participation in a higher, all-encompassing reality, "beyond the Earth," as it is sometimes said. The existence of these special terms, such as *satori* (Zen Buddhism), *fana*

(Islam), *pneuma* (Christianity), and many others, may serve for us as a sign that this effort of total awareness was always set apart from the normal, everyday goods of organized social life. And while the traditional teachings tell us that any human being may engage in the search for this quality of presence, it is ultimately recognized that only very few will actually wish to do so, for it is a struggle that in the last analysis is undertaken solely for its own sake, without recognizable psychological motivation. And so, imbedded within every traditional culture there is said to be an "esoteric" or inner path discoverable only by those who yearn for something inexplicably beyond the duties and satisfactions of religious, intellectual, moral, and social life.

What we can recognize as psychiatric methods in traditional cultures must surely be understood in this light. Psychosis and neurosis were obviously known to the ancient world just as they are known in the few remaining traditional societies that still exist today in scattered pockets throughout the world. In a traditional culture, then, the challenge of what we would call psychotherapy consisted in bringing a person back to a normal life without stamping out the nascent impulse toward transformation in the process of treatment. To do this, a practitioner would have had to recognize the difference in a man between thwarted normal psychological functioning and the unsatisfied yearning ("that comes from nowhere," as one Sufi teacher has described it) for the evolution of consciousness. Certainly, that is one reason why traditionally the "psychotic" was treated by the priest. It is probably also why what we would call "neurosis" was handled within the once-intact family structure, permeated as this structure was by the religious teachings of the culture.

It has been observed that modern psychiatry could have assumed its current place only after the breakdown of the patriarchal family structure that dates back to the beginnings of recorded history. But the modern psychiatrist faces a tremendously difficult task as a surrogate parent even beyond the problems that have been so thoroughly described under the psychoanalytic concept of transference. For there may be something far deeper, subtler, and more intensely human, something that echoes of a "cosmic dimension," hidden behind the difficulties and therapeutic opportunities of the classical psychoanalytic transference situation. We have already given this hidden "something" a name: the desire for self-transformation. In the ancient patriarchal family structure (as I am told it still exists, for example, among the Brahmin families of India) the problems of living a normal, fulfilled life are never separated from the sense of a higher dimension of human existence. What we might recognize as therapeutic counseling is given by family members or friends, but in such a way that a troubled individual will never confuse the two possible directions that his life can take. He is helped to see that the obstacles to happiness are not necessarily the obstacles to "spiritual realization," as it is called in such traditions. A

great many of what we take to be intolerable restrictions—such as predetermined marriage partners or vocations—are connected to this spiritual factor in the make-up of the traditional patterns of family life.

Can the modern psychiatrist duplicate this aspect of family influence? Almost certainly, he cannot. For one thing, he himself probably did not grow up in such a family milieu; almost none of us in the modern world have. Therefore, the task he faces is even more demanding than most of us realize. He may recognize that religion has become a destructive influence in people's lives because the Path of transformation offered by the traditions has become covered over by ideas and doctrines we have neither understood nor experienced. He may even see that this same process of getting lost in undigested spiritual ideas and methods is taking place among many followers of the new religions. But at the same time, perhaps he sees that there can exist in people—be they neurotic or normal—this hidden desire for inner evolution. How can the patient be led to a normal, happy life without crushing this other, hidden impulse that can bring human life into a radically different dimension—whether or not a person ever becomes happy or self-sufficient or adjusted in the usual sense of these words? For the development of consciousness in man may not necessarily entail the development of what would be called a "normal," "well-adjusted," or "self-sufficient" personality.

According to tradition, there is something potentially divine within man, which is born when his physical body is born but which needs for its growth an entirely different sustenance from what is needed by the physical body or the social self.

Traditionally, then, the term *self knowledge* has an extraordinary meaning. It is neither the acquisition of information about oneself nor a deeply felt insight nor moments of recognition against the ground of psychological theory. It is an act that is in itself the principal means by which the evolving part of man can be nourished with an energy that is as real, or more so, as the energy delivered to the physical organism by the food we eat. Thus it is not a question of acquiring strength, independenc, self-esteem, security, "meaningful relationships," or any of the other goods upon which the social order is based and which have been identified as the components of psychological health. It is solely a matter of digesting deep impressions of myself as I actually am from moment to moment: a disconnected, helpless collection of impulses and reactions, a being of disharmonized mind, feeling, and instinct.

I should like to conclude by asking my question from a slightly different angle. Both among psychiatrists and the general public a widespread sense of crisis has set in concerning the psychological condition of man on this planet. Accelerated changes in the patterns of social life and the threats of war and overdeveloped technology are now more and more being met by the unleashing of powerful ideas torn from the traditional integrative sciences of man, against the background of the swift modernization of traditional cultural environments throughout the world. The mixture of these forces has induced a combination of fear and a visionary mentality concerning the possible evolution of planetary and individual man.

Yet in the private lives of almost everyone these same forces of scientific advance and cultural homogenization continue to produce painful and dehumanizing effects on the quality of our lived experience. The passive acceptance of scientific concepts of time, space, energy—and lately of mind—drives man further and further away from discovering his own space, his own time, his own vital energy, and his own active intelligence. So connected to the species has the individual become that his patterns of thought and feeling are now dictated on a world-wide basis by the needs and sufferings of the biological organism, man-on-earth.

Lost in all this is the human middle zone between the creature of earth and the private universe called "atman" in the Hindu traditions, "spirit" in Christianity, or simply "myself," "I," my original face. This middle zone of human life was once known as the family, the community, the tribe. Through the conditions of family life, the development and interiorization of the self could take place alongside the growth of the individual as a cell in the body of man-on-earth. The middle zone of human life was the product of a religion in which both heaven and earth, as ideas and as possible dimensions of living, could be the everyday environment of human life. The exaggerated influence of scientism destroyed this two-natured environment quite as decisively as it now threatens to destroy the environment of biological man. Against this former, more fundamental environmental destruction, modern psychiatry arose to help bring man back into contact with the life of feeling, a life that at the turn of the century was already being obliterated by dogmatic, intercultural religion, religion also cut off from the middle zone of human life, religion become worldly in the sense of being homogeneous, doctrinaire, and explanatory. In international Christianity, the Church lost contact with the hidden existence in man of an embryonic yearning for the eternal and instead imposed beliefs and explanatory concepts patterned after the species-and-survival knowledge of modern science. In the present era the centuries-long process was completed by which the Christian religion surrendered its ancient quiet influence on the heart of man and gave itself up instead to persuading, arguing, and compelling radical choices on a being in whom the decision to seek for oneself does not have to be *made* but only *heard.*

In the nineteenth and twentieth centuries the concept of mysticism was developed in order to classify a part of the self that science could not explain. Later, the same forces that classified mysticism eventually defined the mind, and, as we have said, the mind became an object of scientific exploration. Mysticism was pushed even further aside while the mind as a whole was naturalized—that is, understood as part of the biological organism. That there is such a mind, which functions as part of the biological organism, was always known and given various names in the traditional teachings; disturbances of this physical, biological mind, the species mind, were always treated by the traditional physician-priests, whose task it was to distinguish the sufferings of the physical mind from the yearnings for growth that emanated from the private mind, or soul.

Today, however, with the influx of fragments of traditional teachings and with the current disillusionment in the sciences, techniques for treating the physical mind of man are being joined without real guidance to ideas and methods that pertain to the individual, private mind that was always understood to be rooted in another level of reality—a mind, a consciousness, that is said to have a life independent of the motivations that constitute the ego of the human being.

At the heart of the great traditions is the idea that the search for truth is undertaken for its own sake ultimately. These traditional teachings in their entirety propose to show man the nature of this search and the laws behind it—laws which, as I have suggested, too often get lost in our enthusiasm for ideas and explanations that we have not deeply absorbed in the fire of living with all its suffering and confusion. Psychotherapy, on the other hand, is surely a *means* to an end—to the goal we have called happiness. Unlike the way offered by tradition, therapy is never an end in itself, never a way of life, but is motivated toward a goal that the therapist sees more clearly than his patient. The therapist may even experiment with invented methods to achieve this goal and often succeeds. But is it recognized that two kinds of success are possible in the process of therapy? One the one hand, the successful result may be a patient in whom the wish for evolution has been totally "disillusioned" and stamped out through the deliberate arousal in himself of the very quality of egoistic emotion which the traditions seek to break down and dissolve. But another kind of success may be possible in certain cases—a patient in whom the wish for evolution has been driven inside, who no longer dreams of a response to this wish from the outside world, but who now has within him an even greater sensitivity and hunger for deeper contact with himself. To the outside observer, such a person may seem to have developed a certain "inner-directedness," but in actuality he is precisely the sort of person who may desperately need what the traditions seek to communicate. The effort of contemporary teachers from the East to bring their message to such people in terms that are neither freighted with dead antiquity nor compromised by modern psychologisms constitutes the real spiritual drama of the present age.

Eastern and Western Models of Man

Ram Dass

One of the basic differences between Eastern and Western models of man is that one comes out of philosophical materialism and one comes out of the mystic tradition. The basic difference can be exemplified by the statement *Cogito, ergo sum,* "I think, therefore I am." Now at one level that's true, because a thought is the way in which you "know the universe." But the basic distinction is that who you are is not an identity with your thoughts. That is *I think, but I am not my thoughts.* And that becomes critical. For example, in meditation there are meditative exercises which involve extricating yourself from attachment to your senses. Many of you for example have had the experience where you are reading a book, and you are so involved in reading the book that you don't hear somebody come in the room. Nevertheless you know as a sophisticated individual that the air—we didn't put ear plugs in—the air is operating, the auditory nerves are functioning, the sound waves are coming, the transmission is occurring, it's going somewhere. But you could say that whoever you are wasn't attending to that at the moment. So the ear was functioning, but you weren't attending to your ear. Well, in the same way there are ways of not attending to your eyes seeing, your nose smelling, your tongue tasting and your skin feeling.

Now imagine that instead of just this random thing completely out of control, where at times you happen not to hear something that goes by, imagine that there were a way, through discipline—which is what meditation is about—of extricating yourself from these senses so that they go on doing their processes. They go on working, but you are no longer busy processing those data. They're just going through but you're not involved. What's left? After all, at that point it's like an anesthetic—you're not experiencing your body, you're not hearing things coming from the outside world, you're not seeing things, although your eyes are open. You're not tasting anything, or smelling it. Well, what's left are your thoughts—what you're thinking. In the meditative exercises the sequence goes—"I am not my body, I am not my organs, I am not my senses," and the final one, the one right at the end of the whole journey is, "I am not this thought." Which thought aren't you? I am not the thought. I am not the thought. I am not the thought.

Vivekananda, one of the Eastern people who came to the West and taught this, said, "The mind is a terrible master and it's a wonderful servant." But for most of us it is our master and not our servant. We are so identified with our own thoughts. So this process is the process of bringing your mind to one point. Let me explain. I go into ten-day courses where sixteen hours a day, this is what I do. You focus right on the tip of your nose and you note the breath going in and out. You don't follow it into your body and you don't follow it out into the *akasa,* into the universe. You just notice it right here. You're like a parking lot attendant. And your job is merely to notice a car that goes in the factory and one that goes out. You don't care where it went or who, you know, you're just a checker. Just check—it went in and that one came out. This one goes in—ah—there's one coming out. That's all you do—you just sit right there and notice it. That's all you do—you just sit right there and notice it. That's all you've got to do.

You can at least get a feeling for what the game is. Now imagine that you are a sophisticated, rational, Western person and you go into a course and you sit down and the man says, "All right, now, for the next sixteen hours with breaks every forty minutes to walk around the room a couple of times, you will just follow this breath going in and out of your nose." Well, you literally psychologically climb the walls.

You sit down and you think, "Right, fine." The next thing is "Gee, my knee hurts." Thought. Just another thought. For the first few days they are very kind to you. They let you, when your knee hurts, move your knee. Later the instructions are for the next forty minutes you're not to move at all. Your knee hurts, and that's just a stimulus. After all, your knee isn't going to fall apart if it hurts for a while. Each time you deal with pain, you bring your consciousness back. It gets caught again, and you bring it back. If it gets caught, you don't get violent with yourself. You don't beat the elephant. You just constantly remind it that it's hooked to this post in the ground, so you just keep coming back. It's called a primary object. You just keep coming back to the primary object. You go through "My knee hurts." "Oh, I'm hungry"—that's another one. Then there's another one: "For this I got a Ph.D.?" That's a great one, you know, like "What am I doing here? After all this training here I am sitting watching my breath. I mean, I ought to be in a mental hospital." And, "Who sits around all day long watching the breath at their nose?" I mean, its obviously some totally compulsive individual who's afraid he's going to stop breathing or something. And to take that on as a chosen discipline—sixteen hours a day—day after day?

But the funny thing is, we will spend millions and millions of dollars on creating these incredibly complex computers, and filling our mind with knowledge, but the actual tool, which is the tool of our conscious awareness, we spend very little time training. We don't even understand in the West what it *means* to train consciousness, or what it means to develop these disciplines of one point. Because it is literally true that, were you able to keep your consciousness in the same place, on one point—literally on one point for twelve seconds—you would be in one of the highest forms of *samadhi.* You would be one of the most enlightened beings. Twelve seconds, that isn't much. That's how out of control we are. And what it does is, over the course of some days or some weeks you begin to notice your mind operating. You begin to notice how your desires keep manifesting in thoughts. You'll be sitting there and suddenly get incredible sexual rushes and fantasies. Keep in mind now that who you know yourself to be is only a function of your thoughts or your conceptual models of who you are.

Ego is really a conceptual structure of some sort, and if your mind is thinking about the same thing all the time, what happened to the ego? Because the ego is really based on part of those seventeen trillion mind moments being filled with redefining the game—over and over again. "Well, really I'm Ram Dass, really I'm Ram Dass and I'm doing this and I'm somebody who gets hungry and I'm . . . and there's the world out there and I'm here . . . I'm just . . ." We're using all of our senses and our associative stuff to keep the game together—to keep our conceptual framework of the universe in order. The minute you bring your mind in to one point, what in effect you're doing is over-riding the existing program in the computer. And when you do that, there is an incredible amount, of course, of the computer trying to re-assert itself, so that the thoughts get more insistent, more demanding—suddenly you've got to go to the bathroom in the worst way, even though you just went ten minutes ago. There is a book called the *Bhagavad Gita* in India which is a book that is concerned with a battle—supposedly a battle out in the battlefield. But one way of understanding that book is it's this inner battle about who's going to run the game. Are your thoughts going to be your master or are you going to be master of your thoughts? I would like to have programs available, one of which is the Ram Dass Program, but I would like not to have it run my life. Because it turns out that isn't who I am. That's who I thought I was.

What happens is that when you try to bring your mind to one point, at first it speeds up incredibly and each thought is saying, in effect, "Think of me, think of me, I'm important, I'm important." Like, "What was that noise outside?" You know, "I've got to get up—oh, I forgot to call so and so."

What you start to do is run your old tapes. You remember—I used to sit and think about all the people I ever knew and I'd go back to kindergarten, and all the people I had ever known. Then I'd take one of them and try to remember all the things about him. Then I'd go through all the best restaurants that I've ever eaten in my life. Then I'd go through all the places I still wanted to visit, then I'd go through all my theoretical models of what I thought was happening, and I *still* had days left. The mind would just keep creating this stuff and this stuff and this stuff. I was doing this in a temple in India and—after all, I had closed the door of the temple, this was a voluntary thing. So you try to bring your mind down and quiet your mind and of course these thoughts get more and more dramatic and more and more crisisey and more and more pulling and the most vicious thoughts are the thoughts, "This is never going to work." That's a good one and the other kind of thought that hangs you up is "It's working." See what happens is you're doing it and you quiet your mind just a little and you get these incredible rushes. You get these ecstatic feelings of incredible bliss—even to incredible calm. And you've never felt this kind of "ahhh." Of course, all those experiences are just more thoughts.

All those experiences are just more thoughts. "Oh, got me again. Got me again." They are more subtle all the time. They keep taking you just where you least expect them to. And it's only after some time that you stop drinking in the ecstasy or stop going through the struggles and you start to get calmer and calmer and calmer and let the mind *just sit quietly* and do its thing. It's the awareness which starts to approach what the Buddhists call "pure mind." The thoughts are still there but they are floating by just like clouds. They're not grabbing at you. Now, the question of why thoughts arise is concerned with human motivation. Motivation is what in the Eastern tradition is called attachment or desire—clinging—and attachment or desire or clinging is the root of the problem. Now here's my predicament, see. I was trained as a motivation psychologist, and I worked in the field of achievement motivation, dependency motivation, nurturance, succorance, power, affiliation, etc., sexual hunger, thirst, the drives and needs. I used to teach courses in human motivation.

I come from a tradition where, from a psychological point of view, motives are "givens" in man. Everybody's got drives and needs and so on. Now I come into a tradition where motives are seen not as necessary things, but as part of the package, if you will—*not who you are.* As a motivation psychologist, I defined who we are in terms of motivation. Now I'm seeing that motivation is part of the package, but it isn't who we are.

What you see as a solid is not really solid. It just looks solid because of the frequency of wavelengths that your eyes are capable of perceiving. You begin to realize—just like with hearing, there is a certain frequency, a range of frequencies that you can hear that are audible, and a dog can hear one you can't hear, and so on. If you were a different receiver mechanism, it would all be quite different to you, because were you tuned up to a different kind of frequency or perceptual sensitivity, everything would look like it was in movement all the time. If you get out further and further in that dimension, you would get to the point where you would see—first of all you would see this stage like a cloud, and you'd see these different entities as clouds, just like you see clouds. They are made of stuff that keeps changing and you would see the cloud, the cloud pattern. Like looking at figures in Rorschach cards. . . . If you go out yet one move level into sensitivity, you would see that these clouds are all part of a solid—you go in more and more until finally when you look at the level of these quanta of energy, the universe is a solid. It's a solid, and everything is interchangeable with everything else. This isn't any great Eastern mystical discovery—just straight physics.

THE PLANES OF CONSCIOUSNESS

We use higher and higher power microscopes to play these games. And some of us who have had psychedelic experiences have retuned our perceptual apparatus, like a television receiver. Were we to bring in a television receiver and plug it into that plug which just brings electricity in and tune it in, suddenly there'd be someone on channel 3, 4, 5, and 10. It all must be here somewhere—but we can't see it. Now, were we able to tune just slightly differently, we could pick it all up. "I think I'll look at channel 3. Now I'll tune to channel 4." Now, that all sounds facetious, but it turns out it isn't at all. That's what are called the planes of consciousness—when you learn how to break attachments enough to channel 7 to be able to tune to channel 6. That's what a guru is talking about—our attachments to a certain channel, or a certain wavelength, or a certain frequency. Now, let us say this being who I am studying with has now extricated himself from all attachment. That means the body is going along in the same way that your heart is beating. He's not sitting around thinking, beat—or peristaltic contraction, right—whup, whup, whup—he's not thinking any of that—it's just going on. It's the same way you drive a car most of the time. It's all in base brain. Most of the time when you're driving you turn on the radio, or look at somebody, or plan your day's events. You couldn't care less. You're making these exquisitely complex adjustments all the time. I mean, hurtling through space—this huge monster, you know, at seventy miles per hour—and you're not even aware you're driving. That's all base brain. Well, imagine now that everything is on base brain. Your eating is on base brain—your sleeping, your talking to people, is all on base brain. All your thinking is on base brain. When the thinking thing needs to happen, it happens. You don't have to worry about it. It's just an associative run-off.

If you have extricated yourself completely from all the attachments to this particular frequency—in the sequence of training you start to tune to other frequencies. I mean, I have sat with people in India, and I'm sitting next to somebody who is looking at me with their eyes open and my eyes open, and he's talking to somebody I don't see. Now in the West we put that person in a mental hospital. We say he is hallucinating. But after a while you begin to understand that maybe we don't really quite totally know where it's at, and we put somebody away because they don't play the game the way we play. They don't see it the way we see it. And it turns out that we're hallucinating, too, because we're just fixed on a certain frequency. I have a brother who is often hospitalized and sometimes they let me visit him, but the psychiatrist has to be present. And there's my brother on one plane and the psychiatrist on another plane. They both look crazy, in the sense that they are both attached to what they consider absolute reality. Well, from my point of view these are all relative realities. They are not absolute realities at all. All you have to do is shift in one reality once—you just get out of it once, and suddenly your attachment to what you thought was the real thing starts to collapse pretty fast. You say, "Yes, it's relatively real, but not absolutely real." So that is the training. You go from this plane, and as you loosen your attachments you start to move into other planes which, when we are attached to this plane, we often call hallucinatory states. And sometimes it's very delicate: what's a projection of what.

You come into other frequencies where it all looks different—different greens, different entities—you're looking different. What they call your physical body, your astral body, your causal body, these different bodies are at different frequencies and you're attached to your physical body because you are attached to your senses. When you are attached that way, you don't notice your physical body. So the lowest level of the game is where you loosen the physical body from the astral body.

I've had many experiences where I've left my body. You can get your body into the lotus position, and it's perfectly balanced. You can just put your body there and leave and go somewhere—wherever you want to go. You pull yourself back from your senses and from your thinking mind and then, in just the subtle form of your thinking mind, in your astral body, which is this bodiless awareness, you go out. You can look back and you can see the cord of light that links the bodies. It looks like an umbilical cord and it looks like a blue light. Within *that* body is another body, and it gets more and more subtle as you tune your frequency to different planes.

PERCEPTUAL VANTAGE POINTS AND PSYCHOSIS

We live at a plane of reality which we share, it would seem, in which we all agree that certain things are the way they are. And when somebody disagrees with that and disagrees with it with deep faith, under certain conditions we characterize that as psychosis. I would not reinterpret that and say that what has happened is, that the person—and this is not yet saying anything more, it's merely giving us a framework to see an alternative possibility—has moved from one perceptual vantage point to another. A person, through something which might be a chemical change, could be in a trauma of some sort; it might be ingested, or psychically induced, psychogenic in nature—but through some trauma to the system—he moves from one perceptual vantage point to another one, and then gets as attached to that one as we are to the one we're in. Right? He is attached to that and from our point of view he is psychotic. From his point of view, we are. That is because we don't see reality as he sees it. He's seeing another reality. In any kind of Hindu system this would be called merely an astral plane. He's in another astral plane.

My brother has been in a mental hospital, has been considered psychotic, and thinks of himself as the Messiah. I have spent a great deal of time with him. And my relation to him was to be as much "here and now" as I could be. To realize that he is stuck in a reality, just like I get stuck, and that any reality you're stuck in is just as bad as any other reality you're stuck in. And so, one of the things I do is I go into the reality he's stuck in with him. I look around, enjoy it with him, look at the world from that place with him, and then show him that from my point of view, you have to be able to go in and out of all of them, that any one you get stuck in is the wrong one. And if one guy's stuck in one who may be a psychiatrist, he is trying to cure somebody else stuck in another and is, in one sense, just substituting one stuckness for another stuckness. The journey of consciousness is to go to the place where you see that all of them are really relative realities and these are merely perceptual vantage points for looking at it all. When one looks at the universe from within the spirit, which is another "take," one sees that the entire universe all makes absolutely exquisite sense, but it's all slightly different because you're looking at it from an entirely different perceptual vantage point.

There are some beings that we call psychotic who in India would be called "God-Intoxicants." They are people who have experienced compassion outwardly and then their entire energy turns inward to inner states that they are experiencing. We see them as catatonic. Because we are not getting an elicited response out of them, we project into them a certain kind of psychological state. Now in India they project another kind of interpretation into that, surround the person with another environment, which changes the nature of his experience, because of their models of what it is that's happening to him, you see? So that a God-Intoxicant is treated with great reverence and respect. Ramakrishna, a very famous mystic in India, was often God-Intoxicant. I would say that probably most catatonics are not God-Intoxicants, but there are some that we're confusing, and we've got them in the same category because we don't have these differentiations at this point.

Psychotherapy is just as high as the psychotherapist. If your psychotherapist happened to be Buddha, you would get enlightened in the process, see. When you cut aside all the melodrama, you will get as free of your particular role-attachments as the psychiatrist is free of his. Because if he is still attached to his particular role, all he can do is give you one role to substitute for another, which is primarily his. So that generally Freudian patients end up Freudianized and Jungians end up Jungianized. Now most therapists have a model of what they think they're doing and how it all works, so any data that's fed in from the patient goes through this model and out comes a response consistent with this model.

My further understanding is that there is no being at any state of consciousness that one cannot make contact with, if one is himself free of attachment to any specific plane of consciousness. That is, I think that all of us are available at all times. There is a place in all of us that is available at all times, and our inability to make contact with another human being is our own inability to get out of the place we are stuck in. There is much to say for the flexibility of the consciousness of the behavior change agent, to be able to make contact with another human being where he is, without themselves getting stuck in where he's stuck. That's the work on one's self.

The Way Things Are

Huston Smith

In envisioning the way things are, there is no better place to begin than with modern science. Equally, there is no worse place to end, but that is for later; for now it is the beginning that concerns us. Science is the fitting starting point, partly because of its achievements, which according to Herbert Butterfield outshine everything since the rise of Christianity—others have claimed since the invention of language. Even more pertinent, however, is the fact that science dominates the modern mind. Through and through, from premises to conclusions, the contemporary mind is science-ridden. Its sway is the stronger because we are unaware of its extent.

There may be no better way to summarize the scientific view of things than to say that reality is a stupendous spatial hierarchy, a hierarchy of size. In its middle register, the meso-world in which our daily lives are lived, we encounter objects carrying the proportions of inches, feet, and miles. In the microworld that undergirds this meso-world, cells measure on the order of thousandths of an inch, atoms hundreds of millionths of an inch, and their nuclei thousandths of billionths of an inch. As we continue downward, or rather inward, from nuclei to nucleons and their ingredient particles, the orders of inverse magnitude continue to unfold exponentially.

Reversing our direction we enter the macro-world. Our sun revolves around our galaxy at a speed of 160 miles per second, about 23 times the speed a rocket must attain to escape from the earth's surface. At this speed it takes the sun approximately 240 million years to complete a single rotation. If the orbit seems large, it is in fact parochial, for it is confined to our own galaxy, which is but one among estimated billions. Andromeda, our closest sizable neighbor, is 2,200,000 light-years away, and beyond it space falls away abysmally, nebula after nebula, island universe after island universe, until we reach the limits of our known universe, some 26 billion light-years "across," whatever that means in a four-dimensional pseudosphere.

Now it happens that the view of reality that preceded that of modern science was likewise hierarchical. Centering in the human plane, it too opened onto higher realms above and nether ones below, the heavens and hells of the traditional cosmologies. . . .

The two views are at one in sharing a hierarchiacal layout, but the units of measure are different. The scientific gauge is quantity; space, size, and strength of forces can all be reckoned numerically. The comparable "yardstick" in the traditional hierarchy was quality. It had, over the millennia, two distinct readings that overlapped. To the popular mind it meant essentially euphoria: better meant happier, worse less happy. Reflective minds, on the other hand, considered happiness to be only an aspect of quality, not its defining feature. The word "significance" points us in the direction of the feature they considered fundamental, but significance too was derivative. It was taken for granted that the higher worlds abounded in meaning, significance, and importance, but this was because they were saturated with being and were therefore more real. *Sat, Chit, Ananda:* Being, Awareness, and Bliss. All three pertained, but Being, being basic, came first. In the last analysis, the scale in the traditional hierarchy was ontological.

What it means for one thing to be more real than another will, we trust, become clear. . . . For the present we note that the view of reality as consisting of graded levels of being dominated man's outlook until the rise of modern science. As we intend to make something of this point, it will be well to fix it into place by documenting it.

With the possible exception of Claude Levi-Strauss, no one today is more qualified to pronounce on the mentality of precivilized man than is Mircea Eliade. Reducing the ontological hierarchy to its minimum to cover all cases of such men, Eliade find this minimum to consist in a dichotomy between the sacred and the profane. "The man of the archaic societies tends to live as much as possible *in* the sacred . . . ," he writes, "because for primitives . . . the *sacred* is equivalent to a *power,* and, in the last analysis, to *reality*. The sacred is saturated with *being."*

That which prevailed for tribes carried over into civilizations: they refined the hierarchical perspective but kept its basic structure. "It has, in one form or another, been the dominant official philosophy of the larger part of civilized mankind through most of its history," writes Arthur Lovejoy in *The Great Chain of Being* (which along with Rene Guenon's *Les Etats Multiples de L'Etre* is one of the two studies devoted exclusively to this concept); taught "in their several fashions and with differing degrees of rigor and thoroughness [by] the greater numer of subtler speculative minds and of the great religious teachers." ...

Having noted the universality of the hierarchical perspective in both tribes and civilizations generally, we narrow in on the civilization that is our own. Here, for philosophy, Plato forged the paradigm. Atop being's hierarchy is the Form of the Good, the most real of the various grades of reality, the "Good Itself." Radically different from our everyday world, it can be described only through poetic images. Nevertheless, being "pure perfection," it is the universal object of desire. It is also, of all subordinate things, their cause. Such ancillary and partially privative entities are logically required Plato's successors (such as Proclus) argued, by virtue of what Lovejoy called "the principle of plentitude;" they are possible, and if any possibility were unactualized it would constitute, as it were, a hole in Being's fullness and negate its infinity. Aristotle elaborated on the graded character of the finite portion of the spectrum; for the *scala naturae* he provided biological specifics and a definition of continuity which came to be applied to the scale as a whole. In the words of Lovejoy's summary:

> The result was the conception of the plan and structure of the world which, through the Middle Ages and down to the late eighteenth century ... most educated men were to accept without question—the conception of the universe as a "Great Chain of Being," composed of an immense, or ... infinite, number of links ranging in hierarchical order from the meagerest kind of existents ... through "every possible" grade up to the *ens perfectissimum. (Great Chain of Being, p. 59.)*

"Down to the late eighteenth century," Lovejoy tells us. Why did the hierarchical outlook then collapse? As it had blanketed human history up to that point, constituting man's primordial tradition and what might almost be called the human unanimity, the force that leveled it must have been powerful, and modern science is the obvious candidate. The timing is right: Bacon, Hobbes, and Newton saw the writing on the wall in the seventeenth century, but it took another century for the scientific outlook to sweep the field. And the logic is inexorable: the structure of the two views is such that it was inevitable that they collide. Modern science requires only one ontological level, the physical. Within this level it begins with matter that is perceptible, and to perceptible matter it in the end returns, for however far its hypotheses extend, eventually they must be brought back to pointer readings and the like for verification. Between their beginnings and their ends the hypotheses may cross foreign waters, for in its micro- and macro-reaches matter behaves in unfamiliar ways. This does not, however, alter the fact that the matter (or rather matter/energy) with which the hypotheses deal remains such throughout, subject to matrices of space and time however redefined: curved space is odd, but it is still space. To whatsoever corner of the universe nature is tracked, it continues in some way to honor science's basic indices:

space, time, and the matter/energy that are convertible. It is virtue of the fact that science fits exhaustively into these matrices that its contents are, in last analysis, of a kind. A spatio-temporal state of affairs is a spatio-temporal state of affairs. Or, at a higher level of abstraction, a number is a number and number is the language of science. Objects can be larger or smaller, forces can be stronger or weaker, durations can be longer or shorter, these all being numerically reckonable. But to speak of anything in science as having a different ontological status—as being better, say, or more real—is to speak nonsense.

Itself occupying no more than a single ontological plane, science challenged by implication the notion that other planes exist. As its challenge was not effectively met, it swept the field and gave the modern world its soul. For this is the final definition of modernity: an outlook in which this world, this ontological plane, is the only one that is genuinely countenanced and affirmed. In religion modernity demythologizes tradition to accommodate it to its one-story universe; if "God" in principle requires more exalted quarters, the nonexistence of such quarters entails his nonexistence as well; hence Death-of-God theologians. Existentialism does its best to give man purchase in a world built for the examination of things, but subjective truth is no match for objective, so in the main philosophy, too, accepts the working premises of science. "The best way to characterize Quine's world view is to say that ... there is fundamentally only one kind of entity in the world, and that is the kind studied by natural scientists—physical objects; and second, that there is only one kind of knowledge in the world, and it is the kind that natural scientists have. Willard Quine is the most influential American philosopher of the last twenty years.

That the scientific outlook should, in Carl Becker's word, have "ravished" the modern mind is completely understandable. Through technology, science effects miracles: skyscrapers that stand; men standing on the moon. Moreover, in its early stages these miracles were in the direction of the heart's desire: multiplication of goods and the reduction of drudgery and disease. There was the sheer noetic majesty of the house pure science erected, and above all there was method. By enabling men to agree on the truth because it could be demonstrated, this method produced a knowledge that was cumulative and could advance. No wonder man converted. The conversion was not forced. It did not occur because scientists were imperialists but because their achievements were so impressive, their marching orders so exhilarating, that thinkers jostled to join their ranks.

We ourselves were once in their number and would be so today were it not for a fact that has become increasingly unblinkable. Strictly speaking, a scientific world view is impossible; it is a contradiction in terms. The reason is that science does not treat of the world; it treats of a part of it only. One world at a time, one hears. Fair enough, but not half a world, which is all that science can offer.

At this point matters grow awkward, for we are conscious of entering upon a hackneyed theme. We beg, however, for the reader's closest attention; we wish he could read the balance of this chaper as if he were encountering its argument for the first time. For its conclusion is one of those things that one knows yet never learns. The conclusion is this: Though man's conversion to the scientific outlook is understandable psychologically, logically it involves a clean mistake. Insofar as we allow our minds to be guided by reason, we can see that to try to live within the scientific view of reality would be like living in a house's scaffolding, and to love it like embracing one's spouse's skeleton.

Every advance in our understanding of the scientific method renders this conclusion more inescapable. Indeed, if there is anything new in the version of the argument about to be presented, it lies in the near consensus of scientists and philosophers of science that can now be invoked in its support.

As a probe toward the way things are, science is a powerful but strictly limited instrument. One wonders if it was during the Battle of Britain that Karl Popper of the University of London, ranking philosopher of science in our generation, hit upon an image that has become standard in making this point. His image likens science to a searchlight scanning a night sky for planes. For a plane to register, two things are required: it must exist, and it must be where the beam is. The plane must *be,* and it must be *there* (where the beam is).

The point of this image is, of course, to make plain the restricted nature of the scientific quest. Far from lighting up the entire sky, it illumines but an arc within it. Norbert Wiener used to make the point by saying: "Messages from the universe arrive addressed no more specifically than 'To Whom It May Concern.' Scientists open those that concern them." No mosaic constructed from messages thus narrowly selected can be the full picture.

These images make their point in a general way, but they provide no particulars. Precisely *how* is science limited? In what ways does it restrict its interests? . . .

Science is not one thing. It resembles a village more than it does a single indiviudal. But villages often have greens, and they are usually located near their centers. Following this analogy, we can move in on science by way of a series of concentric circles. . . .

The outer, enveloping circle is labeled *objectivity.* No knowledge can claim to be scientific in any sense until it enters this domain, which is to say, until it elicits intersubjective agreement. It must commend itselt to human knowers generally, provided only that they are competent in the subject in question. We move closer to the heart of science, however, when we enter the second circle, *prediction.* Taxonomy is a science in some sense, but it

does not command the respect we accord to the predictive sciences. When an astronomer tells us that so many years hence, at such and such an hour on such and such a night, the moon will enter eclipse, and this happens, we are impressed. Not content to describe what occurs in nature, the astronomer has pressed on to uncover its operators. A scientist who goes further and takes command of these operators, throwing switches in the tracks on which nature runs, so to speak, steps even closer to science's center, into the circle marked *control.* It might seem that from the standpoint of pure as against applied science the distinction between prediction and control is small, but in fact it is important. In pure science controlled experiments set the stage for predictions that could not be made without them—science grows exact by being exacting—while in applied science (technology) control is where the money lies. It is to the science that can build missile systems and stamp out polio that the coffers of government swing wide. To overlook the extent to which this affects the shape of science as a sociohistorical enterprise would be naive.

The fourth guideline of science takes the form, not of another circle that hugs its center even more tightly, but of an arrow which, beginning at the outer rim, drives straight to the center itself. The name of this final guideline is *number.* . . .

We are now in a position to see how science is limited. The knowledge with which it is exclusively occupied is, to begin with, objective. It must be intersubjectively confirmable, and since sense data are what men most incontrovertibly agree on after the tautologies of mathematics and logic, the knowledge science seeks is that which at some level of amplification can connect with man's senses. That which so connects is energy/matter, so energy/matter in its manifold forms and permutations *is* science's object. Within its domain science looks especially for precise—which in the end means mathematically expressible—knowledge that is predictive and augments control.

What lies outside this pale?

1. Values in their final and proper sense. Some time ago Bertrand Russell acknowledged that "the sphere of values lies outside science, except insofar as science consists in the pursuit of knowledge," and even his exception is not truly such, for the value of pursuing knowledge, though assumed by science, is not itself scientifically derived. Science can deal with instrumental values but not intrinsic ones. *If* health is valued over immediate somatic gratification, smoking is bad, but the "if" itself science cannot adjudicate. Again, science can deal with values descriptively but not prescriptively. It can tell us what men do prize, but not what they should prize. Market research and opinion polls are sciences, but as the word is used today there can be no science of the *summum bonum.* Normative values elude its grasp.

2. Purposes. For science to get on with its job, Aristotle's final causes had to be banished and the field cleared for explanation in terms of efficient causes alone. Whether the case be that of Galileo and falling stones or Kepler and light, the shift "from the mechanics of antiquity to modern mechanics [comes through] the . . . separation of primary and secondary qualities, . . . the numerical and affective aspects of nature, . . . to remove the language of volition and teleology, and to fortify the notion of 'impersonal,' causal laws of motion." Vitalism is unscientific. Behavioral science traces "purposive behavior" to instincts and conditioning, à la B. F. Skinner; biology tracks tropisms to the codings of genes or chromosomes, à la Monod's *Chance and Necessity*. It is "feedback loops" that render organisms "teleonomic." "The cornerstone of scientific method is . . . the *systematic* denial that 'true' knowledge can be got at by interpreting phenomena in terms of final causes—that is to say, of 'purpose.' "

3. Life meanings. Science itself is meaningful from beginning to end, but on certain kinds of meanings—ones that are existential and global—it is silent. What is the meaning of our days? Does life make sense? Does the cosmic drama have point and purpose? As a human being, a scientist may become engaged with such questions, but his science will not help him answer them. It is as if as scientist he were situated inside a balloon. He can shine his flashlight anywhere on its interior, but he cannot get outside it to see it as a whole or in perspective.

4. Quality. This is basic to the lot, for it is the qualitative ingredient in values, meanings, and purposes that accounts for their power. Certain qualities (such as colors) are connected with quantifiable substrates (lightwaves of given lengths), but quality itself is unmeasurable. Either it is perceived for what it is or it is not, and nothing can convey its nature to anyone who cannot perceive it directly. The most that one can do is to compare things that have a quality with thing that do not, and even then the comparison is meaningful only to persons who know from experience what the quality in question is. Inability to deal with the qualitatively unmeasurable leads science to work with what Lewis Mumford calls "a disqualified universe."

Values, life meanings, purposes, and qualities slip through science like sea slips through the nets of fishermen. Yet man swims in this sea, so he cannot exclude it from his purview. This is what was meant when we noted earlier that a scientific *world* view is in principle impossible. Taken in its entirety, the world is not as science says it is; it is as science, philosophy, religion, the arts, and everyday speech say it is. Not science but the sum of man's symbol systems, of which science is but one, is the measure of things.

With science itself there can be no quarrel. Scientism is another matter. Whereas science is positive, contenting itself with reporting what it discovers, scientism is negative. It goes beyond the actual findings of science to deny that other approaches to knowledge are valid and other truths true. In doing so it deserts science in favor of metaphysics—bad metaphysics, as it happens, for as the contention that there are no truths save those of science is not itself a scientific truth, in affirming it scientism contradicts itself. It also carries marks of a religion—a secular religion, resulting from overextrapolation from science, that has seldom numbered great scientists among its notaries. Science has enormous difficulty dealing with things that cannot be measured (if it can deal with them at all), yet David Bohm, who *is* a great scientist, says that "the immeasurable is the primary and independent source of all reality. . . . Measure is a secondary and dependent aspect of this reality."

Where are we?

Searching for the way things are, we found that the modern reduction of reality to a single ontological level was the result of science. But its psychological, not its logical, result; this was our further finding. Nothing in what science has discovered controverts the existence of realms other than the one with which it deals. Meanwhile our growing understanding of the scientific method shows us that there are things science by-passes. Whether these neglected items belong to a distinct ontological scale, science, of course, does not say; it says nothing whatever about them. The fact that scientific instruments do not pick them up shows only that they differ in *some* way from the data science does register.

As long as modernity was captive of an outlook presumed to be scientific but in fact scientistic, reality was taken to be as science mirrored it. Now that it is apparent that science peers down a restricted viewfinder, we are released from that misconception. The view that appears in a restricted viewfinder is a restricted view.

Since reality exceeds what science registers, we must look for other antennae to catch the wavebands it misses. What other antennae are there? None more reliable than the convergent sensibilities of, in Lovejoy's characterization, "the greater number of the subtler speculative minds and of the great religious teachers" that civilizations have produced; and, we have added with Eliade, that archaic societies have produced as well. Lovejoy's crediting of the hierarchical outlook to the subtler of human minds gains force from the fact that, writing as he did in the heyday of scientism, he thought the hierarchical outlook mistaken. When we combine (a) the fact that it has been the subtler minds which, when not thrown off balance by the first flush of the scientific breakthrough, have gravitated to the hierarchical view, with (b) the further fact that, from the multiple heavens of Judaism to the storied structure of the Hindu temple and the angelologies of innumerable traditions, the view was reached convergently and independently, as if by innate tropism, by virtually all known societies; when, to repeat, we combine these two facts and bring them into alignment, they entitle us to regard a tiered reality as man's central surmise when the full range of its experience is legitimated and pondered profoundly. Constituting until recently, through both rumored and recorded history, what we have ventured to call the human unanimity—the phrase overstates the case slightly, but not much—it presents itself as the natural human outlook: the view that is normal to man's station because consonent with the complete complement of human sensibilities. It is the vision philosophers have dreamed, mystics have seen, and prophets have transmitted.